NEVER PISS INTO THE WIND

by

Jules R. DuBar

PublishAmerica

Baltimore

First printing

ISBN: 1-4137-1970-8
PUBLISHED BY PUBLISHAMERICA, LLLP
www.publishamerica.com
Baltimore

Printed in the United States of America

To all those raggedy-assed misfits, man and dog alike,
who once dared call themselves "Kings of the Coastal Plain"

and

To Hobart W. C. Furbunch, III, who filled in
a lot of the spaces between the lines of my life

TABLE OF CONTENTS

"As you go through life, two rules will never bend.
Never whittle toward yourself, or piss into the wind."

—*An old timer, years ago*

The World's Slowest Train

It was March 7, 1946, and I was on the world's slowest train. We were headed for Canton, Ohio, but as we crept across the flat old glacial lake bottom around Toledo it occurred to me that I was probably going to die of old age long before we got there. Each time I tried to peer out of the dirty little window by my seat I saw the same scene; it was like looking at a framed painting in a museum.

At about 10 a.m. that morning, or maybe it was a year or two ago, I had left the Coast Guard Personnel Center in Detroit with an honorable discharge in my grubby little hand. When I enlisted I was a machinist for the Westinghouse Naval Ordnance Plant, but my real dream had been to be a professional boxing champion. Now, forty-two months later, I was headed home determined to become a professional geologist.

I left the Center with another sailor who also was headed for Ohio. I don't remember much about him, or even how we got to the train station. I was too hopped up to listen to his chatter and I had slept only a few hours since leaving Ft. Lewis, in Tacoma, seven days earlier. I was a walking zombie but didn't realize it. I recall the two of us standing on the sidewalk in front of the station. We were in our dress blues and carrying our sea bags and bedrolls. For some reason I turned to my buddy and said, "I'll go in and check the schedule while you sit here." It was the last time I ever saw the guy. At the ticket window I learned that a train was ready to pull out for Canton so I bought a ticket and got on board. I figured the sailor outside could catch the next train.

As the train pulled out of the station I stowed my gear, sat down and tried to relax, but my brain would have none of that shit. I thought about that morning at the Center. There had been a little half-assed ceremony during which I was awarded a Good Conduct Medal. As the officer handed me the thing he smiled and said, "This is not for three years of good behavior, but rather for not having been caught." The simple shit thought he had made a joke, so I laughed.

11

Actually, he was dead on the mark—I hadn't been caught and I was damned proud of that.

A little later, Lt. J.G. Homer E. McCullouch made a last ditch effort to talk me into re-enlisting. *Christ,* I thought, *you got to give these guys credit—they never give up.* At that moment I wouldn't have re-enlisted for another day if they had made me Commandant of the Coast Guard. But I didn't say that to the Lt. because I didn't want to piss him off. Instead I said, "No sir, I know it would be a great opportunity for me, but I've decided to use the G.I. Bill and go to college and study geology." The Lt. shrugged and gave me a look that said, "Well, I had to give it a shot."

After that he issued my discharge papers, a $10.75 travel voucher, $14.25 back pay, and $100.00 mustering out pay. It wasn't a fortune, but I'd rarely had more at one time in my life.

As we moved through the railroad yards in Greater Detroit, I began to reflect on going home and what it would be like, and most of all what it had been like before I left.

My parents never knew much about what my life in the service had been and, as far as I could see, didn't give a damn. My dad wrote to me four times and each time he told me about his latest political campaign and the union activities in which he was engaged. He always included a dollar bill, so I ended up with $3.75 more than he had given me in the previous 19 years. In 1940 he went to a labor union convention in Cincinnati, but before he left he handed me a quarter. It was the first time he had ever given me any money, and I still have no idea what prompted this unique act of generosity.

Unfortunately my mother wrote several times each week. She basked in the glory of having given her only begotten son to her country. She liked to tell her neighbors and church friends how close we were, and how we shared everything, and how much she was interested in everything I did, and how she loved and missed me. This usually was accompanied by misty eyes and quivering chin, playing her captive audience for the last drop of sympathy. She fed on this kind of shit, and luckily most of her friends were too stupid to figure her out. They thought of her as she wished, as a beautiful, long-suffering, self-sacrificing Christian mother and wife. She liked to tell anyone who would listen how she suffered in silence and how no one would ever know what she had gone through. Hell, with her non-stop mouth only the stony deaf were spared.

Her letters to me were basically carbon copies, describing in detail her woes, privations and terminal illnesses, and all the crises in the lives of her two brothers and two sisters. Her letters depressed and disgusted me, so after a

12

while I threw most of them into the trash unopened. My letters to her were collections of banal generalities laced with silly platitudes and signed, "Your Loving Son." This sort of meaningless stuff satisfied her. She had no interest in my private thoughts, dreams, wishes, ambitions or problems, and I had no desire to share any of my life with her.

That Dad wrote to me at all was an indication that he was making some sort of effort to seek reconciliation with me. He didn't know how to say "I'm sorry", and never learned. Actually, neither of us was any good at reconciliation.

In the summer of 1941 Dad and I had a two-punch fist fight in the backyard. The fight was triggered by his damned drum set, but as I figured out later, there was a lot more to it than drums. My mother's insidious manipulations had set us on a collision course many years earlier.

Dad had been in show business before I was born. He worked the vaudeville circuit before World War I, traveled with a quartet ("The Frisco News Boys") after the war, and when I was four or five he was a big band leader with a regular show on the local radio station. During the Depression he worked at cheap cafés with pick-up bands to earn a little extra cash. The night of our fight he was doing a gig at a bucket of blood called Ray's Café. Earlier in his career he had played the banjo and guitar but during the Depression he switched to drums. That night he ordered me to bring his drum set from the basement to the backyard where he planned to load them into his car. There was no way I could handle the entire set in one trip, so I brought up the two larger drums figuring to make a second trip for the others. When I walked out to the car with only two drums he glared at me and sternly asked, "Why didn't you bring the entire set?" I responded that I was afraid I'd drop one if I tried to carry them all at once. The blood rushed to his face and he yelled, "You defied me; I told you to bring everything!" To emphasize his displeasure he fired a looping left hook at my chin and instinctively I countered with a right over his left. Both punches landed but I had pulled mine to avoid breaking his dental plate because I knew we couldn't afford unnecessary bills.

In a barely controlled rage he ordered me into the house. In the kitchen I walked to the far corner by the cupboard and he stood across the room with his back to the stove. He began cursing me and shouting, "You need to be taught a lesson; you're nothing but a goddamned ingrate. When this is over, you're going to reform school, by God!"

I wasn't sure what was going to happen but I knew there was a fair chance that he planned to jump my ass. The thought scared the hell out of me. We both knew he had little chance against me in a fair fight, but I also knew he hadn't survived fifteen years as a union organizer fighting by any goddamned rules. He had told me many times, "Never give the other guy a chance," and he often expounded on the effectiveness of a knee to the groin and a brick to the head.

I figured it would take four steps to reach me. That would give me time to grab a butcher knife from the drawer by my right hand. Then I planned to kill the sonofabitch. But he didn't come, he just kept shouting and threatening and then one final time he said he would arrange to have me sent to reform school the next day. With that he went outside, loaded his drums into the car and left.

For years my mother had played one of us against the other, but faced with the full effect of her manipulation she stood rigidly in the dining room doorway, pale, wide-eyed, and tight-lipped, in apparent awe of the monster of her making. Perhaps none of the scenarios born of her sick mind had included one or both of us lying dead on her clean kitchen floor.

Dad continued to threaten me with reform school for a week or so and then just stopped talking to me. We didn't speak to each other again until 1942, when I announced that I was going to enlist. That was something we had to discuss because I was under age and had to have his approval. On the day I left for Manhattan Beach he shook my hand and wished me luck.

The Ultimate Graduation Gift

When I looked out my little window again, I was surprised to find that the picture had changed. The landscape had closed in on us—we had left the open, flat, glacial lakebeds. Small streams flowed through narrow, rock-lined ravines sliced into the sides of wooded hills. Rocky ledges fringing the hillsides were clearly visible through the leafless trees. Now and then I caught flashes of rocky road cuts bordering the distant highway. There were flat, cleared areas nestled among the hills where neat farm houses and barns stood watch over fallow fields.

There was no snow on the ground; not even old, dirty shoveled piles lined the driveways. Although a bit unusual for northern Ohio in early March, it was no disappointment for me. It's not that I dislike snow, or that I never dreamed of a white Christmas, but in Canton, fresh snow was soon converted to a depressing black by the heavy soot fallout from local steel mills.

On sunny days the mixture of ice, snow and carbon packed on the city streets melted into slushy, oily pools, and ran in dark rivulets along the curbs. It was common to see pedestrians standing at a street corner, covered with oozing goop, loudly cursing and shaking angry fists at a passing auto. Most drivers sped on ignoring their victims, but a few sadists would turn and laugh, grin and wave the middle digit.

After several decades we reached Wooster. Now we were only thirty miles from Canton and occasionally I could see autos cruising along U.S. 30. It was called the Lincoln Highway nearly everywhere, but in Canton it bore the Indian name Tuscarawas and it passed within a few blocks of my parents' home. No one in Canton could pronounce Tuscarawas so everyone called it Tusc. It was that way on the street signs, too; some people lived there all their lives and didn't know that Tusc was an abbreviation. When strangers sometimes asked what Tusc really stood for, most of us were too embarrassed to try to pronounce the name, so we just spelled it for them. But that caused a problem too, because most of us couldn't spell Tuscarawas.

I hadn't spent much time around Wooster; none, actually. Nevertheless the landscape of long round hills and wide, gentle valleys bore a certain resemblance to the area south of Canton where I had grown up. When I was a kid no one I knew traveled much. For one thing, hardly anyone had a car, for another, few of the older folks, especially the women, knew how to drive. I eventually learned when, as a twenty-nine-year-old geology instructor at Southern Illinois University, I purchased my first car. The few people in our neighborhood who had cars could barely afford the gasoline necessary to get them to work and back. There were buses then, and trains, of course; but no one I knew could afford the fare out of town.

As a teenager, I did manage one real auto trip. When, in June 1941, I unexpectedly graduated from McKinley High, my parents were so astonished and relieved they promised to take me to New York City to see the June 18th heavyweight title fight between the skinny, brash Irish kid from Pittsburgh, Billy Conn and the seemingly invincible Brown Bomber, Joe Louis. Conn was my all-time hero. I had patterned my boxing style after his and more than a year earlier as a skinny sixteen-year-old neophyte featherweight I had predicted that Conn, just a middleweight then, would be the next heavyweight king. The opportunity to witness my dream come true was mind boggling, the great gift of my life—perhaps even a miracle.

Aunt Maggie, my mother's sister, provided her car for the trip and my dad drove. I was never told how the trip was financed, but I suppose the money as well as the transportation was a gift from Aunt Maggie.

When we arrived in New York City, my mother and Aunt Maggie checked into a YWCA and Dad and I at a nearby YMCA. The next day, as I recall, was spent walking the streets of the city and staring at tall buildings. In the evening we drove to the old Polo Grounds and joined the rest of the 55,000 people who had come to see the bout.

Earlier in the day Louis had been installed as a four-to-one favorite, but at fight time my guess is that few of the fans, including those who had come in on the special trains from Pittsburgh, would have been willing to wager much of their own money at those odds on the chances of the 169-pound Conn.

In the first round, pasty-white and looking frightened and fragile, Conn did little to instill confidence in his chances of winning or, for that matter, of going more than two or three rounds. He fought with tentative reserve as if awed by the impossibility of the task he had foolishly undertaken. And I remember well my feeling of horror when in the midst of the round he uncharacteristically lost his footing while attempting to avoid a Louis punch and fell awkwardly to the canvas.

But I needn't have been concerned for Billy. During that first round he successfully dispelled whatever devils of fear and doubt he had brought with him to the Polo Grounds. Moments into round two Conn brought the fans to their feet when he launched an electrifying, audacious assault on the heavyweight champion. The fans remained standing for the remainder of the fight, shouting encouragement to the scrawny contender who round after round did an incredible dance with death. Carrying the fight to Louis, outmaneuvering, outspeeding, outboxing, and at times outpunching Joe, he repeatedly ruffled the feathers of the normally implacable Louis. Then, in the twelfth round Conn stunned Louis with a flurry of mighty blows, buckling his knees and glazing his eyes, coming within an eyelash of flooring the great Brown Bomber.

In the minute between rounds that followed nearly everyone in the Polo Grounds except Louis and his corner man, Chappie Blackburn, thought they would soon witness the crowning of a new world heavyweight title holder. Ahead on points, Conn had only to win one of the remaining three rounds to take the decision and the championship.

Few of us, including Conn's manager Johnny Ray, gave serious thought to the possibility that Conn would entertain the rather fanciful notion that the only proper and honorable way for a contender to separate a boxing champion from his crown was to render him senseless. Nevertheless, forty-five seconds into round 13 it became clear to all present that the relatively light-hitting Conn had decided to cast his fate to the wind and go for a knockout of one of the most dangerous punchers in ring history. Incredibly he almost succeeded.

The battle once joined, was of course, to the death—no quarter asked, none granted. Each man unleashed his full arsenal of bombs and at toe-to-toe range most reached their intended targets with nerve-deadening effectiveness. When perhaps thirty seconds were left in the round, Louis stunned Conn with a very short and very powerful right uppercut flush on his chin. He followed with a barrage of two lefts and four more rights to the head. Conn's body turned slowly to the right and then pitched forward to the canvas where he was counted out by referee Eddie Joseph.

Joe Williams of the *New York World Telegraph* wrote the following day, "Young William David Conn of Pittsburgh is the only fighter we know who ever won the heavyweight championship and lost it in the same night."

For those who enjoy *Reader's Digest* abridged novels, the fight can be summed up effectively in the words of the two fighters. Before the fight, in response to a reporter's question about how he would handle Conn's superior speed, Louis responded, "He can run but he can't hide." After the fight, Conn, reflecting on Louis's punching power, said, "He's dangerous as long as he is standing."

It took a long time for the huge crowd to work its way out of the stadium. When we finally reached the street by a side exit the newsboys were there hawking special editions of their papers which in great black headlines blared out to us what we already knew: "LOUIS WINS, LOUIS KO'S CONN IN 13TH ROUND." In the largest headline letters I had ever seen, 2.7 inches by 0.7 inches, the *Daily Mirror* Extra declared, "LOUIS BY K.O."

As I attempted to read the round-by-round accounts of the fight in one of the papers, a stadium side door opened and three men hurried out and climbed into a waiting cab which soon sped off into the darkness. It had been Billy Conn, Johnny Ray and one of Conn's corner men. Hurrying then lest our coach turn to a pumpkin, we drove back to our sterile quarters at the Y's.

On my return to Canton I began to assemble a record of the fight and of the two fighters in a scrapbook. Through the years I have maintained and added bits and pieces of Louis-Conn lore to the record. Reading the clippings in the book (actually two volumes now) today it tells me that the reality of that evening exceeded the dream brought with me to the Polo Grounds so long ago. The two warriors were destined for the remainder of their lives to share the nostalgic glow of historic perspective and inevitably to become, in their later years, close friends.

In January, 1981, *Ring Magazine* (the Bible of boxing) reported that in an exclusive poll of boxing experts, the 1941 Louis-Conn fight was voted the greatest bout in the history of the sport. In 1954, Louis was elected by the Modern Writers and Broadcasters to the Boxing Hall of Fame and Conn was inducted in 1963.

When Louis died in April 1981, at age sixty-six, he was buried with full military honors at Arlington National Cemetery. A young *New York Times* sports reporter who covered the services identified Billy Conn at the gravesite. "I saw," he wrote, "a tall man with a gentle face and a shock of white hair, who forty years earlier had fought thirteen memorably ferocious rounds with the Brown Bomber."

In May 1993, I perhaps made the last entry in that old scrapbook—the announcement I had cut from the *Austin American Statesman* of the death in Pittsburgh of Billy Conn at age seventy-five. The story released by the

Associated Press of course told how Conn in his memorable fight with Louis fifty-two years earlier had been knocked out in the thirteenth round. He was, the article read, living up to his reputation for being cocky and brash.

My mother's memories of the fight were somewhat different than my own. Whenever reminded of that evening in the Polo Grounds, her face would light up as she recalled her supreme moment of histrionic achievement. For several minutes she had successfully diverted the attention of a substantial number of the fans in our sector of the stadium from the fight in the ring below us. It happened during the second round when most of us stood shouting words of encouragement to Billy Conn as he rained blows on the champion. Suddenly she realized that she was no longer the focal point of anyone at all. It was a condition that from her point of view demanded immediate and dramatic remedial action. For such occasions she possessed a varied repertoire of devices to attract attention to herself at the expense of everyone near to her. That evening she chose the always effective fainting-collapsing ploy.

Before any of us could intervene she had slithered to the floor between my father and me. When several individuals from the row behind us bent forward to offer their assistance and express their concern she fluttered her eyelashes seductively and in her best Minnie Mouse voice asked that someone summon a doctor.

Maggie, Dad and I turned and peered down on my mother in silent disgust. Assured that she would survive, we redirected our attention to the fight. I remember thinking that if she grabbed my pants leg and tried to pull me to the floor with her I would step on her throat and crush her larynx. But she didn't need me—she was in her glory, being fawned over by a dozen or more concerned strangers who had temporarily given up watching the fight to come to her aid.

Not long after she had called for a doctor I heard a voice on the public address asking if there was a doctor in the house. The next time I looked down at her, a man in a business suit was bent over her, one hand on her forehead, another holding her wrist. The doctor, I assumed. If she had died there on that cement floor, it would have been with a smile of satisfaction.

I never discussed that episode with either Aunt Maggie or my father. It wasn't necessary. The expressions of revulsion I had seen on their faces as they looked down on her crumpled body told me more than a thousand words.

Walking into War

Though we may have lacked autos and bus and train fare in the '30s we did have legs and feet and we made regular use of them for walking. Walking was easier than now because most streets were flanked by sidewalks placed there for that purpose. And in most residential areas there was so little automobile traffic one could safely walk in the streets, or for that matter, sleep in them. We walked to the stores, to school, to work if we had a job, to the homes of our relatives and friends, and sometimes we walked just for the hell of it.

At an early age my friend Bob Schario and I became avid hikers. In a few years we covered almost every highway, back road and pathway that existed within a twenty-mile radius of south Canton. When we were old enough and had earned enough money we purchased 22 caliber rifles which we carried on all our hikes, mainly for target shooting.

In our senior year we took Mr. Goss's geology course at McKinley High. Thereafter geological observations played an increased role in our wanderings through the Ohio countryside. We talked then of someday becoming professional geologists, dreamed of exploring faraway lands and one day in our old age becoming members of the Explorers' Club. I did pursue those dreams and was even elected a Fellow of the Explorers' Club in 1979. Bob, following the beat of a different drummer, eventually chose to go into the pharmacological business and to live out his life in Canton.

In 1941 the Canton YMCA announced that they planned to organize a hiker's club and that anyone interested should show up at the Y lobby the following Sunday prepared for the club's inaugural excursion. Although never a joiner and rarely a willing participant in organized, structured, social activities, I had nothing better to do that Sunday so I walked downtown to the Y just to see what kind of people would want to join a hiking club.

I arrived at the scheduled time and took a seat in a distant corner of the lobby

20

where I could hear and observe all that transpired without giving the appearance of being in any way interested in what was going on about me.

It was easy to spot the would-be hikers—they had come prepared, it seemed, for an all-out assault on the South Pole. Even in the winter when I went hiking I dressed with an eye on freedom of movement: long johns, dungarees, denim shirt, field boots, long wool socks, gloves, two or three wool sweaters, and, at times, ear muffs. These people had shown up with horse blanket plaid jackets, snowsuits, knee boots, galoshes, mittens, fur mufflers, long wool scarves, and brightly colored stocking caps sporting obscene frilly tassels. I had no idea how any of them expected to be able to walk at all. And it seemed certain that if any of them fell down they would never be able to right themselves without the help of a derrick.

There were about twenty-five of them, mostly women as far as I could discern. At that time it was my considered belief that no woman was capable of becoming a serious cross-country hiker. The men were, for the most part, soft, flabby, sedentary candidates for heart attacks, at least as hopeless as the women. Worst of all in my mind was the leader, a little Napoleonic twit filled to his eyebrows with exaggerated self-importance. Today I can see him as the perfect Army drill sergeant. He liked to say things like, "Listen up, you people, I'm in charge here. You'll follow my lead at all times. Never leave the group without my permission." I knew if I did go with them on this hike I would stuff the SOB in the first waste receptacle we came across.

Anyway, as I listened to him I learned that they would assemble in the lobby each Sunday at 1:00 p.m. and then at 1:30 they would load up in cars, drive to the public park of the day, hike for several miles and then, by 6:00 p.m., return to the Y.

It was all more than I could handle so about fifteen minutes after the group had gone to find their cars I left the Y and walked home. When I entered the house it was empty; my parents were visiting relatives. Disgusted that I had just walked five miles for no reason I flipped on the radio and threw myself onto the big old leather sofa in the living room.

I became aware of a male voice describing an air attack, somewhere in the world—ships sunk, men dead, planes shot down. Nothing new, it seemed. There was a lot of that going on around the world. I had no idea where this latest battle had been fought. The man had mentioned a few names like Hick's Field and Pearl Harbor, but they meant nothing to me. Then, following a dramatic pause, he said, "This means that a state of war exists between the United States and the Empire of Japan."

21

I bolted upright to a sitting position at the edge of the sofa where I tried to assimilate the man's words and to make sense of them. Gradually a current of excitement penetrated the shock that had enveloped me. It seemed, I thought, December 7 is my lucky day—the damned Japs had booked my passage out of Canton.

Of Footballs and Teapots

Massillon hove into view. Massillon was a dirty little steel mill city in Stark County, eight miles west of Canton. Massillon was famous throughout America for its high school Massillon Tiger football teams, especially those coached by the legendary Paul Brown in the late '30s and early '40s. The chief rival of the Tigers were the Bulldogs of Canton McKinley, who they inevitably met during the fall of each season for the state championship. They were not by any definition ordinary high school teams. They out-weighed the teams of the Big Ten schools, out-drew ninety-five percent of the nation's college teams, and routinely pulverized northeastern Ohio university teams in pre-season exhibition games.

The intense rivalry between the Tigers and the Bulldogs was a holdover from the days of their professional predecessors who had represented Massillon and Canton in the post-World War I years. Knute Rockne had played for the professional Tigers in 1922 and 1923, the years that the great Indian athlete Jim Thorpe had led the Canton Bulldogs to undefeated seasons and to two world championships.

I never met Rockne or Thorpe, but when I was four years old my father one day introduced me to Pete Calac and Joe Guyon, who had played beside Thorpe on Canton's championship teams. I recall them not as football stars but as they then were: towering, broad men in blue; beat cops on the city police force.

In recognition of the role Stark County had played as the "cradle of professional football", the National Football League in 1963 established its Hall of Fame adjacent to Canton McKinley's Fawcett Stadium. Among the first inductees into the Hall were Joe Guyon, Jim Thorpe, Marion Motley (one of my high school classmates) and, of course, Massillon's Paul Brown.

When one considers that during the Great Depression the Massillon Chamber of Commerce presented each newly born male child with a regulation football, one might think a case could be made that the denizens of that small city were just a little wacko. It's a view that seems to gain some credence from the knowledge that during that same period Massillon was as renowned in northeast Ohio for its mental institution as it was for its football team.

In those days a mental institution was formally referred to as an insane asylum. But as heartless kids we usually spoke of the one in Massillon as the Crazy House or the Nut Factory; our parents just called it "Massillon." When adults had particularly bad days they commonly would exclaim with obvious exasperation, "If things don't get better they're going to take me to Massillon." Listeners usually indicated their comprehension and empathy with nods of the head and knowing smiles.

At one time or another most of us considered the possibility that we were imminent candidates for Massillon, but generally we succeeded at concealing our condition from the authorities. Several of our neighbors were not so lucky. Perhaps the most memorable of those was Mrs. Connor, my buddy Ed's mother.

Mrs. Connor's husband had been in the American Army in France during World War I. He returned home physically unscathed but the horrors he had endured left open wounds in his psyche that would never heal. During the many years that I knew him he spoke to me at length only once. Staring off into the distance with vacant eyes and taking no note of me, he recalled battles and retreating armies and stacked bodies in torn woods, and he spoke of the stench of death. I was only ten or eleven years old and too young to understand most of what he was saying. However, instinctively I knew he was re-living experiences so horrible he could never completely erase them from his memory. In any case, I always thought that one-sided conversation went a long way toward explaining some of the odd behavior of Mr. Connor.

By choice Mr. Connor was a friendless recluse who had once succumbed to human frailty long enough to acquire a wife and son. Subsequently he stoically and unfailingly accepted the responsibilities inherent in the commission of such a rash act. He did this much as a zombie might, with no joy and no detectable trace of affection for either wife or son.

Mr. Connor worked in the brickyards on Belden Extension, only a few blocks from his home. When not working he rarely left his house—not even to walk in the yard or sit on the porch. His occasional encounters with neighbors were dispensed with politely but in a manner that clearly stated he did not care to linger for casual chatter and idle gossip. It is doubtful that he knew the names of most of his neighbors after living in the same house for thirty years.

The Connors never entertained and did not encourage visitors. In the many years that I knew the family I was never invited into the house. I think even door-to-door salesmen and hobos avoided their doorstep. For most neighbors contact with the Connors was confined to brief encounters with Mrs. Connor in the grocery store or on a city bus. It was from their son, Ed, that we learned how the family spent their evenings.

After supper, Mr. Connor would permit only one light to be turned on at any given time. This invariably would be the lamp that stood by his living room chair where he read the newspaper. Because this was the only lighted room in the house, it assured a silent hour of "family togetherness" each evening. If, for any reason, one person had to leave the room and turn on a light elsewhere, the living room light was extinguished for the duration of that person's absence.

One morning Mrs. Connor went into her kitchen to prepare breakfast for her husband, something she had done hundreds of time in the past without any unusual disturbances. However, this morning as she reached for an egg, her teakettle volunteered several unflattering observations regarding her attire and general appearance. When she suggested that the pot mind its own business it impertinently responded with a shrill and sustained hissing.

During the following weeks Mrs. Connor had many conversations with her teakettle and she related them to anyone who would listen. It became apparent that she had developed a love/hate relationship with the kettle from which she derived a certain satisfaction.

Sometimes neighbors who had difficulty taking Mrs. Connor's affliction seriously would greet her in the grocery store with, "What's new from the pot?" Oblivious to such attempts at facetiousness Mrs. Connor would unblinkingly proceed to detail her latest adventures in the kitchen while her victims valiantly fought a compulsion to explode in wild laughter.

Mrs. Connor's delusion was the most popular topic in our neighborhood for several months. One small but vocal group insisted the teakettle was possessed and that St. Benedict's priest should be called upon to perform an exorcism on the evil little devil. On the other hand, the majority, including Mr. Connor, adhered to the more pragmatic view that Mrs. Connor was simply wacky.

The county authorities, learning of Mrs. Connor's plight, quickly adopted the majority opinion and two men in white came to her house, gathered her into a waiting vehicle, and took her to Massillon.

I never did learn what happened to the teakettle.

Little Chicago Revisited

The train slowly moved through the suburbs of Canton; the station was only minutes away. When the conductor called, "Canton, next stop Canton," I was up, into the aisle and gathering my gear. As the train ground to a halt the station platform came into view. Fifteen or twenty people were gathered there to either board the train or to greet friends or relatives. I didn't need to scan their faces for someone I knew because, as usual, no one would be there waiting for me. During the war I had arrived at this station four or five times and each time had walked the two and a half miles home alone. One arrival remains vivid in my mind.

When our ship, which had been heavily damaged in a typhoon, came into Seattle for repairs, I had unexpectedly been granted two weeks leave while she was in dry dock. Checking my limited financial resources I found that after purchasing a train ticket I would be left with only a dime. Food or no food, I was determined to make the seventy-two hour trip home. The first twenty-four hours I stood in the aisle of the crowded train. Afterwards I found a seat but still had no food. The third day, in Lima, Ohio, a group of USO ladies carrying baskets of sandwiches and apples met us at the train station. There is little doubt that those lovely ladies saved my life—I hadn't eaten for sixty-five hours.

When I reached my parents' house I staggered into the dining room and collapsed on the floor. My mother, without asking how my trip had been, immediately began to relate the details of her latest illness and disasters. Lulled by the drone of her voice I was soon peacefully asleep. The next moment my mother, obviously greatly distressed, was shaking me, demanding that I wake up. As I stared blankly into her face she asked, with tears in her eyes, "How can you be so inconsiderate and uncaring that you fall asleep while I'm trying to talk to you?"

I was in no mood for politeness as I shoved my way down the aisle, knocking several passengers back into their seats with carefully aimed but subtle shifts of my formidable seabag. I hurriedly forced my way through the crowd on the platform and entered the station. Inside I lost no time heading for the door to Market Street. I felt compelled to reach the street as quickly as possible in case someone was following with the news that my discharge had been a mistake and I was to return to Detroit immediately.

Outside the station I found, with a sigh of relief, that I was alone. Getting a firm grip on my seabag and bedroll, I resolutely headed north on Market Street. With luck I'd be home in thirty minutes.

At first I tried to get my bearings. Physically, it seemed nothing much had changed. The old, bumpy, rutted, red brick street looked familiar and the buildings were as drab and dingy as ever. On closer inspection, however, I noted that many of the buildings, empty during the Depression, now sported prosperous looking businesses and shops. There were customers, clutching purchases and whistling happy tunes, emerging from some of the stores. They, too, appeared prosperous. During the war I had heard much about the miseries of tire and gasoline rationing, but I couldn't help noticing that there seemed much more auto traffic on Market Street than in 1941.

Slowly I was getting the feeling that things hadn't really been so bad for the folks at home. They had often complained of the burden of income tax, and the hardships of long work hours and meatless Tuesdays. I remembered well that these same people a few years earlier didn't pay income tax because they had no work, and that for all of us virtually every day had been meatless.

Those of us in the service encountered civilians like these everywhere we went. They were the people who wouldn't allow us in the better restaurants, or give us a room in a respectable hotel. They were the people who put out the signs in Norfolk, Virginia, that read, "Dogs and Sailors stay off the grass." These were the "patriots" who in private confided to friends that if the war would only last another two years they could pay off the mortgages on their houses.

Sometimes, after weeks of being tossed about on a stormy Pacific, when we were tired and lonely and discouraged and when we had lost all hope of survival, some of us uttered a silent prayer that the Japs might bomb a few American cities and take the minds of the civilians off their terrible hardships.

At Fourth Street, I paused long enough to glance three blocks north to DeWalt Avenue where I was born on June 30, 1923. The house, of course, was long gone, the victim of commercial development. My mother's doctor stayed at the house on the eve of the happy event. He slept in a rocker and snored so loudly that he woke my eight-year-old cousin Pete, who thought someone was mowing the lawn in the middle of the night. Finally, I assume to everyone's relief, I decided to make my entry into the world at 8:00 a.m.

In the next block I looked across the street at the old Windsor Theater. During the war their movies were always free to servicemen in uniform. Perhaps my most pleasant memory of the war years emerges from the evening,when, home on leave, I had put on my civvies, gone to the Windsor, and purchased a ticket for a double feature. For three wonderful and peaceful hours, I sat in that darkened theater creating the illusion in my mind that the entire war had been, after all, only a long and particularly hideous dream.

In the 200 block of Market, I walked past the four-story red brick building that housed the Cootie Club. The Cootie Club, conveniently located one and a half blocks west of the center of the red light district and two blocks east of the city police department, was the principal focal point of illegal gambling operations in Canton. It was also the headquarters of the local Mafia.

When I enlisted in the Coast Guard in 1942, most criminal activity in Canton was controlled by a man known far and wide as Nick the Greek. There were a lot of people in Canton who looked upon Nick as an all-around good guy, a friend, a Robin Hood type, who robbed the rich and other undeserving types and used at least some of his ill-gotten gains to help the needy. He was especially lauded for having, during the years of his reign as Canton's godfather, provided the tuition for numerous young people who otherwise could not have afforded to attend college.

His generosity also was known to extend to such worthy causes as the policemen' s retirement fund, the campaign expenses of certain well-known politicians, and the arrangement of therapeutic sea voyages for stressed-out judges.

The FBI was unimpressed with Nick's philanthropic deeds. Following an intensive investigation into his operations it became their considered opinion that he was, in fact, a very dangerous sociopath who should be confined in a maximum-security cage as soon as possible. By 1943 with the cooperation of the IRS, the FBI had managed to engineer a Grand Jury indictment against Nick for alleged income tax evasion.

While he waited for the Grand Jury to convene Nick holed up in a suite in the Onesto Hotel immediately behind the courthouse on Canton's square. Just across the street from the Onesto on W. Tusc was the Elite (pronounced ee-lite) Restaurant. The Elite was the favored gathering place for an odd assortment of gangland chiefs, high-ranking police officers, plain-clothes detectives, labor leaders, lawyers, judges and prominent politicians. Even to a casual observer it must have been apparent that the seat of political power and influence in Canton centered more nearly on the Elite Restaurant than on the City Hall across the street.

Outside the Elite on the sidewalk there were always, day and night, at least a half-dozen young punks loitering about, cigarettes hanging from the corners of their mouths, laughing, joking, propositioning every passing female, threatening their male escorts. Everyone knew who they were, including the police who did nothing to control them. They were the wheelmen, bodyguards, and errand boys for the gangsters who dined and dealt inside.

They all knew me. I had gone to school for four years with most of them and twelve years with some of them. Whenever I passed by the Elite they greeted me with boisterous male enthusiasm: "Hi, Jules, old buddy, how're things going?" Usually one would walk over, wrap an arm around my shoulder and poke a friendly knuckle in my ribs. Some, knowing I was a boxer, would approach me with a slow, exaggerated fighter's move, a right to the body, a looping left to the head.

With repetition these public displays of affection and comradeship by some of Canton's lowest life forms became increasingly embarrassing. Certain that I was in danger of gaining about town the reputation of being a mob member, I resolved one day never again to go near the Elite Restaurant. It was a sensible stratagem, but one not entirely effective.

From time to time some of my gangster chums were sent out by their bosses to run errands around town. On these occasions they drove big, shiny, black limos known to everyone in town as "mob mobiles". At times when they spotted me walking along the street they would smile and wave, or shout greetings from an open window. Onlookers first gave the car a long look and then would fix a wary eye on me until I was at what they considered a safe distance. Even more embarrassing were the occasions when one of the fellows would pull the car up to the curb and engage me in friendly chitchat or worse, jump from the car and go into one of their stupid male-bounding routines. These unwelcome encounters with the underworld ended only when I left Canton for boot camp at Manhattan Beach in Brooklyn.

While Nick languished in his hotel suite, the FBI kept close tabs on his movements, monitored his phone calls, and identified and checked out his visitors. In an effort to impress on him the futility of attempting something foolish such as leaving town, the FBI periodically provided him with a copy of their surveillance log which detailed his every move during the previous twenty-four or forty-eight hours.

Then late one evening, somehow undetected by the elaborate FBI surveillance network, Nick walked out of the Onesto and entered an auto driven by someone in whom he thought he could entrust his life. Apparently they drove to a warehouse on Belden Extension in southeast Canton, close to the brick kilns where Mr. Connor worked and only seven or eight blocks from my parents' home. Early the next morning his bullet-riddled body was found on the floor inside the building by a warehouse worker.

To my knowledge there was never an official explanation offered for Nick's nocturnal excursion to the warehouse. It seems reasonable to assume that if, indeed, Nick was acting of his own free will, he went there that evening with the expectation of meeting with someone in whom he had considerable confidence. It could have been one or more of his own lieutenants who, fearful that their boss might turn state's evidence, decided to eliminate him.

With the removal of Nick the Greek, the Grand Jury was dissolved and the FBI closed the book on the case and left town. No one was ever charged with the murder. Within the year, apparently having taken over all of Nick's operations, the Mafia set up headquarters in the Cootie Club.

Before I was born, Canton's nationwide notoriety as an incubator of crime and corruption had earned it the title of "Little Chicago". By 1937 when I entered high school that unflattering appellation was no longer in common use although crime and corruption in the city remained as vigorous as ever.

Crime permeated the city from its ghettos to its courthouse. It was spawned in the filth and clutter of its worn and rough streets and narrow, sinister alleys lined by bleak rows of neglected brick buildings and tired, decaying, soot-grayed frame houses. It was nurtured by its sterile, red-brown streams, long ago poisoned by chemical effluents and human refuse and excretion, and its air fouled by voluminous fiery emissions vomited from its steel mills, foundries and brick kilns.

When I was five years old my dad took me downtown to view the place near the police station where a city policeman had been shot to death. In a last ditch effort to evade his assailant the policeman tried to duck down a stairwell leading to the basement of a business establishment. He didn't make it. The killer, standing on the sidewalk, fired several shots at his victim. My dad pointed out two small shatter marks in the cement wall a foot or so above the sidewalk level. He said, "Those marks were made by bullets that missed the policeman or passed through his body."

We stood there for perhaps a minute, side by side, looking into the empty stairwell and the scars in the gray wall. Then Dad took my hand and led me down the street to a large brick building. It was a funeral home. In a room inside he led me to an open coffin. I stared, almost at eye level, into the pale dead face of a man dressed in a crisp, blue uniform. Dad told me it was the policeman shot in the stairwell.

In a few minutes we left and drove home. Dad never mentioned that day again but I was unable to erase what I had seen from my mind. From time to time, through the years, I tried to understand what it had all meant and why I had been shown those terrible things. Eventually I became convinced Dad had been trying to tell me something, perhaps teach me a valuable lesson. But what? Though I often tried I could never discover the answer.

Old Central High School used to be on Tusc two blocks from the courthouse on the square. During my freshman year some of my buddies and I spent many of our lunch hours roaming the adjacent city streets. One day as we approached Bill's Diner on North Cleveland, a prowl car slammed up to the curb in a cloud of dust and two burly patrolmen with drawn nightsticks burst from the vehicle and raced into the diner. In a few moments, as we waited near the curb with a growing crowd to see what was about to develop, the two policemen struggled out of the diner dragging a drunken man between them. When they reached the patrol car one of the policemen released his hold on the prisoner to open the back door. At that moment the prisoner, a middle-aged man in Goodwill Mission attire, suddenly attempted to break free. Instantly both policemen beat the man mercilessly with their nightsticks until he slumped to the gutter, bloody and broken. Did this somehow relate to what my father had tried to teach me at the stairwell?

About two years later I was standing on the crowded square in mid afternoon waiting for a bus. Suddenly a dark, four-door sedan squealed up to the curb and five or six mean looking gang members leaped from the car and charged at a young fellow who stood about twenty-five feet to my left. With no chance to turn and run or to reach for a weapon he was knocked to the sidewalk and with impressively coordinated ferocity kicked and beaten senseless. Before any of the onlookers could respond the gang members were back in their car and speeding down South Market. With no desire to be questioned by the police I walked several blocks up Market to a different bus stop.

I didn't know the name of the victim but I had recognized him as a member of a street gang led by one of my classmates at McKinley High, Frank Perrone, whose brother Patsy had once gone ten rounds with Joe Louis.

Frank and I were taking a joker course called "Occupations". The course, designed for dumb jocks, was taught (I use the word loosely) by the head football coach who confined his lectures to tales of his glorious days as a college star and of his spectacular successes as a high school coach. That the course work was not particularly demanding is indicated by the observation that Jim Inman, the football team's star running back who appeared in class just once during the entire semester, "earned" an A in the course.

When I saw Frank in class the next day I began to tell him of the event I had witnessed on the square. Smiling he held up an arm, palm out. "That's okay, Jules, thanks for the info, but I already know all about it. Everything's covered. Tonight we take out those guys," he said ominously.

During the next class meeting Frank leaned forward from the seat behind me and whispered into my ear, "We took care of them. Caught them in their pool hall on Walnut last night. Busted up the place and kicked the crap out of them. They won't bother anyone again for a while." Perhaps there was connection here with the bullet holes in the wall.

On my first leave after boot camp in 1943, Dad and I drove downtown to the old Grand Theater on Third SE. He wanted to talk with his long-time friend Bill Gieb, who was currently doing drums in the burlesque orchestra. I hung around on the stage while they discussed labor union business. In time, bored with talk, I wandered outside and stood on the sidewalk under the marquee.

The Grand hadn't always been a rundown burlesque theater. In its glory days before my birth, it had reigned as one of the theatrical citadels of northeastern Ohio. My parents spoke often and fondly of some of the great shows they had seen there: O'Neill's *Long Day's Journey Into Night,* Frederick March's *Dr. Jekyl and Mr. Hyde,* and appearances of the acrobatic Douglas Fairbanks, Sr.

At some time, mixed in with such performances, Dad and Gieb had done minstrels at the Grand. For the past twenty years they had worked in Canton as sign painters, but their friendship had been hatched and nurtured in show business, in barbershop quartets, the vaudeville circuit, and big bands.

In 1928 Joe DuBar and his Orchestra had won a regular slot on the local radio station, WHBC. My dad was the leader, played the banjo, and was the featured vocalist. Bill Gieb, of course, was on the drums.

Each Wednesday evening from 8:00 to 8:30 p.m. my mother and I listened to the show on the console radio that resided in a corner of the dining room. Each show opened with the playing of the theme song, *Who,* and concluded with a message from Dad, "Good night, Jules, it's time to go to bed now."

32

One or two evenings each week band rehearsals were held at our home. It was a small orchestra of only six to eight members but with their instruments and the large upright piano that stood against the inner wall they filled our living room and overflowed into the adjacent dining room.

I was always sent to bed before the rehearsals began, but the clamor of male voices, the pounding, blasting, music, and the clouds of cigarette smoke that engulfed our small house combined to keep me wide awake for at least another hour. Sometimes I slipped from my bed, tiptoed across the room and spied on the proceedings until someone headed for the bathroom would discover me crouched in the hallway shadows and send me off to my bed.

I still remember some of the fellows who rehearsed there. Bill Gieb, Sam Unger on bass, Harry Comische on the trumpet and Frank DeVol at the piano. Unger and Comische, a devout alcoholic, enjoyed widespread reputations for their musical skills and were regularly used as fill-ins by the name bands that came into town to play at the Moonlight Ballroom at Meyers Lake. Frank DeVol was only 17 then, but he went on to form his own big band and later carved out a very successful movie career in Hollywood. For many years my father loved to tell anyone who might listen that it was he who gave Frank DeVol his first professional job.

With the stock market crash of 1929 and the onslaught of the Great Depression, Bill Gieb's career as an entertainer as well as my dad's declined rapidly. More and more they became dependent on their skills as sign painters to earn a living. When the sign business, too, folded, they were reduced to standing in government relief lines for handouts and finally, to the ultimate indignity of the WPA Symphonic Orchestra.

Gieb was a man born to entertain. He seemed fulfilled only on center stage in the spotlight facing a receptive audience. During the Depression years he visited our home often. In the living room he would tower over me on unsteady legs and grin at my parents. His look at those times seemed to say, "You can deny it if you wish, but I know for a fact that you have carnal knowledge of large furry farm animals."

Almost as an afterthought he would smile knowingly at me, bend forward, pat my head and then with great earnestness, relate to me a long and involved and quite gross tale that I did not understand. The stories always sent my dad into convulsions of uproarious laughter while evoking from my mother a frowning admonition, "Now Bill, you shouldn't tell him things like that, he is just a small boy." Then all three would laugh uncontrollably until tears streamed from their eyes, prompting me to consider the possibility that all old folks were a bit addled in the brain. When he had once again gained control of himself, he invariably demanded, "Tell me, Joe, do you still hide that blackberry wine in the fruit cellar?"

Among Canton's musicians and sign painters, Bill had gained legendary status for his outlandish drunken antics at parties. I saw him in action only once, but it was a memorable performance. The occasion was one of the sign painters' annual family picnics at Meyers Lake Amusement Park when I was about ten years old.

The festivities centered about a large covered pavilion two hundred yards or more from the lake's edge. As soon as we had finished the big meal early in the afternoon, some of my young friends and I raced off to the lake for a dip. The men, at a more leisurely pace, belching contentedly and loosening their belts, sought refuge in shady nests under nearby trees where, as was the custom of sign painters in such circumstances, they planned during the next several hours to drink themselves into zombified, palpitating blobs.

The women, wives and girlfriends, who had planned the picnic, prepared the food, and who had served the men and taken care of the small children, were left to clean up our mess and to preserve the leftovers.

Several hours later, when my friends and I wandered back to the picnic area in search of cold drinks and snacks we were not surprised to find the men where we had left them sprawled on the grass near the pavilion. Some were inert, but most of them seemed in fine shape, singing, laughing, joking and imbibing with impressive gusto. We were surprised, however, to discover that the women were still in the pavilion, seated now, with their backs to us. But it was their behavior that was most perplexing. They were stamping their feet and clapping their hands in a rhythmic frenzy while emitting the kind of piercing shrieks induced either by intense pain or extreme delight. Creeping more closely we soon discovered that the cause of it all was Bill Gieb, up on top of a picnic table with his pants and shorts around his ankles. He was executing a series of overtly lewd grinds, bumps, and pelvic gyrations as he shuffled awkwardly from one end of the table to the other. At irregular intervals he would reach down to his crotch with his left hand, grab his dangling member, and then flagrantly flap it at the ladies in the front row. With each of these displays the women chanted, "Pass the meat this way, big boy."

We stood there, the three of us, in open-mouthed amazement at such an exhibition. Then, having forgotten why it was that we had come to the picnic area, we returned—silent, subdued, and a little bewildered—to the sanctity of the lake and the relative sanity of childhood pleasures.

* * * * *

The day was gray and dreary; the cold had begun to seep beneath my blues and to slip icy fingers under my skivvies. I wondered if my dad might be ready to leave. I shuffled my feet and shook my arms to stimulate a little circulation.

Then I noticed a shabbily dressed man at the corner waiting for a car to pass. As I watched, a dark, silent figure in a long black coat darted from the alley at my left, ran up to the man at the corner and deftly drew the cutting edge of a long knife across the man's throat. As his victim sagged to the gutter the attacker ran back into the alley.

The body in the street was motionless and, assuming the man to be dead, I moved back closer to the theater doorway. I have no idea who called the police—someone across the street in one of the shops who had witnessed the attack, I suppose. In a few minutes a car with flashing red lights pulled up in front of the theater and two plainclothes men stepped out and headed for the victim. By that time a small crowd had gathered to gape at the body.

The cops made a quick examination of the man, questioned a few of the onlookers, and then one of them walked over to me. "Did you see what happened here, sailor?"

"I sure did," I responded, and I proceeded to brief him on the details. He listened impatiently and finally interrupted me. "Why didn't you chase the guy?"

Looking the detective in his eyes, I said, "Well, I may be in uniform, but I'm not crazy. That fellow just killed a man and he was still packing that big blade." He stared at me for a long second as if he wanted to ask something else but then with a look of resignation, and a cynical shrug of his shoulders, he returned to his buddy at the curb. At that moment my dad who, unnoticed by me, had moved to my side, took my arm and led me down the street to where the car was parked. As we left I caught a glimpse of Gieb's broad back disappearing through the entrance to the Grand. *He isn't hanging around*, I thought, *because he knows damned well there is no way he can steal this scene.*

What, I asked, *has this to do, if anything, with two bullets in a wall and a dead policeman?*

Old Queens Never Die

At the corner of South Market and East Tusc I dropped my seabag and bedroll to the sidewalk and stared across the square. The square, presided over by the ancient courthouse on its west boundary, was then Canton's hub. *Nothing*, I thought, *has changed since 1942.* City buses still came and went and milled about in herds like great noisy hippos in search of a favorite water hole. The square was the main transfer point for the city, and all bus routes converged here.

From early morning to late evening people crowded the square waiting for buses, disgorging from buses, boarding buses or just watching buses. There were the endless greetings and farewells among friends, fellow travelers, neighbors, sweethearts, husbands and wives, school children, business associates, job seekers. There were lively discussions of whatever was of immediate interest: the weather, the NRA, WPA, Union activities, the war, Bob Feller, FDR, Father Coughlin, crime, politics, heartburn. Everyone who could come to the square did so, and many came several times daily. Hang around long enough or often enough and one might meet anyone, including those one might normally hope to avoid.

I think it was in 1940 that Cousin Pete began, from time to time, to show up on Canton's square in full drag. He was there, I assumed, to catch a bus—soliciting two blocks from the police station would have been too risky. Understandably he never mingled with the crowds that waited near the curb, but instead discreetly withdrew twenty or thirty feet to the sheltering wall of the courthouse, where he could avoid close scrutiny.

I'm certain that to anyone else Pete, at a distance of ten feet, seemed to be an attractive young lady: long, flouncy skirt, flowered blouse, high heels, pink satin scarf tied around golden curls, lipstick and rouge. Drag or no drag he was instantly recognizable to me at any distance as Cousin Pete. When he spotted me passing across the square and called out in a feminine soprano, "Julie, Julie," and then fluttered from his lair to greet me, I had no doubt that the entire world knew I was being embraced by a bloody queen.

I grew up with Pete and have always been fond of him. He is the nearest thing I've had to a brother (some might say sister), but such public displays of affection in full plumage were extremely disconcerting and enormously humiliating for me.

Pete, eight years my senior, was born in 1915, the illegitimate son of my mother's youngest brother, Earl, and an Italian hooker named Elinore. When Earl came home from work early one afternoon and found Elinore practicing her trade in his bed, they abruptly and permanently parted company. Unwilling to accept any responsibility for his young son, Earl unceremoniously deposited Pete with his sister Maggie and her husband Paul. Then with no apparent second thought or regrets, he proceeded to devote himself seriously to what would become his life-long avocation—the pursuit of women.

By the time I was born in 1923, Uncle Earl had married and was well on his way to producing two additional children, Betty and Layne. He was divorced when I was in the third or fourth grade and that time his wife gained custody of the children, freeing Uncle Earl to resume his eternal quest for the ultimate woman. To my knowledge he fathered no more children, despite the fact that when he died at age sixty-four he was married to his fourth wife.

In the years I knew Earl, I heard him refer to Pete only once. It was in 1939 when learning for the first time of Pete's sexual preference he announced to the entire family that henceforth he would disown Pete as his son.

As a pre-schooler and grade schooler I spent a lot of time in the home of my Aunt Maggie and Uncle Paul. Maggie was tall and angular with a head full of bright red hair, wore horn-rimmed glasses and had atrocious taste in clothes. She hadn't made it through grade school, could barely read and write, and brutalized the English language. She tended to be too loud and too demonstrative, but she laughed a lot, told great stories, and was fun to be with. She fussed over me, spoiled me, and allowed me liberties my mother would never permit. She was always supportive, always in my corner, always there when I needed her. She was my favorite aunt.

Uncle Paul was a burly man with a large head covered with black hair and a permanent four o' clock shadow. He had ham-sized hands with big hairy fingers. He was brusque and rough and had great difficulty relating to small boys. His playful overtures took the form of painful Dutch rubs and crushing bear hugs that only served to scare the hell out of me. I was sure he liked me, but we never became close. When he died in 1941 I attended the funeral of a man I never really knew.

On those occasions when I stayed at their house I saw very little of Uncle Paul. He worked six days a week as a sales manager at Pearl Ford Motor Co. and in his spare time operated a one-man real estate business and pursued young girls. During the school year, until I entered grade school, I spent many days alone with Aunt Maggie. Parts of those days I played in the basement with the two Airedales, Muggs and Jack. I also spent a lot of time on the floor of Pete's room playing with his neat toys. Pete had more terrific toys than anyone else I knew and he was very proud of them. He was also very fussy with his toys. Toys were never to be mistreated or misused, and each toy had its special place in his room. I didn't mistreat or damage any of his things, but I did have a tendency to spread the toys all over the room and then go away without putting them back in their proper places.

When Pete returned from school late in the afternoon he always went directly to his room to check the mess I had made. Usually at that time of day I managed to be in the kitchen with Maggie having cookies and milk. Knowing from experience what was about to take place I waited a bit nervously for the first wails of anguished distress to sally forth from the room upstairs. Such outbursts were always quickly followed by a rush of pounding feet as Pete charged down the stairs and headed for the kitchen. As soon as he reached the dining room he would cry out in tones of practiced indignation, "Mom, Mom, he made a mess in my room again. All my things are scattered all over the floor. Make him go up there right this minute and put everything where it belongs." Then he would glower at me and in a theatrical tone, say, "I never want you to go into my room again. Do you understand?" When he had concluded his tirade Maggie, making every effort to inject a note of sternness in her voice, would look at me crossly and say, "Now, Julie, you be a good little boy and go right up there and put all them toys away." She never seemed to notice that the next day I would return to the room and once again create chaos on the floor.

Pete never remained peeved with me for long. Usually after I had straightened up the room and we had shared a few cookies and a glass of milk we went into the backyard or the basement to play. He didn't seem to have friends of his own age, so perhaps he felt compelled to put up with the minor annoyances of my irresponsibilities.

For my part I loved to play with Pete. He was an honor student, more intelligent than most of my friends. He was witty, had a great sense of humor (especially when directed at himself) and possessed an unbounded imagination and a natural curiosity about almost everything. He never participated in sports and had no interest in them, but that didn't matter to me, I got enough of that with my buddies at school and in our neighborhood.

Before he was five, Pete had taught himself to play the piano by watching the moving keys on the family player piano. At seven he was hired by the owner of a neighborhood bar to entertain the drunks. He played for tips, coins tossed by bleary-eyed patrons into a tin cup placed on top of the piano. He averaged $70 a week, and for three years was the chief breadwinner of the family.

At age ten Pete was given his own radio show on Canton's WHBC. The same year Frank DeVol, a fifteen-year-old schoolboy with his own orchestra, asked Pete to audition for him. "No, no," Pete responded. "I don't audition, I'm a professional." A little taken aback, Frank gave him the job without an audition.

On Saturdays sometimes we went on hikes which for me were always great adventures. Once we walked to West Tusc and visited Lincoln High School. We didn't go inside; we were afraid to do that, but we walked around the grounds and peered into some of the classrooms through downstairs windows. On several occasions we explored the old abandoned Deuber-Hampton Watchworks, where my paternal grandfather had worked as a watch engraver. The factory had gone out of business before I was born. The grounds were weed covered and the buildings had begun to succumb to time and the ravages of weather. Once we groped through a stand of weeds so we could look into a basement window, and there in the window well, hidden for many years, we discovered a small cache of beautiful, shiny, purple, mineral fragments. We had never seen anything like them and they fascinated me. I scooped them from the well and tucked them into a pocket. Years later, as a senior at McKinley High, I took the crystals to our geology teacher, Mr. Goss, who told me they were fluorite, a mineral used in processing aluminum ore. I never did learn why those crystals had been there in that window well. On several occasions we spent several hours playing in the house that had served as the home of President McKinley. The house, which had been located on north Market, was moved to an empty field on West Tusc and left unprotected by the city. Early in the Depression, with no available money for upkeep or preservation for its historic value, the house of President McKinley was dismantled and sold as scrap.

Unlike today's young kids, as a small boy I knew nothing of sex and had never heard the word homosexual. One day during lunch period a boy in my class dared me to yell out the word FUCK in class. He said it would amuse our teacher, Miss X, and make all the girls laugh. It sounded like the "open sesame" to instant popularity, so that afternoon I did it.

Miss X, who was standing in front of her desk, stopped speaking in mid-sentence, and, with a slightly startled expression, looked down on me in the second row of seats and unwisely asked what it was I had said. Anxious to alleviate her apparent doubt I repeated the word, this time more distinctly and, if possible, even more loudly. Just as my friend had promised all the girls laughed and as an unexpected bonus so did all the boys. Miss X, however, displayed not even the slightest trace of amusement, providing me with the first hint that I might be in some sort of trouble. She fixed me with a strange stare before asking in measured tones if by some chance I understood the meaning of the word I had just used. When I assured her I had not the foggiest idea she asked that I report to her after the close of the day. At 3:30 when the other children had filed from the room, I cautiously approached Miss X who sat at her desk leafing through a book. I was terrified, certain that she would write an account detailing my misdemeanor and demand that I deliver it to my parents that afternoon. My mother would be stunned. She would give me a long, pained stare, tears welling in her eyes as she slowly placed the note on the kitchen table. Then she would lecture me for an hour or more while I stood in the middle of the kitchen floor shifting nervously from foot to foot. In the end she would place me under house arrest for at least a month. The scariest part would be when my dad arrived home. He would read the note, angrily throw it across the kitchen, shout and curse and then beat the ever-loving wad out of me. But when I reached the desk there was no sign of paper or pen and Miss X was smiling. It was then that a glimmer of hope entered my skinny, evil little body. Retaining the smile she said, "I just want you to tell me where you heard the word you used in class today." Assuming that a full confession might help save my seven-year-old butt, I told her everything, including the name of the boy, Billy De Walt, whom I considered to be responsible for the entire mess. "He told me," I said with emphasis, "that if I said it in class you would be pleased."

"Well," she said. "I'm happy that you have been truthful with me, but that is a very bad word you used and it certainly did not please me. I want you to promise me that you will never again repeat the word." When, with great sincerity I had promised, she dismissed me. Assuming then that I would live to screw up another day, I hurried home so that I would not provide my mother with reason to inquire why I was late.

The next morning while walking to school I asked Billy to tell me the meaning of the word, but he refused and when I pleaded he laughed and told me to go away. After that, for several days, I sought out each of my friends and asked them to explain the word to me, but most were as ignorant as I and no help at all. The few who professed knowledge of the word responded as had Billy with a laugh and a refusal to comment. Eventually, having failed to satisfy my curiosity, I gave up the quest and moved on to other diversions.

A few years later a family from Wheeling, West Virginia, moved into our neighborhood. They had a boy my age named Willy, who I soon learned used the F word with reckless abandon. So one day I asked him to tell me what it meant. He laughed and reaching into his jacket pocket extracted a mechanical cut-out model of Olive Oil and Popeye. There was a small knob on the back of the thing, and when Willy turned it a most astounding sequence of events ensued. Olive Oil bent over on her hands and knees and Popeye leaned forward and executed a vigorous, dog-fashioned mounting.

Though Willy's visual aid had not provided a fully comprehensive definition of the word it rather dramatically demonstrated why my use of that word in the second grade had failed to amuse our teacher.

During the summer when I turned 12, I was playing one day in a large apple tree with Bob Schario and his 14-year-old brother Bernie. Bernie was sitting on a limb a few feet above our heads when he abruptly unbuttoned his fly, whipped out his member, and instructed us to follow suit. When we had, he told us to grasp the thing in the palm of a hand and gave it a gentle massage. "If you do that," he said as he demonstrated the technique, "you'll soon get a really funny feeling." Then, with the look of wisdom that comes with advancing age, he said, "That's what's called 'jerking off'." My sex education had taken a giant leap forward.

Before I was 10 or 11 I can recall no time when my parents, or Pete's adopted parents, or any of our uncles and aunts indicated in any way that they thought Pete was particularly odd or strange. I do recall an incident, however, when Pete was 13 or 14 that I can see now clearly indicated that Maggie and Paul had been somewhat concerned about the direction in which he was headed.

We were in the backyard talking or playing when the girl next door popped out on her porch and struck up a conversation with Pete. When she had gone back inside Pete turned to me with a worried look and confided, "Mom and Dad keep pestering me to take her on a date but I don't want to do that. I just don't like girls." That he would not like girls didn't seem strange to me—at age six I didn't much care for them myself.

During the next four years the relationship between Paul and Pete, never very meaningful at best, deteriorated rapidly. More and more often Paul seemed to go out of the way to provoke Pete, ridicule him, demean him, and challenge his manhood. During that difficult period for Pete, it was Maggie, my mother, and their sister, Nett, who consoled and soothed him and who assured him that no matter what they would always love him and be at his side. My dad, who for years had watched all this without comment, one day announced to my mother that she, Nett and Maggie had to face the obvious: Pete was a goddamned queer. My mother was enraged and forbade him ever to use that word again in our house. If she hoped to hide the fact from me it was too late, I heard the word and although I was unsure of its full implications, I knew instinctively it was not one to be shouted at my fifth grade teacher.

Soon Paul openly accused Pete of deliberately choosing his disgusting life style and he ordered him to give it up immediately. Pete retorted that his sexual orientation was not a thing he could alter; it was genetic. He argued that he was born that way and would always remain that way.

It became a standoff that led to protracted and bitter arguments during which Paul shouted, accused, threatened, and Pete shrieked, wailed and whimpered. Commonly such a battle ended only when Paul strode from the house and drove away in his car and Pete fell limply into the comforting arms of his mother.

Pete graduated from McKinley High in 1933 at the height of the Great Depression. Unemployment was at its peak and there were few available jobs, especially for a 17-year-old effeminate boy whose professed interests were literature, French, and classical music. However, with uncommon wisdom and foresight, he had for several years studied business administration, bookkeeping, shorthand and typing, which enabled him to quickly secure a secretarial position with the Timken Roller Bearing Company. During the next few years, to counteract the tedium of his work routine, he used his leisure hours to sharpen his skills at the piano, to compose piano music, and to complete a novel written entirely in French but never published.

In 1939 Pete's biological father, Earl, was between wives and living with his sister, Nett, and her husband Charles, a few blocks from Pete's home. Long a health freak, Earl had purchased the Charles Atlas Dynamic Tension Correspondence Course. When I expressed a keen interest in the program he invited me to work out with him. For 16 weeks, each Friday after school I walked two miles to Aunt Nett's house and then spent an hour or two with my uncle becoming familiar with the latest set of exercises that had arrived in the mail that week. It is both ironic and sad that during those 16 weeks I spent more time with Pete's father than Pete had in his entire life.

It was only after Paul's death in September 1941, that Pete felt free to invite a few of his friends to his house. The most frequent visitor was Robert, a concert pianist. During the subsequent year I saw Robert at the house three or four times, but my memories of him have yellowed with the passing decades. I remember a neatly dressed, clean-cut youth with black hair combed straight back from his forehead and a pair of dark, aesthetic eyes. He was quiet, perhaps shy, but always friendly, pleasant and very polite. I recall no specific conversations that we may have had, but I do know that his favorite topic was music. On one occasion he treated us to a brief but completely enjoyable piano recital. At that time I thought of the relationship between my cousin and Robert as purely one of friendship; later I learned otherwise. When Robert moved to Hollywood in 1942 he wrote regularly to Pete, who sometimes shared the letters with me. It was only then that I learned Robert and Pete were lovers. Robert always referred to Pete in his correspondence as Kay, and he constantly urged "Kay" to join him in his Hollywood apartment. I knew that Pete wanted to go but was afraid to leave his job and his mother. In 1942, after I had joined the Coast Guard, he finally left Canton and went to live with Robert in California. Pete and I did not correspond during the war so I heard none of the details of his life with Robert at first hand. From comments in letters written to me by my mother and Aunt Maggie I learned that shortly after his arrival in Los Angeles he began to play in recording orchestras for MGM, Warner Brothers, Universal, and Columbia. At the same time he dabbled with acting, appearing as a bit player in numerous movies. During his years in Hollywood, Pete became well acquainted with many of the legendary motion picture actors including Mae West, Anthony Quinn, Greta Garbo, Gilbert Roland and Cornell Wilde, with whom he allegedly had a brief affair.

The dates are a little hazy, but I think in late 1943 or early 1944 Pete received an invitation to attend a masked ball at the home of Cary Grant. Pete's actor friends June Havoc and June Allyson, thinking it would be quite a joke on Cary, made up and dressed Pete as a woman and introduced him to Grant as "Kay Keys," rising young starlet. Though Pete wore a mask, Cary reportedly was immediately enamored. They danced together repeatedly that evening and soon after the guests unmasked at midnight Cary and Kay became lovers.

The affair ended abruptly and dramatically in late October 1944 when Pete was arrested for engaging in homosexual activities in the men's room of a restaurant at a Los Angeles hotel. Despite the efforts of his defense attorney, hired and paid for by Cary Grant, Pete was found guilty. However, he avoided a jail sentence when he agreed to leave California immediately and forever.

He returned then to Canton and to the tenuous sanctuary of his parental home where Maggie lived with her ex-convict boyfriend, Bob Black.

For Pete and Bob it was unconditional hatred at first sight. Determined not to be driven from his home by a hostile stranger or by the smothering love of his mother, Pete found a secretarial position in town and, in his spare time, returned to one of his true loves, the composition of piano music. When not at work or at the movies, he listened to 78 rpm records of operatic music on his Victrola. His favorite was his latest acquisition, Puccini's *Madame Butterfly*, which he had had few opportunities to hear during the war because, incredibly, its sale and live performances had been forbidden in this country on the grounds that the story was anti-American.

In the end, however, Pete was forced to confront the truth: his hopes of finding peace, serenity and happiness in his mother's home had been born of wispy self-delusion. The frequent bitter arguments with Bob, the bickering and quarreling between Bob and Maggie, and Maggie's efforts to control his life proved intolerable.

In 1946 he once again packed his bags and left Canton. This time it was New York City where he found an apartment which promised privacy, if not happiness, and a secretarial position in the French division of a large import-export corporation. In New York, Pete was able to renew his relationship with Lillian Gish, to meet many of the Metropolitan Opera stars, and to become a close friend (so he claimed) of Eleanor Roosevelt.

In a letter written to my mother on July 4, 1950, Pete attempted to explain why he had left Canton. Revealingly he seemed to place most of the blame on his mother rather than on Bob Black:

> *Many an evening I sit here in my room and meditate. I worry about hurting Mom. I know she does not want me to be away from home, and I honestly do not wish to do anything to hurt her; but I nearly lost my mental balance in Canton. I was so stifled and bottled up. I couldn't find work. I could not feel free in my own home ... I know Bob does not like me and that causes friction with Mom, then with Mom ailing all the time I had to tip-toe around and could never have any company, and all in all it preyed on my mind until it affected my health. I couldn't sleep a wink, and I had no appetite and when I did force something down I got indigestion so badly and heartburn I nearly passed out. I don't want to sound like I am complaining but I just couldn't stand that sort of existence any*

longer. After all, I am now thirty-five and I have a right to live my own life. Other people cannot live it for me and it is definitely wrong to treat me as an automaton and pull the strings. Mom always meant well but she really was doing me a great wrong and injustice by regulating me.

In 1964 Pete was unable or, perhaps, unwilling to bear any longer the growing sense of guilt imposed on him by his aging, ill, and unhappy mother so he left New York City to return to Ohio. Aware that he could not hope to peacefully share his mother's house with Bob, he wisely elected to take a position at a small college in Akron and to confine his visits to Canton with Bob and Maggie to selected weekends. It was an arrangement not entirely satisfactory to Maggie, but it permitted Pete to retain some control over his own life and at the same time to siphon off some of his pent-up feelings of guilt.

When, in 1967, Bob, a victim of cancer, passed on to the Big House in the sky, Pete decided it was safe, if not entirely sensible, to return to Canton. With that in mind, he accepted a position at Canton's Malone College and moved into his old second floor bedroom in his mother's house.

At that time Maggie's sole income was a $175 monthly Social Security check, the last of her savings having been used to cover Bob's hospital and doctor bills. To Pete's chagrin, Bob had engineered his final con by sticking Pete with his funeral and burial expenses.

After Bob's death Maggie's physical condition deteriorated rapidly. In 1975 she was functionally blind, extremely deaf and only marginally ambulatory. She had great difficulty climbing the stairs to her bedroom so spent most of her days and nights on a recliner in the dining room.

In 1978 the physical and mental strain of holding down a full-time job and meeting the increasing needs of Maggie became too much for Pete so he resigned his position at Malone College. In early January 1979, Maggie survived major colon surgery, but afterwards required round-the-clock care. It was then that Pete placed her in a nursing home, where she died on June 18, 1981. With his bank balance reduced from $175,000 to $12.00, Pete borrowed to cover funeral and burial costs and repaid the loan in small installments from his meager Social Security income.

Since 1981 Pete has lived alone. In that time he grew fat, nearly blind, and increasingly cantankerous. A shut-in now, reduced to using a walker to negotiate his living quarters, he sleeps in the dining room in Maggie's old recliner, and twice daily makes the laborious and sometimes adventurous climb to the second floor bathroom to empty his slop jar.

It is not entirely accurate to say that Pete has lived alone since Maggie's death. For the first ten years he shared his house with April Sunshine, a Boston Bull terrier. When April died in 1991, she was succeeded by Christopher, a black kitten who appeared as "Mr. October" in the 1991 and 1992 Friskie's Feline Calendar of cute cats.

It is accurate to say that Pete has few human visitors. He has one friend, Herb, a seventy-five-year-old widower who owns a car and is in good enough health to drive it. Herb comes to the house once or twice a week to check on Pete, to run small errands for him, to help tidy the house and to chauffeur him to doctors' appointments. Pete's half-brother and sister and his cousins who live in Canton rarely visit him. This is in part because of Pete's conspicuous effeminism and his often flaunted life style which long have been sources of considerable embarrassment for all of them. There is one other reason. Though his eyes and other body parts rapidly fail him, Pete's acute facility for uninhibited and relentless expressions of utter contempt for his closest living relatives has only sharpened with the passing years.

So Pete is left too often with only his memories, the good as well as the bad. The latter relate to times spent in his mother's house, the former to his years of freedom in New York and California. When he ventures into his upstairs bedroom he certainly pauses to admire the many beautiful gifts from former lovers that adorn the surface of the dresser and night stands. And sometimes he must go to the closet and dig out the tattered scrapbook brought back to the house from Hollywood in 1945, a book packed with fading photos of Cary Grant and Cornell Wilde and with yellowing news clippings which report the details of their glamorous lives which he once shared.

Several years ago during my most recent trip to Canton I visited with Cousin Pete. When I was leaving he called after me, "Good luck with your book, Julie," and then with a smile of confidentiality, added, "You know I haven't always been old, fat and ugly. Someday I'll tell you the truth about my wicked, wicked youth." So far he has not done that, although during recent phone conversations he has leaked a few tantalizing details.

Sometimes I worry that one day, too immobilized by injury or illness to summon help, Pete will die there alone in that sad, dreary old house. At such times I am invariably reminded and even a little reassured by the words of a female impersonator delivered in 1943 from the stage of Howdy's Nightclub in New York City, "Old Queens never die, they just blow away."

Addendum: Cousin Pete died after this chapter was written, of heart failure in a Massillon hospital, twenty-nine days following his eighty-second birthday. He never got around to telling me the story of his "…Wicked, wicked youth."

Against All Odds

Standing there on that corner I thought, *God, I'm home, home against all odds. The damned nightmare—it's over.* Somehow I had survived for three and a half years and was still in one piece, still semi-sane.

Earlier aboard the PF-9 I often lay in my sack and considered the unpleasant probability that I would not survive, that we would invade the Japanese home islands, that the Jap resistance would be maniacal—"To the last man," I would say to myself. "And they'll take a million of us with them, and I'll be one of that million." Strangely, at the time it seemed a small matter. I knew no one gave a damn if I made it or not, and at times I didn't either.

But I had been wrong. With two atomic explosions Harry Truman had saved my ass and a million others. Unfortunately the bomb and Harry came along a bit late to save some of my buddies. Most of my friends made it one way or another, but some ended up in flag-draped boxes. I tried to remember why we had been friends. It was confusing. There were so many who had gone, gone to so many places and done so many things. We were all too busy to track each other for three and a half years and sometimes when we wrote it took so long for the letter to get there the guy was gone or was dead. I realized that I wasn't very sure who had and who hadn't made it.

Still looking across the square I saw myself, home on leave in 1943, standing in front of the courthouse with Jimmy Frieda, home on furlough from the Army. I had grown up with Jimmy and his brother Louis and the three of us had spent endless hours together at their father's tailor shop on West Tusc while our fathers engaged in clandestine discussions of politics and union activities.

Jimmy died at Normandy, on D-Day. He probably wouldn't have been there at all if our fathers and Louis hadn't been so damned bull-headed. Jimmy believed it was his duty to atone for the disgrace that Louis had brought to his family when, to avoid the draft, he had enlisted in the National Guard. When our fathers had learned of Louis's intention, they had gone to great lengths to dissuade him and when reason and cajoling had failed they forbade him to go, but he defied them and did it anyway.

Our fathers hadn't objected to the National Guard because it was a draft dodger's haven, but, rather, because its chief function, along with the Pinkertons, had been to break strikes and because the National Guard had murdered so many good union men, good Americans. Jimmy had not died for his country so much as he had died in an effort to restore the good name of his family.

I would never again see Jimmy, I knew, and I didn't much care to see Louis who had, of course, survived the war.

Jim Focht, with whom I had many fights during our years in grade school, was another I wouldn't see again. He had been a B-29 pilot shot down over Formosa. His death eventually had more effect on me than I realized at the time—I married his former fiancée in 1947.

I met Eugene Greenfield during our senior year at McKinley High. I liked him a lot, but I never got to know him well; no one did. He was a loner, basically, quiet and probably shy. When he did say something, though, it usually had been carefully thought out and always seemed to make sense. One day in May 1941, as we walked together on Belden near his home he quietly and logically told me of his decision to enlist in the Army when he graduated in June. "There are no jobs now," he reasoned. "That is, none that are worth anything. And there's no money for college. The Army can be a career, a job, an adventure." It all seemed a good idea that day, but I know he hadn't included Corregidor in his plans or the Death March, and I know he hadn't figured to die in a Japanese concentration camp.

Then there was happy-go-lucky, handsome Larry Baskin. We were on McKinley's track team together for two years. Our crystal balls had been hazy—war was as remote and unexpected to us then as the eventuality that the grass next to Fawcett Stadium, where we stopped each day after school to put on our running shoes would one day be covered by the NFL Football Hall of Fame. I could never face his family after the war because I knew they wondered why it had been Larry and not me, and I had no answer to the question.

And there was Carl Eggleston who lived across the street from us. We went to grade school together for eight years. The Egglestons had a flat-roofed garage behind their house where on Saturdays Carl and I sometimes played. We pretended the roof was a ship's deck and that we were under attack by scores of villains: bearded, scarred, one-eyed, peg-legged pirates with gravelly voices, a hook in one arm and a great sharp cutlass in the good hand. Carl was a lieutenant in the Army and an expert in bomb disposal. He survived the war in Europe only to have his luck run out while trying to defuse a Nazi bomb that had buried itself unexploded into the soft soil of a Normandy farm.

Mellon Marshalek was an example of war's ironies. During our pre-enlistment days I would stop by Schuman's drug store where he worked as a soda jerk and listen to his dreams as I drank the milk shakes he dispensed. Mellon wanted to be a pilot and glowed with enthusiasm as he talked about flying. The army refused to send him to flight school but, noting his interest in airplanes, sent him to Burma with a unit whose job was to rescue downed pilots. A year of recovering charred, semi-decayed bodies from crashed airplanes was enough to convince Mellon he'd consider himself lucky if he never saw another plane. It was then the Army sent him to flight school. His experiences had destroyed the confidence and enthusiasm necessary to a fighter pilot and it was as a reluctant trainee that he crashed his plane in a rocky field. He died in Texas, but the dream had died earlier in Burma.

As I moved off Market onto E. Tusc I recalled an incident that had occurred at that very spot about two years earlier. Home on leave again, I had been walking west toward the square. It was about 2:00 a.m. and the streets were deserted except for two drunken sailors walking parallel with me but across the street. They were talking loudly but at first I paid no attention to them. Then one of them made some garbled comment about "shallow-fucking-water-coasties". This was followed by raucous laughter and then various comments about what they intended to do to this sad-assed pansy Coast Guardsman. About that time they started to angle slowly across the street toward me. Having been through similar situations in the past I turned to face them, while slowly backing to the wall of the building behind me. I felt my waistband, reassuring myself that the four-inch blade I always carried for such occasions was indeed in place. As they neared me I suggested that they back off and go some place for another drink.

With that remark they both grinned and the short, chunky one with the beady eyes snarled, "Oh, we'll get a drink later, after we have your pansy ass." Slowly and unsteadily they moved forward until we were about three feet apart and then they stopped and looked me over somewhat appraisingly. I waited tensely for their next move, my right hand moving slowly to my waist. Then the taller, sallow-faced kid turned to his buddy, and, grinning again, said, "Oh shit, he ain't worth it," whereupon they turned and swayed across the street. Relaxing I took a deep breath and thought, *Well, at least I didn't have to kill the silly shits.* When I think of that I can only wonder if it had anything to do with what my dad had tried to tell me at the stairwell.

Continuing down East Tusc about a half block I noticed a familiar department store across the street. It was in front of that store that I had taken the most humiliating beating of my life. Right then while trying unsuccessfully to dodge punches I resolved to become a boxer. I was 16, a junior at McKinley High, and a veteran of scores of street fights, but no boxer. On my way home from school one afternoon, three older hoods I had never seen before followed behind me as I walked down Market Street. They began to taunt me, to call me names, and then to loudly discuss what they intended to do to me. I tried to ignore them, hoping they would give it up and bug off. But they continued to follow as I turned down E. Tusc and as we reached that department store, the tallest fellow stepped around me and punched me in the face. He was not only older and taller, but at least forty pounds heavier. Worse, he obviously had some boxing skills.

Later I would learn to step inside long, looping hooks and disembowel an opponent with short chops to the body. That day, however, I foolishly stayed at arm's length and stopped his punches with my head and body.

Finally, mercifully, the guy got tired of the fun or just got tired. Either way he backed off, and with his two henchmen disappeared into the crowd that had gathered to watch the slaughter. Standing there, bleeding, I resolved never to let anything like that happen again. A little middle-aged man came over to me and identified my attackers. "That was Jake Stearn who whipped your ass. You shouldn't fuck with him. He'll come back for you." At that moment I thought, *I don't want to fuck him, I want to kill him.*

The next day my dad and I went to see Mr. Potoroff, principal of McKinley High. Old Potty had reason not to like me, but he listened patiently as I related the events of the previous day. When I had finished my story, Potoroff called in an aide and instructed her to locate and bring Jake Stern to his office. In a short time a surly Stern was ushered into the principal's office. Immediately Potoroff confronted him with my allegations and to my surprise he admitted his guilt. Then, without further ado, old Potty expelled the bastard from school. As he left the office, Stearn stared hard at me and his eyes said, "Your days are numbered, sucker."

The next day I enlisted a half Cherokee friend of mine to give me a crash course in boxing, and at the same time I arranged with another friend, a Diamond Belt middleweight champion, to walk me to and from school. A few weeks later I began formal boxing lessons at the YMCA, determined to one day be a professional fighter.

I never saw Jake Stearn again, but a few years later, after I had completed the Coast Guard boot training at Manhattan Beach in New York, I was selected for Jack Dempsey's commando school. On my first day of training I met my martial arts instructor, Babe Stearn. I never did tell Babe that I had once met his younger brother.

Whether or not this episode had anything to do with what my dad had tried to tell me at age five, it had altered my life in a dramatic manner.

As I reached Rex Avenue, still toting the bulky seabag and bedroll, I automatically turned and looked up this infamous alley. Here resided the most notorious red-light district in Ohio—it was only a few blocks from both the courthouse and the police station and it was run by our beloved ex-mayor, the dapper Jimmy Seccombe. The district extended for several blocks on each side of Rex and spilled over onto Walnut Avenue. The girls worked in old two-story frame houses that lined both sides of the street and each house had its madame.

Teenagers were discouraged from entering the district, but, of course, most of us had sneaked down there in the evening just to satisfy our curiosity and relieve the boredom on hot summer nights. On one such evening several of us decided that we ought to check out things on Rex Avenue. We had never been there at night and were amazed at the carnival atmosphere that greeted us. Scores of men wandered up and down the brightly lighted streets, engaging in banter with the madames who, standing on their porches, hawked their wares and explicitly described available services. Scantily clad girls hung out of most of the upstairs windows enticing the men in the streets to come in and sample the merchandise. One madame announced a new girl, "Come on guys, try out our new young chicken, a virgin just in from New Orleans. Get it while she's hot!" We all laughed, but I suspect we were each secretly shocked by what we saw and heard. But it was a new and exciting experience and beat the hell out of hanging around the house.

The basic price of admission to one of the houses was two dollars and we didn't have a half-buck among us. Finally one of my buddies, caught up in the carnival-like atmosphere, produced a quarter and, waving it over his head, called out to one of the girls framed in an upstairs window, "How about jacking me off for a quarter." We all laughed nervously as we awaited the girl's response. She leaned out the window far enough for us to see two white globes pop into view and called back, "Go home kid, jack yourself off and save the quarter."

Somewhat subdued we walked on down the street and eventually a patrolman showed up and suggested that we get our asses out of the district or we'd find ourselves in juvenile court. We didn't have much to say as we walked home. We had briefly entered the world of our fathers and learned that, after all, we were still just boys.

At Cherry Avenue I passed the infamous Golden Pheasant Tavern. Anyone dumb enough to stand on the corner here for several days running would be treated to the sight of most of Canton's middle and lower echelon low-life sleaze balls passing through the tavern doors.

Among the patrons of the Golden Pheasant were the Norcia boys. The Norcia brothers formed the core of a particularly vicious street gang. My contacts with these characters had been purposely minimal. I did play baseball against their team several times and each game ended in a riot. These guys had been born mean and enjoyed the riots a lot more than the games. Their leader, Nick Norcia, was the meanest of all. One night when Nick was about twenty he walked into the Golden Pheasant, whipped out a gun and shot a member of another gang. He was tried, found guilty of murder, sent to prison, and for unknown reasons was released six months later.

A few months after his release Nick returned to his house one night with his girlfriend. As the two walked onto the unlighted front porch a dark thing, faceless and without discernible form, rose slowly from the bushes by the porch where it had waited patiently for this moment. Shimmering in the darkness, arm-like appendages materialized at the diffuse margins of this sinister apparition; they cradled an elongated, menacing object that, like a giant compass needle, rotated until it was directed at the unsuspecting couple on the porch.

Possibly the couple detected the slight movement in the bushes; Nick may even have uttered a cautious challenge. It is possible also that they heard the twin explosions a split second before two rapidly expanding bundles of buckshot blew off their heads and splattered their brains and skull fragments along the front wall of the house, over the window panes, across the wooden flower box on the banister and finally spreading them into the neighbor's lawn.

As I proceeded down E. Tusc I wondered if perhaps I knew now what my dad had been trying to tell me. As I walked I could almost hear his voice. "Son," he was saying. "Don't look for a meaning in any of this because there isn't any." Then I realized that my mother had always been saying the same thing when she explained the inexplicable with her platitude, "It's God's will, son."

As I walked south from Cherry my thoughts dropped back to 1935. The Great Depression was still running rampant. Dad, like most of the men in our neighborhood, hadn't held a steady job in five or six years. The bread lines were gone by then, replaced by a thing called "The Family Service". On Saturday mornings Dad drove my mother and me down to the Gressner-Milner Sign Shop or the Jackmides Tailor Shop in my grandmother's car. My mother and I, carrying wicker baskets, walked from there to south Market to the Family Service headquarters for our weekly handouts of food while Dad stayed behind and discussed politics with his friends. Dad was too proud to personally accept handouts, so he delegated the job to us.

At a warehouse we stood in a long line of destitute, emaciated men and women whose families, as ours, would have starved if deprived of the flour, oleo, wilted vegetables, stale bread, beans and other goodies that were dropped in our baskets by the people who worked there. Then, with overflowing baskets, we walked back to our meeting place with Dad. When we arrived he was never ready to go so we waited another hour or two for a ride home. By then our Saturday was just about shot, but we'd eat for another week.

In 1936, I got my first regular job. Mrs. Miller, who lived on Eighth Street, baked pies in her basement and hired young boys to sell them door to door. We each were provided with a wicker basket with two movable handles. The baskets were loaded with the number, sizes and flavors of pies that we expected to sell. On weekdays we carried two sizes: the five-centers and the eight-centers. After a few weeks I had developed a four-mile route that included about 15 regular and 10 semi-regular customers. I walked the route each afternoon making one cent for each pie sold. Any day I sold twenty pies or more Mrs. Miller gave me a free pie which I usually ate as soon as I left her house. I also took orders for larger 25 cent and 35 cent pies to be delivered on Saturday morning. I pushed these pretty hard because my cut was five cents each.

In a typical week I made about $1.25, but the hitch was that my father maintained absolute control over every cent. I was required to keep an accurate book on all my finances which he closely checked once a week. No purchases were possible without his authorization. This meant that I could never spend money for important things like candy, ice cream, and Big League chewing gum, only dumb stuff like rabbit food and school supplies.

After a few months in the pie business I branched out. I bought a magazine route from a kid for two dollars. On Tuesdays after school I delivered *Colliers, Saturday Evening Post, Liberty,* and *Ladies Home Journal* to about 25 regular customers spread over a five-mile route extending from the northeast corner of Canton to the First National Bank building on the square. At two cents a magazine I made 50 cents a week and for half the take I had a buddy run my Tuesday pie route.

When my savings had grown to $12.00, my dad okayed the purchase of a bicycle. With growing hysteria I had anticipated this moment for several months. Bernie Mahalick, a neighbor, had just what I needed and he sold it to me for $3.00. It was old, a bit battered and rusty, and needed a 75 cent tire, but I thought it was the most fabulous bike in the world. Thereafter I delivered pies in half the previous time and with infinitely greater pleasure. Of course I still walked the magazine route because Dad wouldn't allow me to ride a bike in town.

That beautiful hunk of metal and rubber served me with distinction until I entered high school. The long walk from Central High didn't leave time to carry my routes any more, so at age 14 I retired from the pie and magazine business. A few months later I sold the bike for $3.75. It would be 15 years before I acquired my next set of wheels—a shiny, new Dodge. By then I was an instructor in the Geography-Geology Department at Southern Illinois University.

At Hartford Avenue I was closing in on home. Four blocks to my right stood the old red-brick Hartford Grade School where I had been a reluctant prisoner for eight years.

I vividly recalled my first day at Hartford in September 1929. My mother walked with me to school and, taking my hand in hers, led me into an office on the first floor where we met Miss Elizabeth Swope, principal of the school. As my mother introduced us, Miss Swope stood behind her desk coldly assessing me. It was a stare that scared the shit out of me. She was tall, angular and austere, with her hair skinned back on her head and tied in a knot at the nape of her wrinkled neck. As her eyes burned holes through me like laser beams I thought, *Here is a woman who would enjoy watching little boys boiled in oil.* Then, without acknowledging the introduction she snapped her head toward my mother and, through stiffly drawn lips, observed, "Little boys who place most of their weight on one leg never amount to anything." Thus she fired the first shot of our eight-year war.

In 1934 when I reached the sixth grade, it was common knowledge that I was a hard-core problem child and a general pain in the ass. That year, for the first time, Canton school children were given IQ tests. When the results for our school were in, Miss Swope and her staff must have been at least a trifle surprised to learn that among Hartford's 600 students I had recorded the highest score.

Old Swopey sent one of her teachers to break the news to my parents. It was a "good news-bad news" situation. The good news was that I wasn't stupid after all; the bad news was that, in Swopey's opinion, the school system could in no way be held responsible for my poor performance in the classroom.

I had, the teacher explained, willfully chosen to fritter away all my golden opportunities to receive a meaningful education by endlessly engaging in dallying daydreams, fanciful fantasies, and playful pranks. Her advice to my parents was that they bear down on me, press my little nose to the old grindstone, and see to it that henceforth I give my undivided attention to schoolwork. As an 11-year-old boy it seemed to me that being smart might prove to be an affliction worse than chicken pox.

As my eight years at Hartford drew to a close my mother and I were requested to meet with one of my teachers to discuss what might lie ahead for me in high school. At some point during our conference the teacher turned to me and asked, "What do you wish to be when you grow up, Jules?"

Without hesitation, I answered very seriously, "A geologist." It was the funniest thing she had heard that week. When she managed to control her laughter she looked at my mother, who also had found my answer hilarious, and reassured her, "Don't you worry, Mrs. DuBar, he'll get over that notion soon enough."

I had made my first mineral and rock collections at age four, could accurately explain the processes of soil formation at seven, and at eight I had actively begun to collect fossils. At age twelve it seemed unlikely to me I would ever get over geology. In 1949 I graduated from Kent State University with the first degree in geology awarded by the university.

I remember equally clearly my last day at Hartford. Old Swopey strode into our eighth grade classroom and, brushing aside our teacher, proclaimed, "I have dropped in to congratulate those of you who will be going on to high school next September. That is, all of you except Jules DuBar and his friend Eddy Conner who I never again wish to see." After eight years the old lady had made a wish I could gladly grant.

Crossing Hartford Avenue I glanced left at the First Brethren Church which I had attended with my mother for 12 years. The congregation was a bunch of bible-thumping, ignorant, misguided, bigoted misfits that for some inexplicable reason thought they had been chosen as God's children. What He might have wanted with them beat the hell out of me.

One day in the fall of 1930 my mother told me that starting the next Sunday she and I would begin to regularly attend church. At age seven I had never been in a church and had no interest in starting—it sounded too much like school to me. I was wrong though, it was much worse. It has always seemed to me that my mother made that decision as a diabolical effort to antagonize my atheistic father and grandmother whom she detested. Years later while on a ship in the middle of the Pacific Ocean I realized that I had been my mother's pawn in her war with my father and that she had never really given a damn about me.

On a Sunday morning when I was ten or eleven, our minister delivered a sermon during which he described in some vivid detail what Heaven is like. It struck me as a terribly boring place where everyone sat around all the time admiring the pearly gates and golden streets, while strumming lackadaisically on harps. There must be, I reasoned, a better way to use all that time. So I asked my mother if it would be all right with God if I floated around through space, exploring the Universe. She didn't have an answer to my question but she took me to the church elders and I asked them the same question. They were puzzled. They hadn't heard that one before, and it didn't seem to be covered in the Scriptures. After some agonizing deliberation they decided it probably would be all right with God if that was what I really wanted to do. I was greatly relieved after that and told all my friends what they had said. All my friends thought I was weird.

Later when the preacher tried to convince me that Charles Darwin had been an evil man I decided that he and most of his congregation were lunatics. I also concluded that their concepts of Heaven, Hell, God and life in general were nonsense. After that I disassociated myself from all religions.

At the edge of my old neighborhood I paused at Schumann's Drugstore and took a long look north along Belden Avenue. The street sliced its way sixteen blocks through the heart of the ghetto to the gates of Hell—the Republic Steel plant.

The ghetto was home for thousands of southern Europeans and Balkan immigrants who had come to America in search of a better life. They had found little more than poverty, squalor, and the rejection of the established citizens of Canton. They quickly learned they would be kept out, would always be outsiders.

When the Italian army invaded Ethiopia on October 3, 1935, the Sicilian immigrants were elated and quickly overcome with patriotic fervor for their homeland and unbounded adulation of their conquering hero, Benito Mussolini. Each day when the Italian language newspaper reported fresh defeats of the spear-bearing Abyssinians, the headlines were posted in store windows and the people danced with joy in the street. I think it was during that time that my dislike of Sicilians grew to hatred.

In 1937, when I was 14, the steel workers union went on strike against Republic Steel. When the strikers set up picket lines at the plant gates the scabs and Pinkertons, who had been brought in by the company, were trapped inside for the duration of the strike. While the scabs did their best to keep the plant in operation, the Pinkertons, to earn their keep, took up positions at upper level windows and sniped at the pickets with powerful and silent pellet guns.

But violence tends to beget violence, and the strikers, who were not particularly saintly, were quick to adopt the credo, "An eye for an eye". To prevent the company from bringing in reinforcements the union placed groups of men at strategic points along all roads in the immediate vicinity of the mill.

Vehicles suspected of transporting scabs were intercepted and the passengers usually worked over severely. Unfortunately some of their victims were innocent passersby with no involvement in the strike. One evening a man and his seven-year-old son were driving home to their nearby farm; they were halted by the strikers, dragged from their car, and in the ensuing melee the young boy was struck on the head with a large rock, barely escaping with his life.

Eventually the Governor called in the National Guard, and the troops were bivouacked in Belden Elementary School. Each evening, in a show of force, they double-timed down Belden Avenue with fixed bayonets. The residents always gathered on their front porches to watch and to jeer and shout obscenities. Sometimes I would go down there with one or two of my buddies to witness the spectacle. One evening, as the troops approached, an elderly man came off his porch to the curb where he stood and cursed the passing soldiers, and saluted them with a stiff middle finger.

Suddenly, as we looked on, three or four guardsmen broke ranks, rushed to the curb, and with the butts of their rifles beat the old man to death. The next day the *Canton Repository* reported that the man had died of a heart attack. Years later when the Ohio guardsmen were exonerated of the murders of the Kent State students, I was enraged but not surprised.

The men who had remained on the job during the strike were rewarded by Republic Steel with cash bonuses and promotions, but when these men returned to their homes they were met with such hostility and sustained resentment from their neighbors and former friends they were eventually forced to move their families from the area. Even so, unforgotten and unforgiven, they carried with them the stigma of scab to their graves.

The Beginning

I turned left at Girard Avenue and entered my home turf. St. Benedict's church and grade school at the corner reminded me that I had grown up in a Catholic diocese. Most of our neighbors were Catholics and their sons and daughters had been my childhood chums.

It was a neighborhood six blocks wide and twelve blocks long, its unpaved streets lined with twenty-five-year-old maple trees, carefully tended lawns and flower gardens and a mixture of two-story frame houses and small bungalows built during the decade following World War I. There were also numerous open fields where housing had been planned but those plans had died with the Great Depression. During the years of unemployment and stark poverty the fields had been converted to vegetable gardens, but with wartime prosperity the gardens were gradually abandoned and replaced by lush stands of assorted weeds.

Our neighbors were religious, God-fearing, industrious, unimaginative and plodding, reasonably responsible, and, with the exception of several dedicated drunks, they did their boozing in moderation or not at all. We had our fair share of petty crime, but most of the serious stuff was concentrated in a few families of degenerates who, fortunately, spent much of their time in jail or in the booby hatch. When the kids got out of line, retribution was usually swift and memorable. Our parents enthusiastically adhered to the axiom, "Spare the rod and spoil the child," and they were quick to enlist the aid of the city police when offended by the actions of a neighbor's kid.

All the older folks were first or second generation Americans who originated from German, French, Czechoslovakian, Polish, Scandinavian and Irish stocks. Most of them hadn't completed grade school and could barely read or write, but could curse fluently and loudly in one or more languages. They considered themselves good Americans. They resolutely supported organized labor, voted a straight Democratic ticket, and faithfully attended church services on Sunday mornings. Even though they were mostly blue-

59

collar workers low on the economic and social scales, they took solace in the conviction that they were vastly superior to all the niggers, kikes, dagos, hunkies, spics, arabs, and chinks who inhabited the surrounding ghettos.

Lives of the older generation were austere and barren. The constant, unrelenting struggle to survive afforded little time to smell the roses. When the men left for work they carried dingy, battered lunch pails, packed by their wives in the wee hours. Lunches weren't fancy—slices of bologna between slabs of homemade bread, a thermos of hot coffee, an apple, and maybe a cookie. They wore rough, drab work clothes, often threadbare, and always a mosaic of patches; steel-tipped work shoes with glued-on rubber soles; and slouchy old, narrow brim hats. They walked eight to ten blocks to the bus stop and rode the buses in silence with lunch boxes perched on closed knees. No one drove a car or rode in a car pool because none of them had ever owned or expected to own a car. When they returned home their clothes and their hands and faces were streaked with the grime of hard labor.

They reeked of sweat, garbage, chemicals, smoke and sewage. They walked from the bus stop with a deliberate, weary gait, lifeless arms dangling at their sides and aching shoulders slumped forward in what would in time become a permanent stoop. At home they would be in no mood for light banter with the wife or the playful antics of their children. They expected supper to be on the table at 5:00 p.m. and after that to find the evening newspaper, if they could afford it, beside their favorite living room chair. Their lives were molded to a dreary, lethal routine. They never retired. There were no golden years or golden watches. When they were too old or too tired or too sick to work they just quietly died and their families were left with no father, no savings, no insurance and no hope.

Wives managed the house and raised the kids and they catered to their husbands' wishes and whims and to frequent abuses. The expression, "A woman's work is never done" could have originated with these women. Interludes of free time were rare, brief and coveted: a family picnic at Meyers Lake, a church social, a wedding, a funeral, or an hour on the porch swing on a hot summer night. At times pleasure could be combined with chores. A little gossip with a neighbor while hanging the wash in the backyard or listening to Cheerio, Father Coughlin or Ma Perkins on the radio while scrubbing floors, making beds, ironing, baking, canning garden vegetables, cleaning the wallpaper or mending torn clothes and altering the kids' hand-me-downs. Occasionally they broke the monotony by making themselves a new dress from patterned flour sacks purchased at the local grocery/feed store on 5th Street.

With only occasional whimpers they accepted the hardships and their subservient roles with the philosophical acknowledgment that this life was imposed on them by custom, God, and the necessity to survive. There were no divorces—the Catholic Church and economic dependency saw to that. And for wives and husbands alike, hope and expectations rested in the lives of their children and in the hereafter.

I turned into the alley that led to my parents' house. With slightly quickening steps I passed weedy fields where we had played as kids. Images of those days flickered through my mind as I walked—flashes of pick-up football and baseball games played by whoever happened to be hanging around at the time or whoever had a bat or a ball. We had built a succession of unsightly clubhouses in those fields, built from old pieces of scrap wood and junk. Sometimes other kids would knock them down out of meanness, but usually they were so flimsy that they eventually collapsed from fatigue or with a little help from a light breeze. We used to play in the snow in the winter out there in those fields; we made snowmen, built snow forts, and had spirited snowball fights. Sometimes we skated when the pond water at the corner iced over and at other times we hooked our sleds to the back of the horse-drawn baker's wagon and took free rides around the block. There were hardly ever any cars in the street so we played there a lot. You could sleep in the streets on a summer afternoon and never have to worry about being run over.

We had a lot of fights in those fields and in the streets, too, usually over really dumb things. I remember once when Bob Schario and I had gotten pissed off at something Bill Balzer had done. For punishment we tied him to a tree and beat him with sticks until my hysterical mother intervened.

Sniffing the warm air I thought I could detect a hint of spring. Soon, I thought, violets would be straining to pop their little purple faces above the tangle of matted weeds, and robins would be arriving to search for juicy worms and glossy, plump mates. Kids would soon materialize outside their houses and with brightly colored kites they would race to the fields as we had done a long time ago.

I remembered a few verses of a poem I had written on board the *Pocatello* in the Pacific:

> *Once again the robins sing,*
> *and lilacs bloom in full,*
> *And violets spring like nymphs*
> *from layers of brown leaves dull*

Once again spring had come,
in budding, pure new life,
With blanket fresh and green
O'er scars of winter's strife.

At last I reached my parents' driveway, two parallel tire-wide ruts in the grass that passed beneath overhanging branches of apple and peach trees and that ended abruptly at the back porch of a one-story home. The rarely used garage fronted on the alley and was separated from my grandmother's tiny house by a narrow driveway that led to the front of my step-grandfather's shop. He had worked there seven days each week from 3:00 a.m. until 4:00 p.m., refinishing and repairing antique furniture for rich clients who lived on the northwest side of town. When a client delivering a sick antique parked a big shiny new car in the alley, small crowds of kids and a sprinkling of parents invariably gathered to stare in awe.

My uncle Bud built the two-story house in the lot adjacent to my grandmother's house in 1937. He had planned to bring his new wife there from Chicago, but he died of lung cancer before they could make the move. He was buried in Canton and the house was sold by his widow.

As I stepped onto the porch I dropped the seabag and bedroll, opened the door and walked inside. My mother wasn't expecting me. She was bending over the stove, cleaning a burner and hadn't seen or heard me until I stepped into the kitchen and was standing at her side. She jumped, and turned, startled, and cried, "Julie, you're home!" As I responded, "I'm out, Mom, out for good," she threw her arms around my neck crying and slobbering kisses on my face. Her phony displays of affection always nauseated me so I brushed her aside, announcing in an emphatic tone that I wanted to get out of my uniform as quickly as possible. She followed me into the dining room as I strode ahead into my old bedroom. Closing the door behind me I noted that the room was as tiny as ever. My little cot-like bed still paralleled the back wall. I used to lie on that thing on warm days and with the barrel of my 22 rifle pointed out the window I shot rats that ran in and out of our garage. Occasionally I loaded the rifle with birdshot and popped pesky dogs and cats in their posteriors. They always left in a hurry, screaming and yelping as they charged down the street. Most never returned but there was one determined big, black tomcat who liked it so much he came back frequently for additional treatments.

A small chest of drawers stood against the wall close to the tiny clothes closet, and a large glass-fronted bookcase covered the opposing wall by the door. There was a little nightstand by the bed that held a dilapidated old lamp. The floor was covered with ugly, faded, yellowish linoleum, tough on bare feet in the winter, and over it, parallel with the bed was a multi-colored rag rug made by my grandmother. It wasn't much, but it had been mine for fifteen years.

Having quickly surveyed the room and its contents I ripped off my shoes and uniform and dropped them on the floor. I jumped up and down on the heap with sufficient vigor to break the glass castors that cradled the legs of my bed and to tilt the pictures on the walls. Then, taking careful aim, I kicked the disheveled pile into a far corner of the room.

In my skivvies I belatedly began a desperate search of the closet for a reasonably presentable set of civvies. There was little from which to select, and two inches taller and fifty pounds heavier than when I had enlisted in 1942, the prospects of a trim fit were remote. Nevertheless, with considerable determination and resourcefulness I managed to squirm into a permanently stained pair of brown work pants and a faded gray sweat shirt, and then painfully forced my flattened feet into a narrow pair of steel-tipped shoes worn while employed as a machinist at the Westinghouse Naval Ordnance Plant.

Thus, more-or-less prepared to enter my new life as an unemployed twenty-two-year-old civilian, I threw open the bedroom door and stepped into the hallway. My mother was still standing there facing the door, now with alarmed eyes and slightly parted lips as if she were about to speak. She didn't say a word; she was totally silent for one of the few times in her life. As I passed by her I announced emphatically, "I'm going outside; I'll be back sometime."

I walked around the yard for a while trying to settle down, trying to comprehend that it was all over, trying to convince myself I wasn't dreaming. Then I stopped walking and, smiling broadly at the old, faded garage, I thought, *Christ, after twenty-two years I've finally found the beginning.*

The Coup

In August 1951, I moved to Southern Illinois University from the University of Illinois where I had completed a year of work on a Ph.D. degree in geology. My appointment at Carbondale had been for one year and I was expected to teach the courses in mineralogy. I never managed to teach a mineralogy course there, but I did come close to finding a home in the hills of southern Illinois. Had those hills been etched from marine fossiliferous Cenozoic rocks instead of Paleozoic coal-bearing rocks I might never have left.

In the spring of 1953 R.C. Moore invited me to come to the University of Kansas to teach a few paleontology courses while completing my residency requirements for the Ph.D. Such an invitation from the world's foremost invertebrate paleontologist could hardly be refused, so I took a year's leave of absence from SIU and moved to Lawrence for the 1953-54 academic year.

In the autumn of 1954 I returned to the SIU campus where for the next two years I taught courses and worked on my dissertation. Then in September 1956, with the completed dissertation in hand, my wife, Phyllis and I met R.C. and Lillian Moore at the French Motel in Mexico City, where we had gone to attend the 18th International Geological Congress. For the next eight days Moore and I spent an hour or so each evening sitting on the edge of his bed, working over my masterpiece. Finally, to my great relief, Moore announced that I had done an acceptable job and that as soon as I had made the relatively minor alterations in the text that he had suggested (mandated) he would schedule my dissertation defense in Lawrence.

With the dissertation out of the way and the Ph.D. virtually in my pocket, I made the decision to leave SIU at the close of the 1956-57 academic year. To accomplish this, all I had to do was to find a suitable university located in the Gulf or Atlantic coastal plain with a geology department that had an urgent need for a Cenozoic biostratigrapher and which was willing to hire me. A wiser, more mature individual may have entertained doubts that the plan could work but I was neither very wise nor mature so, of course, I succeeded at my very first attempt.

In March 1957, I led my Invertebrate Paleontology class on the annual field trip to western Tennessee and Mississippi to study Cretaceous and Cenozoic fossiliferous localities. On the way out of my office I grabbed the latest issue of *Geotimes*, a professional newsletter, which had arrived that morning and slipped it into my field pack for later scrutiny. That evening, balanced on the edge of my motel bed, I flipped through the little magazine to the section entitled "Vacancies". As usual there were only a few openings listed, but one announcing an opening for a Cenozoic biostratigrapher in the geology department at the University of Houston caught my eye. The position seemed tailored for me, so, wasting no time, I wrote a letter to the Search Committee in which I expressed my interest in the position, briefly outlined my qualifications, and requested additional information.

About a week later in Carbondale I received a response to my letter from Dr. John Wang (name has been changed), Chairman of the Geology Department at Houston. His letter, dated March 29, stated an interest in my possible candidacy for the position, provided a brief description of the department and staff, and enclosed necessary application forms.

While awaiting a response from Houston, I discussed my plans with R.C. Moore. It was his opinion that the Houston geology department was "up and coming". He also mentioned that Henryk Stenzel was a professor in the department and that the opportunity to work closely with this highly regarded biostratigrapher would be a valuable experience for me. I had not met Stenzel but was familiar with his publications and also aware of his formidable, near legendary reputation as a meticulous and brilliant master of Gulf Coast Cenozoic geology. The unexpected opportunity to be his professional associate was an added incentive to join Houston's geology department.

Another man at the university I was anxious to meet was Tom Pulley of the zoology department. Tom was the foremost authority on the ecology and distribution of mollusks living in the Gulf of Mexico. For several years we had corresponded and during that time I had unashamedly picked his fertile brain for data on the living species that would help me to better understand the lifestyles of some of the fossil species I regularly encountered in my Florida studies.

A letter from John Wang dated June 29 stated that the position was mine at the rank of Assistant Professor and a monthly (nine months) salary of $600.00. On July 3, I telegraphed my acceptance of the offer. During the first half of the summer I taught the SIU summer field course in southern Illinois and the St. Francis Mountains of Missouri. The latter half of the summer was spent in Florida in my role as a consultant to the State Geological Survey.

In the fall, Phyllis and I with two nervous, hairy cats moved into an apartment near the University of Houston campus. Two days later I was ensconced in my office on the second floor of the Roy Cullen Building. Before I had unpacked all my books and lecture notes I was stunned to learn from one of the staff members that both Stenzel and Pulley had left the university in June. Stenzel, my informant said, had resigned following a major heart attack and had since recovered sufficiently to accept a position with the Shell Development Company in Bellaire, Texas. Pulley, he explained, had accepted an appointment as curator of the city's Museum of Natural History, when he had been informed that his teaching contract at the university would not be renewed for the 1957-58 academic year.

It was an ugly and bizarre story that eventually emerged—one far removed from the layman's usual perception of the pristine ivory tower. It was a story told with emotion shaded by strong feelings of hatred, personal betrayal and raw anger. It was a story told by men who despised Stenzel and by those who admired or even revered the man.

Houston's geology department had been in existence for about twenty-five years. In that period of time it had gone nowhere. Academic standards had been low, the faculty less than distinguished, and accomplishments of graduates insignificant. In a quarter of a century the department had gone through more than 100 faculty members and had failed to produce a single student who earned a Ph.D. Most disturbing was the failure to establish a meaningful working relationship with the oil industry. One might have expected the department to have reaped at least modest advantages from its location in the oil capital of the world.

In 1953 the university administration belatedly decided to woo local oil companies. They began by requesting the geology department to recruit a group of prominent (rich) oil geologists who would be willing to serve together on an advisory board. The stated purpose of the group was to recommend steps the department might take to achieve national visibility as a leading center for geological studies. An unstated objective of the administration was to develop close ties with a group of rich men who might eventually feel inclined to bequeath some significant part of their fortunes to the university. For an institution that had been founded by a wealthy oil man, Hugh Roy Cullen, this objective had obvious merit.

One of the first recommendations of the eighteen-member advisory board was that the department needed a dynamic geologist of substantial national and international stature to serve as chairman. Following a period of collective head scratching, a decision was reached to approach Henryk Bronislaw Stenzel, then a highly regarded research geologist with the Bureau of Economic Geology in Austin. Stenzel accepted the position but demanded an annual salary of $18,000. It was an unusually high salary for a professor in the 1950s, and the university refused to go higher than $9,000. The difference was made up by contributions from several of the major oil companies. Thus, as a blend of academic and industrial cooperative effort, Stenzel became chairman of the geology department in the fall of 1954.

Stenzel was born in 1897 in Pabianice, Poland. He attended school in Breslaw, and received the Ph.D. degree in geology magna cum laude from Schlesiche Fredrick Wilhelm University in 1922. In 1925 he accepted a position as Instructor of Geology at Texas A&M College. In 1934 he joined the Bureau of Economic Geology in Austin, Texas.

There were compelling reasons to select Stenzel for the position of Chairman of Houston's geology department. His research accomplishments in the field of Coastal Plain Cenozoic biostratigraphy had earned him well-deserved professional acclaim. In Texas he was particularly admired and highly esteemed throughout the oil industry as a man of exceptional character and as a superb scientist with a formidable work ethic. It probably seemed self-evident to the advisory board that such a man was tailor-made for the job.

On the other hand, there were facets of Stenzel's personality that made his selection as chairman tantamount to placing Genghis Kahn in charge of the Salvation Army. He had no tolerance for colleagues he considered to be professional sluggards, and he was quick to bluntly and at times colorfully express his contempt for research he considered to be the product of unclear thinking or unscientific procedures.

Hardly anyone who knew Henryk Stenzel in 1954 would have envisioned his becoming a lovable, mellow old professor. To those who knew him best it was clear that he was neither lovable nor a master of diplomacy. On a good day he could be grumpy, gruff and startlingly blunt. Even some of his closest friends, when pressed, were obliged to admit that he was an egotistical, strong-willed, domineering, uncompromising, opinionated, dogmatic and autocratic taskmaster. Some, who did not count themselves among his admirers, tended to characterize him as an arrogant, intolerant prick with a personality composed of ground corundum and castor oil.

From the first day of his chairmanship Stenzel began to alienate his staff. If he intended to conceal his general contempt for the professors and graduate assistants he failed miserably. Instead of inspiring the faculty his badgering and bullying tactics succeeded only in shocking and demoralizing everyone.

Stenzel's first notable edict was, by most accounts, also his most memorable. All faculty members were ordered to actively conduct research projects and to publish the results of their work at least once a year.

To most of the staff the word "research" was vaguely recalled as a distasteful exercise they once endured as an inescapable prerequisite for the Ph.D. They had discovered that research was a pain in the ass that required a great amount of time better directed to more creative activities such as sleeping. That some members of the staff could produce a research paper possessing the scientific quality acceptable to a major professional journal was slightly more improbable than their chances of shacking up with Marilyn Monroe.

One member of the staff determined that for him there would be no research or research papers and that eventually there would be no Stenzel. This man, a wily Chinese professor of geology whose Americanized name was John Wang would ultimately prove to be the lethal factor in the plans of Stenzel and the advisory board to elevate the geology department to world class status.

During the first year of his chairmanship Stenzel began to recruit additional geology faculty. Eventually he hired three bright young men with impressive research records. At the time there was an obvious need to bolster the department's academic strengths in several disciplines not adequately covered by existing faculty expertise. Stenzel, apparently with advisory board approval, ignored those needs and opted to bring in three macropaleontologists. It is difficult to understand this decision unless the goal of the board was to establish Houston's geology department as a major center for paleontological studies. The only residual effect of this tactic that I could detect on my arrival on campus was that most of the staff had developed a keen aversion to the subject of paleontology.

In November 1956, Wang and his allies decided the time to attack had arrived. Stenzel had left the campus to attend an annual meeting of the Geological Survey of America where he was scheduled to chair a technical session. In his absence a covert, Watergate-type operation was ordered by Wang. A small group of professors and graduate assistants broke into and ransacked Stenzel's office. Among the documents removed was a list of names of the old guard faculty which indicated the order in which they were to be fired.

At that moment Wang moved swiftly. He prepared a petition demanding Stenzel's removal as chairman, which was quickly signed by all the pre-Stenzel faculty and each of the graduate assistants. The petition was then delivered to the office of the Dean of Faculty who immediately ordered a work crew to remove all of Stenzel's personal items from his office, box them and stack the boxes in the corridor. As soon as the work crew was finished a locksmith changed the lock on the office door.

When Stenzel returned from the GSA meeting he was met at the airport by the Dean of the Faculty who bluntly informed him that he was no longer departmental chairman and that his contract would not be renewed for the 1957-58 academic year. Shortly thereafter Stenzel suffered a massive heart attack which he narrowly survived.

Following Stenzel's heart attack Shell Development and all other major oil companies operating in Houston blackballed the geology department. No longer would they hire their graduates or provide any financial or material aid. For the geology department it was a virtual kiss of death.

In two years Wang had thwarted all efforts of the advisory board to help the department reach academic respectability. He had unseated a chairman fully supported by the oil industry and propelled him to the edge of his grave. Nevertheless he emerged from the two-year civil war unscathed. He was the only member of the old guard who had not put his signature to the petition to strip Stenzel of the chairmanship.

Wang could not have unseated Stenzel without the blessing of high-level administrative personnel. Before the episode was concluded one might have reasonably assumed some active involvement of the university's chancellor. It also would have been necessary for Wang to work around the Dean of the School of Science, a paleontologist himself, who had hired Stenzel and who had remained a staunch supporter of the irascible old Pole.

In the official view of the administration Wang's solid judgment, rare wisdom, astute diplomacy, and his steadfast role for two years as conciliator between the two warring department factions more than warranted his appointment as Stenzel's successor to the departmental chairmanship.

One of Wang's first assignments as department chair was to notify the three young paleontology professors hired by Stenzel that their contracts would not be renewed. At the same time Tom Pulley, a close friend of Stenzel, was dumped by the zoology department and the Dean of the School of Sciences received his walking papers. I never heard an official explanation for the coup, if one was ever offered by the University of Houston.

Wang was forty-five-ish, round face, short rotund body; black, straight, slicked-back hair, and a Ph.D. from the University of Iowa. His wife was shorter than John but less rotund—more angular. She was a professor in the chemistry department. Both had been born in China and neither spoke English well. I usually could understand most of John's words but the way in which he strung them together often baffled me. When he talked to me I always figured there was a hidden meaning in his words. I became so paranoid about this that when he said, "Good morning, Jules," I went to my office, sat at my desk and tried to figure what exactly he had meant.

I was surprised to learn that the Wangs were devout Southern Baptists. I've never heard the circumstances of their conversion but always assumed that they had been victimized as children in China by predatory missionaries. They were serious about their religious convictions and frowned on card playing, booze, dancing, and other mortal sins. They were dedicated Creationists and each year John embarrassed our faculty by presenting a series of public lectures designed to expose the fallacies of the modern theory of organic evolution.

There was reason to believe, however, that John was not so devout as his spouse. At faculty parties attended by the Wangs, the host, when serving John a drink, seemed to make a point of saying, "Here's your lemonade, John." I noted with curiosity that as he sipped those drinks he soon acquired an air of serenity I found difficult to attribute to the possible effect of a concoction of sugar, water and lemon juice.

Finally one evening when we were all at the Greenwoods for cocktails, I caught Bob alone in the kitchen. "What's this stuff about Wang and lemonade, Bob?" I asked. He smiled knowingly. "That's not lemonade, Jules, it's gin. John's wife would divorce him if she knew he was drinking something alcoholic."

Wang enjoyed telling jokes but he usually screwed up the punch lines. This got a lot more laughs than the jokes deserved and encouraged Wang, who never caught on, to continue to tell his stories at every opportunity. His best joke was not intended to be funny; it was his frequent reference to his latest research project in a seemingly desperate attempt to convince us, or himself, that he really was a scientist. We all knew John never did any research and that is what made it so hilarious.

John taught the course in sedimentation, and one year, to our complete surprise, he announced he would take the class on a field trip. This was strange because it was something he had never done. He claimed he was doing a study of the gravel deposits of the Colorado River and he wanted the class to see what he was up to. On a Saturday morning, he loaded the students into a university vehicle and they drove the sixty miles to Columbus, Texas, on the banks of the Colorado. When they arrived he walked with the students to the water's edge and pointed at a gravel bar which lay mostly submerged in the river, ten or twenty feet from shore. "Ah!" he announced proudly. "There it is—gravel. You see?" When everyone agreed they could see the gravel bar he turned and led the puzzled students back to the bus. Loaded aboard they made the return sixty-mile trip to the university.

The Wangs had two boys about six and eight-years-old who were thoroughly Americanized. They often appeared in the department attired in full, star-spangled cowboy regalia with chrome six-shooters holstered on each hip. When bored (most of the time) they ran up and down the halls with drawn revolvers shouting at each passerby, "Bang, bang, you're dead, y'all."

In time I learned that Wang left no paper trail. When he was chairman he never sent anyone a memo or posted a notice on the bulletin board (actually, we had no bulletin board). There was no budgetary accountability, no record of undergraduate or graduate course or degree requirements, no lists of undergraduate majors or graduate students (master's candidates), no departmental newsletter, and no written record of any departmental policies.

He presided over our infrequent departmental staff meetings where he rarely expressed an opinion on any topic more substantial than the weather. And, of course, no minutes were taken at such meetings.

There was at least one departmental meeting in which Wang repeatedly expressed an opinion. The subject was a female applicant for the position of departmental secretary. Her predecessor had been fired because of her addiction to listening in on the private telephone conversations of the staff.

The candidate, I soon discovered, was a well-endowed young widow, whom everyone except me had already ogled. There was a lengthy, detailed and animated discussion of her physical attributes (big boobs rated near the top) in which Wang was an enthusiastic participant. At one point several of the professors, including John, volunteered to personally supplement her salary if that would induce her to take the job. Most of those present were glassy-eyed and drooling on their unused notepads when I managed at last to shock them out of their sexual fantasies. "Can she type?" I asked.

With anguished expressions that might have been induced by *coitis interruptus,* all faces turned to me. Finally Wang regained sufficient composure to respond, "Well, no, Jules," he said solemnly. "She can't, but I'm sure she can learn."

The motion to hire her carried with only one dissenting vote. As an epilogue to the story I can say that although she never did learn to type, no one ever seemed to give a damn.

A Geological Einstein

When I was a student at Kent State University I was hired as a laboratory assistant by my geology professor, Carl Savage. One day during my senior year, Savage called me into his office for a "chat," as he put it.

"Next year," he said, "you will leave here to attend graduate school. It doesn't matter so much where you do your master's work, but the Ph.D. is different. A Ph.D. is your union card. It's essential, then, that your doctoral studies be done at a first rate institution under the guidance of the very best man in your chosen field. He must be a great teacher and a great scientist." Then he asked, "Who is the greatest invertebrate paleontologist in the world?" I only had to ponder the question for a second. "Well," I answered,. "That has to be Raymond C. Moore of Kansas." Smiling and nodding his head in agreement, he said, "It's settled then, isn't it? You'll go to Kansas and study with Ray Moore."

Even as an undergraduate I was aware of the legend that was Raymond Cecil Moore, the Einstein of the geological profession. I also had heard of his reputation as a formidable taskmaster who brooked no nonsense from his students or his peers. And I had heard the tales of how he could, on occasion, with a glacial stare or cutting sarcasm, denude entire forests and cause water to flow uphill. At that moment a bout with Rocky Marciano for the heavyweight title seemed less intimidating. For a kid off the streets who had only squeaked through high school, the knowledge that I would become the first member of my family to earn a college degree was a bit mind-boggling. A Ph.D. seemed a distant dream; that I might one day work with R.C. Moore surely would require a miracle.

The road to Moore would prove long, circuitous and, at times, uncertain. In the end the miracle did happen, but it was Moore who found me.

Late in the spring of 1953 we were having a party at our Carbondale home for a large number of Southern Illinois University geology majors, their wives and girlfriends. At about nine o'clock a vigorously contested game of darts was in progress in the den. The noise level was deafening. Just then the phone rang and one of my students answered it. He called across the room in a booming voice, "Dr. R. C. Moore calling from Lawrence, Kansas; he wants to talk with you." When I took the receiver I laughed, well aware of the practical jokes some of the students enjoyed playing on me.

But when I said hello, a well-modulated voice at the other end said, "This is Ray Moore, calling from Lawrence, Kansas, I've been hearing good things about you. I want you to come to Lawrence in the fall and teach our undergraduate courses in paleontology. Of course you can complete residence for the Ph.D. at the same time. I assume you would elect to do your dissertation under my direction."

It was an offer I couldn't refuse. I accepted immediately. At last I would follow Carl Savage's advice and study under the world's greatest invertebrate paleontologist.

In the fall I arrived in Lawrence ready to take up my duties as an Instructor of Geology. During the summer I had completed field studies for my dissertation, the paleontology and paleoecology of the Caloosahatchee Formation of Southern Florida.

My dual role as a student and a faculty member moved along smoothly for about a month. That was when I received a summons from the Dean of the Graduate School to appear in his office post-haste. When I walked into his office it was obvious he was greatly perturbed. Without a perfunctory salutation he went directly to the issue. "You have deliberately violated a rule of this university. It is a policy that no one who is a student here can at the same time hold a faculty appointment. I don't know how you did it, but it is a situation which must be correctly immediately."

When I explained that I had no idea about the details of the appointment he looked at me scornfully and said that I was a liar. I was stunned. I was not accustomed to being referred to as a liar. More important, if I lost my position as an instructor I would be forced to drop out of school.

As he droned on I realized that it was quite possible that he had never been informed of my special situation. Moore had made all the arrangements. At that time Moore dealt directly and exclusively with the University Chancellor and had undoubtedly cleared my appointment with him. The Chancellor may have felt no need to inform the Dean.

Still uncertain of my fate and extremely disturbed, I went directly to Moore and explained what had occurred in the Dean's office. He smiled reassuringly and said, while patting me on the shoulder, "It will be all right. I'll see to that."

I continued to teach my courses without further harassment. However, at the end of the semester I was once again requested to report to the Dean. When I entered his office he stepped from behind his desk and, with a cordial grin and hearty handshake, greeted me as if I were his long lost brother. Making no reference to our first meeting, he said, "Jules, I wish you to know that it is a pleasure to have you at this university. Your outstanding grade record [straight A's] marks you as an exceptional student. We are very proud of your accomplishments."

It was my last encounter with the Dean. Moore, as promised, had taken care of the situation. The Dean's role in the administrative scheme of things had been completely clarified.

A graduate course taught by Moore was notable for a variety of reasons. For one thing, there were two textbooks, one written in French and the other in German. Moore had little sympathy for students who could not read, write, and speak several languages.

Moore was usually late for the class which was entitled "World Geology." One day after we had waited for him at least ten minutes he huffed into the room waving a printed pamphlet. "Just received this reprint today," he said excitedly. "Haven't had time to read it closely, but it's going to fit right in with our discussion of the Paris Basin. I need a volunteer to review it for us at our next meeting." A young fellow in the front row, who did not know Moore well, waggled a hand in the air indicating his eagerness to accept the assignment. "Good," Moore said, as he handed the paper to the fellow.

Perhaps half a minute later, the student who had been looking at the article, emitted a loud cry of anguish followed by, "This paper is written in French!"

His lecture effectively interrupted by this outburst, Moore looked down at the student and said, "So?"

The student protested indignantly: "But I can't read French."

With a withering glare Moore responded, "Well, learn it son."

At our next class meeting Moore strode into the room waving another reprint he had just received in the mail. "This is a very interesting paper," he announced. "It's in Japanese, so as soon as I brush up on the language I'll summarize it for the class." We were all greatly relieved that he hadn't chosen to assign the damned thing to any of us. We were also aware that he was setting an example for all of us.

Our graduate seminar in paleontology met one night each week. At the meetings Moore assigned each of us a paper to review at the next session. At the first meeting I drew a work by Roman Koslowski on graptolites. I had nothing against graptolites, but there was a gigantic problem with the paper. It was written in Polish, and I didn't know one word of Polish. A French abstract at least provided some notion of the topic, but scarcely formed the basis for a substantive review. I was well aware that I could hardly show up in class and beg off with the lame excuse that I couldn't read Polish. I also knew that my future as a Moore student probably hung in the balance.

For two days I worked with a Polish dictionary at the library, but that proved a tedious and ineffective approach. Then I began a frantic search of the campus for someone who was fluent in Polish and who would be willing to help with the translation. I found two people who each had a smattering of the language, but who were completely ignorant of paleontological jargon. After a week of blood, sweat and indigestion, I appeared at our seminar with a summary of the paper even I considered only marginally satisfactory.

In the classroom we sat around a big table with Moore presiding. The plan was for the student to his right to give the first review and for the rest of us to follow in a counterclockwise sequence. Following that scheme I would be the fourth speaker. Such an arrangement provided more than enough time for my brain to become a gelatinous mass. When finally it was my turn my mouth was powdery dry and I could barely swallow. Speaking would be a challenge.

Moore gave me an expressionless look before he asked which paper I was prepared to discuss. I responded that my subject was Koslowski's graptolite paper. Moore nodded his head thoughtfully. "If you don't mind, Jules, I think we will pass on that one and go on to something more interesting."

In any serious consideration of the essential ingredients of great teaching, one must never summarily dismiss instilled fear and raw intimidation. Moore used both effectively and constructively. Jack Dempsey, commanding officer of the Coast Guard commando school at Manhattan Beach and former heavyweight champion, used the same tactics. His approach to teaching physical conditioning was direct, dramatic and memorable. One of his favorite devices was to walk up to an unsuspecting sailor and drive a sledgehammer blow to the man's midsection. Towering over the crumpled heap on the gym floor he would say with a tight smile, "You don't seem to be in very good shape, pal."

I reviewed many scientific papers for class presentation, but there are none I recall so vividly as that damned paper by Roman Koslowski.

I was more than a little worried about the course in Stratigraphic Paleontology I was scheduled to teach during the spring semester. I was uncertain how to organize the laboratory sessions and had no idea how Moore might want them structured. Pondering the problem for several days led to no satisfactory solution. So I dropped by Moore's office and explained my dilemma. He was quiet for a minute, wheels, I assumed, spinning. Then he said, "I'm thinking of a series of exercises where the students walk to the blackboard and study several stratigraphic sections. When they have finished they return to the work table and construct a geologic map."

Without the foggiest notion what the hell he had just said, I thanked him for his assistance. "Not at all, Jules," he said cheerily. "Glad to be of help." With some effort I had refrained from asking for elucidation; I was too aware of one of his inviolate axioms: "If I tell you once and you do it right, that's good, but if I must tell you twice that's bad."

Acting as best I could on his cryptic instructions I eventually put together a set of exercises that made use of stratigraphic cross-sections and geologic maps. I never learned if they came anywhere close to what Moore had in mind, but they worked and I used those exercises in my labs for thirty years.

I failed the German exam at my first attempt. Thereafter, at all social and professional functions which we attended together, Moore introduced me in the same manner to everyone: "This is Jules DuBar, he failed his German exam." Needless to say I passed the exam on my second attempt.

Moore had a distinctive way of registering displeasure with the work of a student who had failed to meet his standards of excellence. On one occasion a young doctoral candidate had, following many months of hard toil, completed a draft of his dissertation which he submitted to Moore for appraisal. Moore told him he would look at it that evening and discuss it with him in the morning.

Predictably anxious to learn of the revisions that might be requested, the fellow was at Moore's office door at 8:00 the next morning. When he entered the room Moore was busily working at his desk. Without looking up from the papers spread before him, Moore pointed to a small table near the door and said, "It's over there." The student picked up his weighty tome and nervously began to flip through it looking for the expected penciled marginal comments. Instead, to his horror, he discovered that Moore had poured black India ink over every page. It was a critique of the dissertation calculated to reduce the poor fellow to a moldering heap of mulch. For each of us who were students of Moore, the incident served as a vivid reminder that even one's best effort provided no certain insulation from the scorn of the master.

During the spring semester Moore taught a course in field stratigraphy. A few weeks before mid-semester he confided in me that he just didn't know about the students in his class. "They aren't getting it," he complained. "They don't seem to give a damn. Really not taking it seriously."

I went to one of the students enrolled in the course and told him Moore was very displeased with their work and advised him to pass the word that they all should get on the ball.

Apparently my admonition went unheeded. The day after the mid-term exam Moore expressed his opinion of their efforts by driving large nails through the stack of exam papers and tossing them onto the floor of the hall outside his office.

Horacio J. Harrington, an Argentinean, was South America's most illustrious geologist. His wife was a member of the Spanish royal family. The Harringtons had been special favorites of Juan Peron, who lavished Horacio with money, accolades, plush research facilities, and a small army of young student assistants conditioned to heed Horacio's every beck and call. For unknown political reasons, in 1952 Horacio was forced to flee the country. Sometime thereafter Moore arranged to bring Horacio to the University of Kansas as a professor of geology.

During the spring of 1954 Harrington occupied the office adjacent to mine. Although he was an internationally recognized authority on trilobites and the geology of South America, he had very little experience with, and no taste for, manual labor. Because I was near at hand and because he outranked me, he called on me occasionally to perform odd jobs for him. He always enlisted my services when he needed someone to haul down boxes and drawers of trilobites from the upper shelves of the storage units which lined the walls of his office. Doing his flunky work was a little irritating but I found Horacio to be an interesting man and I enjoyed his company and our frequent conversations.

One day a highly agitated Don Hattin, one of Moore's favorite doctoral candidates, burst into Moore's office. "Dr. Moore," he exclaimed. "Dr. Harrington just asked me to sweep out his office!"

Moore fixed Don with a cold stare. "Do you know how to use a broom?" he asked.

"Well, ah, yes, of course I do."

"All right, then," Moore said. "Use it."

A few days later we learned that Harrington had called Moore and asked him to come upstairs and empty his wastebasket. There is no known record of Moore's response, but thereafter Harrington never asked any of us to do odd jobs for him.

On one afternoon in the fall of 1953 Moore stopped me in the hall outside his office. He was carrying a great stack of papers under one arm and smoking a cigarette. "You don't smoke, do you?"

"No," I replied. "I don't."

He paused to appraise me for a moment, and then, with a note of hope in his voice said, "But do you drink?"

When I assured him that I indeed did drink, he nodded approvingly and said, "Good!"

Moore had a reputation of being a man who rarely, if ever, wasted time. Several years before my arrival on the Kansas campus the president of Phillips Petroleum Company, one of the principle financial donors to the university and especially to the geology department, arrived unexpectedly at Moore's office.

"There is a matter of some importance I wish to discuss with you, Dr. Moore," he stated.

Glancing up impatiently from a manuscript he had been editing, Moore said, "All right." Then laying his pocket watch on the desktop, he added, "You have three minutes."

Early in 1954 Moore's mother died at her Washington state home. On his flight from Lawrence, Moore put the finishing touches on a manuscript he had written, and during a layover in Denver he mailed it to the journal editor. Then, making certain his stay in Washington would not be a total loss, he edited a second manuscript during his mother's funeral.

While at Kansas I visited with the Moores at their Stratford home many times. I learned early on that each invitation carried a specific purpose, and that no other activity or subject was permitted by Moore.

Following his return from his mother's funeral, Moore invited a dozen or more guests to the house to view color slides he had taken while in Washington. As we all huddled in the darkened living room, Moore narrated his slides. About halfway through the show, his wife Lillian, who sat at my right, commented on something unrelated to the slides. Moore looked up at her from his seat by the projector and gave her a withering look: "Lillian, that's not the topic for this evening."

Sometime during the winter of 1954 Moore decided to purchase a TV set. He arranged to have four sets delivered to his house on approval. He called me that day and asked that I come to the house in the evening and help him decide which was the best. When I arrived four large console models were lined up in a row in the middle of the living room, all tuned to the same channel. We stood together in front of them and studied the quality of reception, color, etc. of each TV. In a few minutes he asked, "Which do you think is best, Jules?"

"Well, in my book, the RCA has the greatest clarity and definition."

"All right then, the RCA it is."

After that I had a standing invitation to the house every Friday night to watch the boxing matches with him. When the fight ended the TV was clicked off and I took my leave. Friday nights with Moore were exclusively reserved for boxing.

Boxing was not the only sport Moore enjoyed. He liked basketball, especially while Wilt Chamberlain was on the university team; he acted as an official timer at UK track meets; and he was an enthusiastic football fan. In the fall of 1960 he drove to Houston, Texas, to attend the initial Bluebonnet Bowl with me. When Kansas defeated Rice he was elated.

One day when her husband was out of town on business Lillian invited Phyllis and me to the house for dinner. At eleven o'clock we were still sitting in the kitchen talking when Moore burst into the room carrying the galley proof of Bassler's work on bryzoans, soon to be published as volume I of the Treatise on Invertebrate Paleontology. Without bothering to say hello, he began to distribute detached segments of the text to each of us. "We've got to complete the index for this thing by morning," he announced. "I'm certain that if each of us do our part we can accomplish the task with no difficulty."

When, at dawn, we had managed to finish our assignments, Moore gathered up all our contributions, dumped them into his briefcase, and without breakfast or even a goodbye, charged off to his office in Lindley Hall.

Looking back on that morning I am reminded of a Civil War historical marker at the Manassas battlefield, "We who fell, the dead, the dying and the disabled, held the field."

On a rainy winter night Moore was driving a load of graduate students (myself included) through the wet streets of Lawrence to a destination long since forgotten. The young fellow seated to my left, who had little previous contact with Moore, asked, "Dr. Moore, when you were a visiting professor at Utrecht in the Netherlands, in which language did you lecture?"

Moore directed one of his frigid stares into the rearview mirror sufficiently powerful to penetrate the darkness of the back seat. "Son, I always speak the language of whatever country I am visiting."

Moore, Phyllis and I were at the faculty lounge for lunch. When our orders had been filled, Phyllis noted that we had a plate of butter but no bread. Moore immediately summoned a young bus boy to the table. "Would you mind," he asked, disarmingly, "telling me what this butter is for?" The busboy stared at the butter for a moment, and then scanned the contents of the table. Without a word he wheeled and scurried to the galley. A minute later he was back with a heaping basket of bread.

Several of us were gathered about in Moore's office one morning having coffee and chatting when R.C. strolled in wearing a big grin. In obvious good spirits he flipped a gold plastic credit card onto the table. "That is a prestige credit card given to me today by the President of Phillips Petroleum Company."

The card was passed hand to hand among our small group and then returned to him with the appropriate expressions of admiration.

Later in the day Moore decided to drive into town and try out his newest status symbol at a local Phillips gas station. He returned to the office an hour later clearly in a foul mood.

He had gone to the Phillips station and had the tank filled. When he handed the fancy card to the attendant the man stared at it, turned it over several times, and then, completely puzzled, asked, "What kind of card is this?"

From his seat behind the wheel Moore responded impatiently, "If you could read you would know that it is a Phillips 66 card issued in my name, R.C. Moore, by the president of the damned company."

Still puzzled and clearly unimpressed with Moore's explanation, the man once again flipped the card over and re-examined it. Finally, obviously ill at ease, he said, "Well, sir, I ain't never seen a card like this one before and I don't think you can use it at this station." Then, a little apologetically, he added, "If you want to wait around I could call the District Manager and we can see what he makes of this."

Fighting back his rage, Moore grabbed the card from the guy, whipped out his wallet and paid his bill in cash. In the fall of 1953, most people in the small town of Lawrence, Kansas, still preferred cash to prestige.

Moore had a sharp eye for attractive ladies. Those who worked for him were accustomed to his hands-on treatment of them. He found it difficult to converse with a women without placing his arm around her shoulder, or gently patting her behind. The girls in the office learned never to wear a T-shirt with a logo spread across the front. Moore loved to slowly spell out the words as he traced each letter with his forefinger.

Most women who spent much time around Moore regarded his antics and familiarities as a minor embarrassment, and a few considered them amusing. Some considered him a dirty old man, but were willing to leave it at that. Today

Moore's treatment of his female employees would certainly have invited official complaints and possibly even a lawsuit or two. Such reactions would have made absolutely no sense to Moore.

Generally overlooked was Moore's generosity. In 1952, when John Frye, Director of the Kansas Geological Survey, could not find funding to attend the International Geological Congress held in Algiers, Moore anonymously covered John's transportation and expenses from his own pocket. And when he died, Moore left his million-dollar estate to the University of Kansas Endowment Association.

Upon completion of residence requirements at Kansas I returned to my post at Southern Illinois University as Assistant Professor of Geology. My annual salary remained less than four thousand dollars, and it wasn't possible for me to maintain an extensive wardrobe. I don't think my peers thought I dressed shabbily, but at the same time it is unlikely that anyone saw me as a fashion plate.

During my final two years at Southern it was necessary to return to Lawrence on several occasions: preliminary exams, German exam (twice), consultations with Moore about my dissertation, and eventually to defend the dissertation. On all those visits I was a guest at the Moore home. At some point Ray and Lillian made a decision to take over responsibility for my wardrobe. On each visit Lillian, at the first opportunity, took me upstairs to their bedroom where she rummaged through Moore's dresser and closet, pulling out various items of apparel—socks, underwear, shirts, ties, and suits—which she would decree Moore no longer needed. On one of these visits she gave me the brown tweed suit he had worn when lecturing at Utrecht.

At SIU I strolled into class one day wearing the Utrecht suit. "Before I begin the paleo lecture today," I said, "I want you all to know that I stand before you dressed inside and out, head to foot, in clothes once worn by the legendary Raymond C. Moore. If for no other reason the lecture I am about to deliver you may perhaps regard as memorable."

At the 1956 International Geological Congress in Mexico City Phyllis and I and the Moores occupied adjacent suites at the French Motel at Hamburgo 96. It was a small motel, conveniently located and quite pleasant, a private place whose owner catered only to French and American guests. It proved to be a tiny island of serenity set in the very midst of the hustle and bustle of the downtown area. It was clean, cheerfully cloaked in an air of easy-going congeniality, and operated with unobtrusive efficiency. A delightful breakfast was served from 7:00 a.m. to 9:00 a.m. and a bevy of young Mexican girls did our laundry each day. There was something to be said about the security of the place as well. Concrete walls ten feet high and eighteen inches thick surrounded the grounds, iron gates at the entrance were locked at 10:00 p.m. and mean-spirited dogs led by armed guards patrolled the inner perimeter from dusk to dawn.

At the same time the Russian delegation of 300 geologists were housed together in one hotel leased by the Soviet Union and carefully guarded by scores of KGB agents. None of the geologists was permitted to leave the hotel alone. Watched closely by their ever-present keepers, they were escorted en masse to meetings and other functions previously approved by the chief of security.

The convention, which continued for a week, was attended by several thousand geologists originating from many countries of the world. So many technical sessions were scheduled on the campus of the University of Mexico it was possible to attend only a small percentage of them. The Mexican government provided a variety of irresistible social events: ballets, native dances, lunch at Montezuma's Palace, and numerous cocktail parties and dinners. There were endless meetings of international committees. I was involved in none of the latter, but Moore was up to his neck with them. As a result he had little time for recreation, sightseeing, or even meals and sleep.

On the fourth day of the convention, Lillian, Phyllis and I persuaded Moore to join us for dinner at an elegant downtown restaurant. Moore was so exhausted he was almost unable to order. While waiting to be served he took out a cigarette, placed it between his lips, and held a flaming lighter near its tip. A half minute later he had not moved; the flame burned brightly, the cigarette remained unlighted. Moore was fast asleep.

Moore earned a reputation as an erratic driver, something to which I can attest. As most geologists, he preferred to watch road cuts rather than the road. When drunk he did both poorly. In Mexico City in 1956, he, Lillian, and Phyllis and I were preparing to drive into town when I expressed reluctance to face the city traffic. Impatiently Moore said, "All right, I'll drive, it's just like any other place, traffic is traffic." As soon as we were all loaded into the car Moore roared the Dodge onto Hamburgo, a one-way street – the wrong way. Unabashed, he sped toward town seemingly oblivious to the honking horns, hoots, and wide variety of obscene gestures of the Mexican drivers.

A few years earlier Moore took a faculty member with him on a tour of the western states, where they planned to visit and study classic Paleozoic rock exposures. For a week or more letters and phone calls to his office repeatedly referred to the complaints of his companion concerning Moore's driving. Then one day he called from some place in Oregon. He told us to be on the lookout for Professor X, whom he was sending back to Lawrence by Greyhound bus. "Hell," he said. "I couldn't take his continual bitching about my driving. You know the fellow actually thought I was going to kill him. Odd sort of chap."

Excellent brands of liquor were very inexpensive in Mexico City. Moore and I wanted to avail ourselves of as much of the bargain booze as possible. Moore, of course, had no time for shopping, so he gave me a wish list, a fist full of pesos, and delegated me to make the purchases. At that time each of the U.S. states had its own limit on the amount of alcoholic beverages its residents could bring into the country. When we entered Mexico the Illinois limit had been twelve liters. Accordingly, when the Congress adjourned, Phyllis and I loaded twelve bottles of booze into the trunk of our car: six for us, six for the Moores. We would deliver the Moores' share to them on our next trip to Lawrence.

At the Laredo Point of Entry I declared the twelve bottles only to learn that during our stay in Mexico the State of Illinois had lowered the import liquor quota to three liters. We were now stuck with nine illegal bottles. Outraged, I asked the officer what the hell I was to do with the extra bottles. "Well," he said with a big grin. "You can stay on the Mexican side until you drink all of them, or you can turn them over to me for proper legal government authorized disposal. That means I'll pour the stuff down the official drain."

It seemed to me that his options left something to be desired. It also seemed grossly unfair for the State of Illinois to have changed its rules in the middle of the game. For another thing, I had, for the past ten days, been held in the grip of Montezuma's revenge and just the thought of alcohol passing my lips sent my stomach into snarling convulsions of nausea.

Finally, making the only plausible decision available to me, I stood by helplessly and watched in somber silence as the contents of three of my bottles and all six of Moore's flowed into the government sewer.

After we moved to Houston in 1957, Moore, then a consultant for Humble Oil and Refining Company, was a frequent guest in our home. He burst into our house late one afternoon flushed with excitement. He passed quickly through the kitchen and flopped down on the den sofa. "Do you have a copy of my paleo text handy?" When I returned from the study with the book he placed it on his lap, opened it to the chapter on crinoids, and motioned for me to sit beside him.

"On the drive down here from Lawrence, I worked up a hypothesis concerning the evolutionary development of one of the orders of crinoids and

I need to talk it out with you." It was his way of saying that he would do the talking and that I would serve as his sounding board. As the world s authority on Paleozoic crinoids, he really didn't need my input.

For an hour or more he reviewed the reasoning and evidence which formed the basis of his hypothesis. As he spoke he illustrated some of the intricate features of crinoid morphology and anatomy with pencil sketches along the margins of the pages of my book. I could hardly object to the doodling in the text; whether or not his hypothesis had merit he was transforming my dog-eared book into an historical document.

When at last he decided his case had been made he signaled that it was time to break out the liquid refreshments. Work before play—an important lesson.

Before mixing the drinks I asked that he autograph the book. With firm hand and bold strokes he signed his name, Raymond C. Moore, on the cover page. After an hour of bourbon I brought out a copy of the second edition of Moore's Historical Geology text and requested another autograph. This time, with shaky and uncertain strokes of the pen, he scribbled:

> *To J.R. DuBar*
> *Raymond C. Moore*

Later, when we had decided to call it a night and hit the stack, I handed him my copy of the first edition of his historical text and asked, a little apologetically, for yet another autograph. By this time Moore was almost unable to grasp the pen; the inscription was nearly illegible and my name was misspelled.

On one of his trips to Houston, Humble Oil installed him at the Rice Hotel. Several hours after he had checked in I drove downtown, picked him up and brought him to the house for dinner. He had been drinking in the room and was already fairly well sloshed, but as soon as he walked into our kitchen he grabbed a bottle of Jim Beam and poured us two very large drinks. When it was time for refills I was startled to find the bottle empty. We had consumed half a fifth of bourbon in less than thirty minutes.

At about 1:00 in the morning, having finished another fifth of old J. Beam, I loaded Moore into the Dodge and drove him to the Rice Hotel. It was raining hard and cold, the streets deserted when we arrived. Moore showed little sign of life so I went around to the curb side of the car, opened the door, and dragged him out, but as I attempted to stand him up and walk him toward the front of the Dodge he went completely limp, slipped from my arms, and rolled face down into the gutter.

For maybe twenty seconds I stood astride his inert body watching the murky drainage water flow around him. Then I spoke softly: "R.C. Moore, you really aren't a god—great man perhaps but only a man." At that moment our relationship changed forever. The burden of obligatory worship I had borne for several years dissolved in the cold rain leaving me with a strange almost eerie inner warmth. I knelt beside him then and lightly slapped his cheek. "Come on now, old man," I said. "We've got to get you out of here before you drown." To my surprise he raised up on one elbow and with his help I was able to lift him to his feet. Then with his left arm over my shoulder and my right arm around his ample waist, we swayed and staggered together, two drunken buddies, into the warmth of the hotel lobby.

During another of Moore's visits to Houston we decided to have a small party in his honor. The guests were Hal Fisk, Russ Jeffords, and Bob Langford.

Jeffords, a research scientist with Humble Oil specialized in the study of Paleozoic corals. At forty he had sold his soul to the company. Thereafter he had spent his weekends trying to find the meaning of his life in the bottom of a bottle, while dreaming of early retirement. Russ, one of Moore's former students, was also one of his favorite drinking buddies.

Fisk, a big, raw-boned man of about fifty, was Chief Geologist in charge of Humble's research lab in Houston. Hal was admired around the world for his painstaking work on the Mississippi Delta complex, work which served as a model for much of Humble's petroleum exploration. At the same time he was hated and painted as a flame-throwing, horned devil by some geologists of the midwestern states who denounced as nonsense his explanation for the origin of lower Mississippi Valley loess (silt) deposits.

As a man, much as Moore, he was revered by many of his colleagues and despised by many others. When confronted with what he regarded as professional ignorance, stupidity or carelessness, he did not hesitate to publicly express his disgust. He was quite capable of being brusque, volatile and unforgiving. On occasions he could cause a granite wall to tremble before his steely glare. I knew that side of him, had seen it often, but none of it had ever been directed toward me. I knew him as a firm but gentle man, critical yet receptive to others' views even when they were at odds with his own. He was a complicated man but he was my friend and mentor. He stood, I knew, on feet of clay as all men, but he was a cut above the others. He always stood tall, a man of honor, integrity and courage.

Bob Langford was a young and gifted professor of geology at Rice Institute. For more than a year he had been helping my students and me make

NEVER PISS INTO THE WIND

sense of our east coast foraminifer assemblages, and I had spent a weekend with him dredging the Gulf of Mexico sea floor off Galveston. I had found him bright, personable, outgoing, and partial to Canadian Club.

By the time our guests arrived at about 8:00, Moore, who had been drinking steadily and heavily since 3:00, was well into his cups. The group assembled in the den: Moore at an arm end of the sofa, where he had resided for hours, sat in a growing stupor, hands in his lap cupping a water glass of Rebel Yell. Langford, at his side, hovered over a bottle of Canadian Club on the coffee table. Fisk, Jeffords, and I huddled in chairs around a card table several feet from Moore. Phyllis, a non-drinker, acted as our roving barmaid.

For an hour we drank, ate potato chips and talked about our jobs and our common professional interests. As alcohol permeated our bodies and soaked our brains, conversation, once controlled, sedate and erudite, slowly mounted in volume and diminished in quality. Soon we reached the familiar stage of inebriation where everyone becomes stony deaf and each simultaneously begins to launch into earnest, confidential, and generally incoherent attempts to express statements of keen insight, great profundity, and world-shaking impact.

It was then that Phyllis, with some difficulty, drew our attention to Moore, who had slumped over the arm of the sofa where he appeared to be fast asleep.

As we towered over Moore's limp body he half opened two glazed eyes and mumbled something like "beddy-bye time." He made a gallant effort to lift his bulk from the sofa, spilled his drink on his crotch, and slowly slid back down onto the sofa. Fisk and Langford grabbed him under the arms, and half dragged him to the bedroom. Unceremoniously he was dropped like a gunnysack of beans, backside down, onto the bed where he remained in a sprawl of peaceful oblivion.

Having thus disposed of the guest of honor, we returned to our stations in the den. Reunited with our drinks and chips we tried unsuccessfully for the best part of an hour to ignore Jeffords' seemingly endless and highly imaginative account of his exploits as an amateur boxer. More times than he could recall (fortunately) he had, with stout heart, valor, and consummate skill, against all odds, defeated brutes of steel, twice his size. Exercising more than usual common sense, I endured his tedious boasts without giving way to an urge to invite him into the garage for a few quick rounds.

Sometime in the midst of Jeffords' filibuster, Fisk leaned toward me and, with a drunken leer on his ruddy face, whispered into my ear: "You know, Jules, I think you are right, the Tamiami Formation probably is of Pliocene age."

Until that moment I had thought Hal was handling his booze rather well; now I was uncertain. If the Pope had issued an edict that henceforth all men's rooms in the Vatican would be equipped with condom dispensers it wouldn't have been any more startling than Hal's whisper. For some years Fisk had led a group of geologists who, for reasons unclear to me, vehemently contended that no Pliocene deposits exist in the Northern Gulf of Mexico region. In their opinion, the Tamiami Formation of south Florida was a much older Miocene deposit.

My suggestion a year or two earlier that the Tamiami was of Pliocene age had been met, as expected, by the condescending benevolence usually reserved for the feebleminded. Could it be, I wondered, that a hicky had erupted within the conventional body of wisdom? Before I could savor that intriguing possibility we were all brought straight up by a resounding thud in the bedroom where we had deposited Moore's then peaceful, serene, and to all appearances, inert body.

The five of us dashed spastically into the bedroom where we found the bed rumpled but empty. Moore had fallen to the floor in the narrow space between the bed and the wall. With difficulty I climbed over the bed and positioned myself on the floor over Moore's somnolent shiny bald head. At the same time Fisk stationed himself over Moore's feet. On a prearranged signal Hal grabbed Moore's ankles and I slipped my hands under Moore's armpits. Together we succeeded in raising only the extremities. Moore's torso, limp as warm jello, assumed the dead weight of a freight car, which in some improbable manner, had fused with the floor. Faced with defeat, Jeffords and Langford sprung into action. Russ climbed up onto the bed and, in a kneeling position, leaned over its edge and clasped both hands under Moore's belt. At the same time Langford slipped behind Russ and wrapped his arms around Jeffords' waist. Lacking a block and tackle this sort of teamwork was our only hope.

Even so, our work was cut out for us and our initial efforts were in vain. Finally, amidst a volley of heave ho's, grunts, raspy groans, shouted instructions, and words of encouragement we hauled Moore's hulk onto the bed. Puffing and wheezing we again filed back to the den leaving Phyllis to spread a blanket over our unconscious friend.

Up at 7:00 the next morning, with thick, fuzzy tongue and throbbing temples, I stumbled into the kitchen in my shorts. Phyllis was washing dishes at the sink. I asked, "Have you checked on Moore?"

"Oh!" she replied. "He was up at 5:00, had breakfast, and left a little while ago. Said he would drive straight through to Lawrence."

I took two aspirins and went back to bed.

Eighteen years following the Congress in Mexico City, R.C. Moore, the son of an itinerant Baptist clergyman, who had earned a Ph.D. summa cum laude from the University of Chicago at age twenty-three, was dead. I made my first attempt then to characterize the man and to record some of his professional achievements.

When he entered Dennison University he was a Greek scholar, a track star, a gifted artist, an ardent master of bridge, and fluent in six languages.

As a teacher Moore demanded the best possible effort from each of his students at all times. He taught by example and by intimidation. Though he never hesitated to denounce faulty or lazy thinking, he always dealt fairly and justly with his students. Some students (usually the less serious types) feared him, others idolized him. Some regarded him as a remote, god-like figure, but others came to know him as a human being.

A plaque presented to him by his students reads: 'Professor Raymond C. Moore, in appreciation for teaching us to sharpen the mind by dulling the pick.'

For his seventh-fifth birthday, former students from around the world contributed to a commemorative volume entitled, Essays in Paleontology. It was the perfect tribute, one he would appreciate above all others.

Today, Moore's students permeate the geological profession and in the final analysis may prove his greatest contribution to the science.

He was generally regarded as the greatest invertebrate paleontologist in the world, and he was the most decorated and honored geologist in the history of the science. Of all his honors he once told me that he valued most the cherub-faced doll presented to him by the Soviet Union geologists as a tribute for 'being a human being'.

Moore's energy and powers of concentration were legendary and his organizational abilities challenged the most powerful computer. These qualities were perhaps best exemplified by his work as the originator and editor of the Treatise on Invertebrate Paleontology. These volumes stand as the most monumental contribution yet made to the science.

Life magazine once termed Moore... one of the brightest minds in the world' and Walt Kelly referred to him in his comic strip 'Pogo'. His fame was so great that letters addressed to Raymond C. Moore, U.S.A. were delivered to him in Lawrence. The achievements and activities of Moore would fill several large volumes. But who might be the author of such volumes? Moore shared his life with hundreds of people, each of whom possess only a fragment of the complete story. Today many of these people gather in small groups in bars and taverns throughout the world and over a few beers exchange stories of their relationship with the man. Such anecdotes have come to be termed 'Moore Lore'. A compendium of these tales would doubtless constitute fascinating reading, but still might fail to fully characterize him.

Perhaps he is best remembered simply as Raymond C. Moore, Lawrence, Kansas, U.S.A.

When he died in 1974 Moore was buried in Pioneer Cemetery on a serenely green hill slope overlooking the Kansas Geological Survey Building which bears his name. In 1984, when I visited the gravesite, petite, sassy, sharp-witted Lillian lay at her husband's side, the graves guarded by a small stand of stalwart oaks. I stood there for a long time, a light warm breeze dancing playfully about me and over the graves, a breeze fragrant with the scent of spring blossoms and the reassertion of life. I stood there and tried to remember the Moores as they once had been, and I recalled how much our time together had meant to me, how much my life had been enriched by them. So much they had given me lingers yet, enmeshed in the fabric of my being.

Then, as the shadows of the young oaks stretched long and narrow across the graves I bid a fond and reluctant farewell to the two people I had earlier come to regard as foster parents. When I left that place I took with me an indelible memory of my last visit with the Moores and two acorns I would plant in my yard in Texas.

On a Wing and a Ten Dollar Per Diem

I was lying on my bed at the Lakeview Motel staring at the ceiling while attempting to digest a gristly hamburger and a watery chocolate malt gulped down at a fly-infested dive a few blocks down the street. I had left Houston before dawn and driven the 500 miles to Jackson, Mississippi, stopping only for gasoline and candy bars, but now I was too hyper to feel tired. It hadn't been difficult to leave my wife that morning. I was anxious to get to South Carolina and to begin work on the research project. Also I was looking forward to three months away from Phyllis—three months without criticism and rejection. When I received her perfunctory kiss in the morning I'd had little doubt that she would have no difficulty handling my absence.

Our twelve-year marriage had been most of the way down the sewer for several years and I had no idea how to salvage it. I wasn't altogether sure that I wanted to salvage it. Now, at least, I'd have time and opportunity to put things in perspective and possibly to find a few answers. Actually I had little hope that anything would come of it all. For the past year or more Phyllis and I, although living in the same house, saw very little of each other. She worked days as an executive secretary for the Arthur Anderson Company, while I taught night and Saturday morning courses and was frequently out of town on field trips or at professional meetings. We did sleep together a few hours a night when I was home, but rarely had meals together and our social activities involved either her boring friends or my "disgusting" friends.

Shortly after we were married in June 1947, Phyllis had announced that we would have fun the first two years and after that we could start on the four kids I had in mind. There had never been much fun during the first two years or during the ten that followed. I soon discovered that she disliked being touched and that she had no intention of uncrossing her legs in my presence. My suspicion that she didn't even like kids was reinforced one day when she told me that kids just grow up and become ugly adults. Nevertheless, she explained

91

repeatedly that the real reason we should not have children was that I was certain to prove a pitiful father.

Thinking that she might have a real fear of childbirth I had at one time suggested adoption. Glaring at me while she spit out her words between clenched teeth, her response left little doubt of the merit of that idea: "If you think I want to raise someone else's little brats you're mistaken!" For my most recent masochistic act in late 1958 I had purchased a how-to sex book and presented it to her with the suggestion we sit down and read it together. Holding the book as if it were a fresh cow patty, she snarled, "This is trash—nothing but trash." Then slamming it to the den floor she stomped off to the bedroom and closed the door, leaving me standing there feeling that I had just been exposed as a sicko sex deviate.

With a sigh I thought perhaps three months of separation was exactly what we both needed.

Suppressing feelings of chagrin, bitterness and defeat, I turned my thoughts to the events that had led to my presence in Jackson on that day.

At the beginning of the 1958 fall semester, the dean sent word to John Wang, our department chairman, that Camp Wallace, a World War II military base located on the coast near Galveston, was up for grabs. The dean asked that we think of a productive use for the property and then go to the National Science Foundation to acquire the land.

We soon made the decision to promote the old base as a potential marine geology and biology teaching and research facility. Bob Greenwood, Professor of Geochemistry, and I were assigned the job of on-site assessment of the land. We mapped the base and existing facilities and made recommendations relative to possible sites for classroom, dormitory and research buildings and for location of boat slips.

Karl Keital (name has been changed), our structural geologist, had appointed himself project director, and had accepted responsibility for preparation of the NSF proposal. Three months later he had not written a word. This was no surprise to me—Keital sported a crew cut, wore bow ties, voted for Nixon, and insisted that the blinds on all department windows be at precisely identical level above the sills—hardly the stuff of great expectations.

To be completely fair, I must report that Keital did eventually complete the proposal. About a year later Dr. William Benson, NSF Program Director for Earth Sciences, visited with me at the university. During the day he met with the geology department staff and announced to us that our request for the Camp Wallace property had been approved. Looking directly at Keital, Dr.

Benson said, "The proposal you submitted was, perhaps, the most poorly written I have ever seen. However, in spite of that, and because it is my belief that wherever possible universities should be given land, I approved your request."

By Christmas break I had become disgusted with our lack of progress on the Camp Wallace project and could foresee little chance that the proposal could be completed before the January 10th deadline for submission to NSF. That year Phyllis and I spent Christmas with her aunt and uncle in St. Petersburg, Florida. On December 26 I sat down in a chair in their living room and completed a proposal to study the Waccamaw and Croatan deposits of the Carolinas. NSF guidelines at that time allowed twenty percent of the budget to be applied to "indirect costs" (an overhead allowance later notoriously abused by Stanford and other institutions). However, I concluded that because I would be doing much of the work in the field there would be no legitimate indirect costs connected with the project so I requested none.

When I returned to Houston the proposal was typed, copies made and approval to submit the proposal was obtained from John Wang, and our dean. Neither of these men made note of the absence of a request for indirect costs.

My proposal was received in Washington in January 1959, and assigned to William E. Benson for evaluation. On June 9th Dr. Benson informed me by telephone that the proposal would be funded by July 1. On the strength of this information the University Bursar issued me an advance of $500.00 so that I could head for the Carolinas as soon as final exams were concluded on June 16th. In July when the university officials discovered that the budget did not include indirect costs they informed NSF that they could not accept the grant. This caused me a few anxious days until I learned that NSF had told the university that they would indeed accept the grant if they hoped to receive NSF funding for future proposals. At that point the university acquiesced but for two or three years thereafter when instructing faculty members on how to prepare research proposals, Joe Krump, Director of Research, used my proposal as his primary example of "how not to do it."

As I lay there on my motel bed in Jackson I could only hope that William Benson was truthful when he told me that the proposal would be funded. The possibility that I might eventually need to return the university's $500.00 advance had less appeal than a bad attack of diarrhea. *Oh, what the fuck,* I thought. *I don't have time to worry about such trivialities. Tomorrow I'll be driving to Tupelo to pick up my field assistant, Jim Solliday, and after that we will have a hell of a lot of work to worry about.*

Shortly after submitting the research proposal to NSF I began to look over the current crop of graduating seniors in our department for a potential field assistant. To my dismay none of the available students seemed to meet either my standards or expectations. I wanted someone like Roy Staton, who had assisted me in Florida. Someone who could handle primitive conditions, someone who could stoically endure heat, snakes, biting insects, sweat, dirt, long hours, and hard work. I needed someone with considerable physical endurance, who was mentally alert, responsible, resourceful, geologically knowledgeable, willing to work for low wages and exceptionally motivated to make a career of geology. I didn't want an introverted bookworm who might have trouble dealing with people, who lacked basic conversational skills, or whose idea of a wild time was a game of checkers. He would also need to be a person who could tolerate a notorious taskmaster and sometime SOB. After all, I had to live in close proximity with the individual twenty-four hours a day for three months.

My choice was James Richards Solliday, a senior in geology at Southern Illinois University. During 1956 and 1957 he had been in several of my classes including summer field camp. He was an active and constructive member of the departmental geology club, and a lively participant in our frequent student-faculty social events. I was completely confident that he was the man I wanted, so in February I contacted Jim and invited him to come to the University of Houston to work on a master's degree and to act as my field and laboratory assistant during the next two years. He was instantly receptive so I mailed him the obligatory application forms along with my assurance that he would be granted a graduate assistantship in the department. The day that Benson informed me that the proposal would be funded, I telephoned Jim with the news and instructed him to pack his gear and meet me in Tupelo, Mississippi, on Wednesday, June 18.

Jim was an inch or so under six feet and, at a lean 150 pounds, he was an exceptionally well-coordinated athletic young man. His clean-cut features were well accented by a pair of bright, somewhat mischievous brown eyes and a bristly crew cut cap of dark reddish-brown hair. In later years as a more mature, well padded, 190 pounder, he wore his hair much longer and usually sported a bush of reddish facial hair, but the mischievous glint of the eyes persisted.

From observations of Jim in the classroom, field and in social encounters he had struck me as a man who possessed the ingredients of a first-rate geologist. He was intelligent, quick-witted, imaginative and he obviously loved geology. Jim wasn't an A student and that bothered him because, as he confided in me, he always strove for perfection.

"Well, shit man," I said. "Only a few of us are perfect, besides a B average is considered pretty fair credentials in most of the better places." He had responded to my attempt at humor with a bewildered shake of the head.

"I know I can do better, it's just that—well, I clutch on exams. I think I'm well prepared when I walk into the room, and when I look at the test paper and find there is something I've overlooked or forgotten I just clutch—go blank. Then I write some things that are wrong or dumb even though I know better. That's when my A goes down the tube."

I had pointed out that he was experiencing the symptoms of a common affliction among students—especially the better ones, the ones strongly motivated to do well. "Just relax a little," I had advised him. "Learn to play as hard as you work—get some balance in your life and I think everything will work out okay."

He had looked at me with a gleam in his eyes and a tight smile on the lips. "Work hard, play hard, eh? That' s the way you do it?"

In later years as a college instructor, Jim often admonished his students, "What you people need to do, as old Professor DuBar once told me, is to work hard and play hard—get a little balance in your lives."

Jim had been born in Springfield, Illinois in 1932, but was raised, along with four brothers, on the banks of the Wabash in Mt. Carmel, a small community located about forty miles south of Robinson, Illinois, the birthplace of the author James Jones. Shortly after his discharge from the Navy Jim married Janet, a striking brunette and a bit of an ingénue who worshipped the ground upon which her husband strode. Janet was disturbingly confident that Jim could do no wrong. In 1959 Jim and Janet were parents of a one-year-old girl named Pamela; they later added James, John and Jennifer.

Looking forward to joining Jim in the morning (in the hometown of Elvis the Pelvis) I switched off the bed lamp, rolled into a fetal position and slipped off into never-never land.

We didn't have interstate highways in those days so it was a four or five hour drive from Jackson to Tupelo. When I pulled up in front of the Tupelo Hotel at about 11:00 a.m. Jim was sitting on the hotel porch steps surrounded by his gear. He looked just as he had in 1957 and on our drive to Atlanta I quickly learned that he was in every way the same Jim Solliday I had known in Carbondale. As we walked toward one another to shake hands and exchange male-type greetings, I noted with dismay that his stack of gear included a large wooden footlocker. Footlockers like that are a problem to handle in the field. They are awkward, difficult to lift, and they don't fit readily into a car, boat trailer or small motel room; in short, they can prove to be a pain in the ass. I explained all this to Jim and suggested he leave the damned thing at home next year. I could see that he was a bit stung by my comments, but before the season ended he had come around to my point of view.

As we drove across the northern corner of Mississippi on the way to Atlanta I briefed Jim on our financial situation and our modus operandi for the summer. I reminded him that the proposal had not yet been officially approved, so for a week or more we would need to live on the $500.00 I had borrowed from the university. "But what if the study isn't funded?" he asked apprehensively.

"Well," I replied, "it will be funded. Benson has assured me of that. I don't think we need worry much about it. Of course, if for some unforeseen idiotic reason it isn't funded we both are going to be sucked down the toilet bowl like two big turds." I could have told him right then he could catch the next bus back to Carbondale if he had real doubts but I knew Jim well enough to be confident that he had signed on for the duration.

I glanced over at Jim slumped in the passenger seat of my old '53 gray Dodge and said, "You know, of course, even when the money does arrive this will be a no-frills operation. You'll get the $300.00 a month I promised and I'll get my regular salary, but when it comes to expenses we won't be living high on the hog. We get ten bucks per diem to cover both of us. That means we eat on five dollars a day and we average five bucks a day for lodging. Any day we exceed the budget we cut back another day, even if it means sleeping in the car and living on peanut butter sandwiches. Expenses on the road, like now, will run higher so by the time we get to Columbia we'll already be in the hole. I figure if we avoid motels and restaurants when possible we'll do all right. We have to rent cheap apartments by the week and do the grocery shopping at supermarkets. We can take turns cooking the evening meals, pack lunches and ad lib breakfast."

When I had finished my little speech Jim looked over at me and with his face in the grin mode said, "Hell, Big Daddy, that's why I signed up for this duty—I knew how you like to go first class."

By the time we entered the Atlanta city limits we had agreed that peanut butter sandwiches and cockroaches could come later—tonight we were going to have a little recreation.

We stayed in Atlanta for two nights, partly because we were having fun, but also on the morning following our arrival there we were too tired and hung over to even contemplate the drive to Columbia. I could only hope that it had all been worthwhile. Our hotel bill of $19.84 combined with sizable restaurant and bar tabs had condemned us to at least a week in peanut butter purgatory.

We spent most of the first night at a lounge on Peachtree Street a few blocks from the hotel. In the first hour we had hooked up with wives of two officers stationed at the Goldsboro, North Carolina Air Force base. In no mood to reveal our true identities, especially to another man's wife, we adopted recreational aliases for the evening. It was the beginning of a practice we were to follow for two years. After two years of deceit I decided the resulting stress and hassle dictated a more direct and honest approach.

That night, however, I introduced myself to the ladies as Don Taylor and Jim became Bobby Gammil. Don and Bobby were real people—students in my paleontology and stratigraphy classes. I wasn't particularly perturbed about using their names this way because I knew what while taking the university summer field courses in Silver City, New Mexico, Don was well known to the local females as Jules DuBar, and Bobby as Frank Barber (name has been changed), our departmental Professor of Petrography. As I look back on that night it seems the best thing that happened was that the ladies were liberated to the point of paying their own tabs.

On our way out of Atlanta Thursday morning I felt satisfactorily purged and beset by slight twinges of guilt, but geared up and eager to get on with the future. In fact my hormones were so robust I spontaneously broke out in ribald song:

> *Do your balls hang low,*
> *Can you drag them in the snow,*
> *Can you tie them in a knot,*
> *Can you tie them in a bow,*
> *Can you throw them over your shoulder*
> *Like a good American soldier,*
> *Do your balls hang low?*

Such spontaneity was commonplace in the field and away from my wife. However, in the three years we worked together I don't think Jim ever quite adjusted to my outbursts. Like a dutiful student he nevertheless displayed commendable tolerance for his professor's idiosyncrasies no matter how weird they may have appeared to him. There was little doubt I had picked the right man.

By the time we reached Columbia it was quite late and I made a spur of the moment decision to keep going toward the coast. I was eager to see the area I had selected for study and to savor the salt air. I figured it would be profitable to spend a few days checking out the country around Conway and Myrtle Beach. After that we could return to Columbia, locate some low-rent lodging and visit with Henry S. Johnson, Jr., the State Geologist. We had corresponded during the previous year or so, and he was expecting our arrival in Columbia sometime soon. I wanted to brief him on our summer's plans and to solicit whatever aid he would be willing and able to provide at the time. I could not have foreseen the importance of that meeting, or known that Henry and I would become best of friends and work together in the lower coastal plain for more than twenty years.

At 1:00 a.m. we sleepily decided to abandon our goal of reaching Conway that night. Instead we checked into the Evans Motor Court in Sumter. The manager had retired for the evening but had thoughtfully left a note for late arrivals: "Please sign in on the register, take a key and go to your room. In the morning return the key to the desk with your payment."

When we checked out at dawn no manager was in sight, so as instructed, we left the key and the $7.21 for a double on the desk. Then we hit the road for Conway and Myrtle Beach.

In Conway we stopped at a grocery for a doughnut and milk take-out breakfast, and then with deep satisfaction we crossed over the chocolate brown waters of the Waccamaw River on the 501 bridge. It was an exciting moment for me. Even though I had never before been there, I had a strong feeling of returning home following a long absence.

We drove the twelve miles to Myrtle Beach with a vague notion of checking into a motel for a day or two, while scoping out the town and the surrounding area. It was possible we would elect to adopt Myrtle Beach as a base of operations when working the Waccamaw River and Intracoastal Waterway exposures.

We strolled the downtown streets for an hour or so before concluding that the place had little to offer us. The town seemed a Mecca of brain-damaged teenagers and herds of bovine, red-necked tobacco farmers with faces uniformly frozen in expressions of awed amazement. The uniform of the day was clearly gaudy Bermuda shorts spread tightly over generous, jiggling buttocks; wild Hawaiian shirts worn open in front by the men to reveal lobes of hairy, sweaty fat; crumpled baseball caps with upturned bills; canvas sandals strapped to bony flat feet; and rimless, dime-store sunglasses. In addition to the tourists the chief attractions consisted of a motley array of penny arcades, amusement parks, a broken-down movie house, beachwear and souvenir shops which peddled the uniforms of the day and other atrocities, and gift shops which specialized in tourist trap junk.

Before leaving town we agreed to sample the one item that held some appeal, the foot-long Coney Islands. They were pretty good. During the next few years, despite my first negative impressions, I found there were a lot of things in Myrtle Beach that I could like, even love.

We checked into a motel in Conway and for the first time managed to stay within our budget. For the remainder of the day and much of Sunday we scouted the surrounding countryside.

As we traveled the back roads we passed the neatly tended tobacco fields with their working mules, tobacco sleds and not so neat ramshackle curing sheds that surrounded Conway. During hot summer afternoons when electrical storms exploded over the low country, the black field hands took refuge in the metal curing barns, where some died, electrocuted by lightning bolts drawn to the highly conductive metal roofs and walls of the sheds.

We skirted the white sand rims of the mysterious Carolina Bays, which from the air resemble great oval bowls filled with dark swamp water, stands of tall hardwood trees and a dense undergrowth that affords refuge for myriads of twittering birds, slithering snakes and incredible numbers of biting insects and other wildlife.

We drove through sleepy little towns named Red Hill, Shell, Hand, Longs, Grisset and Wampee. We crossed the humate-stained, sluggish waters of the Waccamaw on a one-lane bridge at Red Bluff. From open windows of tiny white frame churches, half hidden in roughly cleared recesses in the woods, the rich, spirited, rhythmic sounds of black gospel songs drifted across the countryside on warm, soft Sunday morning breezes. These were sounds and sights forever imprinted on my mind. When the day had ended I knew that I had at least made fleeting contact with the soul of the Carolina low country.

One incident that occurred during the tour remains vividly stored in my memory. We had set out to find the type section of the Waccamaw Formation, which, according to the old literature on the subject, was located at Parker's Landing on the north bank of the Waccamaw River only a few miles upstream from Red Bluff. County Route 905 more-or-less parallels the north side of the river between Longs and Conway; at Parker's Landing the river meanders to within about 200 yards of the highway. Clocking the mileage from Longs, we pulled off the road at a point we calculated lay directly opposite the type section location. We had hoped to find traces of a trail or lane leading to the landing, but instead found a dense entanglement of insect-infested briars, vines, palmettos and shrubs beneath a canopy of tall trees. Undaunted we cautiously began to work our way through the dark, imposing maze toward the riverbank. Soon we were stumbling and thrashing about in the thick undergrowth, cursing and unsuccessfully fighting off insect attacks while our ankles were ripped by briars; and low-hanging, malevolent tree branches tried desperately to gouge out our eyes. Our faces became layered with creepy spider webs that clung tenaciously to our sweaty skin. After a fifteen-minute struggle we somehow succeeded in breaking through to the riverbank. We stood there puffing, sweating, bleeding, clawing at itchy insect bites and trying to brush away clouds of persistent Carolina gnats that hovered around our eyes. Slowly the truth seeped through to our overheated brains: against all reason and commonsense we had apparently emerged precisely at the old Parker's Landing. There, beneath our feet in the bank of the river, were the gray, marly, shell-studded deposits of the Waccamaw Formation in all their pristine glory. A month or so later when we worked this part of the river by boat we studied the exposure in detail, dubbed it locality WA-17, and pronounced it to truly be the type locality of the Waccamaw Formation.

Since then, when I recall that moment of discovery I can only regard it as a minor miracle. In the years that I worked the coastal plain I searched for many old sites that had been reported in the literature. Finding any one of them was never easy and even today after years of sporadic search, the locations of some remain a mystery. In the remote areas where the best localities usually occur, along banks of tortuously winding streams, the exposures in time become overgrown, obscured by bank failure and fallen trees, or eroded into oblivion by shifting river currents. The job of finding these old outcrops was also commonly complicated by the fact that the early workers using inadequate maps had mislocated the localities, or more often they had placed them in terms of ephemeral landmarks that had long since vanished or been rendered unrecognizable by the ravages of nature and the passage of time.

As the fly that walks on the ceiling we neophytes to the region had found this locality in less than thirty minutes simply because we didn't realize that such a feat was impossible. However, an epilogue to my tale suggests that the little miracle may actually be slightly tainted. Years later Frank Swain of the U.S. Geological Survey, confided that one of my published maps shows the location of WA-17 to be several hundred yards west of the true site of Parker's Landing. Chances are he was right.

Pink Cabins and Fried Bologna

On Monday morning we returned to Columbia where in a few hours we managed to find lodging of sorts at the Cabin in the Pines on the east edge of town. The cabins were tiny, barf pink boxes occupied by characters one wouldn't want to meet in a dark alley or, for that matter, on a lighted thoroughfare. Inside there was barely room for the double bed, a lamp and two rickety wooden chairs. Most of the minuscule floor space was piled high with our gear. The narrow passageway between the bed and the wall was effectively blocked by Jim's goddamned footlocker. We had two routes to the john; one involved crawling across the bed, and the other jumping over the footlocker. In the bathroom there was just enough space to stand between the john and the sink. One didn't really sit on the john; it was more a matter of wedging one's body into the available space between the door and the tank. Neither of us was ever tempted to sit there and read a book. It was clearly not what we might have preferred, but, hell, at $21.00 a week, we could afford the rent.

The worst feature of the place was that we could not cook our meals there. Fortunately, Henry Johnson unwittingly resolved that hickey the next morning.

Henry had managed to find working quarters in the basement of the chemistry building on the University of South Carolina campus. As soon as we saw the hot plates and Bunsen burners we knew we were going to have hot meals after all. And there was plenty of floor space where we could lay out our topographic maps and air photos, and there was table space where we could sit down to read or write. We could hardly have asked for more.

Henry introduced us to the Geology Department's librarian who granted me library privileges. This was a windfall that allowed access to relatively rare books on the paleontology of South Carolina not available in the University of Houston library.

While we marked time waiting for funding I wanted to compile a list of all Waccamaw or possible Waccamaw localities in the Carolinas reported in the literature. Each locality would be spotted on the topographic maps and air photos as accurately as the available data permitted. When that task was completed we would be able to sit down and refine the preliminary work schedule prepared in Houston and to settle on a realistic time frame in which we could complete various goals. At the same time we needed to determine exactly the equipment we needed to purchase and to check out the local availability and prices of these items.

Despite the dreary lodging in the bilious pink cabin in the pines, a diet heavy on fried bologna and the overriding concern about the status of our funds, we set to work and accomplished all our goals. The spring session had ended so we were never interrupted by curious students or faculty members. After the first day even Henry, who had obligations elsewhere, did not visit us again. That suited us because we weren't sure of his reaction to cooking meals in the chemistry quarters. Henry, a tall, strapping, former Marine, was friendly, polite and cooperative, but we thought somewhat stuffy and a bit aloof and we weren't very certain that he wholly approved of us anyway. We agreed that the less we shared with Henry about our activities, the better. We decided to keep him informed only of our general plans and itineraries for the summer. In that way there would be no chance he could pay us a surprise visit. This was part of our standard procedure maintained for the next three years. Return addresses were always in care of General Delivery, commonly in a town where we were not currently in residence. We never provided anyone a phone number where we could be reached in an emergency and we made all our calls from pay stations. Our motto was, "Don' t call us, we'll call you."

On Wednesday, June 25, I received a telegram from my wife: "Grant came through, Krumpf called this afternoon—Phyllis."

To say that a load had been lifted from our bodies and minds would barely do justice to our reaction to the news. Nevertheless we valiantly resisted a strong temptation to interrupt our work for a celebration. We did pause for a moment to snigger at the spelling of Joe Krump's last name, and for years thereafter we usually referred to Joe as Dr. Krumpf. On Thursday, when the university's check for the comforting amount of $1,400.00 arrived it was even more difficult to resist the urge to party, so I suggested to Jim that we purchase tickets for the Patterson-Johansen heavyweight title fight to be telecast at a local theater. My spirits were only slightly dampened when the chin of my hero insisted on engaging in fatal encounters with Johansen's "toonder". As we left the theater I confidently informed Jim that Ingemar's luck would run out in the return match.

We finished work in the chemistry basement on Sunday afternoon. On

Sunday evening there had been an unwelcome break in our routine. An unidentified intruder had broken into one of the cabins and stolen the occupant's wallet. The police had been called shortly before we reached the motel, so we hung around with the rest of the gathered crowd for their arrival. As we waited the victim, a fat, ugly lady of about thirty dressed in an outlandish purple playsuit, began to hysterically accuse a young man who apparently lived in the unit adjacent to hers. He, in turn, just as hysterically, denied the charge. By the time two Columbia policemen arrived we had a disturbing scene in progress. To our relief the policemen were able to calm the lady and man without resorting to violence. Then most of us who were standing around were questioned but none, including us, could shed any light on the case, with the result that the wallet was not recovered and no arrest made.

As the police cruiser pulled away the fat lady once again began her accusations but by then the young man had disappeared into his cabin. The last thing I recall was the woman screaming something to the effect, "…There is no fucking justice in this fucking world, but by God I'll do something about that—just wait and see!"

As unpleasant as the scene had been it added a little color to our stay at the Cabin in the Pines and it served to confirm our original judgment of the tenants.

Monday morning we moved out of the cabins and into the relatively spacious but more expensive Orton Court in Columbia. In the evening we completely shattered our budget with two hefty steak dinners. Soon after dropping off our gear at the Orton we found an Army Surplus store and made our first purchases: khaki slacks and shirts, Frank Buck hats, wading shoes, mosquito netting and machetes. In the afternoon we drove to West Columbia to pick up the most important and expensive items—a fourteen-foot aluminum Arkansas Traveler, a 10 hp Evinrude and a boat trailer. Then we added two oars, an anchor, two life jackets, a captain's chair for the skipper, a five-gallon gas can and a large aluminum cooler.

The cost of the entire package was a little less that I had budgeted so when I peeled off the eight crisp hundred dollar bills we were able to wait smugly while the chunky, ex-Clemson football player behind the counter counted out our change.

Monday evening we packed most of the gear into the trailer and the Dodge in anticipation of an early departure in the morning. As we headed for Wilmington, North Carolina on Tuesday, the morning air felt fresh and cool and the red glow of the rising sun had begun to wrap around the city. There could be no doubt about it; it was a great day in the coastal plain. Thinking back on that morning it seems a rather inauspicious beginning for a journey that would prove to consume much of my life for the next twenty-two years. In 1971 I summed up the first twelve years of that journey:

> *In 1959 Jim Solliday and I arrived in South Carolina prepared with the aid of an NSF grant and the assistance of the South Carolina Division of Geology to whip out the geology of the Cape Fear Arch area of the Carolinas in two years. My studies in south Florida had directed my attention to the possibility that the Caloosahatchee Formation was indeed the same age as the Waccamaw Formation of the Carolinas. It was my notion that the study of all existing outcrops, supplemented by ten or twelve shallow drill holes would provide all the information needed to resolve the question. With the Carolinas dispatched, I intended to resume work in Florida.*
>
> *During the first two years we discovered the Carolina coastal plain relinquished her geological secrets begrudgingly. By 1961 I viewed the Cape Fear Arch as a battleground and had begun to appreciate the resourcefulness of the enemy. It was time to quit or to call for reinforcements and renew the battle. I chose the latter course and the war was escalated. I enlisted the aid of students and colleagues and plotted our strategy. Twelve years later more than twenty-five papers have been written concerning various aspects of the geology, nine or ten master's theses, and three doctoral dissertations have been completed; approximately 900 holes have been drilled, hundreds of surface sections measured and described, tons of fossils and sediments collected and analyzed, scores of maps and cross-sections prepared, and nine or ten more papers are in preparation and others planned.*
>
> *It would be difficult (but possible) to find a square foot of this 15,000 square-mile area that has not been the recipient of at least one drop of our perspiration. If one examines closely, one may find stains in the sands that vaguely resemble our blood. Our footprints, hammer marks and slurry piles are everywhere. State, federal and private agencies have supported our efforts with grants, salaries, expenses, and equipment. More than 150 people have been involved in the study and the labor; some have since departed to follow other trails, new troops arrive yearly.*

For some of us the battle has become a way of life, we are determined to prevail, we believe we've made progress and optimistically continue to see the end of the struggle in 'another two years'. We readily admit we don't have all the answers, but at least we've learned many of the questions. We can be frustrated at times to have to confess that some of the original 1959 questions remain unresolved, but take solace in the fact that we can now endlessly spout learned reasons for not having the answers.

We can say proudly that this is one of the most intensively studied segments of a coastal plain anywhere in the world. It is reassuring to note that other geologists have opened additional fronts so that now the entire Atlantic Coastal Plain is under organized, systematic attack. Although not all the active investigators agree on details, it is clear that a rational interpretation of the geologic history of the region is rapidly emerging.

It has been a long war and there is more to come. Even though some of us may never complete the job and achieve the victory it won't really matter, for we will have been well rewarded by the opportunity to 'give it a try', by the comrades we have come to know, and by the many pleasant memories of times, places and people. We refer to ourselves as 'the Old Pros' and we recognize the 'Battle of the Coastal Plain' as the sum and substance of our lives. Instinct and low cunning have been added to logic and book learning, with the result that we are more properly fitted for the job to be done. In a way we have become part of the Coastal Plain, a part of its golden sands, its dark, mysterious streams, its torrential downpours, blazing sun and eternally ill-tempered insects.

Perhaps, in time, the enemy will merely absorb us and our identities will merge imperceptibly into the legends and folklore of the land. A man could do worse.

White Sneakers

On the way to Wilmington our only scheduled stop was at the Columbus County Courthouse in Whiteville. No boat license was required by the state of South Carolina, but we had to have one to operate the boat in North Carolina. We hadn't wanted visible identification on the boat and for that reason had no plan to give her a name. Now, of course, the license number would need to be painted on both sides of the bow. Later we decided to prefix the number with the letters U.H. for the University of Houston. Thereafter, for some strange reason, a lot of people we encountered assumed the letters stood for University of Hawaii. It was a notion we rarely discouraged.

While we were standing in line at the courthouse a wiry little black man about forty, dressed in a ragged T-shirt and torn blue jeans moved close to my side. I looked down on him assuming he was trying to edge his way into line. But when our eyes met he smiled and asked, "You gonna do some fishin?"

I hadn't realized that everyone in the coastal plain who discovered we had a boat would ask the same question. "Well, no we aren't," I said. "We're going to be doing some scientific work along rivers around here." The next segment of the conversation was no surprise. We'd heard it at every gas station, café and country grocery store that we had visited since leaving Houston.

"Where you men from?" he asked.

"Well, we're from Texas—Houston, that is." With that I steeled myself for the inevitable response.

"Long way from home, aren't y'all?"

Suppressing simultaneous urges to smile and to cry I responded, "Yes, a long way from home all right." All three of us now entirely caught up in the local ritual nodded our heads solemnly and Jim made little clicking sounds with his tongue adding emphasis to the profundity of the moment. Each of the scores of times that I have observed this ritual I've had a vague feeling that I was on the verge of discovering a universal truth, but try as I might I could never figure out what the hell it was.

106

I wanted to drop this conversation; I was at the counter now and a sweaty, surly-looking redneck waited impatiently for me to make my request. So, ignoring our new friend, I filled out the proper form, paid the fee and at last had the boat license. When I turned to leave I noted with relief that the pesky little fellow was nowhere in sight. However, as we reached the exit there he was standing on the walkway, grinning, with shining dark eyes fixed on me. *Shabby little beggar, and persistent as hell*, I thought, and wondered what he was really up to. Maybe he'd be on his way if I offered him a buck.

As we emerged from the courthouse and headed for the car he fell in step behind us like a dog that had been to obedience school. In a moment, however, he drew even with us and, looking up into my eyes with a particularly plaintive expression, he said, "I was here looking for a job of work to do so I could buy a pair of shoes."

"Shoes," I replied, a little surprised. "You've got no shoes?" As I asked I looked down at two black, dusty feet and ten dirty toes. "I guess you're right," I said. "You really don't seem to have shoes." Then I stupidly asked, "You have no money for shoes?"

"That's the truth, man, I got no money to buy me a pair."

"Well," I said. "I can't give you a job, but suppose we walk across the street and get you a pair at that store over there."

"You gonna buy me shoes?"

"That's right—one pair—you can't run around like that in your bare feet even if it is summer."

At the little store we picked out a pair of white canvas sneakers and a pair of white socks which our friend put on immediately. On the way back to the car he tagged along, grinning and staring at his feet.

"If you give me a job I'll work hard," he pleaded. "And you don't need to pay me much. I'll work cheap. Maybe y'all take me back to Houston with you and I'll take care of your yard." He seemed desperate and I was rapidly becoming so. I motioned Jim to get into the car and I climbed behind the wheel.

The little man was leaning over my open window now, his face in mine. I thought he would try to climb into the car unless we got underway soon.

Shaking my head, I said with true regret, "I'm sorry fellow, I'd like to help you but I can't take you where we are going, and we aren't going back to Houston until September." Then I added, "We're in sort of a hurry so need to hit the road." With that I started the engine and slowly pulled away. The little man stepped back obviously dejected but apparently resigned to his fate. When

I looked back he was still standing by the road looking forlorn and abandoned. His damned white sneakers glistening in the searing Carolina sun seemed the brightest things in Whiteville.

The Perfect Birthday

Solliday was slouched in the seat beside me; the plug of my little transistor radio protruded from his left ear as he tapped out on his knees the beat of a seemingly silent tune only he could hear. Inability to share the music with Jim usually irritated me, but at that moment my thoughts were directed elsewhere.

With the boat and trailer securely in tow and the boat license safely in the glove compartment, full realization that the research project had been funded was rapidly seeping into my brain. Now we had money and equipment, I needn't be concerned about the $500.00 loan from the university, and in a few days we would be busting our butts in the field. As I considered our work schedule I suddenly realized that it was Tuesday, June 30—my thirty-sixth birthday! *Damn*, I thought, *what a hell of a great birthday!* Then with no warning I bellowed at the top of my voice, "It's the best goddamned birthday I've ever had!"

I had momentarily forgotten Solliday, but was quickly and dramatically reminded as he ripped the plug from his ear and bolted wide-eyed upright in his seat.

"What, what, what the goddamned hell is happening?"

"It's okay, Jim, I just remembered that today is my birthday, that's all."

Looking at me in disbelief, he retorted, "Your birthday, your fucking, goddamned birthday? Jesus fucking Christ, I thought we were doing a head-on with a fuckin' semi."

"No, Jim, I'm sorry, just sit back and relax, it was a red-blooded burst of exuberance. Most of my birthdays haven't been worth a shit, but this one is something else."

A bit relaxed, Jim said, "Well, mine's December 11; remind me to return the fucking favor."

Ignoring him, I continued, "I don't even remember most of my birthdays. Actually, there's only two I can think of and both were disasters. When I was a kid I didn't have parties or get presents; just some crummy cards from two aunts and my grandmother. But my mother always baked a cake for me—no candles—just a cake but her cakes were great. The one cake I remember was the devil's food she baked for my fourteenth birthday, in 1937."

"That's a fucking long time to remember a fucking cake."

"Well, that's because I didn't get any of it. That was the year my Uncle Bud died of lung cancer and his funeral was on my birthday. All of our relatives from Cincinnati came to town for the event. They all moved into our house like a bunch of barracuda. They ate everything not nailed down."

"Your cake, too, I assume."

"Right. My mother had baked this big beautiful thing the day before and put it in the cake keeper in the cupboard. There was no room in the house for me so I was staying next door with my grandmother. On the morning of my birthday I came over to our house ready for a big slab of chocolate cake, but my mother stopped me short of the counter. With a pained expression she said, 'There's no cake, Julie, it's all gone.'

'What?' I asked. 'What do you mean there's no cake? I saw you bake it yesterday. I know there's a cake in that thing.'

'Well, of course I baked it, and for you too, but our guests ate the entire thing last night.'

'All of it?' I asked incredulously.

'I'm afraid so, Julie—it's gone and such a shame. They're just pigs.'

"In disbelief I began a desperate search of the kitchen for the piece I knew must have been saved for me, but all I found were a few smudges of chocolate icing on the inside of the container. To this day I've never forgiven those people—I had never seen them before, and with a little luck will never see them again."

Staring now at the car ceiling, Jim remarked, "That's it? You said there were two disasters—I figure the second one has to be more interesting than the first."

"There was a second one—my twenty-first birthday. You might relate to this one."

"Probably. Most people remember their twenty-first birthday. Why was yours so special?"

"I know, but probably most people remember it for different reasons. I was nineteen when I enlisted in the Coast Guard and I learned right away that I couldn't legally buy a drink in a bar until I was twenty-one. The worst part was that I looked sixteen so bartenders were quick to check my I.D. Most of them would let us have one drink before they checked, so I did a lot of bar-hopping. I had to go to five or six bars just to get a good glow. Sick of that kind of shit, I began to dream of my twenty-first birthday, when I figured I'd find a nice joint, lay my I.D. on the bar and then drink myself into legal oblivion—the perfect birthday."

"So what happened?" Jim seemed at least a little interested now.

"Hell, on June 30, 1944, I was on the *U.S.S. Pocatello* in the middle of the fucking Pacific—not a bar or a drink in a couple thousand miles—just albatrosses trying to shit on my head. Anyway, this one makes up for the bad ones. I might even forgive my relatives now but it'll take a while before I forgive the Japs."

Before Jim could hook into the earphones again the road sign for Lake Waccamaw loomed ahead on the right.

"Looks as if we can take that road on the right up there to get back to the lake."

"Not today, Jim. We'll be back here soon enough. Horace Richards has some Waccamaw and Duplin outcrops plotted on the north bank that we need to find and study."

Jim was peering at our road map now. "That looks like a fair-sized lake—should be a good place to test out the Arkansas Traveler."

"Yeah," I responded. "It's one of the largest of the Carolina Bays—about four or five miles long, I think. There are thousands of the bays on the lower coastal plain from Georgia into southern Virginia; most of them are nearly perfectly oval with clean white sand rims that really show on the air photos."

Jim was intrigued now, as most people when learning of Carolina Bays. "What the hell are these things, these bays? How did they form?"

Hunching my shoulders in an impatient attempt to shrug while steering, I said, somewhat thoughtfully, "Who knows, maybe you could do a study of them for your M.S. thesis. A lot of people have conjectured on their origin and there are about as many hypotheses as speculators. One interpretation or hypothesis actually field checked is that they are the result of a meteorite shower. Doesn't seem to hold up though; no meteorite debris has been found in or around them and, as far as anyone can tell, the underlying rocks don't seem to be disturbed the way you might expect from a high velocity impact.

"Unless they have been drained and cleared for tobacco, most of the bays are densely vegetated swamps. When I was a kid Francis Marion was one of my very special heroes. During the Revolution he led a band of South Carolina guerrillas that operated in the bay country inland of Charleston. They were all natives of the area who could live off the land and who knew the terrain so well they could avoid stumbling into one of these swamps even at night. Of course, the redcoats didn't know the country at all, so when they tried to pursue Marion's men they invariably ended up mired in the muck while the South Carolinians made their escape. I guess that's why the British called him the Swamp Fox."

Jim gave me a look of exaggerated incredulity; it was a look I would see many times during that summer and in later years. "You really think the British dubbed him with that moniker—could just as easily been his mother..."

"His mother!" I retorted. "Man, fucking sarcasm is supposed to be the exclusive domain of your valiant and brilliant mentor. I suppose I'm going to have to put up with shit like this all summer."

Smiling knowingly, Jim said, "I always said you were a lucky fucker."

"Well, that may be right, but it sure isn't all good. Anyway, it doesn't matter how Marion became the Swamp Fox, or for that matter, how Carolina Bays formed. Our first objective is to locate every damned recorded and unrecorded Waccamaw outcrop in the Carolina Coastal Plain."

Jim's low, wet whistle was followed by an observation that our objective sounded like a lot of work.

"It certainly will take a lot of time, but the total number of localities is probably fewer than a hundred. On the bad side, the damned things are scattered over a hell of a big area. Worse yet, some of them are probably long gone. The fertilizer pits, for instance, haven't been operative for thirty years so most will be grown over, weathered to hell, or plowed under. And some of the river outcrops will have been eroded away or covered with slump. Outcrops in the coastal plain tend to be very ephemeral."

"Well," Jim mused. "If the rivers can erode them away, they can expose new ones at the same time."

"You're right, that's why we got a boat so we can run the rivers and check every inch of the banks. The same sort of things hold for the pits—there will be new ones to replace the old ones. Istvan Ferenczi put me onto two road metal pits last year. One is at Old Dock, south of Lake Waccamaw, and the other is south of Wilmington. I'm sure we'll find others but it will take time and effort. Our real work starts when we find an outcrop. We will need to measure each section and delineate, measure, describe and collect each unit. Then we have to get the huge fossil collections safely back to the lab in Houston. That's why we're going to work seven days a week, twelve hours a day."

"What about the literature?" Jim asked.

"What about it?"

"Well, can't we get a little help there? There must be measured sections and fossil lists and that sort of thing."

"Forget it," I said. "The people who have done the work in this region were glorified shell collectors with PhD's. They didn't give a shit about detailed stratigraphy and paleontology, and never heard of paleoecology. They got their rocks off on new species—they loved to write papers entitled 'New and Otherwise Interesting Species From—' you can fill in the blank. We can't get diddly out of most of the stuff they wrote. Hell, they didn't even bother to accurately locate the goddamned outcrops."

Registering a little surprise at my spirited outburst, Jim commented, "Sounds like really shitty work for professionals. Were they really all that bad?"

"Unfortunately as far as I've determined most were. It's like an incestuous cult where the brains of the followers are controlled by a few dominant assholes—guys like G.D. Harris at Cornell and William Healy Dall at the Smithsonian. Both of them are dead but they live on in the bodies and minds of C.W. Cooke, Wendall Woodring, and their buddies. One thing is certain— they all have low tolerance for new ideas.

"While we are on the subject of our work out here I should warn you that we are going to be operating in the Bible belt. The rednecks tend to be gun toting, Bible-thumping, fundamentalists who believe every word in the fucking Bible came directly from God. They figure the universe and humans were created by God less than 10,000 years ago and they won't take kindly to hearing some scroungy, foreign, heathen, smart-ass college guys trying to tell them about evolution and all that sort of shit."

Big-eyed, Jim stammered, "But, but what the hell if they ask us what the fuck we're doing out here. Some are bound to ask us that—what do we say then, Big Daddy?"

"Anything except the truth, my man—anything but the fucking truth. Telling those guys we're collecting soil samples for the state works pretty well."

"Yeah, but what do we know about the damned soils?"

"Don't need to know anything. Just tell them we collect the samples for those smart-ass college professors in Raleigh or Columbia. All we know is the state is trying to figure out how to raise better tobacco, peanuts, rice or some such shit."

"They gonna buy that?"

"Hell, the dumb fucks will buy anything except the truth. Of course we'll meet a few smarter people along the way, I hope, and if it serves our purpose we can give them a different story."

Sinking back into his seat and staring down the road, Jim muttered, "This is gonna be one fuckin' summer."

Discussion of our work plans terminated when Solliday spotted the Wilmington city limits sign. "We're home!" he cried.

"Not quite home—we need to check into a motel, dump our gear and start looking for an apartment. On $10 a day we can't hack motel rates. We need a cheap place, where we can work, park the boat, store our gear, and dry our samples."

Looking a bit doleful, Jim asked, "Did I hear you mention food?"

It was somewhere near high noon when we checked into the Live Oak Motel south of town on the Wrightsville Beach road. I picked the place because we planned to hit the beach for a swim in the evening. With misgivings, I paid the desk clerk $9.27, accepted the room key and motioned to Jim to pull the car and trailer as close to the room as possible. We needed to unload our gear, grab some chow and begin the search for a suitable apartment as soon as possible. There was no way we could afford to stay at the Live Oak two days. On our budget, we needed to find a place with weekly rates.

While Jim was bringing in our gear I noticed that we seemed to have a double bed rather than the twins I had requested.

"I hope you don't mind sleeping with me tonight, Jim, there's only one bed. The Navy wouldn't approve of this arrangement at all—strictly against the rules."

"No," Jim responded. "There are two beds, they're just shoved together."

Checking more closely I saw that he was right, but when I tried to pull them apart I discovered that they were Siamese twins connected to a hinged headboard. We tried to disconnect them but when that failed we spread-eagled the bastards so that while the heads of the beds were close together, the feet touched opposite walls. At least only our heads would be in close proximity.

We picked up a local newspaper at a nearby café and checked the classifieds while gorging down hamburgers immersed in generous globs of mayonnaise and cole slaw. The classifieds were definitely more rewarding than the lunch. There were several apartments listed that appeared to hold promise. Our first pick, a large brick complex accompanied by endless rules, beaucoup residents and high rates, wasn't for us. Opting for the low-rent district on the shabby side of town we soon found an old two-story house converted to four three-or four-room apartments.

Our second floor apartment matched our needs: two bedrooms, a living room easily converted to work space, and a kitchenette. As a bonus our new landlady agreed to allow us to use her garage where we could park the boat and trailer and store gear and samples. Best of all the entire setup went for $12.00 a week. This was definitely our kind of place—home sweet home.

Sitting on the edge of my bed it seemed to me at the time that everything was working out and that tomorrow we could begin the search for a boat landing on the Cape Fear. In the morning we would need to lay in some food and supplies, and, in view of the 100° temperatures I decided to look for a portable air conditioner or a window fan. Need for these items ended the next day when a hurricane struck Wrightsville Beach and day time temperatures dropped to 75° or lower.

Returning to the motel room after our moonlight swim at Wrightsville Beach, we wasted little time in occupying our respective halves of the Siamese twin beds. Assisted by a six-pack of Country Club Malt Liquor Jim had consumed at the beach, he was snoring contentedly in thirty seconds flat. On the other hand I lay wide-eyed, staring at the dark ceiling. It wasn't the project this time but rather thoughts of Jim and his family.

Jim was here with me in North Carolina and his wife and baby were in Houston because I had convinced him that he should pack up his family and possessions and join me as my research assistant. I had done this despite not having official notification the project had been funded, just so I could get an early start on the fieldwork. Man, what if the damned proposal hadn't been funded? As painful as it might have been I could have repaid the university, but what about the Sollidays? What would they have done? It had all worked out as anticipated, but I definitely had been a little reckless with their lives.

I was never a devotee of the hard sell when it came to recruitment of geology majors. I wanted to be certain that the students understood what might be ahead for them both in college and later as professionals. It was essential that they be highly motivated, even passionately motivated for geology and not by prospects of money, and that they possess the necessary determination and ability to persist and eventually succeed. Most of all, I wanted to think that the decision was theirs, not mine, or as it happened at times, the decision of their parents. The specter of meeting a former student, five or ten years later after their graduation, to find that they had become disenchanted with geology as a way of life haunted me and remained close to the surface of my consciousness. Only those who enjoy playing God can accept such responsibility lightly.

On reflection it seemed to me that I need not be too concerned about Jim.

The decision had been largely his. All I really did was open a door. His enthusiasm for geology was evident and, from what I had observed of him, he would both persist and succeed. Reassured, I allowed my head to sink into the pillow, closed my eyes and dreamed of the great adventure that lay ahead for both of us.

AAA to the Rescue

After a four or five hour search of the Cape Fear we had located nothing resembling a boat landing and local residents had unanimously expressed the opinion that none existed in Columbus County. Despite the dreary prospect we continued looking because there were considerable advantages to a landing located near the principle outcrops to the alternative of a daily 100-mile round trip by water to and from Wilmington.

Our determination paid off when Solliday spotted a forlorn trail that seemed to lead off into the woods toward the river.

"It ain't much," I said. "But, what the hell, let's give it a try."

"Sure," Solliday replied. "Nothing to lose but your car."

Jim's dour observation proved unwarranted. Encountering no obstructions such as fallen trees, we drove slowly but unscathed to the river's edge. Descending from the car we were presented with the most God-awful ugly boat landing in the entire coastal plain, but at that moment it appeared beautiful to us. Cut in a steep, ten-foot bank, and obviously not used in years, it was muddy, rutted and partially grown over with an assortment of weeds and small trees. Even so we knew instantly it would do the job.

Despite the condition of the landing we had no difficulty launching the boat. In minutes we were in midstream opposite the site of the Reiglewood paper pulp mill whose belching fumes provided downwind residents with an atmosphere laden with the rich fragrance of rotten eggs. From there we moved upstream seven or eight miles to the County 141 Bridge. High, steep banks cloaked in thick stands of vegetation rose sharply from the water's edge. Here and there, where floodwaters had eroded the banks and removed the vegetation, we could catch glimpses of Late Cretaceous sand and clay overlain by a thin layer of younger, unfossiliferous sands. Though interesting, these deposits did not seem to be relevant to our project so we retraced our course to Reiglewood and proceeded downstream toward Wilmington. Here also the high, steep banks were supported by Cretaceous clays and sands, but even

117

from our distant vantage point at water level we could discern the chalky white fossils packed in the overlying golden sands and gray limestone layers. These were the famous Waccamaw deposits of the Neils Eddy Landing area that I had read about and which had led us to the Cape Fear. Suppressing a reckless impulse nurtured by weeks of anticipation, we reluctantly decided not to land the boat and make a mad dash up the bluff to the fossil beds. It was late in the afternoon and I knew a fresh start in the morning would better serve our purpose.

Proceeding down river four or five miles we spotted an interesting, dark gray outcrop at the water's edge. On our knees, picking at the outcrop with hammers, we quickly recognized that this was a limestone packed with oysters that had lived sixty to seventy million years ago in the Cretaceous bay or lagoon. Although the Cretaceous was not the prime target of our project, I decided to get the field study officially underway by designating this locality WA-1.

On the return drive to Wilmington our spirits were high. There had been no problem getting the boat out of the water at the landing and then onto the trailer. It appeared that we were now in position to begin serious field studies in the morning.

"When we get to the apartment, Jim, we should make certain everything we need for tomorrow is ready to go—I don't want to run up and down those bluffs any more often than necessary."

"I'll go along with that," Jim said. "What exactly do you have in mind?"

"Well, in addition to our lunch, we'll need an ample supply of assorted sample bags, hammers, chisels, picks, notebooks, pencils, bug repellant, mosquito netting, and don't let me forget my cigars. Nothing keeps the Carolina gnats off a sweaty body like cigar smoke."

"I can take care of all that stuff, but you'll have to smoke the fucking cigars. How about a rope—will we need a rope?"

"Yeah, we'll need the rope, but not to scale the bluff. There are places up there, though, where we may want to steady ourselves on a line while sectioning. Also the rope will be useful in lowering burlap bags filled with samples and gear. One thing is certain, we don't want to bring a ladder. I assume Ferenczi carried his ladder overland and lowered it down the side of the bluff."

"Knowing you I figure we'll be on the river at the crack of dawn."

"Maybe not at the crack," I said, "but shortly thereafter. We should be at a filling station to load our ice chest and our gas can by 6:00 a.m. I want to be on the Cape Fear by 7:00 a.m."

Glaring over at me with a trace of a smile, Jim responded, "You must be getting soft, you always had us up at 5:00 a.m. in field camp. I'll never forget those goddamned aerial bombs you fired every morning at 5:00 a.m. The fucking sound reverberated all across the St. Francis Mountains for several minutes. Everyone was out of their sack, big-eyed and jumping into their pants in about two seconds flat."

"Oh, hell," I replied. "That was boot camp. I'm not getting soft, I just think you've earned the right to lay around in bed in the mornings."

Looking straight ahead now, Jim said, "Since you're such a sweetheart I'll get the gear arranged tonight, but you'll have to cook supper."

Grinning, I replied, "I was hoping you'd say that, and while you're at it, clear space in the garage where we can lay out our wet samples tomorrow night. While you're having all the fun I'll open a can of beans if you promise not to fart in the car tomorrow."

"How long do you think it will take to do the river?" Jim asked.

"Depends on what we find, I guess. If all goes well, I suppose two days will do it."

"What then?"

"I want to hit Ferenczi's Old Dock and Town Creek pits, and then we'll check the north shore of Lake Waccamaw, look for a couple of old fertilizer pits and try to find Horace Richards' localities. I can't promise anything, but we should be able to wrap up everything in the Wilmington area by the 10th or 11th, then as soon as we've packed and shipped the dry samples, we can head south for Conway and the Waccamaw River. One thing's sure with this type of work, we can hardly expect to maintain a rigid schedule, but we'll do our best."

Still in a state of euphoria we crossed the U.S. 17 bridge over the Cape Fear River and joined the rush hour flow of traffic into downtown Wilmington. The euphoria evaporated a second later when the car came to an abrupt stop in the southbound lane. Pumping the gas pedal and cursing failed to provide the desired results. The brakes apparently were locked.

Jim roared, "What the fuck are you doing? You can't stop here in the middle of this traffic. You'll get us killed!"

"Hell," I said. "We don't have much choice. I think the old girl just expired." Then I noticed an AAA Gulf station directly across the street. Help was at hand.

"Stay here, Jim, I'm going over there for help." Before he could protest I was nimbly dodging passing vehicles as I raced across the busy street. I found the manager by one of the gas pumps, hunkered down over a wounded tire. The owner of the patient, a paper-pusher type in white shirt and bow tie, stood over him discussing the manager's prognosis, when I drew up behind them.

I didn't wish to appear impolite, but it seemed my problem was a trifle more urgent than a flat tire. Excusing myself, I interrupted the discussion, explained my predicament, and asked for assistance. Nothing, however, that I said seemed to register. The two men, ignoring me, continued to stare at the fucking tire. I tried again, but by then it was clear that I was intentionally being ignored. While I contemplated my next move the manager stood up and the two men began to walk toward the office. I followed, pointing out at the same time that I was an honest-to-God, card-carrying, paid-up member of AAA. No response.

Though struck with the absurdity of speaking to two unresponsive, sweaty posteriors, I gave it one last shot. "My friend is out in the car. We need to get out there and move the thing before there's an accident and he's injured or killed." But without the slightest sign they were aware I was there, they slowly walked into the office and slammed the door behind them.

Enraged and frustrated I returned to the car, stopping only long enough to brief Jim. Then I raced up the street to a pay phone I had spotted a moment earlier.

When I dialed the local AAA office I was greeted by the genteel, dignified voice of a matronly southern lady. Fortunately I had the presence of mind to realize that the indignant outburst I had been prepared to deliver was somewhat inappropriate. Summing up latent reserves of self-control, I calmly related to her our circumstances, the location of the vehicle, and pointed out the treatment I had received at the Gulf station.

A slight pause at the other end was followed by the lady's assurance that the man's behavior seemed a bit unusual and that she would look into it.

"Unusual?" I responded, controlling my voice as best I could. "I should think outrageous and incredible would better cover it."

"Well," she replied. "Even so we need to take care of your problem. I see that Bill' s Garage is situated about three blocks south of your location on Main Street. I'm certain Bill will take care of you but it is nearly closing time so you must hurry. Please call me if you have further problems."

Thus dismissed, I ran back down the street toward Bill's Garage. As I passed our car I could see Jim still hunched in the front seat. I waved and gave him the victory sign and as I sped by his head emerged from the window. The bellow he emitted was a bit incoherent; however, I clearly heard the words,

"Jesus Christ hurry up. I'm going to get killed out here." By then I was nearly out of earshot, but he did seem to repeat the word "beer" several times.

Making a silent resolution to get myself into better shape, I charged into Bill's Garage, sweaty, disheveled, and gasping for breath. Bill was in a back room preparing to close shop. He looked up at me, startled, but before he could grab a weapon I blurted out the essentials of our problem. Amazingly, the man not only looked at me and listened, but he smiled.

"Run all the way, eh? Well, well, I guess we better rev up the old tow truck and go rescue your car and friend."

With the Dodge and Solliday safely in the garage, Bill agreed not only to repair the car but to store our boat and trailer until the work was completed.

Following a quick examination of the vehicle, he turned to me and said, "Not much of a job, I'll have it ready and as good as new by four tomorrow afternoon."

Greatly relieved that the damage wasn't terminal, we walked the eight or nine blocks to the apartment.

Left in limbo without a car we spent a rainy morning updating our maps and planning sorties to several selected areas of interest. In the early afternoon I turned to some of the old literature on the geology of the area. Jim elected to clear space in the garage for the samples we expected to collect. Actually I figured it was a shabby excuse to tap his seemingly inexhaustible supply of Country Club Malt Liquor. I was tempted to join him, but vivid memories of past beer-generated hangovers discouraged me. Anyway, I wanted to take an operational brain to the Cape Fear the next morning.

At about 3:30 we walked to Bill's Garage and true to his word the car was ready to go. Driving back I thought that we were lucky; all we had lost was one day on the river and $28.95 for auto repairs. I was certain there would be nothing but clear sailing ahead.

No, girls, we don't need any help!

It was Saturday, July 4th, and we had arrived at the landing at about 7:00 a.m. as planned. The drenching rain of the previous day had cooled and cleansed the air but also had converted our sorry landing to a treacherous, slimy quagmire. Surveying the situation it was clear that we would have to remove all the gear and carry the boat down the slippery bank to the water. Then it would be necessary to transport all the damned gear down the same bank and to reload it into the boat. Worse yet, in the evening when we arrived with the boat loaded with bags of heavy samples we would need to carry all that shit back up to the car and trailer. It was a nasty problem that I didn't want to contemplate at that moment. For just a little while I wanted to nurture that new sense of euphoria brought about by the prospect that we were finally ready to do some real fieldwork.

Staring at the boat, I was impressed with the neat and orderly way Jim had organized our gear and supplies. He had risen at dawn and carried all that stuff downstairs to load it into the boat despite obvious symptoms of extreme physical distress. It seemed a shame that we would mess it all up when we carried it down the bank.

During the weeks ahead Jim would provide many examples of his considerable organizational skill essential to the smooth operation of our project. In time I would come to regard him as the best ever of all my field assistants, but that morning as I listened to the guttural groans and heart-rendering wails emanating from a nearby clump of brush, I had reason to wonder if, in fact, he would survive the day.

Solliday, who had, with considerable determination, consumed a large part of his summer's supply of Country Club Malt Liquor the previous day, awakened blurry-eyed and doubled over by surging gas pains. As soon as we had backed the trailer to the edge of the bank Jim rushed from the car to the clump of brush to relieve himself. From where I stood beside the trailer I could just make out

122

the strawberry-tinted burr that capped his aching head. Although I could see little of him I had no difficulty hearing his anguished cries, mutterings, and curses. Ignoring as best I could his expressions of distress I concentrated on the serenity and beauty of this morning on the Cape Fear. The crisp air, cleansed by the recent rain, the azure sky, the fluffs of pink-tinted clouds, the lush greenery that flanked the yellow-brown waters of the river, the twittering of feeding birds, the stately trees—we could have been a thousand miles from civilization.

It always seemed to me that days like this one constituted memorable payoffs in the lives of field geologists. Dwelling on that thought for a moment I burst out at the clump of brush that partially concealed Solliday, "Goddammit man, it's a great day in the Coastal Plain! This is the life, this is why I was born! Just think of those poor fuckers in Houston out there on the freeway, fighting that traffic to get to their boring jobs. Then they sit on their asses wearing stupid suits and ridiculous ties and shuffle piles of nonsensical paper all day."

At that moment I detected a rustling in the brush and Solliday's head emerged above the leaves. Even from where I stood it was clear that his face wore a blended expression of disgust, anger and pain.

"A great fuckin day, you say," he challenged. "What the fuck is so great about it? I'm dying and freezing and you think it's great!"

"You may be dying but you can't be freezing. The way your shit is steaming at least your ass must be on fire."

Disregarding my remarks, Jim continued, "Nice day, you think. What about that fucking paper mill? The air smells like shit to me."

"Well, it's your shit that smells, we're upwind from the mill and over here the air smells sweet as a rose."

"Goddamnit," Jim growled. "Your nose must be up your ass."

Finally, Jim arose from his private little retreat, his face red, trunks crumpled about his ankles.

"Toss me that roll of toilet paper on the back seat of the boat, will you?"

Feigning shock I replied, "You know better than that. Haven't I taught you anything? That's fossil wrapping paper. Hell, you'll never make it as a paleontologist."

Indignantly Jim responded, "Come on, come on, smartass. You can call it what you want, but it's goddamned toilet paper, and I need to wipe my ass before this stuff seals off my asshole."

Jim's geologic hammer rested on the seat by the paper and on impulse I picked it up and waved it at him. "Here, maybe you can use this to ream it out when it dries."

"I don't need a damned hammer, I got one right here between my legs."

"Man, if you call that a hammer you' re in trouble. You couldn't stuff cotton in an aspirin bottle with that thing. Anyway, have you ever tried to bend it around and stick it up your ass? Don' t try, though, because it would never reach. Shit, what you need is a cherry bomb. You could fix your problem and celebrate the Fourth with one colossal bang."

It was then that Jim began to shuffle toward me. The red trunks twisted around his ankles permitting only short, mincing steps so that he looked like a naked, grimacing savage engaged in some sort of tribal rain dance.

"Forget the damned fossil paper," he growled. "Hand me that bug repellant. The fucking green-headed flies are dive-bombing my ass."

Green-headed flies, a particularly mean-natured and vicious enemy of all coastal plain geologists, are not to be taken lightly, so I quickly scrambled for the spray can kept in the boat for such emergencies. I was too late. Lunging desperately to grab the can from my hand Jim suddenly pitched forward. His outstretched arms partially broke his fall but then his hands slowly slid forward and his face descended into the slimy muck. Standing over my fallen comrade I frantically directed the spray can over his bare ass, but as I watched the red welts rise on his white upturned cheeks I knew that once again I was too late.

After a quick dip in the river and a judicious application of Solarcaine, Jim, looking subdued and a bit forlorn in his soggy red shorts, joined me in unloading our gear from the boat. Grateful to the gods that a fourteen-foot aluminum Arkansas Traveler weighs only about 120 pounds, we hoisted the damned thing from the trailer and tentatively carried it to the water where we lowered the bow into the river and allowed about three feet of the stern to settle securely into the mud at the base of the landing. Reloading the gear proved less of a hassle than I had feared. Jim stood by the boat and I was able to hand or slide most of the gear down to him. The 10 hp engine was a tougher proposition, but together we packed it down the muddy bank without mishap.

Skimming along with the current toward Neils Eddy Landing I was once again in high spirits and even Jim, I thought, was exhibiting signs of life. He was in the stern at the tiller and I in the bow where I could scout the banks for outcrops and suitable landing sites, and, at the same time, keep an eye out for floating or submerged obstacles that were best avoided.

I had used this seating arrangement in Florida when Roy Staton and Vince Vanstrum had been my assistants and continued to employ it as long as we worked the rivers.

Separated as we were by the length of the boat, with the wind in our faces and enveloped in the roar of the engine, our conversations were limited to a variety of shouts, arm waving and finger pointing. Generally these primitive methods of communication worked satisfactorily, however, when I sighted Neils Eddy Landing ahead on the right bank, in my excitement I forgot the glowing cigar in my mouth.

Waving my arms and shouting as I turned in my seat to attract Solliday's attention I inadvertently struck the lighted end of my cigar with my right forearm. To my horror a shower of red sparks shot aft like tracer bullets, striking Jim in the chest and face. In his attempt to protect his face and body, Solliday took his hand off the tiller and the boat suddenly veered to port, nearly throwing both of us into the water. As we headed for the left bank Jim, cigarette dangling from his lower lip, continued to beat his chest like an enraged gorilla. Then adding to the confusion, he began screaming at me, "What the fuck are you trying to do to me? This fucking river is cursed; I'm going to die out here!"

In an effort to alert him to the impending danger of running aground and gutting the thin aluminum shell on the hard rocks at water level, I tried to shout over his screams, "Grab the fucking tiller, man—we're going to crash—grab the tiller!" As I watched, nearly hypnotized, Jim finally grasped the situation, managed at the last possible moment to grab the tiller and, nearly tossing me over the side again, swung us back toward midstream. As I tried to re-light my cigar, I couldn't help wonder what the odds might be against us surviving the day.

Despite our dismal start, we completed the work at Neils Eddy Landing and four other nearby sections. To the best of my knowledge, it was the first and remains the only systematic stratigraphic study ever made of these Waccamaw deposits.

At the boat landing that evening we were hungry and tired but despite the improbable events of the morning we were satisfied that we had accomplished our mission.

Feelings of smugness were quickly dispelled by the unexpected return of our gremlins. After unloading and transferring the gear ashore, we discovered that the Arkansas Traveler had been transformed into a Missouri mule stolidly determined to resist all efforts to move her up the landing. Uncertain footing at the water's edge made it difficult to gain any meaningful leverage or balance. Most attempts to either push or pull the boat up the slope caused our feet to slip from beneath us, dropping us into the murky gray goop where we thrashed about like two crazed salamanders.

While struggling with our defiant boat I became aware of a feminine greeting from the bank above us. Two pretty fourteen or fifteen-year-old girls on bicycles were looking down on us with obvious interest and curiosity. I had no idea how long they had been up there but considering our language I could only hope they had just arrived.

"You fellows need any help?" one asked.

It was then standing in the river in apparent cold defeat, covered with mud from head to foot that I chose to draw myself into a stance of imagined macho dignity and utter one of the most memorable and completely stupid pronouncements of my life: "No, girls, we don't need any help."

These words, which would haunt me the remainder of my life, had summoned down upon us the full wrath of what we later called the "Curse of the Cape Fear." The girls, still astride their bikes, looked down on us a bit dubiously, then each smiled sweetly, waved goodbye and disappeared into the shrouded lane which led to the highway.

About forty-five minutes later, battered, bruised, covered with slime and near death, we mustered all lingering resolve and determinedly gave it one final heroic try. With magnificent grunts and curses we managed to dislodge the SOB and then, stumbling, sliding, and slipping, to pull and push it up the landing and with one final heave-ho for God and country we hoisted it onto the trailer. I am sure at that moment of success we were filled with a deep-seated and completely misplaced sense of pride in having exhibited one more time the magnitude of our combined manhood. And we had done it alone, without demeaning ourselves by accepting help from two frail females.

In April, while leading a class field trip in eastern Texas, I strained my lower back unwisely lifting a huge boulder of the Oakville Sandstone. Adopting my customary macho attitude toward injuries, I paid little attention to the problem, assuming it would clear up in a few days. But in June, when we arrived in South Carolina, the pain had stubbornly persisted. Now, driving to Wilmington, I became aware that the level of pain had intensified. "Must have pulled another muscle," I complained, "fucking with that goddamned boat."

Jim interrupted my thoughts at that moment. "How about going out tonight for a drink, after we unload and eat?"

"Yeah," I responded. "But you have forgotten that Wilmington is dry as a dog's bone."

"Not entirely," Jim smiled. "The Elk's Club isn't and I'm a member. All the clubs have a bar and as my guest they'll serve you, too."

"Sounds good to me; maybe a little alcohol will grease the muscles in my back. Besides, we won't be going out tomorrow so we can lay in bed until 7:00 a.m."

Surprised, Jim asked, "Why aren't we going out? You surely aren't planning to take in a church service."

"Well, that would be a cold day; we need to organize our samples and then plan our attack on land-based localities of the area. Monday I want to search the woods above Neils Eddy for the old fertilizer pits. I think all of Julia Gardner's fossils came from those pits and not the outcrops we collected. Then if time permits we'll hit Ferenczi's Old Dock pit southwest of Lake Waccamaw."

Are all the Elks Clubs this exciting?

The Elks Club was housed in a two-story colonial-type brick structure located in a quiet residential neighborhood. When we arrived at about 9 p.m. the street seemed deserted so I parked at the curb directly in front of the club. A good parking place ordinarily might be considered a minor convenience, but that evening it was to prove essential to our ultimate well-being.

When no one responded to his knock, Jim opened the door and we tentatively stepped into a well lighted and clearly deserted hallway which led straight ahead to another closed door. On our right the hall opened to an equally deserted but inviting library-reading room.

"Are all the Elks Club this exciting, Jim? Where do they hide the bar? Don't tell me, behind one of those bookcases, I'll bet."

In his personal element now, Jim ignored my attempts at sarcasm and took command of the moment. "Why don't you step into the parlor and eyeball a magazine? I'll check the back rooms for signs of life—there has to be some action around here someplace."

It seemed I had barely settled into an easy chair and started to flip through a stack of magazines on the marble table before me when Jim returned. From his expression it was evident he had good news.

"Find the bar?" I asked.

"No bar, but there's a poker game under way back there and the guys want me to sit in. A bunch of redneck farmers with their own bottle." Then, a bit anxiously, he said, "You won't mind sitting out here for an hour or so while I rack up some ready loot from these hicks? You could read a book. I know you hate card games."

I responded with a resigned shrug of the shoulders. "Why the hell not? I didn't really need a drink anyway, probably wouldn't serve anything but embalming fluid in this place. Try to keep it to two hours max, though, I've got a few things I'd like to do at the apartment tonight."

With that Jim vanished down the hall and I strolled to the nearest bookcase.

Having selected a promising title I settled into my chair and before I got past the first page I was sound asleep. When I awoke I yawned, stretched my legs and groped for the book which had slid to the seat beside me. Then I looked at my watch. I had been asleep for 2 ½ hours and no Solliday. Reluctantly I decided to drag my body from the chair and go look for him, but before I could rise Solliday suddenly emerged from the door at the end of the hall and hurried toward me. As he came abreast of the library he didn't slow down.

"Let's go," he hissed. "Move it."

Responding to the obvious urgency of his words, I leaped from the chair, tossed the book to the floor, and hurried after Jim who by then was disappearing through the front door. I caught him on the verandah and we raced together down the walk toward the car. "What the hell is going on?" I gasped. "Who's after us?"

"Never mind," he snarled. "Just get in the car and get us the fuck away from here!"

Grabbing the car keys from my pocket I ran to the street side of the car and in one fluid motion opened the door, leaped inside and started the engine. When I glanced across the passenger side I saw, with horror, that the door was locked and that Jim was trapped outside on the curb. He was yanking at the door handle while screaming at me to unlock the fucking thing.

As soon as I opened the door Jim leaped inside still clutching the outside handle he had torn from the door. In that moment I caught a quick and frightening glimpse of eight or nine brutish looking angry young men pouring out of the club. When they spotted the car they halted on the verandah, pointed and shook their fists, and just before we roared down the darkened street I heard one cry out, "There they are, let's get the motherfuckers!"

Leaning forward in his seat, peering straight ahead, Jim, more calm now but still clutching the door handle, said, "Don't turn on the lights and stay on the back streets. I don't think they can catch us, their cars are parked out back."

I was way ahead of him; I'd seen and heard enough to know that whatever the reason those guys wanted our blood. About two blocks down the street I turned the car into a dark alley and headed for downtown Wilmington, still without lights. When I thought we had safely effected our escape I glanced over at Jim; "Now maybe you'll tell me what the hell that was all about."

"Well, shit," he responded apologetically. "I had this fantastic hand, no way I could lose, so I bet fifty bucks."

"Where the hell did you get 50 bucks?" I asked. "You must have had a good run."

"Hell no, I lost everything, didn't have a nickel."

"You couldn't cover your ass when someone beat your hand."

"Yeah, I never would have figured I could lose, goddamn it."

"I suppose that's when you told then you'd run out to the library and pick up the cash I was holding for you."

"Well, something like that."

"Christ you could have gotten us killed, and what's more you're still holding the handle of the door."

"Oh, fuck, you worry too much; they didn't get us and we'll get the damned door fixed."

We drove in silence until we reached a lighted, busy street where I remembered to turn on the headlights. At the first intersection, two young women were waiting to cross the street. Jim quickly rolled down his window and as we drove by, to my horror, called out to the women, "Let's fuck, ladies."

From there to the apartment Jim propositioned every woman we encountered. Rip-roaring drunk and virtually unmanageable, the more I tried to quiet him the louder and more obscene he became. Our only hope was to get to the apartment before the local law drew a bead on us.

When we reached the apartment I doused the headlights and concealed the car behind the garage. My feelings of relief were short lived. Jim leaped from the car and strode to the house crying out, "Let's go man. Let's get those broads in the apartment downstairs and have a party!"

I called after him, "It's no use, Jim, they'll be in bed now."

"Bed," he yelled. "That's fucking where I want them!"

At that point he began to vigorously bang on their door and shout to the girls to rise and shine—party time!

It occurred to me then that the best thing was to go upstairs to our apartment and attempt to ignore the entire affair. If the girls called the cops I could always claim I had been there all evening and that I really had only a nodding acquaintance with the drunk SOB downstairs.

At my kitchen table/desk I went to work on updating my expense records. I sometimes tended to put off this chore, but at that moment I thought it would serve to take my mind off the evening and what might be in progress downstairs. The pounding and shouting had ended, and Solliday hadn't returned, so I assumed he either had gained entry or had passed out in the lower hall. After 15 or 20 minutes I heard him ascending the stairs. In a moment he popped into the apartment surprisingly calm and seemingly pleased with himself.

"Guess what?"

"You laid both of them."

"No, no, what kind of guy do you think I am?"

"I've been mulling that over."

"Well, brace yourself," he said with a smile. "We' re going on a picnic at the beach tomorrow. The girls are going to fry a chicken and we'll supply whatever else."

"But," I protested, "we need to work here tomorrow—we've a lot to do."

"Nonsense," he replied. "Tomorrow is Sunday—nobody works on Sunday except preachers. Anyway, it's all settled, I can't tell them that you're going to play hard to get now. I think we need a little R & R after the days we've had."

As Solliday spoke my resolve to remain in camp on Sunday began to erode. It was not the two girls (a dull pair, I thought), but the allure of surf and sand that worked to alter my earlier plans. Deprived of the sea for long periods of time, my zest for life tends to seriously corrode.

Signaling time out, I interrupted his soliloquy. "Oh, OK, you win, you're right. I'll go. When do we leave?"

Looking greatly relieved, he responded, "About noon. You can get some work done in the morning while I pick up some goodies and help get everything ready."

Keep Punching, Kid

Jim was up early the next morning and out of the apartment with the keys to my car and the 20 bucks I had given him. I settled down to my maps and books and began plotting the fieldwork that was now postponed until Tuesday.

Shortly before noon, Solliday came into the apartment and announced that all was ready and that the girls were outside by the car waiting for us.

"Did you pack towels and suntan lotion?" I asked.

"Yeah, yeah, everything, just come on I'm getting hungry."

As we descended the stairs Jim, without looking in my direction said quietly, "Oh, by the way, the girls have a cousin visiting for the weekend and she's coming along. You don't mind, do you? Her name is Mildred and she's a Marine sergeant from Camp Lejune."

Suddenly I was filled with apprehension. "A Marine sergeant! What kind of a woman is a Marine sergeant?"

She's okay," Jim assured me. "Lots of fun—I met her last night."

I was still mentally trying to visualize a female Marine sergeant when we stepped into the front yard and saw what kind of a girl is a Marine sergeant.

Mildred stood between her two cousins, all 175 brutish, muscle-bound, hairy pounds of her, dressed improbably in a goddamned GI camouflage playsuit. At first I thought she was smiling, but as we approached more closely the smile became a leer and it was directed toward me, causing my head to swim and my legs to become gelatinous. I knew at that moment I had unwittingly committed a mortal sin for which retribution was about to be exacted.

It wasn't an apparition as I had hoped, but a barracuda prepared to attack and tear the flesh from my bones; the curse of the Cape Fear had taken semi-human form and had elected to accompany us to the fucking beach. At that moment I should have turned and run, but instead, mesmerized, I moved forward inexorably to my perdition.

As cousin Mildred extended her hand to me I detected an unmistakable lascivious gleam in her dark, beady eyes that sent a shiver down my spine.

"Jim tells me that you're a professor—that sounds so exciting!"

Considering the bizarre events of the past few days, I had to admit to myself that she had a point. "Well, ah, actually," I stammered. "Most of the time it's fairly routine—nothing like the Marine Corps, I suspect."

"Maybe," she answered. "But in the Corps I don't get many chances to be with a Ph.D."

Then with feet rooted to the driveway and a hand crushed in her vice-like grip, I was astounded as Mildred's face began a transfiguration. I watched spellbound as a heavy cover of dark bristly stubble slowly spread across her cheeks, chin and upper lip. The nose spread and flattened and the brow ridges thickened until they protruded over dark, menacing eyes rimmed with yellow patches of scar tissue.

Though I had not seen that face in fifteen years, there was no question, it belonged to my old shipmate, Johnny Mattero, the pride of Long Beach, California.

Johnny, a professional prizefighter, was a short, powerful, mean SOB, whose brain had been hammered to mush in the ring. Early in his career he had elected to dispense with any pretense of cuteness and had adopted the primitive philosophy of kill or be killed.

Oblivious to his own pain, his face bloodied and battered, some primeval instinct drove him relentlessly forward through savage barrages of nearly lethal blows with the single purpose of getting close enough to his opponent to launch one left hook. It was no ordinary left hook; when it reached its target the recipient was invariably reduced to a broken, crumpled, brain-damaged heap of unconscious shit on the canvas.

Aboard the *U.S.S. Pocatello*, Johnny was generally avoided by the enlisted men and the officers, who regarded him as a dangerous psychopath. His moodiness and frequent outbursts of terrifying rage seemed to lend substance to this view. In any event, in or out of the ring, Johnny managed to scare the shit out of almost everyone. Predictably he was eventually shipped ashore to a psycho ward and then issued a section eight discharge. Unfortunately, this all happened too late to do me any good.

One late summer day in 1944 Johnny and I happened to be standing side by side pissing into the ship's communal trough. We were both staring straight ahead at the gray bulkhead when Johnny broke the silence with his usual husky growl: "You're a slick fighter, kid, probably the best prospect I've seen in the country."

I knew he had seen a few of my bouts but he had never before offered an opinion of my skills. Flattered and startled, I glanced over at him, making certain my eyes were on his face.

"Oh, yeah, you think so?"

"I know so, kid. But you got a serious problem."

"Problem, what kind of problem?"

"You don't punch enough—too cute—gotta punch more kid. Punch, punch, punch, keep punching. Got it, kid?"

Shaking the last drop into the trough, I decided to humor him.

"Got it, Johnny. Punch, punch, punch, keep punching. I'll try to work on that—good advice."

He was with me as we walked out of the head toward the galley.

"You'll remember okay kid, I'm going to help you remember. Starting tomorrow you and me are gonna work out and I'll show you what I'm saying."

I didn't care for the sound of that, it had to be more fun going into the ring with a rabid pit bull. I figured the only thing I was going to learn was fear. The slickest boxer in the world makes mistakes and against Johnny that could prove fatal. I had to be certifiable to accept his offer, but if I turned him down he might get a little peeved and I'd seen him peeved.

"Work out, you say? Sounds, er, ah, great, Johnny, but you probably got better things to do."

"Naw, kid, I ain't got nothin' better to do. You're a real comer but you ain't gonna get there unless I teach you to punch more. I'll meet you on the fantail tomorrow—you bring the gloves."

For the next three or four weeks Johnny and I worked out several days each week. All the sessions were the same. He'd come in on me growling, "Punch, kid, punch!" Moving in on me he was a wide-open target. I had no difficulty hitting him with every type of punch I knew, but nothing slowed him down; nothing even made him blink. Short of jumping overboard, there was no way I could keep him off me. And all the time he would keep growling, "Punch, kid, punch!" Once inside he would fire the damnable left at my head and although I was always quick enough to slip the punch, the breeze that missile generated as it tore past my ear tended to turn my legs to jelly. It was only with the utmost self-control that I managed to fight back the urge to break and run. I knew that sooner or later one of those blows would find its mark and I would be left a vegetable for the remainder of my life.

Then one memorable day I met Johnny lumbering through the mess hall. When he spotted me he gloomily wagged his great shaggy head. "Bad news, kid," he said. "We gotta quit the workouts—sea's too choppy, the way the fantail is jumping around you could fall and hurt yourself. We'll pick it up again when the sea calms."

Trying to look disappointed and injecting a note of regret into my voice, I sighed, "Guess you're right, Johnny, but I'm sure going to miss the fun. Anyway, you've pretty well taught me to punch—really Johnny, I've learned a lot these past few weeks."

With a rare smile, he gave me a friendly slap on the back that nearly knocked me to the deck. "You did good, kid, you're slick okay, but don't forget to keep punchin'."

Mildred, in the fine tradition of the Corps would surely prove a formidable opponent, and much like punchy Johnny Mattero. I could assume that she would relentlessly propel her short, powerful body toward me as she attempted to close for the kill. It was clear then, the defensive strategies that I had used against Mattero were my only hope—keep moving, don't allow her to corner me or catch me on the ropes, and by all means slip the big ones. Johnny, of course, would have said, "Keep punching, kid," but it's also true that every time you throw a punch you create an opening. *No punching for me*, I thought. *I'll just run and try to hide.*

As Johnny's face slowly faded, it was replaced by the leering, bovine features of Cousin Mildred, who still crushed my hand in her vice-like grip. Fortunately, Solliday at that moment was urging everyone to get into the car so we could get the show on the road. With uncharacteristic insight he herded the three girls into the back seat as I hastily climbed into the passenger seat beside him. With a sigh of relief I realized that the inevitable confrontation had been temporarily postponed.

My recollection of our day at the beach remains somewhat of a blur. As soon as we had emerged from the car Mildred was at my side. I didn't dare sit down or even stand in one place for more than a minute. Following my plan to keep moving, I quickly headed out on a five-mile search of the lower beach for seashells. Mildred was at my side each minute, and when I began to chase ghost crabs across the upper beach she eagerly joined in the new sport. Then we killed more time watching butterfly clams burrow into the wet sand at the water's edge. Several frisbee contests and a broad jumping competition with Jim and the two girls killed another hour or more. I was pretty good at the standing broad jump but by that time my legs were gone and Mildred beat me easily.

After several hours of these Olympian heroics I felt old and exhausted with my lower back disintegrating, and I was out of ideas and hope. Throughout the afternoon Cousin Mildred, emulating Johnny Mattero, had stayed with me step for step and, driven by an unremitting animal passion, she had joined me in each of my frantic escapades with appalling vigor and undiminished enthusiasm. She was a match for old Johnny any day. It occurred to me that the Marine Corps must be very proud of her.

As I sank to the warm sand it seemed a man in my state should acknowledge defeat and accept his fate with resolution and whatever dignity he might muster. I looked up at Mildred, braced to endure the leering smile of victory and anticipation, but to my astonishment she was looking with concern at the watch on her powerful, hairy arm. Disregarding me completely she turned and called to Jim and the girls who were lying nearby on a beach blanket, "Hey you people, it's past four o' clock, we've got to haul ass or I'll never get back to the base on time tonight."

Only slowly I began to comprehend that I had been saved by the bell. Just as with Johnny Mattero, I had prevailed not by superior skill and endurance but by sheer dumb luck.

I Wish I Were a Little Rock

We stayed at the apartment Monday morning to plot our field strategies for the week and to compose the weekly obligatory letters to our wives. Aware that Phyllis and Janet would regularly share news of us, it was imperative that accounts of our extracurricular activities be properly innocuous and most importantly that they agree in essential details. It was also wise to occasionally admit to minor indiscretions, knowing that both our wives were well aware that neither of us were particularly saintly by nature.

During the past few years, before I had admitted to myself that my marriage to Phyllis had become a deadly trap, I could not have indulged in this kind of deceit. Now, however, I regarded it as a necessary but bothersome ploy to prevent Phyllis from interfering with my quest for freedom. Unlike myself, however, I think that Jim came to regard his deceits as expressions of a defective moral fiber which one day was bound to extract from him final retribution.

Early that afternoon we were deep in the woods over the bluff at Neils Eddy Landing, in search of the old fertilizer pits that I was certain provided Julia Gardner with the fossils described in her monograph.

I didn't have high hopes of locating the pits. After all, 40 or 50 years was more than enough time for them to have become deeply weathered and overgrown by a dense cover of vegetation that would effectively obscure any obvious traces of them. Nevertheless, I felt obligated to give it my best shot. Gardner reported species from Neils Eddy that I had not seen in the bluff outcrops and it seemed important to verify their presence in the Waccamaw deposits at this locality.

Several hours of searching yielded only a weathered slope on the back side of the bluff that exposed sandy sediments with a few chalky fossils that seemed typical of the Waccamaw of the bluff face. We collected two bags from the small exposure, designated the site WA-6 and shoved off for home. The meaning of Gardner's anomalous species would probably forever remain a mystery.

On Tuesday morning our target was the Liston Spivey property near Old Dock, a few miles west of Lake Waccamaw. According to my Hungarian friend Istvan Ferenczi we could expect to find a recent excavation in the woods there that had cut into a Waccamaw shell unit.

For the legendary crow it was a breezy 35-mile flight from Wilmington to Old Dock; for earth-bound geologists required to follow roads that skirted the Green Swamp it was close to a 60 mile drive. It wasn't an unpleasant drive but before the day ended I had concluded that it had been a waste of time.

Instead of one large pit that exposed a full section of Waccamaw fossiliferous units, we found three isolated cleared areas where Mr. Spivey, using a bulldozer, had scooped the upper foot or two of dark soil and tan sand into low, undulating ridges. From the air it probably looked as if a big cat with diarrhea had passed through the area.

There were no exposures of shelly beds; however, the dozer had, in a few places, nicked the top of a fossiliferous bed so that a few shells had been scraped onto the ridges where they lay scattered and mixed with soil and sand.

Dutifully we numbered the three sites WA-7, WA-8, and WA-9, and at each we collected several bags of fossils from the ridges. Because none of the fossils were collected directly from Waccamaw units, their scientific value was severely limited. However, the collection did provide evidence of the Waccamaw at shallow depths beneath the surface and clues concerning the environment in which they had been deposited.

Solliday and I completed the return drive to Wilmington in relative silence. Jim had quickly clamped the earphone to his head and then had slithered down into his seat in an apparent state of semi-comatose bliss. My disappointment in Ferenczi's pit registered as a sullen funk. Had I possessed the gift of clairvoyance my mood might have been quite different.

Later that year Mr. Spivey, apparently abandoning a dream of becoming the landfill czar of Columbus County, sold the Old Dock property to the State of North Carolina, which had a keen interest in acquiring a large source of shelly sand to use in construction and repair of local highways. By June, 1962, a large pit had been opened in the woods at Old Dock. The Waccamaw was exposed to its base, which rested on the time-hardened ancient surface of the Cretaceous PeeDee Formation.

The pit had been an unexpected windfall that held the promise of vastly broadening our understanding of the Pleistocene history of the region. Aware of its potential importance my studies at the pit had commenced on the day of its discovery and continued at a high level of enthusiasm and expectation for its 16-year life span. Hell, that's longer than most marriages last these days....

On a warm, humid mid-summer morning in 1980 I left Susan and our kids at Holden Beach, where we were visiting with the maternal grandparents, and headed across the low country to Old Dock. The time had arrived, I knew, to bid a last farewell to an old and now defunct friend—the shell pit at Old Dock which had in so many ways enriched my life.

Encroachment of the woodline threatened to soon choke off the lonely old sand access road and the small remnant of the original pit left open by the quarrymen was nearly filled to its brink with ominous-looking, murky, stagnant run-off. The great sandy heaps of spoil once studded with thousands of sun-bleached shells which glistened blindingly in the merciless Carolina sun were reduced to a scattering of subdued, lonesome, rust-stained hummocks nearly obscured by a cover of sickly yellow-green weeds, straggly brush and small, scrawny trees that struggled to gain footholds in the infertile sand. Small open patches and the old service road were liberally strewn with discarded artifacts that told me Old Dock now was the domain of beer drinkers, loiterers, target shooters, fishermen, and clandestine lovers. It seemed that my old friend deserved better.

Though depressed by the fate of Old Dock, I left the car and walked to the edge of the murky pond where my mind traveled back through the years, conjuring images of the way it had been and of the people who had been here and who had shared moments of their lives with me.

A sizable slice of my life was tied to this old hole in the ground. And there was a bucket load of memories—memories of sweat and incipient heat stroke, of sitting out electrical storms and watching the pit fill with run-off, and of slipping and staggering up the wet pit banks loaded down with dripping, water-logged bags of fossils. Memories, too, of the comradeship of colleagues: Terry Wescott, Harry Hoge, Jim Howard, Henry Johnson, Jim Fowler, Larry Otwell, Nelson Garner, Gary Spicer, Blake Blackwelder, and Willard Berry, and of my drilling crew with whom I spent a memorable two weeks in 1962.

Susan worked with me at the pit and throughout the Coastal Plain from 1967 to 1981. Our daughter was two years old when she was introduced to field studies and our son Scott began his field days at age six months. During those years they each logged more hours in the field than many seasoned professional geologists. Perhaps it is not surprising that as adults neither Nicole or Scott have retained more than a casual interest in the science of geology and that each are seeking careers elsewhere.

And there were memories of young men and women of my undergraduate classes I sometimes brought here during the spring to study coastal plain geology, and there were groups of mature geologists, participants who came on field trips as members of professional societies. Old or young most would have professed that a desire to learn had brought them to the lowlands of the Carolinas, but they were equally attracted by the opportunity to escape the confines of offices and classrooms, to stretch their legs, to fill their lungs with fresh clean air, to enjoy the companionship of fellow earth scientists and to bring a small sense of adventure into their lives.

Solliday, who had come here with me twenty-two years earlier was gone now—gone since the morning of November 11, 1976. His personal life in shambles, despondent over recent twists in his professional career he had seated himself at the kitchen table in his Houston home, written a farewell note to his current mistress, then pressing a revolver to his right temple he had squeezed the trigger.

In the afternoon after Jim died his lady friend called from Houston. In a faltering, subdued voice she said, "I have bad news about Jim."

"Oh," I responded, assuming Jim had been injured in another drunken driving mishap.

"Jim is dead," she said. "Shot himself this morning at his home."

Later the initial numbing shock was replaced by a growing sense of frustration and to my surprise, an undeniable touch of anger and feelings of betrayal. "Why the hell," I pondered, "would he do such a fool thing without first talking to me? Shit, if he had called and explained his problem, we could have worked it out together. Hell, we had worked out a lot of things in the past."

Through the years Jim had been my touchstone, always there to reassure me of the reality of our shared past; the euphoria and pain, victories and defeats, hopes and disappointments, good times and bad times. Then with one swift and irreversible act he had removed himself, my chief witness to those first incredible years in the Carolina Coastal Plain.

The following day I found my anger unabated. When a lady called from the florist shop to inquire what message I wanted to put on the card with the floral arrangement we had ordered, I hesitated for only a second before blurting out, "Good-bye, Dumb Shit."

Standing there at the pit edge, gazing into 1959 I asked aloud, "Where have you gone Jimbo? Hell, didn't we have some glory days in the old swampland?

We were kings of the coastal plain!" It was then that a soft, warm breeze brushed my cheek and in passing a voice whispered, "We sure did, Big Daddy; you can hope to shit in your flat hat we did."

ANOTHER DAY

I wish I were a little rock sitting on a hill,
Doing nothing all day long,
I'd never eat,
I'd never sleep,
I'd never even play,
And when a billion years had passed
I'd say, "Another day."

By Dr. James Richards Solliday (1932-1976)

I kicked the toe of my sneaker into the mucky sand at my feet in an idle search for a surviving fossil, some tangible trace of the past. Then I remembered Istvan Ferenczi. Ferenczi was gone too. Istvan and his wife were refugees from Hungary where he had been a prominent geologist. In the U.S. during the mid-1950's he was unable to find a position compatible with his credentials. After a series of demeaning consulting jobs for which he was rarely paid, Istvan was offered a temporary teaching position in 1956 at North Carolina State University in Raleigh. Knowing that in a year or two he would be back on the street at age 68 with $103.00 a month Social Security benefits as his only income, he began or, perhaps, continued a frantic search for a more substantial and certain source of income. His efforts included research proposals to state and federal agencies, applications to petroleum companies, numerous universities and to the U.S. Geological Survey. No one wanted him.

My first encounter with Dr. Ferenczi was in 1956 when he wrote me and asked if I would assist in identification of some Caloosahatchee fossils he had found in the collections at North Carolina State. Our subsequent correspondence quickly turned to a mutual interest in the Waccamaw Formation and eventually to his bewildering personal problems.

In November 1958, Ferenczi was ill and deeply depressed. He had virtually given up all hope of employment and reported to me that suicide seemed the only solution. I responded with a list of suggestions that might help ferret out a job, and at the same time invited Ferenczi and his wife to come stay with us in Houston until his fortunes reversed.

Then I initiated a nation-wide letter campaign in which I introduced Ferenczi, briefly summarized his problems, and asked members of the geologic profession to assist me in locating employment for the man.

Perhaps encouraged by my support, Ferenczi hung in, working on several short-term, minimum wage assignments for the State of North Carolina, while continuing to conduct his own search for employment. Finally, nearly a year following introduction of my little campaign in Istvan's behalf, I received a letter from Dr. Siemon Muller, himself a Russian refugee, stating that a curatorial position in Stanford's geology department was open to Dr. Ferenczi When I responded to Dr. Muller's letter, thanking him for his very kind and considerate offer, I was able to pass along the very good news that on his own initiative Dr. Ferenczi at age 69 had succeeded in securing a permanent position with the military branch of the U.S. Geological Survey in Washington, D.C.

Istvan and I had shared a common interest, and we had shared some dark moments that had bonded us in friendship. We corresponded from 1956 until his death in the early 1970's, but regrettably we never met.

Life is a blend of memories and hopes: I was in fine fettle as I drove back to Holden Beach that day. It had occurred to me that if the future were to provide as many great moments as had Old Dock I had one hell of a lot of living yet to do.

The Ph.D. and the Peon

It was about 6:15 a.m. and we were crossing the NC 87 bridge over Cape Fear headed for Acme in northern Columbus County. On such days as this, when working outcrops from the land, it was unnecessary to pull the trailer and boat or to take time to fill the five-gallon can with gasoline for the 10 hp Evinrude. However, without exception, we loaded our cooler with ice at a gasoline station, grocery store or one of the old-fashioned icehouses that sold ice by the block.

When not pulling the trailer, some gear normally stowed in the boat was shifted to the car trunk. Jim always took care of this task, and in the three years he was with me we never arrived at an outcrop without all the equipment needed for the job.

Wednesday and Thursday we had worked one of Ferenczi's sites about twenty miles south of Wilmington in Brunswick County. It was a state highway department road metal pit that apparently was in the early stages of a shutdown process. Spoil piles were still large and fresh, pit walls were clean and vertical and much of the excavation equipment was still on site although no workmen were present. We designated the pit locality WA-10; a year or two later Walt Wheeler, University of North Carolina, referred to it as the Town Creek pit for a nearby stream and that name prevailed.

From our point of view the pit presented a few serious problems. Water was 10 to 15 feet deep and the 14 feet of nearly vertical pit wall that rose above the water level offered no secure footholds where we could stand and sample and describe the units. Height and steepness of the walls also precluded getting our Arkansas Traveler into and, most importantly, out of the water. We considered going over the side on a line, but a rope is awkward to work from and the loss of lateral mobility would have made the job of tracing individual units around the pit tedious at best.

After an hour or so of deliberation we devised a plan of action, the first step of which involved a return to Wilmington to purchase an auto tire inner tube and a cheap snorkel set. This meant that work at the pit would be delayed until the next day. Early Thursday morning we were back at WA-10 armed with the new, sophisticated scientific equipment. Smugly confident of success we were eager and ready to test the plan.

To measure, describe and sample four sections of the upper 8 to 19 feet of unfossiliferous sand we lowered ourselves over the side on lines. Working side by side as a two-man, fourhanded team, this part of the operation went fairly smoothly and was completed in about two hours.

To work the fossiliferous units below the sands we abandoned the rope technique. For this phase, I remained topside and Jim entered the water where he was suspended under the armpits by the inflated inner tube. From my vantage point I was able to direct Jim's activities, record in my notebook his verbal descriptions of the units, lower labeled sample bags to him on a line and retrieve them when they were filled. I was also in position to pass on the occasional word of advice or encouragement as well as good wishes for his well being.

Jim's role in the grand scheme was somewhat more tricky, requiring substantial physical agility and endurance and considerable patience in the face of frustration. To sample the uppermost shelly unit Jim needed to grip the Estwing hammer in his right hand and fully extend his right arm above his head. At the same time an opened sample bag held in his left hand was positioned below the hammer to catch the dislodged sediment. From his position in the water, dangling from the inner tube, it was extremely difficult to wield the hammer with either authority or anything approaching pinpoint accuracy. To catch free-falling sediment and shells in a bag that diabolically insisted on collapsing around the rim proved notably vexing. Instead of dropping neatly into the bag most of the sediment splashed into the water or cascaded into Jim's upturned, sun scorched, bewhiskered face. In time, however, accompanied by a growing crescendo of cries and curses of frustration and sundry indescribable animalistic utterances, Jim managed to fill the bags and eventually complete the upper shelly section.

As I lowered the snorkel to Jim I figured a few words of encouragement were in order. "Great job, Jim. It's fun time now; I think we got this thing knocked."

Jim's reaction was less enthusiastic than mine. Looking up at me with one of his classic, long-suffering expressions accented by his matted hair and the tiny white shell particles embedded in the creases around his eyes, he plaintively asked. "Why the fuck do I get all the shit work while you stand up there like God Almighty with his fingers up his holy ass?"

With what I hoped was a serious expression I replied, "You shouldn't be complaining; looks to me like you're having all the fun splashing around in the nice cool water while I risk a sunstroke."

Unimpressed Jim continued his lament. "You always get the good deals while I get the shit. Hell, I'm just a peon to you."

Still feigning seriousness I said, "That's because I'm a fucking Ph.D. professor and you're only a B.S. student." Continuing, with a smile now, I added, "You ought to be careful when you mention peon. When it comes to peeing on someone I'm in a hell of lot better position than you."

My attempt at humor failed dismally. "All the fucking sand and shit in the face and eyes is bad enough, but there probably are slimy leeches down here. I hate leeches—they grab hold and suck your blood and they're tough as shit to pull loose."

Jim had a tendency to be panicked by his own weird fantasies, and I recognized that this was one of those situations.

"Hell, Jim, there are no leeches down there; if there were they'd be all over you by now."

Jim responded indignantly, "How the hell do you know so much about leeches? Maybe they're like sharks and circle your ass for a while before they move in for the kill."

"Well, you're right, I don't know much about leeches but I doubt they're much like sharks. Anyway I look at it though, it would be best if you put on the damned snorkel and finish the sectioning. If you keep moving maybe they won't attack."

Now driving toward Acme I smiled to myself as I recalled that scene at the pit. Somehow it seemed particularly amusing as I looked over at Jim peacefully snoring at my side. He had finished the sectioning and no leeches had attacked him, but, according to him, it had all been sheer luck.

Wearing the snorkel Jim was able only to section and sample about three feet below water level. There was probably another 10 feet of Waccamaw below his reach that would never be seen unless the pit was one day drained.

I visited Town Creek many times during the next fifteen years and it was never drained. In 1964 I arranged to have Diamond Drilling Company drill a series of holes in southeastern North Carolina. In June when most of the drilling was to be completed it was necessary for me to be in Reno establishing Nevada residency preliminary to my anticipated divorce from Phyllis. In my absence

I placed Henry Johnson in charge of the project and hired Larry Otwell to assist him.

Two holes were drilled at the Town Creek site with the hope of learning more about the lower Waccamaw deposits that we had been unable to sample in the pit. Unfortunately recovery from each hole was very poor so in the end all I could glean from the meager evidence was that the Waccamaw at WA-10 was about 16 feet thick and that it rested directly on the hardened surface of the Cretaceous PeeDee Formation. My plan to return one day for another attempt never materialized.

Stalking the Elusive Equus

I had a special interest in the old fertilizer pit at Acme, North Carolina, so I was determined to locate it if possible. In 1931 Charles W. Berry reported his discovery at this pit of a metatarsal of a fossil horse. The bone, according to Berry, was found mixed with shallow marine Waccamaw shells, sand and clay. The metatarsal was identified by the eminent vertebrate paleontologist J.W. Gidly, who stated that it was part of the right hind foot of *Equus complicatus*, a species very closely related to, or the same as the South Florida Caloosahatchee horse, *Equus leidyi* Hay. Neither of these species of horse or any closely related species are known to have lived prior to the Pleistocene.

Berry's paper was titled "Metatarsal of *Equus* from marine Pliocene of North Carolina." Neither he nor any of the contemporary paleontologists who worked with Atlantic Coastal Plain geology seemed to regard the occurrence of a Pleistocene horse in older Pliocene sediments as a trifle odd.

When I began work on the Caloosahatchee Formation of south Florida, the unit was universally regarded as the type marine Pliocene of eastern United States. In 1953 I discovered a suite of Pleistocene vertebrate fossils, including *Equus leidyi* Hay, distributed throughout the type Caloosahatchee deposits. Because of the presence of these fossils and the absence of substantial contradictory evidence I eventually concluded that the Caloosahatchee was, indeed, a Pleistocene rather than a Pliocene formation.

I had assumed that some of my colleagues would challenge my view of the age of the Caloosahatchee, but even so, in my naïveté I could not have foreseen the intensity of the negative reaction from some quarters. When the Florida Geological Survey published my report in 1958 the "Old Guard" including C.W. Cooke, Wendall Woodring, Druid Wilson, Horace Rich-ards, Axel Olsson, and many others, especially those affiliated with the U.S. National Museum of Natural History, locked arms and in one unified, strident voice proclaimed my madness.

Fortúnately, I did not stand alone. R.C. Moore and J. Brooks Knight had earlier endorsed my conclusion, the Florida Survey immediately adopted my age classification, and, as I gradually learned, many stratigraphers employed by major oil companies agreed with me.

Unknowingly, however, I had been sucked into a vortex of controversy that I had not wanted and from which I could never escape.

From the time it was studied and named by William Healy Dall in 1892 the Waccamaw Formation had been thought to be a northern age equivalent of the Caloosahatchee Formation of south Florida. It was thus apparent to me in 1953 that if the assumption were true then reclassification of the Caloosahatchee as a Pleistocene unit dictated a similar reclassification for the Waccamaw deposits.

The question regarding the age relationship between the two units substantially contributed to my decision to take a close look at the Waccamaw Formation. Armed with a modest National Science Foundation grant (the first for the University of Houston) I was prepared in January, 1959, to invade the Carolinas.

I had no idea where to begin the search for the damned fertilizer pit. The only locality data I could glean from the literature was, "On the Butler farm near Acme," and Ferenczi's map was next to useless. Patrolling the few streets that traversed the tiny hamlet revealed no sign of excavations, old or new.

It seemed certain that the pit long ago had become overgrown with weeds and hidden in one of the small wooded areas in and around town. Julia Gardner, of the U.S. Geological Survey, had published a report on the fossils of the pit in 1943, when the town was known as Cronley, but she had neglected to publish a precise location for the site. There was little to do but to drive directly to the Butler residence and hope someone there could and would provide the needed directions.

I was never very comfortable making inquiries of local residents when in the field. Almost invariably people tended to regard rumpled, bewhiskered and dirty strangers with suspicion. Also, attempting to convince them that I was in real life a relatively harmless university professor always made me feel silly.

In this case Ferenczi had paved the way. In 1957 he had written to me that he would never have located the pit without the help of Mr. Butler and his sons. I took this to mean that the Butlers were friendly and cooperative and that they would not be put off by a friend of Dr. Istvan Ferenczi.

The Butlers lived about a mile east of Acme in a large, well-weathered two-story farmhouse, surrounded by cultivated fields and grazing plots for a few head of cattle. Gnarled, spreading live oaks close to the house offered the only protection from the sun.

With unaffected southern hospitality and congeniality we were invited by Mr. Butler's daughter, Beth, into a somewhat Victorian parlor where an elderly gray-haired gentleman, introduced to us as Mr. Butler, sat in a large wing-back chair. He gave us a friendly smile, stretched out a large bony hand and apologized for not standing.

"Been having some trouble with the old legs lately. After more than eighty years of excellent service they've kind of gone into retirement, I guess."

"No need to apologize," I said, unaware that in a few days, my own legs would dramatically announce their intention to go on a sabbatical.

The Butlers immediately recalled the visit of Ferenczi, which seemed to have been associated with pleasant memories. They had no recollection of visits by earlier geologists such as Julia Gardner and Horace Richards.

Both the old man and his matronly schoolteacher daughter appeared pleased that we thought their old fertilizer pit held some scientific value. Mr. Butler seemed embarrassed that he could not personally lead us to the site and that his sons were not present. He assured us, however, that his daughter would be able and happy to take us there.

Ms. Butler drove her Olds and we followed in the Dodge. In Acme we pulled up in front of a little two-room shanty with a rickety roof and peeling, dingy white paint. The shack sat amidst a maze of rusting wire fences that from a distance resembled pictures I had seen of World War I battlefields. Upon close inspection I saw that the fences enclosed a series of small, roughly square plots of ground that contained an assortment of farm animals. In some squares chubby little pink piglets with cute curly tails pranced about in apparent delight at the prospect of new playmates. In other enclosures adult porkers, big brutes with beady red eyeballs, glared sullenly and grunted belligerently at our passage.

As a city boy I was a bit surprised as the prim and proper school marm scurried ahead without hesitation or comment, over and around the wire entanglements and assorted critters, across a stretch of brush behind, and into a small clump of woods. I had to remind myself that this school marm was, after all, merely reverting to her roots and that her culture and apparent primness only thinly concealed the farm girl that lurked beneath.

About 50 feet into the woods we stepped out into a clearing instantly recognizable as the site of an old excavation. With outspread arms Beth exclaimed, "This is it gentlemen, the old Acme Fertilizer Company pit or at least what is left of it. As you can see there are plenty of shells. I just hope you find what you are looking for, but I'll let you determine that—I've got to get back to Father now."

Before she turned to leave I hastened to thank her for her courtesy and assured her that without her help we would never have found the site. As she was leaving I called out to her retreating back, "If we find anything of special interest we'll let you know."

Twenty-eight years after Berry's discovery the chance that we might find additional bones or teeth at the long inactive Acme pit seemed remote. However, because vertebrate fossils, especially mammalian remains, offer the greatest potential to provide accurate age estimates of the Waccamaw deposits, it was essential that we closely examine whatever outcrops and spoil material that had survived the years.

The tired old pit was small, probably 200 feet by 300 feet, and although it had not been worked in decades it was in surprisingly good condition. Slumping had covered some of the pit walls but in several places these slopes were clean and each unit penetrated in the excavation was clearly visible for study. Ms. Butler had been right, there were two densely fossiliferous Waccamaw units and the spoil piles surrounding the pit were also packed with fossils.

During the first several hours Jim and I crawled on hands and knees over the surface of the spoil piles and along the faces of the outcropping units in search of bones and teeth. Finally, frustrated, hot, and tired, I turned to Jim and said, "We might as well give it up, Jim., I think Berry found the only bone that was ever here."

A sweaty, equally tired Solliday stretched his legs and looked at me with an exaggerated, pained expression. "There must have been more of the horse; where did it go?"

"Hell, Jim," I responded. "It could be any place: trucked out and dumped with the rest of the fertilizer in some damned peanut field, picked up by one of the old paleontologists or some farm kid, or most likely it's still in the ground out there under those trees. Let's just section and describe the outcrops and get out of here. We gave it our best and that should be good enough for anyone."

Shaking his head negatively, Jim retorted, "One thing is certain, Daddyo, there is no doubt about it, you are a master at stating the obvious."

"Well fuck, man, someone needs to state the obvious and since I'm in charge the responsibility to make certain that the obvious isn't overlooked is all mine."

Broadly smiling, Jim asked, "Why the hell does anyone need to state the obvious? If it's obvious, it's obvious and shouldn't need to be stated!"

"Oh shit, Jim, grab some sample bags and a marker and let's get to work or obviously we'll never get out of this damned hole."

Though Acme had nothing more to offer in the way of old bones, our efforts there were not entirely in vain. My records show, for instance, that the collections made that day yielded 71 species of mollusks, 27 ostracode species, 47 foraminifer species, and that corals, bryozoans, barnacles and echinoids were each represented by one species.

Such data properly analyzed in combination with data analyses from many pits, outcrops and drill hole samples would eventually lead to a comprehensive understanding of the origin of the Waccamaw Formation and to its temporal and spatial relationship with the Caloosahatchee Formation and other Pliocene and Pleistocene deposits of eastern United States. After all, that was the point of the project.

Persistence finally paid off in 1972 with discovery of a varied vertebrate assemblage preserved in Waccamaw marine sediments exposed in a new pit near Calabash, North Carolina. Not unexpectedly the animals represented were very similar to those of the Caloosahatchee Formation suggesting the Pleistocene age equivalence of these two units.

With Pointed Finger

Friday evening I told Jim that we would stay at the apartment Saturday. Our work along the Cape Fear was nearly completed and we needed to pack and ship all the dried samples before heading south to Conway, South Carolina. Sunday, I figured, we'd finish our work in the area with a study of the outcrops on the north shore of Lake Waccamaw. Richards had reported Waccamaw deposits overlying outcrops of the Duplin Formation there, and we had not observed that relationship at any of the localities we had visited.

Saturday morning we went down to the garage where the boat and trailer were parked. The eight to nine hundred pounds of samples we had collected were arranged on the garage floor between the wall and the boat. Most of the samples were dry now; wet samples collected at Town Creek and those to be collected at Lake Waccamaw Sunday would be carried to Conway with us on Monday.

Usually we shipped the samples by railway freight which meant that they were en route about three weeks. In that amount of time wet samples mildew the bags, rotted labels become illegible, and the scientific value of the collections is irretrievably lost. In rare circumstances when it was necessary to ship damp samples I have used Railway Express which was much faster but also much more expensive. Even so, I had to make certain that there would be someone at the other end to check the sample bags for incipient mildew and rotting.

We had brought shipping boxes, mailing labels, tape and marking pens from Houston, but I needed a stack of newspapers to use as packing material. In 1953 I had shipped my Caloosahatchee fossils from Florida to Kansas packed in Spanish moss, but had learned since that crushed newspaper provided a cheap, readily available and effective protection against shock and crushing of fragile fossils. I was going to need a lot of newspapers, so I handed Jim a fist full of change and instructed him to drive into town and pick up at least 15 copies of a big city newspaper.

152

We had accumulated a few old papers since arriving at Wilmington so I planned to begin the packing while Jim was gone. Looking at the crowded floor I decided the first thing to do was to move the boat and trailer out into the driveway to give me room in which to work inside the garage. It was one of the simple, innocuous decisions we all make a hundred times each day, but this one permanently altered the quality of my life.

As I twisted to my left and reached down to grasp the trailer hitch my back exploded. Blinded by dazzling streaks of white light and nearly immobilized by mind-altering pain, I slumped against the gunwale of the Arkansas Traveler. I had no idea what had happened but instinctively was certain it was lethal.

When I was about 16 years old, *Life* magazine carried a photo of a wounded geologist being carried by native litter bearers somewhere in the Amazon Jungle. He was sitting upright on the litter looking straight ahead, expressionless. A spear had completely pierced his body so that about 2 or 3 feet of the shaft protruded both from his chest and his back.

Oddly, instead of being repulsed by the grotesque scene I found it particularly fascinating. It seemed to represent the essence of the excitement and adventure that I hoped one day to experience as a professional geologist. In fact, at the time I half expected the caption to read: "Hurt? Well, only when I laugh."

Holding that old *Life* photo in my mind's eye I slowly drew the palm of my right hand over my chest and stomach. Finding nothing unusual I inspected my back. It, too, was free of foreign objects and blood.

The problem, it appeared to my dazed mind, was internal rather than external; in some mysterious manner my spinal column had seriously malfunctioned.

Faced with unabated, excruciating pain, I had an irresistible urge to cry. Unwilling to do so where passersby could witness the spectacle of a grown man weeping, I inched myself along the gunwale toward a crate that sat invitingly in the shadows of the far corner of the garage.

I knew in my present state that to sit down on the crate or anything else could pose a special problem. Fortunately, I was already in an ape-like crouch, stooped at the knees and bent forward from the hips. All I needed to do was back up to the crate, position my posterior over the target and let my body drop 3 or 4 inches. Seated, I cupped my chin in the palms of my hands and, proceeding as planned, I cried. Tears of pain mixed with those of despair as I considered the possibility that we would be unable to complete the field studies.

Eventually Jim returned from town and when I turned my pain-contorted face in his direction he dropped the bundle of newspapers he had been carrying. He stared incredulously for a moment and then asked, "Jesus Christ what happened to you?"

"I'm not sure," I responded weakly. "It's my back. I tried to move the fucking trailer and it felt like my spinal cord snapped."

"Your back? Can you walk?"

"Hell, I don' t know that either, haven't tried. Maybe if you give me a hand we can make it to the car and find a hospital—I definitely need a hospital."

Jim moved near to me and put an arm around my shoulder and a hand under my armpit, then carefully pulled me semi-erect.

"You doin' okay?"

"Yeah, I guess so."

"Well, let' s try walking."

Slowly Jim half dragged me to the car. It was a memorable ordeal but couldn't compare with the pain induced when he lowered me awkwardly into the passenger seat. Still bent forward at the hips I remained motionless, mentally preparing for the jostling motion of the moving car. I remember nothing of the ride or how Jim found the hospital; I only recall sitting in a wheel chair in the emergency room of the James Walker Memorial Hospital. There were nurses and orderlies about but no Jim. Then he appeared from someplace to report that he had arranged a private room for me.

Not totally comprehending what he was saying, I asked, "How?" Why? A private room?"

"Hell, I just told them you were a mean shit and probably would kill anybody they put in with you."

His response surprised me, but I realized he knew me pretty well. *Even so*, I thought, *I'm going to need to improve a hell of a lot before I can even think of killing anyone.*

A few hours later, tucked between crisp white hospital sheets, it occurred to me that this was not exactly where I had expected to end up when I arose at 5 a.m. that morning. Painkillers and muscle relaxants administered an hour or so earlier had ameliorated both my physical pain and mental anguish. Nevertheless it still hurt like hell to move so I lay there nearly motionless, flat on my back with legs slightly bent at the knees. This was the position the orthopedic surgeon had strongly suggested I adopt.

Dr. Sheppard seemed a somewhat benign cherub type, soft and plump with chubby, rosy cheeks, watery blue eyes, graying, wavy blond hair and a thin, almost apologetic smile.

"Just lie there," he had said, "flat on your back with your legs raised slightly at the knees. In two weeks we'll examine you and determine if surgery is required." Then, with a slightly broader smile, he added, "This type of treatment is widely known as 'the magnificent nothing'."

I suppose in his way he was trying to comfort me with a touch of humor, but he failed miserably. One of the few things of which I was certain was that there was no way I would lie in bed for two weeks. I reminded myself not to trust Dr. Sheppard; I hadn't really told him who I was or why I was in Wilmington and I had no intention of doing so. No matter how charming he might be and seemingly interested in my welfare or concerned about my condition he was, after all, a surgeon. I always figured that sooner or later a surgeon would try to do what he was trained to do—whip out a blade and start carving the turkey.

If I was going to escape my prison I needed a plan. First, it was apparent that lying motionless was going to work against me. I needed to move as much as possible and especially I needed to get out of bed, try to walk, take care of bodily functions, shower, and shave so that I would not be dependent on nurses for anything. Hell, I'd even supply my own food. There was no reason Solliday couldn't bring in real food—hamburgers, shakes and candy bars. I didn't need cigars because in those days I only smoked them in the field specifically to keep Carolina gnats out of my sweaty face.

In the afternoon when Solliday visited I outlined my plan. In addition to food I asked him to bring in my copy of the GSA volume on ecology. There was no reason to just stare at the ceiling and walls. Most important was completion of the Cape Fear segment of our work. The only chores left were to section exposures on the north shore of Lake Waccamaw and to pack and ship our collections. I asked Solliday to take over both jobs immediately and to plan their completion in two days. I figured Jim, with a minimum of guidance from me, could handle the assignments. He had observed my *modus operandi* long enough to function on his own, and besides this would allow him to rise at least briefly from his role of "peon" to "honcho." It seemed to me that with a little luck we could meet our work schedule and be off to Conway by Tuesday, July 14.

The first stage of the plan went into effect when Jim arrived in the evening with the ecology text, a hamburger, chocolate malt and a stack of candy bars. I explained to him what he needed to accomplish at Lake Waccamaw and we agreed that he would go there Sunday morning to do the job. That would give him plenty of time to pack and ship the samples to Houston before Tuesday morning when he was scheduled to break me out of the hospital.

I woke at 5 a.m. on Sunday morning, determined to escape the bed and walk to the bathroom. I got a more realistic notion of how tough that might prove to be when I sat up and dangled my legs over the edge of the bed. The effort and pain involved in such an obviously simple act left me physically and mentally drained. I sat there staring off into the darkened emptiness of my room for several minutes. The next phase of the operation proved beyond my capabilities. I did manage, after several failed attempts, to slide off the bed and stand erect but at that point the nerves in my back and legs sent a message to my brain: "Take one step and you're dead."

Still determined to get to the bathroom I opted to try crawling. If I made it, I reasoned, I could pull myself erect by clutching the edge of the washbowl for support.

It was 8 or 10 feet to the bathroom, but it took me at least 10 minutes to crawl there suppressing, as I struggled along the floor, constant urges to sprawl on my face and scream like a wounded hyena. Positioning myself in front of the sink I grabbed the edge of the bowl with both hands and hoisted myself more or less erect. Now all I had to do was an about face and take 2 or 3 short steps to the john. As I stood looking numbly into the toilet bowl it occurred to me that there was no way I was going to be able to gently lower myself to the seat. Any such attempt would clearly lead to a disastrous free fall. Getting properly lowered onto that goddamned seat was crucial to my plan and it was getting more crucial by the minute. Reluctantly I returned to the sink where holding onto the bowl, I once again lowered myself to the floor. Then I rotated my aching body, and while whispering volleys of curses, crawled to the toilet, raised up on all fours and positioned my posterior over the rim of the seat. From that undignified position I was able to slip onto the seat. There for several minutes I relaxed in silent bliss. A bombardier couldn't have done a better job.

The following 30 or 40 minutes are somewhat obfuscated; I know that somehow I managed to shower and shave, then adopting a mincing, stiff-legged shuffle, I slowly negotiated the 8 or 10 feet back to the bed. Getting into the goddamned thing was a hell of a lot easier than getting out. Using the old privy reverse technique, I backed up to the side of the bed and carefully lowered my carcass to the mattress.

Exhilarated by success I rolled onto my back, picked up the GSA monograph and smugly began to read. The nurses wouldn't show up at my door for another 45 minutes.

As the day unfolded it seemed that, under the circumstances, I was feeling pretty damned carefree. At the time I assumed my mood was attributable to the early success of the escape plan. I not only felt well but had become strangely loquacious and perhaps, I speculated, a little charming. My room became the fun center of the third floor. Populated by a steady stream of nurses, orderlies, interns, doctors and stray ambulatory patients, the room hummed with sounds of chatter, laughter and general high spirits. In such an atmosphere of gaiety, festivity and pleasant confusion the ecology text Solliday had delivered to me lay on the bedside stand in a nearly pristine state. All pretense of assuming a supine position on my back was forgotten; even if I had wished I could not have laid down because at any given time 3 or 4 people lounged on the bed engaged in animated discourse.

Considering the degree of my newfound popularity, I thought, *Hell, maybe I'm really not the mean fucker that Solliday has made me out to be.*

A few days after I left the hospital when the supply of big brown pills the doctor had prescribed dried up, my euphoria and my recently discovered charm began to corrode. During the brief transition from Dr. Jekyl to Mr. Hyde I made the connection between the pills and the extraordinary personality transformation. The goddamned fag doctor had me on happy pills—narcotics. In two weeks I could have become a dope head. It was a scary thought; mind-altering pain I could deal with but mind-altering drugs (other than alcohol) were something else. That single experience with drugs left a lasting impression. When I was finally forced to submit to back surgery in 1973, I refused all medication.

On Sunday evening a freshly showered Solliday appeared in my room eager to brief me on the results of his first day alone in the field. I settled back in the bed in my most receptive posture and began to munch on the hamburger and sip on the chocolate malt he had remembered to bring with him. When Jim had finished his story and we had examined the field notes and sketches, I found myself quite pleased; Jim had done a fine job.

Jim had put the boat in at the landing and scouted the north shore of Lake Waccamaw early in the morning. Then he selected three exposures to measure, describe and sample. These we designated localities WA-14, 15, and 16. Solliday's work showed that the Waccamaw exposed along the lakeshore rested directly on a formation of sandy limestone younger than the Cretaceous PeeDee Formation.

Before Jim left I assured him that he had done well and that I was proud of him. I reminded him that he needed to pack all the dry samples stored in the garage and get them shipped to Houston on Monday. This was essential, I pointed out, because we would be leaving Wilmington on Tuesday for Conway, where I hoped to study the Type Waccamaw deposits exposed along the banks of the Waccamaw River in Horry County.

When Jim had gone I spent a little time reflecting on the geological significance of his observations at Lake Waccamaw. If he and Horace Richards were correct, the Waccamaw at the lake rested directly on the Duplin Formation. At all other localities where we had seen the base of the Waccamaw it was in direct contact with the underlying PeeDee Formation. We had not seen any evidence anywhere of the presence of Duplin rocks.

Both PeeDee and Waccamaw rocks had been laid down in oceans that had once covered the entire region. The PeeDee was deposited about 65 or 70 million years ago. Therefore, at most localities, there was a gap in the rock record between the two units of more than 60 million years. What, I asked myself, was going on around these parts during those 60 million years? It was apparent if any sediments had been deposited during that time interval they had been removed by surface processes, most likely running water. One logical explanation for their removal was that the region had been uplifted above the level of the sea by powerful forces within the crust of the earth.

The Duplin couldn't be dated precisely but it almost certainly was deposited 2 to 10 million years ago when the inner edge of the sea had inundated at least a part of the region. The Duplin at Lake Waccamaw could represent a local remnant of the formation that had somehow escaped removal by erosion. But if true that meant the area may have been uplifted and eroded twice; once after the PeeDee had been laid down, and again after the Duplin beds were deposited. How many episodes of uplift might there have been? I asked myself. Maybe the Goddamned region moves up and down like a fucking yo yo. Clearly I had few answers to the questions raised, so we were going to need a hell of a lot more facts, more data. Perhaps the study of more exposures would provide useful bits and pieces of the puzzle, but outcrops are few and far apart in the lower Coastal Plain, and pessimistically it seemed then that my quest could prove in vain. There was one thing certain, eventually we must come in here and drill a hell of a lot of 50 to 100 foot deep holes if we hoped to get the data needed to answer all the questions.

But drilling would need to wait; there was no money for that now. Before dozing off I made a mental note to go to Lake Waccamaw one day when Jim would not be with me and to look at that alleged Duplin myself. I'd never tell Jim that I had done this. He would be certain it showed a lack of faith in his judgement. I had no desire to trifle with his already fragile ego.

On Monday morning Sheppard padded into my room wearing his usual sickly smile. As he stood at the foot of the bed I realized that I really disliked the man. He was not just soft and blubbery, he was effeminate. Fat effeminate people always made me feel uneasy like esthetic pollution. But this man was worse; he was a fat, effeminate, butcher—the kind I would have expected to find in charge of the sick bay at Buchenwald.

Disregarding the fact that I was sitting up on the edge of the bed instead of lying flat on my back as ordered, he blithely proceeded with the obligatory litany of bedside bullshit: "How are you today, young fellow? Sleep well last night? Have they been feeding you well?" He didn't pause for answers and I volunteered none. Then, giving me a knowing look, he repeated his inane platitude about the magnificent nothing. By that time I had a strong inclination to barf.

As soon as I could cut into his monologue I announced firmly, "I'm leaving tomorrow morning. Feeling much better now and have things to do and places to go."

The wispy little smile melted like hot butter. "Leaving? But you, ah, you've only been here two days, you need at least a week or more of bed rest and even then you may require surgery. Surely you don't want to, ah, risk additional complications." More firmly he added, "As your doctor I must urge you not to be precipitous just because you are feeling better. A lot of that is merely the effect of the pain pills and relaxants."

"Well," I responded. "I don't like hospitals and I never was any good at laying around picking my nose, no matter how magnificent that might be, so I will be leaving."

With a look of resignation he said, "I guess if you have made up your mind there is little I can do, but in my judgment you are making a mistake. Perhaps, if you insist on leaving, you'll do me one small favor."

"Sure, why not, if I can."

"Well it's no great thing. Before you leave tomorrow would you drop by the Wilmington Orthopedic Clinic and get fitted for a back brace? A brace will give your back some needed support until it heals and it may well prevent additional damage. The things are lightweight and fit the contours snugly. I don't think you' d find wearing one much of a bother."

I pondered his suggestion for a moment or two. I wasn't very keen about being strapped into a harness. When I was about six years old I developed a groin hernia and was forced to wear a truss. I was always ashamed of that and finally when I was 16 I took it off one day, tossed it in a trash bin, and went out for the high school track team. I thought it was better to die than to wear that damned contraption one more day. I definitely didn't want to wear a back brace, but on the other hand, if it allowed me to finish the field season, maybe it was worth it. After that I could shitcan it as I had the truss.

"Okay doctor, you have a deal. If you point me in the right direction I'll stop by the place tomorrow."

With a look of relief Dr. Sheppard said, "Good. I'll call and tell them to expect you."

With that I figured our conversation had ended, however, Dr. Sheppard made no move to leave. "There's something I meant to ask you earlier. Do you have a doctorate?"

He took me by surprise with that one. "A doctorate," I repeated. "Hell, I barely made it through high school."

Looking a bit nervous now he explained, "Well, I, ah, overheard your friend call you ' Doc' a few times, that's why I asked."

Nodding my head and grinning, I responded, "Oh, that—Jim does that when he's being sarcastic. Pay no attention to him, it's sort of an inside joke."

"Ah, well, that's it then—didn't mean to pry, just had my curiosity piqued."

As I watched his back disappear into the corridor I knew he hadn't believed one damned word I'd said. But that was okay with me, it was none of his damned business.

Jim appeared in the room about 10 a.m. on Tuesday morning. According to him the car was packed and the motor turning so we could make our getaway as soon as I was officially checked out.

To placate my nurse I agreed to ride downstairs in a wheelchair, but on the ground floor I insisted on walking to the business office where I quickly discovered that, although I had forgotten the "Curse of the Cape Fear" it had not forgotten me. My hope of a routine check-out ended when the embarrassed clerk informed me that my health insurance carrier, Blue Cross, had refused to pay the in-hospital bill because the injury had occurred outside the state of Texas. When I finally regained my composure, I paid the bill in cash, and Jim and I headed for the orthopedic clinic. Walking to the car was no fun, but I did it.

Six months later, following a lengthy exchange of nasty, threatening letters, Blue Cross finally reimbursed me for the $80.00 hospital bill, but they refused to cover the cost of the brace. Happily, NSF permitted me to list the $40.00 for the brace as a field expense. Even if I had been required to assume the cost myself it would have proved one of my all time best buys. The brace worked beautifully and served me through the remainder of the summer as we completed studies of the Waccamaw River and the Neuse Estuary. During the past 30+ years it has come to my rescue many times, the most recent being a few months ago as I began to write this section. No friend has ever been so constant.

In Conway I wrote to Henry Johnson recounting the events of the previous few weeks and updating him on our plans for the remainder of the season. I vividly recall the last line of that letter, "With my pointed finger and Jim's strong back, we will complete the studies as scheduled."

The Loose End

Shortly after my arrival in Houston from Carbondale in 1957 I learned of a departmental museum located somewhere on the third floor. I was told, usually with a wry smirk, that the curator was a curious old codger by the name of Asa L. Mathews. Although no one actually made any derogatory comments about the quality of the museum I was left with the impression that most didn't regard it worth a climb up the stairs to the third floor.

Nevertheless, the presence of a museum close at hand was of interest to me because I thought there was a possibility I might be able to use some of the displays and collections as teaching aids for my physical geology and paleontology courses. Eventually I found a free hour to visit the mysterious Asa Mathews. But first I needed directions to the damned museum. A quick trip to Wang's office diagonally across the hall, I thought, would just about do it.

When I tapped on John's partly opened door, he looked up, smiled and motioned me to enter. "All I need, John," I said, "are directions to the departmental museum. Thought I'd drop by and take a quick look and meet Mathews."

"Ah, so," Wang responded, the smile fading a bit, "You want to visit with old Asa? That would be a waste of your time you know. No one ever goes up there. Old Asa is senile. If he traps you in his den you'll have to listen to nonsense for hours. He goes around in some sort of fog all the time—never has any idea what he's doing or saying."

He had turned in his swivel chair toward me then and the smile had entirely faded. "You know, confidentially, that is, that so-called museum is a mess, just a pile of junk. Complete waste of valuable space. One of Henryk Stenzel's brainstorms you know." Then with a sly, conspiratorial smile... "Stenzel and Mathews were two of a kind."

I had only asked for directions so had not been prepared for such a vitriolic diatribe. "Well, ah, er," I stammered. "I didn't realize it was all that bad. Had a little time so figured just to pop up there. Can't do any harm, just to take a peek."

Wang shrugged. "Okay, Jules, suit yourself, but you'll see what I mean. Just go up those stairs down the hall there and then take a right at the top. It's way down at the far end."

The upstairs hall was dark except for the yellow glow of a low-wattage bulb in the distance that, I presumed, marked the entrance to the museum. I had the feeling of having just stepped inside one of the spook houses at an amusement park, but I made it to the door beneath the yellow light without a ghostly encounter. The room inside was a black hole; in a few seconds I located the switch on the inside wall. It worked.

It was a small room only about 20 by 30 feet, but it was clearly the display room. Two casket-like glass display cases stood in the middle of the floor and three-tiered shallow wooden shelving hugged two of the walls. The cases were nearly empty and much of the shelf space covered only with dust.

Two minutes of close inspection of the displays on the shelves served to demonstrate that Wang was wrong on one score—this stuff wasn't junk. The displays were clearly the work of a skilled craftsman. Even more, they bore unmistakable touches of artistry and loving care. The man responsible for this work was surely not incompetent. Stunning mineral crystals and elegant fossils were artistically and delicately balanced on glistening, clear, freeform plastic mounts accompanied by attractive and informative labels.

There was no sign that Mathews had been around lately, so I decided to return another day to visit with him. But just then I noticed the door at the far end of the room. A workshop? Perhaps Asa was inside putting together a new display. Curiosity won the day and I opened the door. Another black hole, another wall switch. Asa wasn't at home. It was a workroom all right—a storage room as well, but to the unpracticed eye it could just as well have been merely a cluttered closet.

A small, forlorn, pea-green table stood in the midst of the cramped quarters; a rickety, dingy, beige wooden chair lurked behind it. There could be no doubt, this was Mathews' command post. The table was strewn with the familiar accouterments of the old-time curators. A battered gooseneck lamp hovered over an assortment of essential tools and supplies: an old hand-held magnifier, two crumpled tubes of glue, a can of shellac, two small camel hair brushes, a 100 ml beaker, paint thinner, several small cans of paint, a cluster of assorted probes and dental tools, a variety of plastic mounts, dozens of blank cardboard labels, a bottle of India ink, and several pens and pencils. I looked in vain for a small pocketknife before realizing it would be in Asa's pants pocket. No ashtrays or scattered ashes—not a smoker, unusual for old-time geologists. One might have expected a pipe.

An old, faded yellow, straw broom leaned dejectedly against one end of the table, a battered, rusty dust pan lay on the floor beneath the table next to a large tin can that appeared to serve as a waste receptacle. Apparently not even the janitors dared invade this inner sanctum.

A rough-hewn but sturdy work bench stood defiantly against one pallid wall, its surface submerged beneath dusty, bulging boxes and assorted containers of mineral and fossil specimens. More pregnant and battered cartons were shoved beneath the bench and along the other walls.

A visitor wishing to sit had the choice of one of the few uncluttered floor spaces or a very low, mean-spirited looking three-legged brown stool. Tentatively seating myself on the little monster I found my chin precisely level with the top of the table. From that position Mathews, even if a dwarf, could sit in his chair and assume the role of a stern grandfather towering over a cowering grandson who had just wet his pants. I decided that if I did eventually meet Mathews here I would remain standing at all times.

Browsing through some of the boxes on the bench I soon discovered some interesting things. The collections, though dusty, were carefully labeled so that with a little care and patience it was possible to determine the identity and origin of the contents of each box. One box contained a batch of fossils originally described by R. C. Moore and Frank Plummer. These were type specimens (new to science) which probably should have been at the U.S. National Museum of Natural History. Then I made the big discovery—a collection of Devonian fossils from the Falls of the Ohio, identified and labeled in the handwriting of James Hall, the "Father of American Paleontology." A collection lost, I suspect, since the last century. I could only wonder how it had found its way to Mathews' cramped quarters. Asa was old, I knew, but surely he had never worked with James Hall.

This was all heady stuff for me—the room seemed to reek with the history of my science. Where the hell was the "junk" Wang had told me I would find?

Wang had been right on one count; no one ever visited the place. Even Bill Berry, our bright young paleontologist, student of the renowned Carl Dunbar, told me he had little interest in "whatever trash might be up there in the attic." I could understand his attitude, Bill had, after all, done his doctoral studies at Yale's great Peabody Museum.

I didn't meet Asa Mathews for several weeks following that first clandestine invasion of his laboratory.

My recollection of Mathews has dimmed in the thirty years since we first spoke. Even then I was not certain of his age, but he had to have been on the long side of eighty. I was aware that he had published research papers on marine Triassic fossils of western United States before I was born. Whatever his chronological age, he had been around for a while—a fossil among fossils. As I reach into the recesses of my memory and sort through faded images, I see a man thin, bent, and brittle, who walked slowly with calculated deliberation. I see a small head with sprouts of wispy hair, white and sparse; a diminutive aquiline nose set firmly between sunken cheeks of a skeletal face; and pale blue eyes which stared always beyond me into some other place and time. I know that he spoke softly but distinctly; however, if he called out to me from his grave today I would not recognize the voice.

When I visited with Mathews he invariably deserted his worktable to show me the results of his most recent efforts. New displays were appearing on the museum shelves with regularity and a few had made their way into one of the glass coffins.

With obvious pride he showed me the new exhibits and explained each in elaborate detail. Then he would turn to the items in progress and tell me the reasons for his choices, his plans for them, the intricacies of achieving a certain artistic effect, and the importance of proper placement on a shelf or in a cabinet. It never seemed to occur to him that virtually no one cared, that hardly anyone would see any of his work. He seemed to do it all for himself, for the sheer joy of it. In a way I suppose it was a futile exercise in self-gratification.

Removed from any need to contribute to the conversations I had plenty of time to observe and contemplate the man as well as his work. At no time did Mathews seek or seem mildly interested in my advice or observations. His "conversation" was a stream-of-consciousness triggered by my presence— a warm mannequin would have served him equally well.

The only things real and certain to Mathews seemed to be the fossils and minerals in his tiny workshop: the specimens he fussed over, cleaning, shellacking, gluing, brushing and polishing, the specimens he lovingly and adroitly positioned on clear plastic mounts with elegant multi-colored labels that succinctly stated the age, geographic origin, biologic affinities or mineral composition. All of these things he knew and remembered even when he had forgotten what he had eaten for breakfast or if indeed there had been a breakfast.

For Mathews his shabby little workshop was a safe house, a cocoon of reverie, a shelter from the distractions and confusion of the alien world about him. His fossils and minerals represented a fragile thread which linked him to his roots and provided the substance of his waning life. Then it had been morning, bright and clear, filled with hopes, dreams and great expectations born of youthful naïveté. He had been prepared to step forward then and face the challenges of life with bold resolution and boundless energy. But now night had blurred and all but obliterated the visions of the morning. His life had been, after all, just one long day which would soon draw to a quiet close.

The passage of time had left Mathews with a myriad of unordered memory shards which flashed rapidly, brilliantly and then extinguished as so many fireflies on a warm summer night.

In his waking hours and in his dreams, difficult at times for him to separate, broken and blurred memories danced tantalizingly before his aged eyes. There were moments when, in impressive detail, he recalled events, adventures, intrigues, times and places. At other times he saw the faces of colleagues, mostly gone now, and he remembered names, but it was hard for him to match the faces with the names.

And there were women from the misty past and just yesterday. His wife, a girlfriend, a clerk at a pharmacy, a nurse who had cared for him at some long-forgotten hospital, his sister, his mother, his landlady at the apartment where he lived, his sixth grade teacher and the check-out girl at the supermarket.

But he confused his wife with the clerk, his sister with the nurse, his landlady with his mother and his sixth grade teacher with the checkout girl. And then he would remember suddenly that it was all nonsense—all these women were dead now, or were they?

When I was with Asa in his little room he quietly spoke of his collections and displays in progress. But when he descended from his den on the third floor to visit faculty offices he was invariably consumed with a particular political or social predicament he regarded as threatening or in some aspect outrageous. These conversations were characteristically animated monologues which directed the eye of his victim to the nearest clock.

In succeeding months Wang intensified his efforts to discredit Mathews and to ridicule the museum. In this endeavor he was enthusiastically abetted by his perennial co-conspirator Mary Pope. Implementation of the plot was considerably enhanced when the fly inadvertently blundered into the spider's carefully woven web.

I first became suspicious that Mathews may have exceeded the bounds of conventionally accepted reality the day he toddled down the stairs from the third floor wearing a surgical mask. As he eagerly explained to those of us polite enough to listen, World War III was imminent and we all could expect to be nuked at any moment by the Russians. Our only hope for survival was to follow Asa's example and don a surgical mask until the danger had passed. If, indeed, missiles were launched it was reassuring to know the gauze would protect us from the harmful effects of nuclear radiation.

I asked Asa if it wouldn't be sufficient just to carry the mask in a pocket. "When the sirens sound the alert," I said with a hopeful smile, "we could whip it out like a gas mask and slip it over our mouth."

"Too risky," he replied thoughtfully. "One might not hear the siren or the siren might malfunction. No it's best that it be kept on at all times. One whiff of the stuff and you're dead, you know."

"But what about eating?" I protested. "Surely one could remove it then."

"Not necessary," he replied. "Do as I do—eat only liquids: milk, broth, that sort of thing. A straw slipped under the mask works quite well."

Listening to Mathew's muffled reasoning, I began to imagine the reactions of our students when we all appeared in class looking like clones of Dr. Kildare ready to demonstrate the latest procedure in the removal of a diseased gall bladder. Actually, I thought, it could be exactly what we needed to add a little zip to our otherwise boring lectures.

"Yes, of course," I said. "But it does seem a bit of a bother."

Asa looked at me with his best expression of pity. "Wearing one of these masks for a few weeks seems a small enough price when one's life hangs in the balance."

Put that way, I had to admit he had a point. "But what if there is no attack after a few weeks—do we continue to wear the things indefinitely?"

"Hell, man" he retorted with surprising vigor. "It could happen any moment. Get a mask now. I don't think there is time to waste. Drop everything and get one today. You hear?"

Following that somewhat bizarre conversation I was forced to admit that perhaps the time had arrived to consider finding a replacement for Asa. Even so, I was still not prepared to share my conclusion with John Wang.

For the next two weeks Asa, attired in his white mask, made repeated sorties to the second floor to spread the word that civilization as he had come to know it would soon end. Whenever one of us spotted him painfully and, fortunately for us, slowly negotiating the stairs from the third floor, we sounded the alarm, "The Lone Ranger is coming, the Lone Ranger is coming!"

In seconds the corridors reverberated with the sounds of slamming doors and a moment later the halls were deserted and the offices dark and still.

I not only switched off the light in my outer office but also retreated to my inner office and remained there working on pressing chores until someone sounded the "all clear" or I was forced to sneak out to a classroom to deliver a lecture.

During this period when all of us were preoccupied with efforts to avoid Mathews he had conceived a special fossil display—his *piece de resistance*. So proud of it and so certain that it would prove to be the recipient of universal admiration, he resolved to house it in a glass display cabinet located in the main second floor corridor where it would be seen by the faculty, visitors and hundreds of students each day.

I was mildly surprised one morning to discover Wang and Frank Barber at my office door. Wang's round face was locked in a broad smile and that surprised me even more. It also sent a tingle down my spine. I was well aware that the kinds of things that made John smile broadly were pretty scary to those of us who knew him best.

"Got a couple of minutes, Jules?" Wang inquired.

"Well, ah, I guess so," I responded cautiously. "What's up?"

"Have you seen Mathews' latest display in the hall cabinet?"

"No I haven't—didn't think he ever displayed anything down here."

"Well, he has now, and we'd like your reaction to it."

Bob Greenwood and two or three graduate students standing by the case moved aside to allow me a closer view of the display. At first glance I saw only a very artistically displayed Cretaceous ammonite (an extinct ancestor of the living Chambered Nautilus). By any measure it was an extraordinary specimen. I had heard of such discoveries but this was the first I had seen. It was easy to understand Mathews' pride in his achievement.

The shell exhibited two quite different growth stages in the animal's development. Initially in the youthful growth stage the tubular shell had coiled tightly in a plane like a piece of rope. Then as the animal reached maturity it suddenly decided to secrete a very straight shaft-like section six or seven inches in length. The fully completed shell had the look of one of those coiled paper birthday favors with a whistle attached at the open end. When a kid blows into the thing the paper rapidly uncoils and then as the air escapes the whistle emits a sound reminiscent of an anguished groundhog. Partly uncoiled those favors look just about like Mathews' beast.

As I stared into the case I recalled Wang's ominous grin and realized he had not summoned me here to admire the specimen. Obviously he and the smirking group gathered nearby had discovered something about the display that was not right, something I had, so far, missed. Puzzled, I bent forward and examined the specimen and the label more critically. Then I saw it.

The damned thing was an artifact of Mathews' imagination! He had skillfully fitted the coiled part of one Cretaceous ammonite species to the straight segment of an entirely unrelated species. The disturbing part was that his label was worded to indicate that the specimen represented the complete shell of a single ammonite individual. Forthcoming explanations for what Mathews had done were bound to be wrapped around such key words as "deceit", "fraud," "incompetence" and "senility." The latter seemed most appropriate to me.

With the episode of the surgical mask and now the hybridized ammonite Mathews had succeeded in making Wang's case. There was little I could do but publicly concede that the time for Asa's retirement had arrived. Even so, I assumed that the changeover wouldn't take place until the end of the fiscal year. Once again I had underestimated John Wang.

A few weeks following the ammonite debacle it was necessary for me to leave town for a week to attend a professional meeting. When I returned early on a Monday morning, Bob Greenwood met me at my office door. He gave me a thin, weak smile and, stammering, inquired how the meeting had gone. Yellow caution lights immediately began to flash inside my head. Bob only stammered when he had bad news to relate or when a big-boobed coed passed by his office. The hall was empty—not even a flat chested girl in sight, so it had to be bad news.

Assuming he would unload on me in due course I responded to his question. "Well, it was the usual thing. The meeting room for the paleontology-stratigraphy session was changed at the last minute; the only available projection screen was smaller than the one I have at home and worse, my talk was built around the assurance there would be two screens. Then the damned room was bare-assed empty so the speakers had to scrounge all over the hotel to find two hundred folding chairs which we were obliged to carry to the room and set up. During my talk the projectionist got some of my slides out of order and half of them upside down or sideways. All in all I'd say that as these meetings go it was about par for course. Every year I vow never to give another talk or attend another technical session; just stay drunk until the post-convention field trip. Incidentally this year's trip was great."

Bob's eyes had glazed over; he hadn't heard a word of my diatribe. His mind was locked into whatever it was he didn't want to tell me—something I suspected I really didn't want to know. Against my better judgement, however, I asked what had gone on in my absence.

"Well, ah," he replied. "M... M... Mathews is gone."

"Gone!" I gasped. "You mean he's dead?"

"Well, not that, but professionally, perhaps. W... W... Wang f... f... fired him after, after y... y... you left for Colorado."

"I can't say that is a complete surprise," I responded. "But I had hoped Wang would have waited until August or at least June. Has Wang mentioned a replacement?"

Bob seemed startled by the word "replacement". "No, no he didn't actually. I don't think there will be a replacement—not really n... n... necessary."

Puzzled I asked, "What do you mean by that Bob?"

"Well, ah, Wang sent wor... workmen up to the m... m... museum to remodel the pl... pl... place just after you left town. I think it's g... g... going to be a... a... an office."

Now I began to stammer. "An off... office? Wh... what about the collections, the displays? Some of that's damned g... good stuff! What are we supposed to do with that?"

He looked at me, seemingly completely shattered. "That's the tough part, Jules. I... I... don't th... think we need give that much thought. The wor... wor... work crew made quite a m... m... mess up there—W... w... walked all over everything, sc... sc... scattered it all. Actually, I... I don't think there's much left to save. Maybe it's best you don't even g... g... go up there. You won't like what you see."

As soon as I could dump my briefcase on my deck I bolted down the hall and up the stairs to the museum. The adrenaline flowed freely. Sweeping the room my eyes transmitted scenes of destruction and devastation that my brain feverishly attempted to reject. Nothing of the order, the symmetry or beauty created by Mathews remained. As I struggled for a rational explanation of the chaos that lay before me, I knew intuitively none could exist. The room was strewn with the shattered remains of a man's life, violated, trampled, dirtied, discarded. Crushed remains of exquisite mineral crystals and fossil specimens, shattered and splintered plastic mounts and crumpled labels were strewn across the museum floor and display shelves and discarded, along with the workmen's debris, in a variety of makeshift waste receptacles.

In a semi-daze, I knelt to the floor, idly picked up two fossils fragments and fumblingly attempted to fit them together until I realized they were pieces of two different specimens. In anger and frustration I tossed the pieces aside, knowing that everything was lost—that nothing would ever again fit together. With tears welling in my eyes and a killing rage surging through my body I called out to the silent walls, "What kind of person could have done this?"

Eventually I pulled myself upright and carefully picked my way through the debris to Mathews' workshop. I still clung to a flickering hope that the collections had been spared. But when I flipped the wall switch I knew that nothing had survived.

Everything—the James Hall collection, the Moore-Plummer type fossils, all of it had been scattered over the floor and the surfaces of the work bench where both fossils and labels had been trampled by heavy-footed workmen. Some specimens had escaped unharmed, but separated from their identifying labels their scientific and historic value had been irretrievably lost.

Sweating and breathing deeply I leaned against the wall bench where I hoped to regain my composure. It was then I noticed the little stool which had somehow survived the holocaust. It crouched warily beside the rusty, abandoned dustbin beneath Mathews' worktable. Rumpled and tattered it retained something of its usual malevolent expression of defiance. Even in its shadowy retreat it managed to convey an impression of a wounded, three-legged pit terrier which might at any moment sally forth, neck hairs bristling, fangs bared in one last kamikaze attack to avenge its vanquished master. I could only hope that it would remember that I had been Mathews' friend.

When it seemed I had capped my emotions, especially the impulse to kill, I decided it was time to visit with John Wang. I figured he owed me an explanation for what had occurred and I wanted his assurance that the guilty parties would be held accountable.

A few moments later I was at Wang's door. He was in his usual slot behind his desk fumbling with a stack of exam papers. When he saw me he smiled and waved me in. Then he began to ask about the Denver meeting, but I unceremoniously cut him off.

"I was just upstairs, John, the museum is a disaster. Looks as if a bomb went off in there. What the hell happened? Who were the sons of bitches who did that?"

A veil of saintly concern descended over his cherubic face, but somehow the expression in his eyes seemed to deny his words. "Ah, yes, Jules. I intended to discuss all that with you at the first opportunity. Terrible thing, isn't it? And a damned shame, too. Those workmen were just inexcusably thoughtless and careless. Somehow," he said, with a perplexed expression, "they got the idea that all that stuff in there was to be discarded anyway."

"Why would they think that?" I demanded. "They should be fired, or sued, or better, they should be drawn and quartered."

"I know, I know," he consoled. "No accounting for some people. But the union, you know, the university must be careful with those fellows. Can't chance a strike. They'll do that you know." Then in a confidential tone he added, "It's all to late, *fait accompli*, you know. Damned shame but that's it. Most of those things Mathews had up there were worthless. That ammonite display was typical. Can't have that sort of thing giving the department and the university a bad name."

As he spoke I knew the subject of the museum and of Asa Mathews was a closed matter. I also knew that Wang had somehow engineered it all.

Enveloped in a sense of abject defeat I dejectedly returned to my office. For several weeks in the sanctuary of my office or while driving the Gulf Freeway to and from my home in southeast Houston, I tried to make some sense of what had happened. Unfortunately, to do that probably required that one understand how Wang's mind worked, something I regarded as impossible. Still, I felt compelled to determine what had so highly motivated Wang to rid the department and apparently himself of both Mathews and the museum. I never discovered the answers to the questions, but it seemed reasonable to assume that it had much, perhaps everything to do with his knowledge that the museum had been Stenzel's baby and that Mathews had been hired by Henryk. Under those circumstances Mathews had lingered in the department as a loose end, an unwanted leftover and a gnawing reminder of the Stenzel regime.

Wang, the master manipulator of others' lives, had to first discredit the man and his work and then erase all trace of his existence in the department by obliterating the museum and its contents. It was, I learned in time, the standard *modus operandi* John Wang used many times with breathtaking success. With the widespread negative reaction of the geologic profession (especially among the major oil companies) to the way in which Stenzel had been driven from the university, Wang probably had decided to bide his time, consolidate his power base as department chairman and then wait until things had cooled down a bit. Alone, old, completely vulnerable, Mathews represented no immediate threat to Wang or to his plans. Wang could deal with Asa at his leisure.

For more than a year Wang had pursued his insidious campaign against Mathews. In that time he had convinced all of the geology staff, except me, that Mathews should be retired. I had remained the fly in Wang's soup until Mathews himself rendered my support for him null and void.

I was not alone, though, in the belief that a museum was an asset to the department. However, Wang's willful destruction of the displays and collections had rendered further discussion of the subject an exercise in futility.

When renovation of the old museum was completed Wang, who always seemed to be at least one step ahead of everyone, caught me off balance yet again. He suggested to my amazement and delight, that I might wish to move some of my research activities up to the third floor. That I was about to be ensnared in another Wang intrigue I didn't doubt. It was unthinkable that this could be an honest expression of good will and friendship, but perhaps I was suffering from an advanced case of paranoia.

It occurred to me that by accepting his offer it might appear a payoff for some clandestine role I had played in a conspiracy with Wang to subvert Mathews. It was also possible that, aware of my close ties with several of the major oil companies in Houston, Wang was simply attempting to placate me and to purchase my silence.

There was an aspect of Wang that at times caused me to regard him as an unsavory Chinese version of the wily old mongoose, Archie Moore. They both struck when it was least expected and they were equally deadly. If it were another of Wang's cons, he had baited the hook most cunningly. I needed the workspace desperately and could ill-afford the luxury of critically looking a gift horse in the mouth. Accordingly, I wasted no time in asking two of my graduate students, Don Taylor (later to become executive vice president of exploration for Tenneco) and Don Beardsley, to occupy the space immediately.

The two Dons were working on Masters' theses under my direction. Their projects were closely related biostratigraphic studies of Pliocene deposits in the Florida Panhandle. It was important that they coordinate their efforts, a task made much easier in a shared workspace. Of course, under such an arrangement my supervision of their work was appreciably facilitated.

In the new quarters work on the Florida Panhandle projects proceeded smoothly and both Taylor and Beardsley had completed most of the laboratory analyses and were well into the more tedious writing stage when Wang's machinations took another baffling twist. He informed me one morning as I arrived at my office that he had deeded our research quarters to the chemistry department and, he added (with humble apologies, of course) that we would be required to vacate within two weeks.

Some of my lingering questions concerning the Mathews affair were resolved when in a few weeks, following the close of the semester, the chemistry department converted our former research quarters (Mathews' museum) into office space for Mrs. John Wang, professor of chemistry. The eradication of Asa Mathews was at last complete.

Hot Chili

When Jim Solliday and I headed for the field in June 1961, my 1959-61 NSF funding was beginning to play out. I had concluded that if we could manage a reasonable degree of frugality enough money remained to keep us afloat until the new grant went into effect sometime in July. I had proposed a study of the geologic relationships among the Pleistocene terraces and shorelines of the Carolinas. Before we left Houston, Richard Benson at NSF had assured me that the proposal would be funded in the amount of $25,000. This time there would be money for food and shelter as well as science. The project would involve expansion of our earlier and current work on the Waccamaw and Croatan formations to include all younger Pleistocene deposits of the region.

The best and most extensively uninterrupted exposures of Post-Waccamaw sediments occur along a 35-mile stretch of the Intracoastal waterway in Horry County, South Carolina. It was there we planned to concentrate our efforts in 1961.

For areas inland from the waterway, where exposures are rare and of poor quality, we would use our butt-busting, hand-powered orchard auger to sample to depths of 16 feet, and, when available, the DOG truck-mounted power auger for deeper (down to 110 feet) drilling.

Before we settled into the Carolina swamplands for the summer we would dip into Florida for a few days. I needed to look at upper Caloosahatchee units exposed along the Caloosahatchee River and to make collections at several localities in the east-central part of the state which I suspected included time-equivalent deposits of the Waccamaw and Caloosahatchee formations.

On the way south we made a four-hour stop at Jackson Bluff in the eastern Florida Panhandle. One of my students, Don Taylor, was finishing a Master's thesis on the Pliocene shell beds exposed in the bluff and his research had alerted me to several interesting stratigraphic possibilities I wished to field check.

Following close encounters with heat stroke at Jackson Bluff, we drove on to Tallahassee where I planned to visit with my friend Harbans Puri, a geologist with the Florida Geological Survey. I had brought along a bottle of Black Label for Harbans, but when we discovered he was out of town, Jim and I retired to a local motel, broke open the bottle, and spent several hours toasting his good health.

The next morning we drove to Ft. Meyers, where we checked into a motel late in the afternoon. My plan was to run the Caloosahatchee to Ortona Lock the next day, a round trip of about 110 miles. To accomplish this we would need to have the Arkansas Traveler in the water at Ft. Meyers dock before dawn. Under the circumstances it seemed a rational idea to hit a nearby burger joint and turn in early. At least that seemed rational before Jim came up with the idea of going into town for chili.

"Hell man," I said. "I think you just saved us from a restful but intolerably boring evening. Let's grab a couple of showers and strike the fucking pavement."

We drove around town for 15 or 20 minutes before Jim spotted a place he declared had a truly sincere hot chili look.

"Looks fine to me," I said. "But remember, it's your call."

Planted on wooden stools and hunched over the counter, we were soon enveloped in a heavy aroma steaming from two bowls of chili and contently sipping on two frosty Millers.

Cautiously I sampled the contents of my bowl. Not bad, should please Jim, but a tad fiery for me. Then abruptly Jim began to emit a series of incoherent sputtering sounds. "What's that?" I asked. "I believe you're trying to tell me something. I suppose you want to say how tasty the chili is, but you shouldn't talk with your mouth full."

With difficultly Jim managed to swallow, but then broke into a series of gagging coughs. When he had washed out his mouth with a half a glass of beer he turned his attention to me. "Tasty," he challenged. "If you think this crap is good you know nothing about chili. This candy-assed shit has about as much punch as anteater piss."

"Tell me how often you drink anteater piss."

"Oh shit, never mind the sarcasm. Let's get out of here and find a place that serves the real stuff—something with a little zing to it."

An hour and a half and four bowls of "candy-assed" chili later, my stomach was a seething, bloated magma chamber and I'd sworn off chili forever. But not Jim—he was prepared to pursue his quest for the perfect chili though it led us to the bowels of Hades. What he needed, I thought was a bowl of paint remover.

At the sixth establishment I watched with little more than detached interest as Jim sampled his latest candidate for the chili hall of fame. The first spoonful was rolled over his tongue several times, savored and finally swallowed. To my relief he didn't gag, he didn't spit it onto the counter. His eyelids dropped to half-mast, a soft sigh escaped his parted lips. Then, tossing his head back he said in a bare whisper, "This is it. I told you they know how to make chili in this town."

"Well I suppose one out of six isn't bad," I commented.

"Oh hell, there you go with your sarcasm again. Remember that we are new in town; we should have asked around."

I didn't doubt that the chili deserved Jim's approval, but it occurred to me that the two attractive young ladies he had spotted at the opposite end of the bar may have added as much zest to the stuff as had the chef. I wasn't surprised when Jim, having cleaned his bowl, excused himself and joined the women.

Assuming I had seen the last of him for a while I moved to a seat beside the only other customer at the bar, a sour-faced, middle-aged guy in a plaid sport shirt, blue jeans and sneakers, who looked as if he needed a little excitement in his life. Even if he didn't, I certainly did. I figured if I goaded the guy for a while he might take a swing at me. Then, in self-defense before witnesses, I could disembowel him. Four bowls of chili and more booze than I needed had definitely put me in a mean mood.

Luck was with me; the guy was a hapless, long-suffering SOB, who endured my insults without a word of protest. He just sat there, hypnotized, drank his beer and ignored me. In time I gave up on him, moved to a different stool, and sulked in my brew.

At about eleven one of Jim's women, a pert brunette, stood up beside her stool and announced with firm conviction that it was time to go home. Her blonde friend stood then and both of them scooped up their cigarettes, lighter, loose change and unceremoniously dumped the stuff into their purses. Swiftly and resolutely they moved across the room to the door, where they paused for a moment to bid us all a cheery goodnight.

Jim was still on his stool at the end of the bar, gloomily toying with a mixed drink, when the blonde came back into the room and called out, "Could one of you men give us a hand? Our car refuses to start."

With surprising agility the mute I had been harassing leaped to his feet and moved toward the door. "Don't worry, young lady, I'll see what can be done. I'm pretty handy with cars." As he and the woman disappeared though the door, Solliday followed in hot pursuit.

Unneeded outside, my first impulse was to wait at the bar until Jim returned. Then recalling our pre-dawn date with the Ft. Meyers boat dock, I decided it would be sensible to pack it in for the night.

In the parking lot the car was purring contentedly, and the ladies were inside the vehicle exchanging parting pleasantries with their two heroes. When the brunette, seated on the passenger side, noticed me standing outside the café, she smiled, waved, and called me to the car. When I walked over and leaned down to look onto the open window she threw an arm around my neck, drew me to her, and planted a large wet kiss on my mouth.

"I'm free tomorrow evening," she said seductively. "Why don't you give me a call tomorrow?" She jotted a number on a small scrap of paper and handed it to me. As the car began to slowly pull away she called out, "Just ask for Sally."

I gave her a weak smile, a noncommittal nod, and then watched in perplexed silence as the car faded into the darkness. I began to crumple the little piece of paper in my hand, thought better of it, and folded and tucked it into my shirt pocket. No harm in giving her a call from LaBelle in the morning.

We began our run up the Caloosahatchee in the darkness of the early morning as scheduled. At LaBelle we tied up at the little wooden dock long enough for me to walk to the pay phone at the drugstore. I didn't need to ask for Sally, she answered the phone. In less than a minute I had agreed to pick her up at her house at eight and take her to a movie. With customary caution I had identified myself as Don Taylor.

The river trip had taken longer than anticipated. By the time I had showered, dressed, and grabbed a meal of stale crackers and fuzzy green cheese which had lurked on the back seat of the car for two days, it was seven-thirty.

Fortunately I was able to follow Sally's directions and found the house with a couple of minutes to spare. It was in a modest, lower middle class development. Several cars were parked in the driveway and along the curb in front of the house, so I parked half a block down the street. On the way to the house I wondered if Sally had arranged a surprise party for me.

She must have been watching from a window because she met me at the door as I stepped onto the small front porch. In the foyer she whispered that the house belonged to her brother and his wife, and that she was just a temporary houseguest. Placing a hand on my elbow she guided me to the rear of the house. "I want you to meet everybody; we're having a Tupperware party in the kitchen."

With the mention of Tupperware I had a sudden upwelling of misgivings. I had a long-standing aversion to things like Tupperware parties, and particularly to the types of people who usually attend such events.

Sally must have read my mind or face. "Oh don't be grumpy! It'll be over soon and then we can leave for the movie."

The kitchen, as I had feared, was packed with chattering, frumpy, fuzzy-haired, lumpy housewives weighed down under burdens of glittering, cheap costume jewelry and layers of caked make-up. The only man sat at the kitchen table. Sweaty, fat, wearing a sleeveless undershirt, two days growth of whiskers, and a look of haggard bewilderment, he was clearly out of his element. He had, I assumed, been hijacked for the occasion by his wife.

When he saw us he stood up, exposing, as he did, an impressive beer belly which oozed forward from under his belt onto the table. He stretched a flabby, hairy arm in my direction. "Bob Fultz," he announced. "Sally's big brother. I guess you must be Don Taylor. Gonna take my little sister to a movie, eh?" Without waiting for an answer and still gripping my hand in his sweaty paw, he pointed his left forefinger in the direction of a chubby, bleached blonde leaning against the gas range. "That there's the missus. Mary, this here's Don Taylor, come to take Sally to the movies."

Mary gave me a girlish giggle and a limp hand wave. "Pleased to make your acquaintance, Don. Take a load off and get acquainted with the girls."

There were no unoccupied chairs in sight, but in a flash Sally dragged one from behind a couple of fat women and shoved it toward me. I sat down, a limp lump, resigned to my fate.

The chatter level quickly tapered off a few moments later and all eyes turned to the head of the table where a large, raw-boned, horsy brunette stood commandingly clutching a puke-green pot in one hand while gesturing with the other for quiet.

"If I may have your attention. I'd like to introduce our fabulous product."

Mercifully, as her voice droned on my eyes glazed over and my mind went blank. Sometime later I was brought back to reality by a hand on my shoulder, and a soft voice in my ear, "Don, Don, it's nine o'clock. The party is running a little long so we must leave now if we are to make the late show."

Sleepily I stood up and followed her to the kitchen door. Big Brother Bob trailed after us. "Don't you kids do anything I wouldn't do," he boomed. In response to this clever witticism, the room filled with an assortment of girlish giggles and knowing sniggers. There was little doubt that the girls regarded old Fultz as an accomplished wit. Well, they were half right.

I recall nothing of the movie except that it was only slightly less boring than Tupperware. In the relative quiet and darkness of the theater I had no difficulty sleeping like a newborn child. Apparently this only annoyed Sally when I snored. She'd poke me in the ribs and hoarsely whisper, "Don, Don, you're snoring again." Each time, certain that my name was not Don, I'd quickly return to my private dreams.

As we left the theater it came to me that I owed Sally an apology. "I'm sorry that I nodded off in there. It was a great movie," I lied, "but I've had a long, hard, hot day in the sun, and I didn't get much sleep last night."

I had decided to drive Sally straight home, but when she accepted my apology with unwarranted grace I made the stupid decision to give it all one more try.

The Ft. Meyers yacht basin seemed an ideal place to park, check out a few boats, sniff some of the Gulf salt breeze, talk, and get a wee bit acquainted. In the twenty-odd hours since our meeting we had hardly conversed at all, and certainly neither of us had said anything particularly meaningful. We were still complete strangers.

When my suggestion was received with a glimmer of enthusiasm I pointed the Dodge in the direction of the basin. My hope of salvaging something of the evening died ignominiously and almost immediately. Before we had cleared the parking lot Sally began to recount the depressing details of her failed marriage, a union consummated in hell, which had mercifully been terminated six months earlier.

Her stream of consciousness was delivered, for the most part, to the windshield and dash of the Dodge. I didn't want to hear any of it, but could think of no way to politely shut her down.

Her husband, Earl, was by her account a first-class jerk and all-around loser. As I listened to her bitter litany I could only wonder why she had married the man, and why she remained with him for two desolate years. She certainly seemed to be a long-suffering individual. I could understand why my snoring in the theater hadn't really upset her.

By trade Earl was an auto mechanic, and by avocation a lush and a dedicated womanizer who couldn't hold a job for more than a few months. During their first six months of marriage Sally was forced to take a job as a waitress just to put food on the table and pay the rent.

When Earl was drunk (most of the time) he was given to violence, which, on several occasions, landed him in jail and other times in a hospital emergency room. During their last year together he began to direct his violent outbursts to the household furnishings, and when that finally became boring, he began to beat the hell out of Sally. Apparently she lived in terror of her husband, a condition not yet entirely under control.

Following their divorce Earl had somehow managed the first two alimony checks before disappearing from her life.

"As much as I needed the money, I could only feel relieved that he was gone," she confessed.

Suddenly Sally seemed to remember that I was seated beside her. She turned her pained face to me, tears welling in her dark eyes. "I didn't mean to burden you with all this, Don, but I've no one to confide in. Bob and Mary think I should just forget it all and get on with my life. They think I was really stupid to marry Earl. I guess I was."

Then she asked me the one question I didn't want to hear, "Are you married?"

As customary, I lied. "No, ah, I, ah, was divorced two years ago." I knew as the words escaped my lips I had made a big mistake. My conviction had been that most women, learning a man has been divorced, do little more than emit a silent sigh of relief. Somehow I knew it would be different with this woman; she would insist on all the bloody details. I was right. Immediately she unleashed a barrage of questions about my former wife, our marital relationship, the problems that led to the breakup, even the details of our courtship. I had no rehearsed scenario to cover such an intensive interrogation, so I was forced into a series of chancy ad-libs.

My web of lies eventually became so complex and entangled I realized that soon I would be caught in embarrassing contradictions. Finally I turned to her, gently placed the palm of my hand over her mouth, and said in a firm voice, "Enough, Sally. This is just too painful. It took a long time, but I've managed to put most of that behind me. Now a lot of it has been dredged up; things I don't wish to remember."

"Oh, I'm so sorry, Don," she said plaintively. "I have no right to pry; it's none of my business and now I've made you feel bad. Perhaps it would be best if you took me home, now. Maybe, if you want, we can see each other again sometime."

We drove in near silence, a dreadful evening coming to a dreadful but welcome close. The street in front of Brother Bob's house was deserted and dark, the party long since over. "I'll walk you to the door," I volunteered.

"No, no," she protested. "Just wait until I'm inside."

She turned and kissed me goodnight. I watched as she walked to the house. On the porch she looked back and called to me, "You'll call, won't you?"

With one last lie, I smiled and drove away.

The night, from my point of view, had been a disaster. Even before I reached the motel I had resolved never again to lie to a woman about my name or marital status.

I was certain that if I honored my resolution I would effectively end all extra-marital relationships. In my naïveté I was convinced that no woman, aware that I was married, would have a thing to do with me. It was a gloomy prospect; with a professional virgin as a wife and a lack of interest in prostitutes I was doomed to a life of celibacy. One thing was certain, I would have a lot of free time, time I might as well direct to a suitable hobby.

On the road to Deland the next day I considered a long list of hobbies that might be pursued both in the field and at home in Houston. Most of them, for some reason or another, simply weren't practical or were very hopelessly dull. I wanted something completely non-geological, something removed entirely from science of any sort. Finally I made my choice. I would, as soon as possible, begin to learn all I could about Adolph Hitler and the Third Reich. I'd been interested in these subjects for quite a while but had never found time to do anything about it. Now time would cease to be a big factor. I already had a foot in the door—a few days earlier, in Tallahassee, I had purchased a biography of Hitler, which lay pristine and neglected, in the trunk of the car. That night I would take it to bed with me and actually read some of it. Hell, in time, I might become an authority on the Hitler gang and write a book of my own.

Had I been thinking at all clearly, I would have realized that Hitler was a piss-poor sex substitute.

The Command Post

By mid-June we were comfortably settled in McCumber Place at the corner of Cassandra and 20th Avenue in Myrtle Beach and ready to assume studies in Horry County.

The little brick bungalow, rented from Hughes-Beale Realty, served ideally its role as a summer field camp. Big time developers hadn't yet discovered south Myrtle Beach, so it was still possible to enjoy the quiet solitude of a pleasant, middle class neighborhood.

Snuggled against a grove of young pines, McCumber reposed in restful isolation among the old sand dunes which adorn the upper flank and crest of a Late Pleistocene barrier bar. From the front windows and the front porch we had a fine view of the ocean two blocks away. We could suck in the fresh salt breeze, and listen to the rush of the surf on the sand beach and the pounding of the waves as they crashed against the Hurl Rocks coquina at high tide.

Our nearest neighbor lived in the two-story, white frame house directly across from us on Cassandra. On the day we pulled our car and boat into the McCumber driveway, he walked across the street and offered to help us unload our gear. He was a short, wiry, white-haired, middle-aged, seafaring man from Auckland, New Zealand. He had decided to spend the summer on the beach, "...To lick my wounds," as he put it.

Despite the unlikely name of Hobart W.C. Furbunch, III, he proved to be one of the most interesting men I have known. Our friendship, hatched that day in June 1961, grew and prospered until his death.

In a small but touching way his memory is perpetuated by the Hobart W.C. Furbunch, III "Traditional Jacobs Staff Award" presented annually by the University of Houston Geology Department to the outstanding student in their summer field course. Names of the winners are displayed on a bronze plaque housed in a hall display cabinet in the geology department. The award is the brainchild of Professor James R. Solliday, who, for several years, taught the field course.

McCumber's fully equipped kitchen allowed us to circumvent, when desired, the inconvenience and expense of restaurant dining. At times, it is true, our cooking left a lot to be desired, but on the whole we ate well and, most importantly, regularly. Ample storage for cold drinks and snacks was a welcome bonus.

The two bedrooms afforded us a modicum of needed privacy. Jim and I were relatively compatible, but being forced to live crunched together in a few square feet of space for twenty-four hours a day for several months can severely test the durability of any relationship.

The living room, which sported an old, tired but functional radio, an ugly, comfortable sofa, and two well-seasoned easy chairs, provided a place for relaxation, reading, reflection, quiet conversation, and entertainment of guests.

We ate at a small table in the kitchen, which freed the dining room for storage, research, paperwork and organizational activities. In short, the dining room became my command post. The long wooden table provided a convenient surface for a variety of tasks. It served, at times, as a drafting table, as a place where we could spread out large maps and air photos, a place to prepare work schedules, to do literature searches, to copy smudged, nearly illegible, field notes, to work on expense records, to make grocery lists and to write letters.

The walls of the dining room, bare when we arrived, were soon covered with our maps, air photo mosaics, charts and geologic cross-sections. We spent many hours staring at the damned things in search of insights into the geologic mysteries of the coastal plain—exhilarated when the picture seemed to come into focus, frustrated when it once again blurred, but always confident that one day it would all come clear and the truth would be revealed.

At McCumber I rarely had difficulty waking at 6:00 a.m. because the sun's rays struck my eyes at about that time each morning and I have never been able to sleep well in glaring light. The sun was my alarm clock, good, faithful and natural, unlike the jangly, vacuous, banging man-made contraptions. Awake, I would reach over to the chair by my bed and turn on the little transistor radio always tuned to a station which played summertime beach music. Then I would get up and head for the bathroom to accommodate bodily functions, shower, shave and dress.

It would be time then to raise Jim, rarely an easy task. While sweeping sand from the floor of the bedroom and having breakfast of Sara Lee chocolate fudge cake and milk, I would make as much noise as possible, including, at times, banging two frying pans together, or once, tossing a lighted cherry bomb under Jim's bed.

While I packed the lunches Jim organized the field gear and stowed it in the car and boat. Usually we were on the road by 7:00 a.m. and at a boat landing or outcrop by 8:00.

Stalked by a Coed

I first became aware of Juanita Richardson on an evening in January 1961. I had just concluded a lecture to my night class in Historical Geology. As usual a small clutch of students had cornered me near the lectern. They came armed, on such occasions, with questions about grades, assignments, exam schedules, and the finer points of my lecture which I had failed to make entirely clear.

I noticed her standing quietly at the rear of the group, her eyes fixed on me, seeming to hang on each of my words. She was plainly dressed and plain looking: slender (almost gaunt), medium height, no make-up, uninspired hairdo, drab, age about 30. When the other students had cleared away she stepped forward and shyly identified herself. I no longer remember what she wanted to know, but I recall that she mentioned, to my surprise, that she had been enrolled in my Physical Geology course in the fall. I had no recollection of her in that class, but night classes were large and most of the students held day jobs so I had little contact with them outside the classroom.

My curiosity piqued, I checked my fall semester grade book as soon as I returned to my office. There had been a Juanita Richardson in my class; she hadn't done well, just barely passing with a D. Curiosity appeased I promptly erased her from my mind.

On a Saturday afternoon a few weeks later I was surprised to find Juanita at the front door of my Houston home. She seemed agitated, uncertain, and almost furtive. I couldn't guess what she might have on her mind. Her words came rapidly. "I thought you might like to come boating with me tomorrow on Clear Lake."

"Boating?" I asked, a bit puzzled. The invitation seemed directed only to me. "Well, I enjoy boating and I'm certain my wife will be delighted to learn of your invitation."

"Wife?" she repeated vaguely. "Oh, yes, your wife." She whirled then and fled to her car parked in the driveway.

185

When I returned to the den Phyllis asked what that had been about. "I'm not sure," I said. "It was one of my students, Juanita Richardson. She wanted me to go boating with her at Clear Lake tomorrow. When I suggested you might want to join us she left."

With a shake of her head, Phyllis commented, "What an odd individual!"

During the next two months Juanita came to my office on several occasions. First she confined her conversation to questions related to my course, but during each visit she worked around to quizzing me about personal things such as my youth, military experiences, my parents, the schools I had attended, my past employment, and even my hobbies.

Then one day the pattern changed. I was at my desk in the back office when she walked in without knocking. She stood beside the desk, and with a thin smile I couldn't at first decipher she spoke softly, almost in a whisper. "I'm in love with you," she declared.

For a moment or two all I could do was stare in stunned amazement. Then stupidly, I said, "Well, I suppose I should be flattered, but you know that I am married and cannot return your feelings."

"Oh!" she exclaimed, putting a hand over her mouth. "Your wife; yes, of course, your wife." Abruptly she turned and scurried from the office, leaving me wondering how she could have forgotten I was married.

Two or three days later she telephoned me at home and once again invited me to go boating with her. "And be sure to bring your sister," she said cheerily. From that moment on Juanita always referred to Phyllis as my sister. In her malfunctioning mind she had solved the problem of an inconvenient obstacle to her future happiness with me. With the transformation from wife to sister, Juanita had erased Phyllis as effectively as if she had placed the muzzle of a loaded gun to her temple and squeezed the trigger.

A few days after Jim and I left for Florida, Juanita called my "sister" and informed her that I had run off to South Carolina with my secretary (I didn't have a secretary). Then she spread the same story around the geology department.

In mid-July I made a perfunctory call to Phyllis. She told me that Juanita's mother had called to tell us that Juanita had disappeared shortly after I had left for the east coast. She had driven off one June morning to go, as usual, to her workplace in downtown Houston. Later it was learned she had not arrived at the office. No one had heard from her or seen her since that morning. Her disappearance had been reported to the police and eventually she was listed as a missing person.

In July I had little time to devote to Juanita's disappearance. I had a lot of things of much more immediate concern on my mind. My top priority was the research project, which required my attention at least ten hours a day, seven days a week. It was true that some of the work was largely cerebral, but much of it fell into the category of hard, backbreaking, physical labor performed in the unforgiving, sweat-wrenching heat of the South Carolina low country.

Then there was the matter of our skinny financial resources. We survived on the leftover dregs of the 1959-61 NSF budget and I still had not learned when funds from the 1961-63 grant would become available.

And there was another small detail—I had fallen in love, or, perhaps, gone quite mad (but who can tell the difference?).

A week or so later the mystery surrounding Juanita deepened. Phyllis received a telephone call one evening from a person who identified herself only as a friend of Juanita. She told Phyllis that Juanita had asked that she pass a message to me. Juanita wished me to know that she was all right, that she was travelling through Kansas and that she had not forgotten me.

When the police were informed of the telephone call, Juanita became the subject of a nation-wide search. Unfortunately, my name and hers became firmly linked in the police files.

Thereafter, once or twice a week Phyllis received calls from the mystery lady, who each time forwarded a message updating me on Juanita's progress through the country—eastern Colorado, the Bay area, western Oregon, Puget Sound, eastern Missouri, southern Illinois.

On an afternoon in August Juanita showed up at my parent's home in Canton, Ohio. When she discovered no one at home she walked into the yard and stared at the house. A neighbor who lived across the street noticed her standing there and, regarding her behavior as somewhat strange, watched her for fifteen minutes.

At that point the neighbor walked across the street, introduced herself, and asked if she might be of assistance. Juanita replied that she was one of my students at the University of Houston and that she had come to see my parents and the place where I had lived as a boy. She appeared to be very nervous— eyes unfocused, weird, very scary. Her reveries having been interrupted, Juanita excused herself and drove away.

When I heard the account of Juanita's Canton visit I began, for the first time, to discern a pattern to her movements of the past two months. If I were correct, Juanita had been tracking my spoor across the country, visiting the places I had mentioned to her, the places where I had lived, worked, studied.

In a sense I was being stalked. It was a sobering thought, but at the time I could do little more than wonder where it might end.

In September after I returned to Houston I received a call from Juanita's lady friend. This time the message was different. She reported they were in Cincinnati where Juanita had decided that I should have her car. The keys and the location of the car were to be mailed to me in the morning. When they arrived, I was to come to Cincinnati and pick up the car.

Juanita had reached the end of the trail. She had tracked me to my roots in America. In the late nineteenth century my great grandfather, his Belgian wife, and their two sons, Louis and Joseph Herman (my grandfather) had immigrated to Cincinnati from Lille, France. In 1887 Joseph Herman married my grandmother, Fanny Scott, of Covington, Kentucky, and they had promptly moved to Canton, Ohio where Joseph was employed as an engraver for the Dueber-Hampton Watchworks Company. The rest of the family remained in Cincinnati where some of their descendants live today.

This latest communication from Juanita was both puzzling and disturbing. I wondered why she would want me to have her car. Several possible scenarios occurred to me: with her pilgrimage over, she planned to commit suicide and had no more need for the car; she thought the car might serve as bait to lure me to Cincinnati (whether just to see me or kill me I couldn't begin to guess). Whatever her purpose, I had no intention of going to Cincinnati to find out.

When the letter containing the keys arrived a few days later, I passed it, unopened, to Juanita's parents. In turn they gave the letter to the detective in charge of the investigation. The Cincinnati police found Juanita at a motel; sometime later she was returned to Houston and committed to a mental institution.

Following Juanita's return to Houston the detective in charge of the case paid a visit to my home. He questioned me closely about my relationship with Juanita, and I quickly discovered he assumed that I had engaged in an affair with her. I assured him that it had been entirely one-sided and that I had never touched her, even to shake her hand—my only feeling for her had been pity. My declaration greatly amused him, and, breaking into peals of laughter, he shook his head and said, "Okay, prof, have it your way." He was still laughing when he left the house.

It was frustrating not to be believed, but I was relieved that the strange interlude was finally over. I never saw or heard from Juanita again; I know nothing nor do I wish to know anything about her eventual fate. I do, however, retain a lingering curiosity about the identity of Juanita's mysterious lady friend.

Georgia on My Mind

On a mid-June evening in 1961 Solliday and I were working over some of our messy field notes at the McCumber dining room table when Furbunch, flushed, sweaty, and a little tipsy, burst through the front door. He was carrying three cans of beer. "What are you gentlemen doing?" he demanded.

"Well, we've been working on ..."

"Working! Hell, that's your trouble, you work too much. Grab a cool one and let's stroll over to Berry's and catch the changing of the guard. All those pretty young waitresses over there coming on and off duty will be heart-broken if we don't show up. You wouldn't want that on your conscience now, would you?"

"Ah, I suppose ..."

"Of course not. Take a can and let's depart. I don't want to hear any damned feeble-assed excuses."

"I wasn't planning to offer any," I protested. "Actually I'm glad you dropped by. I've got to go over there to talk with Tony about the job in Zeb's galley."

"Surely you're not serious about working as a night shift cook for Zeb."

"Serious enough to make sure the job is available if needed."

With money from the old grant running low and funds from the new grant held up for God knows how long, I had to do something. I had asked Zeb Berry one day if he could use an extra hand in his galley during the night shift. At first Zeb had seemed skeptical that I could do the work, but when he discovered that I had done some cooking on a lighthouse and a small patrol boat while in the Coast Guard, he became enthusiastic and told me I could have the job. He asked me to discuss the details with Tony, his head cook.

I knew Tony fairly well and figured I would have no trouble working with him. Tony was a squat, sturdy, young Italian-American, who seemed as harmless as a six-month-old puppy. His steady girlfriend was the daughter of

Zeb's daytime manager, a woman I referred to as Mammy Yocum—craggy, diminutive, and down to earth. Tony and his girlfriend were parents of a baby girl, but any plans they may have had to legalize their relationship ended a little later in the year after Tony was inducted into the Army. He killed a fellow soldier at Ft. Bragg, was convicted of murder, and sentenced to life in prison. Later, when I learned of Tony's fate, I was again reminded that my judgement of human character certainly left something to be desired.

Shortly after the jail doors slammed shut on Tony, his girlfriend put their daughter out for adoption. Then she went to New York City, taking with her some nebulous dream of becoming a songwriter. A year later, penniless, disillusioned, her dream dissolved in the acid realization that she had no talent for song writing, she returned to Myrtle Beach where she did her best to eke out a living waiting tables at a Pancake House and selling a mail order line of ladies' cosmetics.

At the restaurant I found Tony waiting for me in a booth just to the right of the entryway. I slid into the booth facing him, my back to the door. Hobart and Jim wandered into the back room where, judging from the racket, a large group of Air Force boys had gathered for a night of revelry.

Tony and I had begun to discuss life in Zeb's galley when I realized his eyes had fixed on a moving target behind me. I turned to see what had distracted him. I saw four young people, two girls, two boys, flowing in a single file across the room.

But it was the young lady at the end of the line who arrested my attention— a beautiful, divine vision. My reaction was instant and positive. My body tingled, my pulse raced. As I watched she vanished into the back room with the others. Before I could turn my head or erase her image from my mind she popped from the room and went directly to the jukebox. She dropped a quarter into the slot and without hesitation punched out three selections. I remember them still: *Sailor, I Don't Have a Wooden Heart,* and *Stranger on the Shore.*

When I turned to Tony I no longer had the least interest in a night job at Berry's. Tony read the question in my eyes. "The girls are German," he said. "The older one in front is Irmtrauf. She's married to an Air Force sergeant at the base. He's on duty in Puerto Rico now. They have an apartment on the base and a little two-year-old girl. The younger one is her sister, Karin. She flew over from Germany a few days ago. I guess she plans to stay with Irma a few days, and then she's gonna fly to Arizona and marry an Army guy she met in Krautland."

On the walk back to McCumber Solliday told me that he had a date with Irma at her apartment the following evening. "Karin will be there too, with that Air Force guy she was with tonight."

"Don't mention that guy," I cautioned. "I'm already thinking of killing him."

The next evening as Jim was preparing to leave for his date it began to rain, so I loaned him my battered, old, black umbrella. It was one of those little things that sometimes can alter a person's life.

At midnight when Jim returned from the base the rain had long since ended and he had forgotten to bring the umbrella with him. "It's in Irma's kitchen," he said. "But don't worry, Big Daddy, I'll pick it up tomorrow." I really wasn't concerned about the old thing; it wasn't worth a dime. I did realize that forgetting it had given Jim an excuse to see Irma again.

The next afternoon Jim returned from the base with the wayward umbrella. Giving me his best shit-eating grin, he announced, "Got another date with Irma at six this evening."

"That's nice," I said. "You two will be going steady if this keeps up. But don't forget that she has a husband who one day might put a .45 slug into your scrotum."

"Don't knock it, Big Daddy, Karin wants to meet you tonight."

"Geez, Jim," I said apologetically. "I'm sorry I can't go with you. I don't think that would be a good idea."

"What the hell do you mean, you can't come with me? Just last night you told me how great you think she is. The most spectacular female you've ever seen, I think you said. What the hell's your problem?"

"Well, I do think she's spectacular, she is the most attractive woman I've ever seen."

"Well then, maybe you think she's too young for you. She's twenty-one, you know. Old enough to vote."

"Oh hell, Jim, it's not that, although I admit age could prove a problem. It's a lot more than that. I've only seen her twice and for only a total of about thirty seconds, but it's enough to know that I could never have a casual relationship with her. If I start something now it's unlikely I would be able to control myself. I would never be able to just walk away and forget her. That scares the hell out of me."

"Shit, Big Daddy, you can't fink out on me now. Just talking to her for a few hours can't hurt anything. The girls are going to meet us at Berry's. What the hell am I supposed to tell Karin? You know she was already in the shower when I left; she really is eager to meet you."

It was the image of Karin in the shower that did me in. My defenses collapsed; common sense and reason evaporated. "Okay, okay, I'll go with you. But I still think this is a big mistake."

When we walked into Berry's we found Irma and Karin waiting for us in a backroom booth. As Jim dispensed with the introductions we sat down facing the girls. I was nervous and tense, determined to be forthright and completely honest. With some trepidation I told Karin that I was thirty-eight. Relieved when the discrepancy in our ages didn't seem to perturb her, I was encouraged to confess that I was married. She didn't blink. Dropping back to relatively safe ground I told her I had been a boxer. She smiled and asked, "Does that mean you will always be able to protect me?"

"That's exactly what I mean," I replied. Off and running, and gaining confidence, I told her that I was a professor. My first snag.

She frowned. "I don't care much for professors. They are so stiff and so arrogant."

Undaunted, I countered, "But you are thinking only of the German professors. They are that way. In America we are different—casual, humble, and very friendly."

She laughed. Then, somewhat cryptically, she said, "You know it is my way to either hate or to love, nothing in between."

I wasn't sure what she meant. Perhaps, I thought, I am accepted on approval. If so, it was a condition sufficient for the moment. It seemed to be an appropriate time to end my string of confessions and to allow Karin to do the talking. It had been a dangerous game, something akin to Russian roulette. It seemed certain that if I continued my mouth would eventually fire a slug into one of my feet. With a sigh of relief I sat back and listened to the girls.

I soon learned that Karin and Irma were from a place near Frankfort, Germany. When the war had ended in Europe, food and almost everything required to sustain life was in short supply. The girls' father, formerly a sergeant in the German army, sent them out each evening to steal anything of possible use to the family. On nights when they returned empty-handed, they were beaten.

When in her late teens, Irma married an airman stationed in Germany with the American occupation forces. Later her husband was transferred to the Myrtle Beach Air Force base, and it was there that their daughter was born.

Karin confirmed Tony's story. She was engaged to an American soldier who had been stationed in Germany, but was now on a base somewhere in Arizona. In a few weeks she planned to fly there to marry the guy.

After we had filled each other in on our backgrounds we drove to the Clover Club in North Myrtle Beach where the Drifters were booked for a week. When we peeked inside the club and caught a glimpse of the clutter of live bodies and listened for a few moments to the clamor which emanated from the darkened interior, we opted for the relative serenity and intimacy of the Elks Club.

In the Elks we sat in a booth to the right of the bandstand. This time Karin was at my side. Drinks ordered, we were quickly lured to the dance floor by a Jesse Shaw standard. It didn't take long to realize that Karin's attention was directed to the orchestra rather than our dancing.

"Is there a problem?"

"*Nein, nein,*" she responded. "It's just that I've never seen many Negro people. Aren't they beautiful?"

As we continued to dance she quietly listened to the music, and when the piece ended she asked Jesse to play it again.

"I usually don't care for slow music," she said, "but this is different." Then she drew her body close to mine, laid her head on my shoulder, and softly hummed as the vocalist sang: "Georgia, Georgia, no peace I find, just an old sweet song keeps Georgia on my mind."

In the weeks to come we listened to *Georgia* together many times. From that first night it was our song. For nearly two years each time I walked into the Elks Club Jesse Shaw's orchestra interrupted whatever they were doing to play *Georgia* until I was seated.

Back at McCumber that evening I knew that if it were possible I would subvert Karin's intention to fly to Arizona to be married. Five feet three inches, 112 pounds, eyes vivid blue, closely cropped brown curls, no jewelry, no makeup, just natural, breath-taking beauty. I would not permit her to slip from my life so easily.

With no further use for the books on Hitler and the Third Reich, I tossed them into the kitchen wastebasket. This marvelous little girl whose father had fought for Hitler would provide me with everything I might ever wish to know about Germany.

During Karin's first visit to McCumber we walked together into the kitchen. She stopped to look at the June *Playboy* centerfold taped on the wall by the sink. The girl, wearing some sort of skimpy playsuit, lay on her left side, her head propped up by her left arm. Her right breast looked as if it might burst its fragile restraints at any moment. Without removing her eyes from the picture, Karin said, very thoughtfully, "Ploop," or something to that effect.

Then she turned to me smiling and asked, "Is this your way to like the little girls?"

The first time she drove with me in the Dodge she commented, "This is a very nice car. How many kilometers does it get to a liter of gasoline?" I was taken off guard by her use of the metric system. A long, heavy silence followed while my brain worked desperately to make the conversion from miles and gallons. I was the big shot Ph.D. professor, and I was supposed to know stuff like that. It was very embarrassing.

Karin was fiercely independent, I learned. She wouldn't even accept flowers from men. After we had been together for about a week she decided to apply for a job as a waitress at the officer's club. Before she could begin work she was required to pass a physical exam. The young male medic, who needed to obtain a urine sample, was too embarrassed to clearly explain what it was he needed. He handed her a small plastic container while mumbling something she didn't understand. To his dismay she asked that he repeat what he had said. Again she heard only a string of unintelligible mumblings. Finally after two or three futile attempts to communicate, Karin realized what it was he asked. "Oh!" she said. "You want me to pee in the box!"

After her first day on the job we went to dinner together. "How did your work go today?" I asked.

"I quit."

"Quit! Why did you do that?"

"Well, the men kept trying to give me tips and you know I don't accept gifts from men."

One evening while driving along King's Highway in the Dodge I commented, "You are very passionate Karin."

Puzzled, she asked, "What is this word *passionate?*"

"Fire," I said. "You are full of fire."

She smiled and replied, "I understand; and so are you." Though we spoke different languages we always found a way to communicate.

On an evening about two weeks after we had met, we were sitting in my car outside her sister's apartment. While looking straight at the dashboard, Karin said, "You know when we first met I told you I either love or hate— nothing in between. Now I have fallen in love with you."

Sometime earlier she referred to me as, "Jule with the smiling eyes," but that evening I smiled all over; I smiled from the top of my head to the tips of my toes. The oppressive burden of accumulated stress, anxiety and depression lifted from my shoulders, leaving me with a new and exhilarating sense of weightlessness. I no longer walked; I soared several inches above the ground wherever I went. An awareness of life I had not thought possible enveloped me. The grass became a brighter green, the sky more blue and brilliant, the flowers more beautiful and more fragrant, the songs of the birds more melodious. For the first time I felt completely fulfilled. All the dumb things I had heard or read about people in love were true. My one regret was that my life had not always been this way, that for many years I had endured a living death. For the next several weeks Karin and I were together at every possible opportunity: the Elks, Berry's, the beach, the pavilion, her sister's apartment, McCumber. I even rode with her on the "Wild Mouse" at the amusement park to prove that I wasn't just a stuffy old professor.

I thought then that what we had would never end, but one day as suddenly as she had entered my life she was gone. After that a lot of the working part of my guts turned to cinders. The first time I wandered alone into the Elks for dinner, Johnny, the waiter, came to my table, looked me over, and said, "Dr. DuBar, you look lost without your woman."

With a wistful smile I agreed, "Yes, Johnny, I am lost." I thought then of something I had once said to Solliday, "I may have her for a lifetime, a year, a month, or only a day; in that time, whatever it may be, I will have had something most men dream of all their lives and never find."

In the spring Henry Johnson wrote in a letter to me:

I never knew Karin, but she was very alive for me in those days, and is now a part of the kaleidoscope of things which make us what we are. And I was very pro-Karin in those days whether you know it or not. I developed a loyalty to her, probably because she represented something I had experienced and caught a glimpse of and sought after and longed for myself. Anyway I was for her as you may remember and I almost injected myself into your affairs (a thing I do not believe in doing, and do not ordinarily do) one time in wanting to call her and talk to her at a time when for reasons of your own you could not bring yourself to do.

If You Run Over My Duck, I'll Kill You

On a quiet morning in mid-July, 1961 Jim and I walked the three or four blocks from McCumber Place to the Woodland Esso Station on U.S. 17. Our friend, E.P. Decker, had just bought an interest in the place and had taken responsibility for the servicing of foreign cars.

Deck, a former U.S. Army Air Force Warrant officer, suffered from periodic bouts with boredom and the inescapable fact that on his retirement pay he could neither adequately care for his wife Molly and their five children nor afford the volume of booze required to successfully combat his boredom. Deck was a gregarious animal who needed to regularly mingle and interact with people. These were reasons sufficient to stimulate his active imagination to conjure various schemes by which he might supplement his income.

An accomplished golfer, he had tried his hand as manager of the local "Par One" driving range, but he soon found that this was in no way anything like golf and that the paperwork was more boring than TV. On another occasion, lured by a promise of big bucks and easy, pleasant work, he tested his entrepreneurial skills by managing the efforts of a team of ladies who were to go door-to-door selling a line of cosmetics. This venture failed when the ladies, proving to have minds of their own, discovered that they could manage their operations without the help of a man.

When we first met Deck he told us of his plan to convert the Brockhurst house into a massage parlor. "This is the goose that will lay my golden egg," he had predicted. I hadn't known Deck long enough or well enough to fully realize that he was an inveterate dreamer of impractical dreams. Even so, I viewed this idea as a wee bit far-fetched and fanciful.

Brockhurst, a large, square, two-storied frame and brick structure shrouded by sprawling live oaks, stood gloomily unoccupied and somewhat neglected on a half-acre lot at the corner of 20th Avenue South and the Kings Highway. Deck was certain that the place had served as a whorehouse during

World War II. Actually the house itself bore tangible evidence that this might have been true. The nine Brockhurst bedrooms were especially intriguing; each had Dutch swinging doors with large brass numbers set at each door's base. Also, each bedroom was fitted with a full-length mirror affixed to one wall and each had its private bathroom. Clearly this was no ordinary residence.

Unable to secure necessary financial backing, Deck was eventually forced to relinquish his dream for Brockhurst. In the end his misfortune worked to advantage for me. In 1963, with Brockhurst still unoccupied, Henry Johnson was able to persuade the owner to allow us to use the house, rent free, for a summer field camp.

When we reached the Esso station Deck emerged from somewhere in the back, wiping his hands on a clean, soft, white cloth. Dressed in neatly pressed tan slacks, a beige, two-pocket sport shirt and tan and white dress shoes, he appeared rather dapper, I thought, for an auto mechanic.

He grinned broadly when he saw us and in his usual friendly, effusive style greeted us each with a great bear hug while proclaiming to the gas station attendants that the "Rover Boys" had arrived just in time for a beer break.

As we walked into Zeb Berry's restaurant, Eula Scruggins, the day manager, gave us a cheery greeting. Eula was a dark, wiry little Mammy Yokum type who harbored dreams of having her own place one day. Her husband Stan, Zeb's handyman, was skulking behind the counter, unsuccessfully attempting to repair a leaky air-conditioner. He grimaced and waved as we passed, then returned to his unhappy task. The only customers seemed to be two truck drivers crouched over doughnuts and coffee at the counter and a young couple in the back of the dining area working on a late breakfast.

In the empty back room we slid into a booth next to a window that provided a dreary view of the parking lot. It was my first mid-morning visit to Zeb's place, and I was surprised to find that without the clatter of the evening crowd and the blare of the juke box it was possible to make myself understood without shouting.

Deck was sipping his second beer when he mentioned he had been working on Mickey Spillane's Ferrari when we showed up at the station.

"Mickey Spillane? You mean he lives in Myrtle Beach?"

"Not Myrtle Beach, Murrell's Inlet. He's got a big old house down there on the salt marsh. Likes his isolation these days. He does have a toy store in Myrtle Beach, though—Mickey's."

"Oh, hell," Jim said. "I saw that place a few days ago—just across from

Chapins and the post office."

"Toys," I said, speculatively. "Seems an odd line for someone with his tough guy reputation."

"He likes kids. Sometimes he drives around town checking out the drive-in places. If he spots a load of teenagers drinking beer he stops and lectures them on the evils of alcohol."

"You mean he doesn't drink?" Jim asked, incredulously.

"Only like a fish, he does, Jim, but he thinks it's bad for kids."

"Tell you what," Deck added. "The case in point is that I should finish Mickey's car today and deliver it to him this evening. You guys could follow me down there, meet Mickey, and then the three of us could drive back together."

"Sounds good to me," I responded. "I don't much like his books but I would like to meet him."

Late in the afternoon when we returned to the garage Deck greeted us gloomily. "Sorry gents—have a tiny problem with the goddamned transmission. Looks as if I'm gonna have to work on the car tonight and deliver it in the morning. But not to worry men, I called Mickey a few hours ago and told him a couple of my buddies would be by tonight to meet him."

"He doesn't mind?" Jim asked.

"Told him you were big fans."

"Shit you did!" I said.

"Well, its okay. He's divorced now, the ex-wife packed up the kids and moved home to Newburgh or whatever, so he's all alone down there. I assume he's tired of talking to fuckin' sea gulls by now."

We drove to Murrell's Inlet in the growing dusk. Without the aid of Deck's rough map sketched hastily on an oily scrap of paper, we may not have found our way. Spillane's large frame house is at the end of a winding sand road where it stands half-hidden among the great branching live oaks near the edge of the marsh, just as Deck had described. It was not a place readily found by nosy tourists.

As we pulled in front of the house to park, a duck dashed off the front porch and waddled in front of the car. At that moment Mickey appeared at the edge of the porch above the steps shouting, "If you run over my duck I'll kill you!"

As we walked onto the large front porch I could see that Mickey was holding a can of beer, and soon it became evident it hadn't been his first of the day. Before we could introduce ourselves we were challenged to a duel to the death with swords. When we declined Mickey proposed a range of alternate weapons even less appealing than swords. In a final, desperate attempt to accommodate us he suggested a skateboard race around the driveway. This idea was abandoned when he recalled that his son had taken the boards with him to New York.

Inside the house our first stop was the refrigerator in the kitchen where we were supplied with two cans of Pabst. In the large, comfortable-looking living room a small lean man of about 45 or so sat on the sofa clutching a can of beer. As Mickey began the introductions the little fellow arose somewhat unsteadily and presenting us with a drunken leer, proffered his free hand.

"Meet my drinking partner, Sarge O' Rourke here straight from the Emerald Isle. Retired from the British Army. He was just filling me in on his tour of India."

Mickey couldn't remember our names so we introduced ourselves.

"What brings you to South Carolina?" I asked O' Rourke.

"Retired here," he responded. "Moved in down the way last month."

Before I could ask how the hell he had found his way to Murrell's Inlet, Mickey interrupted. Taking a close, calculating look at me, he commented (rather cryptically, I thought), "Professor, eh?"

"That's correct—geology, University of Houston."

Then ignoring me, he turned to Jim. "And you, I know," he asserted. "You're the philosopher." I assumed the appellation was in reference to Jim's full red beard. At any rate, for Mickey, Jim had become forever "The Philosopher," and thereafter was addressed by him in no other manner.

Once again Mickey turned his attention to me. "Publish, do you?"

"Oh yes—scientific stuff."

"So you are an author then. I'm a writer, you know."

"Yes, I know."

"I doubt it," he retorted. "The critics and professors don't like my stuff, don't consider it literature. But those guys can't write anything that sells—that makes any money. They're authors, like you. I'm a writer and not an author because what I write makes money. That's why what the goddamned critics and professors say doesn't bother me—it doesn't mean shit!"

I didn't respond to his tirade but it seemed it was possible that what the critics and professors said about his work bothered him very much. My suspicions seemed reinforced by his frequent attacks on his tormentors throughout the evening and for as long as I knew him. He was still striking out at the critics in 1990 when during a TV appearance he told the interviewer:

"Critics can't say anything worse than they have. The worst has been said.

199

I'm a mechanic. I put the stories together piece by piece in a very short period of time. The way these college professors tell their students to write isn't how to do it."

His diatribe continued. "You know, I wrote nine books. They sold worldwide and were translated into scores of languages. I was on a talk show once and the host asked: ' How does it feel too have produced nine of the ten most popular books ever written?' I told him I guessed it's lucky I only wrote nine books.

"I thought for sometime that nine is all I would write. Five years ago I became a Jehovah's Witness and gave up writing. It didn't take long before everyone figured I was dead. Then a few months ago I returned from the dead and wrote book number ten. It's called *The Deep* and comes replete with an all new tough guy hero, Tiger Mann. I don't suppose it will bump the Bible off the top ten best sellers list, but then," he added with a mischievous grin, "it might come close enough to make the Pope nervous.

"Hell, he said. "Once I get the plot worked out in my head I write the book in two weeks—the whole damned book in two weeks!" Waving his arms toward the far corner of the room, he said, "Right there's where I do it—on that goddamned old portable typewriter. Did them all on that machine." The typewriter resided on a small table near a window which offered during the day a view of the yard. Behind the table and in front of the brick wall there was a low bookcase packed with paperbacks. I had earlier noticed that the room seemed filled with paperbacks—several bookcases, tabletops, and a fireplace mantle. Nowhere did I see a hard-backed book. It struck me as a bit odd; I had always been admonished by my teachers to buy hardback editions of books because the authors made more money from their sale than from paperback editions. But then I suppose Mickey's books never came out in hard cover and it seemed likely he would consider such advice as the complete nonsense of "authors" who never made any money anyway.

When we finally sat down the subjects of our conversation were quite varied, but most were quickly lost in the fuzzy recesses of alcohol-soaked brain tissue. I recall that he said he had been recently divorced and that his wife and the two children were living in Newburgh, New York, and that he went up there for visits on occasions.

He spoke of his days as a police reporter for a newspaper and he said that he had completed the FBI training in Los Angeles. These were experiences he said had prepared him to realize a long-standing dream of becoming a writer of detective stories.

At one point he and Jim became involved in a head to head confrontational discussion of personal philosophies of life. They were deadly serious, arguing intensely over particular points. I tried to follow the discourse but most of it sounded like drunken rambling that made little or no sense.

Another time I recall Mickey bragged that he could steal any man's woman without telling her that he was a famous writer. I was tempted briefly to allow him to try with Karin but later decided it wasn't a very good idea. What if he were right?

All the time O' Rourke, in what appeared a drunken reverie, sat quietly on the sofa, sloshing can after can of Pabst.

Around ten o' clock, Mickey realized that the beer supply had become dangerously slim, so he decided to run into town for a fresh supply. Jim and I, who hadn't eaten since lunch, asked that he pick up a load of fried chicken for us. As soon as he was out of the door, Jim and I, leaving O' Rourke on the living room sofa, raced to the refrigerator in the kitchen. With the exception of a few cans of beer all I found was a small plastic refrigerator container. Opening the lid I gleefully called out to Jim, "We're saved, it's some kind of hash." With no hesitation I grabbed a spoon and began to stuff my face. In a flash I was reminded that Mickey had cats.

Soon after Mickey returned with the beer and two lovely large boxes of exquisitely prepared southern fried chicken, the three of us, burping and licking our whiskers, shared a table covered with crumpled boxes, greasy napkins, small stacks of naked bones, bits and pieces of chicken skin and six empty beer cans.

"Don't worry about the mess, men, the maid will take care of it tomorrow. Let's go into the living room and see if O' Rourke is alive."

O' Rourke was just as we had left. His left hand still clutched a beer can, but now the little fellow was sleeping peacefully. Mickey shook him. "You all right, Sarge?"

Sarge stirred, opened blurry eyes and began to rise from the sofa. "Yes, yes," he said foggily. "I'm fine, just need to walk out into the yard for a breath and a piss."

"Hell, you don't need to go outside, Sarge," said Mickey. "You can use the facility down the hall."

"Oh, that's decent of you, but I'm in need of a wee bit of night air."

We all helped the tottering Irishman to the porch. Then we watched as he staggered down the front steps, crossed the yard, and faded into the shadows of the live oaks, never (so far as I know) to be seen or heard from again.

With O' Rourke disposed of we were soon back in the living room, locked in a heated discussion of organic evolution. Mickey may have done some serious backsliding, but he hadn't fully escaped the clutches of the Jehovah's Witnesses. It didn't take long to discover that he was a devout Creationist.

With great fervor he contended that scientists had no real evidence to support their view of organic evolution. It was an assessment that served to jar Solliday from his post-chicken lethargy.

"What the fuck do you mean, Mikey, no evidence? There's no doubt that life has evolved for the past three or more billion years. The evidence is overwhelming—it's out of your ass man!"

I had discovered early on that arguments with fundamentalists about evolution quickly degenerated to emotionally charged shouting matches. I recall little of what was actually said that night on the subject of evolution but I am reasonably confident that little of it was worth remembering. The three of us were soon on our feet. Then in close formation we surged about the house to and fro from room to room, like a great three-headed mythical beast with six pairs of appendages. The heads babbled in unison, each to its own purpose, uttering a series of largely unintelligible shouts, groans, moans and vulgarities. In passing, the twelve appendages, with uncoordinated but impassioned fury, lashed out blindly at offending walls and bits and pieces of household furnishings that dared impede the progress of the crazed monster.

Eventually we halted in the small, closed-in back porch. Here the chaotic debate reached its explosive climax. Suddenly, with beads of perspiration glistening on his brow, his face crimson and convulsed with emotion, Mickey exclaimed in a voice calculated to activate his long dead ancestors in New York State, "By God, we'll settle this right here and right now! I'm going to call an authority!"

As he reached for the wall-mounted phone I stepped toward him and screamed into his face, "Goddamn it, Mickey, drop the fucking phone—I *am* an authority."

With that he suddenly went limp and, managing a wan smile, said, "Oh hell guys, let's go back into the living room, sit down, have a brew and cool off. We'll never settle this thing tonight anyway."

We sat silently in the living room for several minutes. When I had recovered my composure I sat my beer aside and said. "You know, Mickey, what we need to do is arrange a boxing match between us and stage it at Madison Square Garden."

He sat up with a startled expression for a moment and then, grinning, said,

"By God that's an idea!"

My comment had been mostly in jest, nevertheless it had struck a responsive chord. Mickey was on his feet now. "Hell, do you know Willie Pep?"

"Only by reputation—one of the greatest featherweights of all time."

"You bet your ass he was—' The Will o' the Wisp' . He and I are great friends. He's up in Hartford—I'm gonna call him and see if he'll referee our bout." He actually headed for the phone but then hesitated, turned and with a gesture of resignation, said, "Oh shit, it's no good—even with Pep there is no way a bout between a 45-year-old writer and a college professor is going to draw."

We left it there. We had spent ourselves. As Jim and I headed for the porch, Mickey stopped us. "I'm having a red snapper cookout for a few friends Saturday evening. Why don't you gents join us?"

By Friday Jim and I had decided that a snapper cookout had considerable merit—especially if we could manage to combine the event with a day of constructive scientific endeavor and a good physical workout in the sun and surf. Our idea was to hike the twenty miles of beach to Murrell's Inlet. We would take our time working our way along, studying shoreline features and searching for new Pleistocene beachrock exposures and fossils reworked into the beach sands. We hoped Mickey would put us up for the night and that we could talk him into driving us home Sunday morning. If not, we could sleep on the beach and get back the way we had come.

About eight Saturday morning we grabbed our packsacks, peanut butter sandwiches, topo maps, sample bags, notebooks and hammers and headed south from McCumber. The sun was big and bright, the sky a classic blue vault, the tide low, the sea breeze light and fresh. It was a great day in the Coastal Plain!

When we had gone about nine miles the tide had begun to slip up the beach, the light breeze had become a gale, and black, menacing clouds moved rapidly across our big blue vault threatening to close down the sun. Thunder rumbled offshore and bolts of lightning bounced off distant white caps. We were very familiar with coastal plain electrical storms, had learned they were not to be taken lightly, had learned they could kill.

There was no visible shelter in sight and it was clear that we would be pinned down on the open beach—an all-around bad deal.

"Christ!" Jim growled. "We're in for it now. We're going to be charcoaled standing out here. I think we best head into the dune field where we won't be quite so bare-assed conspicuous." I didn't argue. As we crouched in a swale beside a small dune, large raindrops began to splatter onto the neatly rippled sand surfaces around us. In seconds there was a blinding flash of lighting and a blast of thunder that reverberated across the salt marsh behind us. Then came the real stuff.

Pounding, breath-sucking torrents of rain threatened to strip the shirts from our hunched backs, daggers of lightning cavorted in a deadly dance across the dune crests fusing sand grains to glassy globules; an uninterrupted crescendo of sanity-shattering explosions that would have put to shame the 16-inch salvos of the old battleship Missouri assaulted our ears. As we were dressed in swimming trunks, short-sleeved shirts and wading shoes, getting soaked to the skin was one of the easiest things we had done all week. We were wearing our Frank Buck pith helmets, on their best day piss-poor umbrellas, which became particularly evident as buckets of water cascaded over the narrow brims onto our shivering bodies. One particularly fascinating rivulet caught my attention as it playfully flowed the length of my soggy cigar to the unlighted end where it dribbled off onto the shoe on my right foot.

In an hour or so the dark storm clouds, having tired of the game, drifted off inland, revealing once again the clear blue vault above and a bright burning sun. By that time my interest in red snapper had dropped off to a weak whisper.

"Jim," I called. "What do you think of a red snapper cookout now?"

His response was short and definitive: "Fuck it."

"Well then, I assume you wouldn't be too upset if I suggest we turn about and retrace our steps to McCumber and call it a day?"

I didn't see Mickey again that summer. Jim and I dropped by his house in late July, but he had gone to New York.

During the following two years though, Henry Johnson and I visited with Mickey on several occasions. One afternoon when we were drilling nearby in Georgetown County we stopped at Mickey's for a chat. He listened attentively while we gave him a quick rundown of the geologic work we were doing. When we had finished he said, somewhat speculatively, "Maybe you guys could help me with a problem. During the past few months the water from my well has become contaminated with red iron oxide. Got any idea what I should do?"

We quickly assured him that we had no suggestions for a quick fix, but that possibly we could conduct a subsurface study of his property that would tell us something useful.

"You might want to give us a hand with the drilling and data gathering," Henry suggested. "When we finish the three of us could publish a paper presenting the results."

Co-authorship of a scientific paper seemed to intrigue Mickey. "The problem is, though," he reflected, "if my name appears on the title page people are going to think it's another Mike Hammer mystery."

"Well," Henry responded. "The origin of the iron oxide is certainly a mystery now, and who's to say that when we've completed the study it won't remain a mystery."

Following a round of hearty laughter, we collectively agreed that with iron oxide as the villain, there was no way the book would make the bestseller list. Sure as hell no rival for the Bible here.

On another of our visits we were surprised to find Mickey in an advanced state of euphoria. "Going to Hollywood in a couple of days," he announced. "We've got a group together that have agreed to make a film version of one of my books. I'm going out there to work on the script and maybe do some of the directing. Hell, maybe I'll play the lead."

Who else, I thought, *should play the part? After all, Mickey was Mike Hammer.*

Thereafter for a period of months, Mickey was gone much of the time. He had hired a young girl as a live-in housekeeper who also looked after his young children when they visited Murrell's Inlet. The girl's name was Ceci, and on occasions Henry and I had the opportunity to talk with her. Our conversations were infrequent, brief and casual. Even so, we could hardly overlook the special light in her eyes or the faint tremble in her voice when she spoke of her boss. It seemed clear to us that Ceci was very fond of Mickey—even, perhaps, in love with him.

Very late one evening Henry and I drove to Mickey's house and found that he had just returned from Hollywood. The three of us stood in front of the house beneath the cover of the live oaks and talked. Mickey said he was going to marry again—a young girl he had met in Hollywood.

As we spoke, Ceci suddenly appeared on the front porch carrying an overnight bag. An older man was at her side. As they passed us in the yard Ceci waved and smiled at us. The man took the bag and placed it in the back of a car parked next to ours. Then he and Ceci got in the front seat and drove off down the dark sand road toward town.

"That was Ceci," Mickey commented when she was gone. "I guess you fellows have met her. Nice girl but now that I'm getting married in a few days it didn't seem such a great idea to have a young live-in housekeeper." He said this with a knowing smirk. I hadn't met his fiancée but it seemed it was she, rather than Mickey, who decided Ceci should leave.

"You going to make your bride cook and keep house, Mickey?" Henry asked.

"Oh, well, I've made arrangements for an older and, I might add, less attractive lady to come in three or four days a week."

Not long after our midnight chat with Mickey, Henry and I stopped for dinner in a Murrell's Inlet restaurant. It was past ten o' clock and the manager was anxious to close. The lights had been dimmed and a young boy busily swept the floor near our table. Ceci had taken a job at the restaurant and that evening was serving our table. We asked her questions about Mickey and his new wife, but then we realized that the topic was painful to her. Henry described that evening in a piece he wrote for BTL. I include an excerpt from "Ceci's Tears":

"…And the questions were like knives in the pit of her stomach and she turned and went blindly to a far corner of the darkened room, and she put her head on a table and cried. At once we felt the hopelessness of life, and the anguish of all mankind poured out in Ceci's tears."

After I left the coastal plain to join the Humble Oil and Refining Company in Houston, Henry met Mickey at the Myrtle Beach airport one evening in 1966. He told Mickey I had divorced and married a student from Duke University and that I was the father of a little girl.

Mickey said he had married as he had told us he would that last night at his house. "Her name is Sherri," he said. "She was a twenty-three-year-old virgin when we married. Now she is in Hollywood making another movie."

When Mickey's plane arrived, Henry told him that I would be in South Carolina soon and probably would stop by to visit with him and the wife.

In August 1967, my wife and I were in Myrtle Beach working on exposures along the waterway. Susan had at times expressed an interest in meeting Mickey Spillane, so on a Sunday with a little free time on hand we drove to his house. No one was at home. We walked around the yard then looking for one of his cats or a duck. As we walked I thought of the times when I had chided him about how Ian Flemming's James Bond had supplanted Mike Hammer as the world's most famous tough guy. He always claimed he wasn't a bit bothered by that, but at the same time never failed to observe that after all, Bond was just an effete socialite, whereas Hammer was a real man.

Thinking along those lines I scribbled a note to Mickey and affixed it to the steering wheel of the red Ferrari parked under a live oak. I no longer have any recollection what it was I wrote, but I do vividly recall that both Susan and I were very amused when I signed it "Ian Fleming."

I've never again seen Mickey so I'm unsure if he shared our amusement.

Two Worlds in Collision

Near the end of July, 1961, I decided to make a quick trip to Houston. A few days earlier I had called the Dean of the School of Arts and Sciences, to check out the status of my NSF proposal. He told me the proposal had been funded but, predictably, he had explained that because the money had not yet been released to the university, it would be impossible to give me a cash advance. The dean seemed especially amused by my reference to impending starvation, but I had expected him to be unsympathetic and uncooperative. Earlier I had sized him up as a full-time pompous ass, who probably ate dingle berries on his oatmeal.

I knew I could only deal with the problem eye to eye in Houston. Forced to follow the chain of command, I would be required to start with my dean. He would repeat the same old bullshit, tell me he understood my situation and explain again that he was helpless under the circumstances. Then I would go to the Comptroller, who would scratch his ass, shrug his bony shoulders, shake his empty head, and sing the same sorrowful refrain, "It's out of my hands. Like to help, but rules, you know, must be followed." The Comptroller was the typical administrator, a petty wimp, who lived by the rules. If the book said to eat dog turds for lunch every Tuesday he would eat dog turds, lick his lips, and declare how tasty they were.

In the end I would go to the Chancellor. He was a political animal, a fund raiser. If there was one thing he understood, it was money. He would understand my need if it were properly explained. I would point out that if I didn't get an advance I would be forced to suspend my field studies which would make it impossible to complete the project by the scheduled deadline. In that event, it would be unlikely NSF would look with favor on future projects I might submit for funding. As a clincher, I would add that, under such circumstances created by the university, NSF might, in the future, take a dim view of *any* proposal submitted to them by anyone at the university.

I wasn't certain that what I planned to say was actually true, but it seemed probable that the Chancellor wasn't either and that he wouldn't take a chance that it might be.

It wasn't just the shortage of money that forced my decision to make the Houston trip. For some time I had been living in two worlds, headed for collision. I had to decide which of the worlds was real, which it was I wanted. I could only make that decision in Houston.

On the morning Jim and I were to leave for Texas, Karin and I drove to Litchfield Beach for a quiet lunch. Afterwards we walked barefoot, hand in hand, on the beach behind the Inn. When we reached the water's edge, the lifeguard sauntered up to us on some pretext. He wanted, I knew, a closer look at Karin. I was a little irritated, but could hardly blame him.

At some point Karin broke free from me and ran to one of the beach swings. She pushed it two or three times and then abruptly turned toward me, eyes large, blue and concerned. "I shouldn't do this, should I? You are too dignified." I laughed, walked over to her, took her hand again and led her down the beach. I almost asked her to marry me then, but I remembered that I still had a wife in Houston. Feeling a little depressed I fought back the impulse, rationalizing that I would find a better time after my return from Texas. I had to be certain.

On the return drive to McCumber, Karin curled into a fetal position at my side, her head on my shoulder. The car soared. I didn't feel at all dignified.

When the time came to leave McCumber, Jim, Irma, Karin and I walked outside to my Dodge in the driveway. We stood by the car for ten or fifteen minutes. With no wish to say goodbye, we said silly things, told stupid little jokes and laughed as if we thought they were funny. At some point Karin gave me a sober look. "We are all smiling; we should be on Candid Camera, but your wife might see us."

"It wouldn't matter," I responded. "She would only assume you were a beautiful actress hired by Alan Funt as a part of the show."

A few minutes later Karin and Irma drove away in Irma's little Renault. The previous evening Karin had counted the days of our separation on her fingers. "One, two, three, four. Won't be so long to wait for you." I agreed. I was prepared to wait for her as long as required.

McCumber was rented only until noon the following day, so it was necessary for us to pack all our gear including the Arkansas Traveler and its trailer, and deposit it with the Deckers. On our return to town we planned to stay with them until another field camp could be located.

Mid-afternoon of the next day I pulled the car off the road at a café for sandwiches and beer. We were in the outskirts of Meridian, Mississippi.

At the counter while munching on a BLT I skimmed through a newspaper left there by another customer. A front-page headline caught my eye. A University of Mississippi professor had unceremoniously dropped dead in his classroom the previous day. The guy was only thirty-eight—my age. I showed the headline to Jim and said, "Damn, I've lived an active, full and, at times, exciting life. I am in love and I think I am loved. No need to feel badly should I shove off today. I'd have no regrets."

Twenty minutes later, cruising west over the wet pavement of the two-lane highway at a steady 65 mph, we suddenly broke over the crest of a long, low hill. A wide valley, green and bucolic, spread before us. A quaint and uncertain narrow bridge spanned a small, sluggish, meandering stream—a calm, peaceful scene on most any day, but not that afternoon.

There had been accident at the bridge, and the road was filled with police cruisers, ambulances, wreckers, and most terrifying, an immobile string of vehicles blocking our lane. Instinctively I hit the brakes with a leaden foot. I took a quick glance at Solliday, silent, eyes fixed dead ahead on the scene below, arm crooked over the door sill, a lighted cigarette held loosely between two fingers. Calmly, I said, "I think we've had it this time, Jim." Jim said nothing.

The people who had been in the cars were now standing along the shoulder of the road—stretching their legs, gawking, playing with the kids. In that first moment I saw a passenger car cross the bridge and begin its ascent of the hill in the left lane. All possible escape routes were now effectively blocked. If we veered right, onto the shoulder, we would strike some of the men, women, and children standing there, possibly causing several fatalities. Straight ahead we would crash into the rear end of the last car in the line; our speed would guarantee our own deaths. To the left we faced sure death in a head-on collision with the car coming up the hill.

In a flash I saw a slim chance of survival for everyone. If I could slow the Dodge enough to allow the approaching car time to clear the immobile line, there was a possibility I could shoot the gap to the comparative safety of the left lane. However, as I clutched the steering wheel and frantically pumped the brake pedal, the car began to swerve wildly over the wet pavement. With about 100 yards of open road ahead, the oncoming car broke free of the stationary line. Our Red Sea had just parted. For a split second it seemed we would make it. Before I could savor that thought, the Dodge chose to fishtail broadside into the path of the oncoming car. As I braced for the sickening crunch of metal and glass, the Dodge swung back parallel with the median line. In that instant the moving car swept by us with only a few inches to spare. For a brief moment I looked into the wide, frightened eyes of the driver. His face mirrored my own terror. In a split second I nosed the Dodge through the narrow gap.

Our problems had not ended; the Dodge was out of control. I could only sit in frozen horror as it careened over the shoulder into a drainage ditch where we came to a jolting halt against a grass-covered embankment. In the first moments of that wild, terrifying ride I'd had time for two thoughts: that I would die, and that Karin would never learn what had happened to me.

Sometimes the gods cast eyes of pity on the hopeless. The clay of the embankment, softened by the recent rains, had absorbed most of the shock of the impact, leaving us shaken but uninjured. Damage to the car, we later learned, was relatively minor, entirely confined to numerous punctures in the radiator.

I sat motionless in the front seat of the Dodge for maybe ten seconds before I realized I wasn't dead. Then I looked over at Solliday. He hadn't moved. His arm still rested on the doorsill, the lighted cigarette was still between his fingers. He stared mutely at the grassy bank. He was breathing.

Something less than 30 seconds had elapsed since we had reached the crest of the hill, but at that moment it seemed like a lifetime.

I looked into the rearview mirror in time to see a patrol car whisk by. His mind focused on the scene at the bridge, the officer ignored us. Then I saw a large number of people streaming toward us from the rear of the parked cars. The charge was led by a young man wearing a yellow tractor hat. He rushed to my side of the car, popped his head into the window, and, without asking how we were, exclaimed, "By God, that was the best piece of driving I ever saw!"

Still dazed, I was in no mood to explain that I'd had little to do with it. I gave the fellow a wan smile; Solliday remained a stone statue.

"Don't worry about a thing," the guy said reassuringly. "We'll have you out of here in a jiffy. I'll bring my pickup over here and hook you up to a tow chain. You'll be back on the road in a few minutes."

Actually it was closer to twenty minutes before we were back on the road, but I really wasn't counting. By the time we were ready to go Jim had fully recovered, the wreckage at the bridge had been cleared, and the long line of vehicles was in motion. The Dodge started without a hiccup. Its life-giving juices spurting from a hundred tiny punctures in the radiator, it had become oddly docile and subdued. It had had its thrills for the day and now, wounded and in pain, it begged for a reassuring pat on the hood and some kind of loving care.

The nearest garage was Howard's about two miles east of the bridge, in the small town of Lake. "You'll make it okay," our friend told us. "But you'd better hurry, Howard usually cuts out for home at five." Looking at my watch I saw we had 15 minutes. If our water supply held up we would have time to spare.

Before we left our rescuer, I asked what had happened at the bridge.

"Oh, a drunk nigger in an old pickup ran into a car with two elderly ladies. Killed the women. The nigger bit off his tongue. Can you believe that?"

We found Howard's garage with a few minutes to spare, but no more than a little steam in the radiator. Howard, a big, red-faced guy in greasy coveralls, was an accommodating fellow. He agreed, to our surprise, to stay on without supper and work on the car until it was once again ready for the road. It wasn't an easy job to find and patch all those little holes, but he had the car ready by ten.

Unwilling to waste more time, we decided to drive straight through to Houston. We were home by dawn.

We stayed in town for two days, long enough to get the advance from the Chancellor (who bought my story), to gather up all 350 pounds of Jim Chaplin, and for me to determine that I would get a divorce from Phyllis as soon as possible.

Jim Chaplin, one of my graduate students, had elected to do his master's thesis on Late Pleistocene deposits exposed in the banks of a section of the Intracoastal Waterway in Horry County. Earlier I was going to send him bus fare to Myrtle Beach, but now he could join Jim and me and escape the boring bus ride. It was a long, two-day trip to Myrtle Beach, but with three drivers it was possible to catch catnaps in the back seat. Even so, late the first day we opted to check into a motel in Jackson, Mississippi. We had agreed that a little R & R would do us a world of good.

Following a quick dinner at the motel restaurant we returned to our room and broke open a bottle of Black Label. Around one in the morning we drove into town in search of a late hours nightspot. With water glasses of bourbon in hand and a full fifth in the back seat we patrolled the deserted streets of Jackson. As any sane and sober person could have predicted, we discovered that Jackson after midnight was a ghost town. Chagrined and disgusted we smashed our empty glasses on the red brick pavement and drove back to the motel.

It was a beautiful, quiet, balmy, night with a full moon. Noting this, Chaplin commented that it was bright enough to read a book by the pool. To test this premise we sent Solliday to our room to fetch some reading material. When he returned with three Pogo books he found that we had placed three chairs and a round metal table mounted with a floppy umbrella in the water at the shallow end of the pool. Stripped to our shorts we slipped into the water with the books and three glasses of bourbon and seated ourselves around the table. We soon learned that drinking Black Label and reading Pogo in a motel pool at 2:00 a.m. is highly boring.

Leaving the furniture behind to baffle guests and motel employees in the morning we climbed onto the walkway at the edge of the pool and plotted our next escapade.

Chaplin concluded that there must be other guests on the motel from his home state of Iowa. Solliday suggested we stroll around the grounds and check all the license plates to test Chaplin's assumption. But Big Jim would have none of that. "Hell, he proclaimed. "I'm from Iowa but I've got Texas plates on my car. So what the hell good would it do to check plates?"

He had a point, of course, but I didn't much care for his next suggestion. "The only way to do this right is to go door to door and inquire."

"Man, you can't do that. It's two in the morning, and everyone is asleep. You do that and we all end up in jail!"

Unimpressed with the logic of my argument, Chaplin took off like a rogue rhino, racing door to door, hammering, pounding, and shouting, "Is there anyone in there from Iowa?" Unable to think of a practical way of bringing down a crazed, 350-pound rhino in wet shorts, Solliday and I (also still in wet boxers) followed at a discreet distance, pleading that he call off the hunt.

For some reason, perhaps because the guests lay in frozen terror beneath their beds, no one summoned the police. Finally Chaplin ran out of steam. The tempest at an end, the three of us returned to the poolside, gathered up our clothes, glasses, bourbon, and Pogo books, and walked to our room where we soon passed into peaceful oblivion.

A few hours later we awoke with throbbing heads and burning thirsts. Feeling as if we had been adrift in the Gobi Desert without water for countless days, we staggered blindly, red-eyed, with parched, blackened and swollen tongues, to the motel restaurant. Seated in this oasis, we began to order a variety of hot and cold drinks. Sight impaired, mental faculties seriously diminished, we were unable to see clearly what was set before us by the waitress, with the result that we continued to reorder the same beverages for some time. When we were ready to leave my vision had improved enough to see that our plates were ringed with a couple dozen cups and glasses, many still full or partially full of coffee, milk, and fruit juice. In as dignified a manner as possible, under the circumstances, we worked our way to the counter by the door, paid our bill, and hurried back to the room.

Whatever the volume of liquids we had consumed with breakfast, it had failed to quench the burning thirsts. On the edge of Jackson we stopped at a supermarket, purchased three quarts of buttermilk, and consumed the contents in the car in the parking lot. Our thirsts temporarily assuaged, our brains semi-operational, we set out to drive straight through to Myrtle Beach. We'd had all the R&R we could handle for a while.

As we cruised along the dark and lonely highways that night we sang songs to pass the time. By the time we reached South Carolina we decided our trio deserved a name. A few minutes later, by common consent, we became "The Three Drunkettes," "Blink" (Chaplin), "Blank" (Solliday), and "Blunk" (DuBar). Through the years we continued to use the names, but, like Walt Kelly's bats (Bewitched, Bothered and Bemildred), each of us became confused about which name belonged to which person and tended to apply them rather haphazardly. Hell, I'm not certain I have them right now.

Shortly before 6:00 a.m. we pulled into the Decker's driveway. Not wishing to disturb the family, who would still be asleep, we went to the small guesthouse in the back yard. Wasting no time, we dropped our bone-weary bodies onto the beckoning bunk beds with visions of several hours of uninterrupted sleep. In seconds we were snoring.

Within minutes, however, we were jolted to wide-eyed sitting positions by the unearthly wails and shrieks of, what I could only surmise, was a sexually disturbed demon.

Slowly, as my blurry eyes began to focus, I saw a tall, lean, figure standing silhouetted in the doorway. It was our host, Deck, his cheeks pouched out like a squirrel with a mouthful of hickory nuts, his face red, and his eyes bulging, blowing a goddamned World War II bugle.

When he was satisfied he had gained our undivided attention he placed the instrument on the refrigerator, and, grinning broadly, shouted, "Drop your cocks and grab your socks, it's party time!" It was 6:15 a.m.

Later that morning I called Karin and invited her and her sister to join Solliday, Chaplin and me for dinner at the Elk's Club the following evening.

When we met the girls at the club, everything seemed as it should, as I had expected it to be. Nothing about Karin's behavior suggested that anything might be amiss. However, after dinner as we all sat watching the floor show, Karin leaned toward me, placed her hand on my shoulder and began to speak softly in my ear. The crowd was laughing and clapping their hands, so at first I couldn't identify the subject. Soon, though, I realized she was slowly, with measured, heavily accented words, disassembling my life. She told me she had been very disturbed that I was married, that she had fallen in love with a married man, and that she might cause a break-up of a marriage. While Jim and I were in Houston she had gone to the base psychologist to discuss her dilemma. He told her that she was quite mature for her age and that an older man might be all right for her, but definitely not a married, older man. "Find a single, older man if you must," he advised. She told me then that, despite her feelings for me, she would follow his advice. Her decision was final.

Stunned, I sat there, speechless, numb, as Karin and Irma walked out of the room. Finally on rubbery legs I arose and followed them outside. When I caught up with Karin in the parking lot I took her in my arms and kissed her goodbye. I stood there dazed, without hope, with no meaning to my life and watched helplessly as they drove away in that crazy little Renault. I knew then I could never have her, could never change her mind. I knew also that I would have to try.

When I walked back inside, Chaplin was at the bar talking with a guy I didn't know. I walked to the bar, pushed between them and asked the bartender to pour me a very large tumbler of bourbon—no water, no ice, just booze. When he handed me the full glass, I downed it without taking a breath, then turned and walked to the men's room. When I returned to the bar Chaplin was alone.

Jim looked up at me from his bar stool and smiled. "That fellow who was here was really impressed with the way you polished off that huge drink. Said he had to admire a man who could handle his liquor that way."

At least there was one thing left I could handle.

The Hideaway

When Jim and I had gone to Houston earlier in the month, we had been forced to give up McCumber Place. On our return to Myrtle Beach, Decker's backyard "playhouse" served as temporary headquarters while we searched for a more suitable field camp. On the third day we found it. It was called "The Hideaway" by its owner, Mr. Keel, who also owned Keel's Music Store in Myrtle Beach.

Keel had named the place well. Ten miles south of Conway and ten miles east of Myrtle Beach, it stood alone at the end of a five-mile narrow, rutted, winding sand road that snaked its way through the stands of young pines from U.S. 501 to the west bank of the Intracoastal waterway.

It was a fine house and not really a cabin. For one thing, there were three bedrooms so there was no problem in accommodating Chaplin. There was a spacious well-furnished dining room perfectly fitting our needs for a workroom, a comfortable living room with a fireplace and a great, fully equipped kitchen. Perhaps best of all, there was a small dock where we could tie up the Arkansas Traveler.

During the first week at the Hideaway, Solliday and I helped Chaplin with his studies along the Intracoastal waterway. On about the 8th of August, Henry Johnson drove the DOG truck-mounted mobile auger to Bob's Motel in Conway. We planned to drill 25 to 30 holes which we hoped would provide us with much-needed samples and data.

Rowdy would be with Henry, I knew. Henry went virtually no place without his forty- pound Airedale. In his canoe, truck, car, at all drill sites and outcrops, or on the beach when we searched for coquina, Rowdy was there at his side. When we photographed an outcrop in the field, it was usually Rowdy who posed for scale. It was a job in which he seemed to take considerable pride.

Henry loved Rowdy, and it was apparent that Rowdy returned his affection. After his first extended field experience with Henry and Rowdy, a geology professor from Buffalo University commented to me rather indignantly that it almost seemed that Henry thought more of his damned dog than he did his human friends, an amusing but quite accurate observation.

In time I, too, grew quite fond of Rowdy although I wasn't certain how he regarded me. I came to accept him as just one of the guys—a member of the field party. However, there was, so far as I was concerned, one small hitch in the relationship. When en route to drill sites, Rowdy sat on my lap on the passenger side of the cab. While we were drilling he sometimes sat or lay in the shade of a nearby tree and watched us or slept. At other times he wandered off through the nearby woods and tobacco fields. When we were ready to leave a site, Henry and I took our positions in the cab and Henry would call or whistle for his fuzzy buddy. Rowdy would come on a full tail-wagging run and without hesitation propel his body through the open cab window onto my lap. If for any reason I had not fully prepared myself for the impact I found that during the following ten minutes I could do remarkable vocal impersonations of Minnie Mouse. I could only fear that long time repetition of the ritual would inevitably produce permanent impairment of some of my essential bodily functions.

In time, however, age and arthritis resolved the problem. During Rowdy's last years it was necessary for Henry or me to lift him in and out of the truck and the boat when we were working the rivers. We also were reduced to pushing and pulling him up slick, steep slopes and to retrieve him when he slipped or stumbled into a river or the waterway.

I was saddened, of course, to witness Rowdy's physical decline, but I could never honestly say that I was sorry when his crotch crunching days came to an end.

I spent a lot of evenings alone at the Hideaway, sulking over the breakup with Karin. Linda Decker and Solliday had been in love for some time, and, during the two days we had stayed with the Deckers, Chaplin had become quite infatuated with Linda's younger sister, Gayle. The four of them double-dated nearly every evening, almost inevitably ending up at the Elk's Club. After a few dates Gayle and Chaplin somehow had settled on their song, "Blue Velvet." At their request Jesse Shaw's orchestra played the piece several times each evening. The vocalist, who knew none of the lyrics and had a short-term memory but a fertile imagination, ad-libbed a fresh set of lyrics for each performance of the song.

The Jims were not unaware of my general state of depression. One evening as they prepared to drive my car into town to pick up their dates, they decided to pause long enough to drink a toast to my lost love. We drank from glasses Jim, Irma, Karin and I had used one memorable evening at McCumber. The toast completed we smashed the glasses into Keel's nice clean fireplace.

I appreciated their thoughtful gesture, but unfortunately it did little to ameliorate my blue funk.

We really didn't treat Mr. Keel's house with the respect it deserved. It was my fault, of course. I plainly failed to meet my responsibility as chief honcho of the field camp. At the time I was drowning in a sea of self-pity and neither Keel nor his house mattered a damn to me. Wallowing in my misery I set a bad example for Solliday and Chaplin, but with my sense of self-worth at an all-time low it didn't seem important.

The day we moved into the Hideaway it had been sparkling clean but in short order we had converted it to a pigsty. On our arrival there was more than an ample supply of clean dishes, utensils, pots, pans, and silverware. Within ten days all of it was stained and caked with dried food. Everything was tossed onto disorderly stacks and piles that covered every available surface in the kitchen.

Unwilling to wash anything, we used paper plates and cups and plastic utensils purchased at a market in Myrtle Beach. As our interest in preparation of proper meals diminished we turned to a diet consisting almost exclusively of milk and beer.

One morning while preparing a breakfast of Sara Lee chocolate cake and milk, I idly lifted the lid from a fry pan that had at some time been shoved to the back burner of the stove. Inside I unhappily discovered a two-week old putrid, rotting, hamburger steak. The stench quickly permeated the entire house and asserted its vileness for the remainder of the day.

On another occasion I sent Chaplin outside to dispose of a week's accumulation of trash and garbage. Not finding a trash receptacle, he dumped the load into the waterway off our boat dock, confident the refuse would float downstream to the ocean, never again to be seen (by us).

Of course he was correct—it did float downstream—but he hadn't taken into account the effect of the incoming tide. The next morning when we went to the dock to load the boat for the day's work on the waterway, we found both the boat and the dock surrounded by our trash and garbage looking as if it desperately wished to return to its birthplace in our kitchen.

A few days before Chaplin was to return to Houston he photographed Solliday and me standing, hung over, in the midst of the clutter of the kitchen. I still have that photo. On the back is written, "From the *Good Housekeeping* Magazine." It marks one of the truly low periods of my life.

Hobart Furbunch invited us to his house for dinner and cocktails on the eve of Chaplin's departure for Houston. By ten o' clock we were in high spirits and primed for a little adventure. We agreed to walk over to Zeb's Restaurant and give Chaplin his last opportunity to observe the changing of the guard.

At the door to the restaurant we decided the occasion called for a dramatic entrance. Forming up in single file we snaked our way inside loudly singing, "Jesus Loves to Cha Cha Cha, Arthur Murray taught Him How," sung to the tune of "Jesus Loves Me." The lyrics were the inspiration of Keith Decker, then age 15.

We wound our way to the counter where, still in a line, we settled on four stools and ordered a round of beers. Wasting no time, Solliday began to give the Air Corps private to his right a particularly bad time. For some reason Jim was in an ugly mood and was determined to pick a fight. Jim, an excellent athlete, was no fighter. Usually when he pulled this sort of stunt he ended up getting badly hurt.

Sensing impending doom, I went over and sat down beside the private. Assuming a calm and confidential demeanor, I said, "You don' t want to pay any attention to this fellow next to you. Actually he's a good guy—just a little drunk; doesn't mean what he's saying at all. He was in the Navy, three years on a carrier. Hell, you must understand how those gobs are. Sometimes on shore leave they get a little crazy—we've all done that kind of thing. Hell, it's a matter of letting off a little pent-up steam."

The fellow gave me a dull, dark-eyed stare. No indication that he had comprehended a word I'd said. *Perhaps he was so drunk*, I thought, *he's numb and can't respond to anything.*

But I wasn't ready to gamble on that possibility, so I bought him a beer and gave it another try. "You know," I said with what I hoped was a tone of confidentiality, "this guy has been having a really tough go of it. I'll admit he hasn't behaved very well, but damn, under the circumstances it's to be expected." I leaned forward toward him and practically whispered into his ear, "He doesn't want to talk about it, but he just lost his wife to cancer and they had been married only a year. I'm sure you can guess how that might affect a guy." For just a moment I thought I detected an acknowledging nod, but it could just as easily been an involuntary nervous twitch.

There was a chance I could reason with Solliday, but in his present condition he would almost certainly resent my interference and become even more belligerent. I decided to take up the matter with Chaplin.

Leaning over Chaplin's shoulder, I said, "You know, of course, that Solliday is going to start a fight with that guy next to him."

"I know," Jim responded. "I've seen him that way a few times. Can't do a damned thing with him."

"Well, I think we ought to take a look around that back room. It's full of flyboys. We need to assess the odds."

We moved just inside the backroom where a large gathering of reveling Air Force officers were boisterously reliving their adventure in the wild blue yonder.

"I count thirty-three of the fuckers," I said. "If Solliday starts a fight they're all going to rush out here to help their comrade in arms."

Jim didn't argue my point, so I continued, "The way I see it, you can handle about six of them and I can maybe take three. Solliday might manage that fellow at the bar but Hobie will just get in the way. At best that adds up to ten. No way around it," I concluded. "The other 24 fuckers are gonna kick the shit out of our asses."

Still assessing the throng of airmen in the room, Jim observed, "I believe you just painted a pretty accurate picture of the situation. So what do we do?"

"Just go back to the counter and you and Hobart keep an eye on Jim. I'll talk with Zeb."

I found Zeb in the galley, talking with Tony, the head cook.

"Zeb, old buddy," I said. "I don't want to interrupt anything here, but we got a potentially serious situation out there." I pointed through the doorway to Solliday and the private at the bar. "That flyboy's a trouble-maker," I explained. "He's trying to pick a fight with Solliday. I tried to talk sense to him but he got nasty with me, too. I just don't think he'll respond to reason. If he starts anything your place is likely to get busted up a bit, you know."

Zeb was concerned. "Can't have that. But stay cool and don't worry about a thing, I'll handle it." Before I could return to the stool next to the private, Zeb was on the phone calling the police. I continued my effort to placate the young man until two burly officers burst into the restaurant. By then I had my arm around the private's shoulder—we had become friends.

I felt a little sorry for the guy as the two cops collared and dragged him outside to the waiting patrol car. On the other hand, I could hardly deny a certain satisfaction in the knowledge that the problem had been resolved by old-fashioned duplicity rather than raw violence.

The next morning the Jims and I drove to Hurl Rocks Beach where we sat in the sand and worked over a rough draft copy of a section of Chaplin's thesis. Furbunch joined us after awhile with a cold six-pack of Millers. We had one last brew together and then, his summer's adventure concluded, we took Chaplin to the bus station.

I let Jim drive back to the Hideaway while I sat beside him in deep depression. In ten days Jim and I would also be leaving for Houston. I dreaded facing another September in Houston. As we drove the sand road to the field camp I was almost overwhelmed with a fear that this would be my last summer in the Carolinas.

Later in my house in Houston I put into words some of the despair I had felt that day in August, 1961:

My summers were times to remember—times of exhilaration and excitement, times of hope and of doubt, times when I had surmounted the insurmountable and ruled my world, and times when I had floundered hopelessly in a morass of my own making.

The summers were times of freedom—freedom from criticism, from old responsibilities. They were times of comradeship and love—times of searching and finding, times also of losing—of almost unbearable loneliness, times of hard sweating work and bone-aching fatigue, times of carousing and horsing around, and times of drunken parties.

And the summers were times of tenderness and gentle caresses—of whispered, passionate love talk and shared dreams of Tomorrow and the New Life.

Most of all the summers were times of real living—tasting the zest and the adventure of life in its fullest measure, when every blade of grass and every sunset had special significance. When every day was a welcome challenge and the soul of man a thing to exalt for it was truly immortal.

But each September when I returned to Houston I was forced to make the transition to the cobweb-draped, mildewed boredom that quickly and surely sucked the life out of me life and left me limp and apathetic. Only the searing memory of the summer past and the expectation of another to come had enabled me to face each dreary day. I had come to hate September, to wish I could strike it from the calendar and live forever in one continuous life-sustaining summer.

Now another summer was rapidly drawing to a close. September was near at hand, a slight chill had crept into the night air, the days had shortened and even some of the trees had begun to show a hint of fall colors. Soon, I thought, it will all end, and this time there will be no more summers. My body convulsed with the painful knowledge that summer's promise was only an illusion that would wither and fade in the face of the hard reality of September. I buried my face in my hands for a moment and then lifted my head and defiantly shook my fist at the sky and cursed all the Septembers that had defeated me, and particularly this September which would know my final defeat.

Then the August winds seemed to join me in an anguished plea,' September, oh September, never come, never come again, September.'

But even as the sound of my words echoed across the swamp I could feel the inevitability of September beginning to settle on my shoulders, slowly pressing me downward toward the gray impersonal timeless earth at my feet.

A King of the Coastal Plain

In August, 1961, following a long, hot, day of drilling with Henry Johnson, I asked him to join me for a steak dinner at the Elks. I felt alone and depressed and sorry for myself. Solliday's romance with Linda Decker was in full bloom and he was with her at every opportunity. I needed solace, someone on whom I could dump a load of misery. During the two years Henry and I had known each other, our conversations had been almost completely confined to our professional activities. He didn't seem eager to talk much about himself, so I figured him for a listener.

Henry had no idea what he was in for when we walked onto the Elks dining room and Jesse Shaw's orchestra rose and gave me the customary *Georgia on my Mind* salute. We sat at a table near the bandstand and Johnny took our order for drinks and dinner. Even before the drinks arrived I began to drop my litany of woes on poor, unsuspecting Henry. Soon, however, he identified with my problem and in short order began to relate details of his own disastrous marriage and his failed love affair with his secretary.

For several hours I became the listener and comforter. When we left for the Hideaway I somehow felt much better just knowing that another person shared my anguish. It was reassuring to realize I was not alone. I remember that evening as the beginning of our friendship.

For three decades Henry and I have each groped with the question of why we would become and remain close friends. At first glance we might seem the prototypes for the odd couple. From time to time we have attempted to put into words our thoughts on the subject. Three letters serve as examples:

From me to Henry, date unknown:

> *I often think of our first meeting in 1959. Each of us with peculiar brands of defense mechanisms which made it impossible to*

really know one another. Probably both very distrustful of the other.

We came from such different backgrounds. You an aristocratic southern gentleman, steeped in southern tradition, and I, a third generation Johnny-come-lately from the gutters of a Yankee steel mill town. We disagreed on a thousand things important to the rest of the world, anyone of which could have caused irreconcilable animosity between lesser types.

But we are both basically romantic idealists and we both seek the same things in the same way. We both hold a vision of a better life; we both search for the truth of life; and we both have an indefinable faith that will not allow us to succumb to adversity. Or maybe it's just that we are a couple of screwballs and hopeless misfits.

Though we can't explain our friendship we do know it began that night in Myrtle Beach Elk's Club in August, 1961.

From Henry to me, March 1, 1964:

Sometimes I ask myself why I picked you as a friend when I have so few friends, if any. I don't know the answer unless it is that sometimes when I look at you I have the feeling of seeing part of me, the inner, hidden part reflected in a mirror. It gives me the ghostly feeling that someone else is living my life, experiencing the same experiences, feeling the same emotions that I feel. I never had a brother, but sometimes I have a strong feeling of the brotherhood of man. I think I feel that way because I know deep inside that my brother hurts as I do. I think it is at such times, when this brotherhood feeling is the strongest, that I am inclined to think of you as part and parcel of all mankind and to refer to you as Brother Jules.

But the hell with all that too.

...Something ere the end, some work of noble note may yet be done.

In 1969 Henry again reflected on the nature of our relationship:

One of the reasons I think I get along with you moderately well is that you write good letters. Damn few people do. I have a separate file on you. Your letters are frequent and always interesting. And none of them shows any sign of strain, or pomposity, or formality or sense of obligation. And I never thought about it before but, as typified by your 17 January remark on suicide, you never offer a judgment or any advice about my personal affairs or decisions. Most people cannot resist telling you where you went wrong and what to do in the future. And in 99.99 percent of the cases they don't know their ass about the facts of the situation, and it is none of their business anyway. And the hell with all this!

In July 1963, Henry and I initiated BTL (Between The Lines). BTL is a collection of personal observations and essays written primarily by Henry and me. At last count BTL contained 272 entries held in four loose-leaf notebooks. Though I wrote the first contribution it was Henry who recorded the purpose of BTL and its meaning to us:

While somewhat in his cups the other night my brother Jules remarked that it was a great pity that increasing emphasis on objectivity and brevity in geological literature is producing papers and reports which are completely sterile in so far as the personality of the author is concerned. They give no hint of the personal and professional problems he faces during the course of the work. 'Editors nowadays' said Jules, 'want only short stark sentences, crisp organization, and an absolute minimum of extraneous background material and general description. In fact, if there were an acceptable one they would want you to use code.

Reading one of these reports, we decided, leaves you with the feeling that it was turned out by a machine. A machine that saw no sunrises or sunsets, felt no ocean breezes, blinked away no gnats, burned under no blazing sun, and knew not the frustration of trying with one mud covered hand to rub a burning mixture of salt, sweat, and insect repellent from the eyes while swatting at a deerfly with the other.

Pondering these things we decided that what is really needed are two reports, one reduced to bare scientific essentials to satisfy space-conscious editors and professional geologists who are in a hurry, and the other, a more human account of what it is really like.

This human report would provide insight into the stumbling, faltering, groping process of working out the geology of a given region. Herein would be found the enthusiasm of the hunter, the sudden burst of happy intuition, the blundering side trails leading only to blank walls, good days when things go right and progress is measured in leaps and bounds, bad days of throbbing head and fluttery stomach from the night before, days of sunshine and days of rain, days of broken down machinery, and days of listless men wondering whether anything is worthwhile.

And the nights. Don't forget the nights. Nights of seeking. Nights of finding. Nights of happiness. Nights of loneliness. Nights of hopeless depression.

Days and nights follow nights and days until they merge into an endless blur interwoven with dimly remembered voices and vague forms.

What is the need of such a human story? And what would be its message? No need and no message. Except maybe the need to live and the message that life concerns people and that without them there is no life.

Whatever the need or the message there isn't much chance of ever seeing such a behind-the-scenes geologic report. Jules' " Prologue..." gives an idea of what one might be like in part, and I never expect to see this in print.

Lacking the human account I think we must develop the faculty of reading between the lines to have any concept of what goes on behind the shield people carry before them. Even this is guesswork, and we can never really know the truth of any life situation. But between-the-lines truth is probably closer to true truth than any other kind. I believe this applies in politics, war, and all forms of human contact. Few things are really as they first appear. Extremes of good turn out to be not so good, and extremes of bad turn out to be something else again.

True truth is somewhere between the lines of life and very seldom do we find it, much less know it when we do.

In a 1968 letter to me Henry had additional thoughts on the meaning and significance of BTL.

I like your phrase 'BTL land'. I had not thought of it like that previously but immediately recognize what you mean and applaud the aptness of the phrase. 'BTL land' is much like Brigadoon—a hazy never-never land, coexistent in time with 'real life' but out of phase with it so that when we step through the mists we enter another world, a world in which our pulses quicken, love and adventure are ours, and all our throbbing senses are heightened and made acutely aware of the fantastic fullness and unbelievable wonder of life. It is a magic formula of pain, bitterness, exultation, and beauty held together and shaped by a framework of remembrance and the incurable optimism of man.

I pity those poor bastards who shoot themselves when things look bad. No man who has tasted BTL land would ever do that. A BTL man is going to be there to the bloody grinding end because he has tasted the nectar of paradise and smelled the scented gardens and known the eternal delights of the houris. As long as there is the remotest possibility of that coming down the road a BTL man is going to be there scrutinizing every line on every page of the book of life so as not to miss a fleeting instant of it ere the final convulsive clutching for a breath not there. By God, cheers for BTL land! I believe I detected a glimmer of it in a far corner of the public room of the Little Pee Dee Lodge the other day.

In the winter of 1963 I gave a talk to a Duke sorority entitled "Between the Lines," drawing on some of our early material. It was a resounding success with the young ladies. Thus encouraged, for the remainder of my teaching career I worked bits and pieces of BTL into my lectures. The students always seemed to enjoy the material and I think it helped convince them that a college professor can, after all, be a human being.

A year later Henry and I established RAMS (Ragged-Assed Misfits Society). We wished to recognize the round pegs in our square-holed world. In addition to ourselves, Hobart W.C. Furbunch, III, Jim Solliday, and Rowdy Johnson (Henry's Airedale), were designated as Founders. Women were specifically excluded from the Society; however, a few were eventually included in something we referred to as "The Woman's Auxiliary." For men there were a variety of membership categories.

As stated in the charter only Founders can vote (Henry carried Rowdy's proxy) and Founders can designate their successors (Divine right of kings of the Coastal Plain). None of the deceased Founders (Solliday, Rowdy, and Furbunch) availed themselves of this option.

Full Members and Honorary Members (real RAMS who were deceased or outside our environmental sphere at the time of election) require unanimous approval of the Founders. All others may be elected by the vote of one Founder. In the thirty-odd years since the inception of the Society, only six men have been elected Full Members. These include my old buddy E.P. Decker and Johnny, the waiter at the Elks.

Honorary Members include Sterling Hayden, actor and expert seaman, Mickey Spillane, Clarence King (first director of the U.S. Geological Survey), William Saroyan (author of *The Human Comedy*) and Guilford Phinney, comrade in arms. There are two Associate Members (those who have shared experiences with the Founders on special occasions): Bob Lunz, the diminutive director of the biological station on Wadmalaw Island, South Carolina, who almost single-handedly fought the fat bureaucrats and other rapers of our earth to preserve South Carolina's wetlands; and Zeb Berry, restauranteur, pimp, and All-American loser in the game of life.

There has been only one Junior Member (one who shows promise of becoming eligible for Full membership), my Duke assistant, Blake Blackwelder.

We have considered many candidates for RAMS who were not elected. Among them was Pat Bellemy, one time constable of Ocean Drive South Carolina and skipper of Ron Tom, fishing boat out of Little River, South Carolina. According to *U.S. Today,* Pat was arrested by the feds for smuggling narcotics into the country. Another failed candidate was Corky Winn, one of my students at Southern Illinois University, who committed suicide when his oil business went belly up.

It is of interest to note that to date (1996), 55 per cent of male members (all categories) are known to be deceased. At the same time, all members of the female auxiliary live on as high-spirited and lovely as ever.

In 1962 I suggested to Henry that RAMS should erect a monument in Myrtle Beach to commemorate the "Glorious Past". "It could be a bronze statue of a dirty, disheveled, drunken geologist helping his dirty, disheveled, drunken buddy out of a dirty, disheveled, drunken tavern. They might be followed by a dirty, disheveled, drunken Airedale."

The inscription might read: "It was men and dogs of this breed who solved the geological problems of the Carolina Coastal Plain, and who brought enlightenment and happiness into the lives of fellow human beings. They are gone now, but they are not forgotten."

In 1960 Henry, Solliday and I drilled ten mobile power auger holes in Horry County. At the time I was convinced the holes would provide all the subsurface control needed for my study. It didn't exactly work out that way. The ten holes taught us how to use the rig effectively and how to interpret the samples it produced, but most of all the ten holes showed us that we would need many more to complete the job.

In August 1961, we were back to drill another 25 holes. Once again I was confident these would be all we would ever need. I was a slow learner. By summer's end we had learned a valuable but somewhat disturbing lesson. We discovered that each hole drilled summoned up more questions than answers about the geology of the area. Eternal optimists, though, we continued to believe that all the answers would come with one more hole. In time our battle cry became, "One more hole and we'll have it all wrapped up." By 1972, when Henry resigned as State Geologist, we had drilled more than 300 holes in Horry County alone. But our optimism never waned. Just before Henry left the state we vowed that in our old age we would return to Horry County and drill one more hole, the one which would provide us with the last, elusive piece of the puzzle.

There were those who asked why we would spend our time and money drilling holes into the coastal plain, or mucking about dirty, snake-infested pits and outcrops to collect a bunch of dirty old fossil shells. My response has always been the same. Such activities have no more justification than efforts to learn the secrets of the universe, to climb the highest mountain, or search for a cure for cancer. It is merely the nature of man to explore the unknown. And if someday such things no longer seem important to us we can all gather together and watch the sun set on our species.

In a letter to me Henry offered a more practical and simple explanation:

I grab small patches of peace and calm from time to time and watch as each day goes by, even in the midst of chaos. For instance, when we are drilling and it comes time for lunch I like to sit in the shade by the side of some low country store in one of the Horry County backwaters and close my eyes and savor a cold Pepsi and feel my hungry stomach take hold on a honey bun, and listen to the drowsy buzz of a bee and the faint sound of a tractor in a distant field, and sense the steaming warmth, punctuated by life-giving little pulses of a cool breeze. At such times I let all the pressures go from my mind and for ten minutes I am calm and utterly relaxed. This relaxation is a thing found in nature more commonly than elsewhere. It is a good world. It's a hell of a pity we waste our time here the way we do."

Our twentieth hole in 1961 presented a memorable dilemma. Actually it came within a cat's whisker of being our last hole. We had set up in a clump of shade at the abandoned Evergreen School four miles southwest of Conway. With the drill bit about 75 feet into the ground, recovery of sediment ceased (nothing was coming up the hole) and the string of rods had begun to swing disturbingly free in the hole. It was clear that the drill rods were not making the expected tight contact with the wall of the hole. To drillers this is bad news, indicating that the sediment of the wall is collapsing downhole, enlarging its diameter. We also noted that the diameter of the rim of the hole at the surface had increased from its normal three inches to six or seven inches.

Henry, who was our drill operator, peered down from his perch on the side of the rig. Sizing up the situation he exclaimed, "By God, I think we've penetrated a limestone cavern! The sand we've been cutting through is caving into it."

Stepping forward then I knelt down and looked into the gaping mouth of the drill hole. There was just enough light to see that the hole seemed to widen with depth. How much I couldn't determine. Lying flat on the ground I reached down the hole. To my alarm I discovered that two feet below the rim I could feel only empty space. The damned thing probably was at least four feet wide. To my discomfort I realized that I was lying on a thin, unsupported and undermined shelf of only moderately hardened, oxidized soil. Worse, the rear wheels of the drill truck rested on the same weak underpinning. A large area around the hole could collapse at any moment.

Backing off cautiously to a safe distance I stood up and described the situation to Henry and Jim.

The way I see it," drawled Henry, "we got two choices. Both are very bad. We can drop the string of rods down the hole and drive the truck off to firm ground. That would mean drilling has ended for the season. No rods, no drilling. If you don't fancy that choice we can stay put and try to save the rods. If the hole collapses before we get them out we not only lose the rods, but we are going down the hole ourselves and the truck will sure as hell come down on top of us. Of course that also will end our drilling for the rest of the summer, but then it won't bother any of us much because we'll already be well on our way to Hades."

Any three sane men presented with these two options would have pulled out, cut their losses and retired to the nearest air-conditioned bar. We, of course, rarely of sound mind, chose to save the rods. None of us said anything. We just moved to the hole, took up position, and went to work.

Unfortunately there is no quick or easy way to extract 75 feet of drill rod from a hole. It is a tedious process accomplished while exercising a certain degree of care and even precision. The fifteen five-foot long rods were locked to one another end to end, by tapered, steel cotter pins; the entire string was attached at its uppermost end by another cotter pin to the drive shaft.

The rods have to be removed one at a time. To do so, the entire flight is raised so that the uppermost rod is clear of the hole. At that point a heavy-duty, two-pronged steel fork is shoved forward at ground level so that its inner edges press snugly against the upper rod still dangling in the hole. This is necessary to prevent the entire string from dropping down the hole when the cleared rod is detached from the string and the drive shaft. With the uppermost rod freed the downhole string is again attached to the drive shaft and raised to clear another rod. To retrieve the entire string this procedure would have to be repeated fifteen times.

If all went well the job would be completed in about 30 minutes. We knew the hole was continuing to collapse and could only hope the surface would hold up for at least 31 minutes.

As we worked with the abandon of the damned, beads of hot, dirty, brown sweat formed into rivulets which streamed over our faces and burned our eyes and amidst a soft and constant chorus of curses and primordial sounds we fought our separate impulses to break and run to safety.

When the last rod with its trailing bit rose above ground level, Henry leaped into the cab and drove the truck off its chocks to safety. Once again on firm ground we stood for half a minute, glowering at the menacing hole which could have swallowed us and drawn us down to a common grave beneath the drill rig. Its surface diameter had grown to 12 inches, but the fragile oxidized clay and sand shelf surrounding it had held.

Then responding to silent, shared impulses Jim and I grabbed picks and shovels and recklessly attacked the ground around the hole. In minutes the shelf collapsed. Backing off to savor the product of our frenzied efforts, we gazed into a funnel-shaped crater twelve feet in diameter at the surface and at least eight feet deep. As impressive as it was, we speculated that with each falling rain it could enlarge and deepen until, in time, it would swallow up the little old school house, some of the adjacent paved road, and the country store across the road. Eventually the descending passageway (our enlarged drill hole) to the limestone cavern would become choked with debris and the depression would fill with rainwater to form a sizable body of water. We then and there christened it "Lake Evergreen."

Even in our facetious mood the prospect of our possible liability for what might ensue did not escape our attention. It was not a pleasant prospect for three underpaid geologists.

In search of the landowner's identity I scurried across the road to the country store. When I explained what had occurred in the schoolyard, the proprietor of the store seemed strangely amused. Though puzzled by this unexpected reaction, I asked the man if he knew who owned the school property. He found my question particularly hilarious. Choking on a gale of laughter, he managed to sputter, "Oh, yes, indeed I do. Lives in Conway." This brief declaration was followed by more boisterous laughter. In control once again he added with a knowing grin, "That would be Mr. William Dixon's land. Bought the place right after the school was closed. You know Mr. Dixon is the meanest man in the county." Once again he pealed a round of hee-haws.

Although I saw nothing humorous in the man's characterization of Mr. Dixon, I thanked the storekeeper for his information and left. I didn't bother to mention that his little store would soon be devoured by Lake Evergreen. I figured the last laugh would be on him.

Back at the drill site, I found Jim and Henry leaning against the truck cab, dirty, sweaty and a little limp, sucking reflectively on a couple of R.C. Colas.

Optimistically Henry dismissed the threat of an angry Mr. Dixon with a shrug. "We'll take care of that when I get back to town. In the meantime, I don't see why we can't work up a little business on the side to pick up a little cash in case he sues us. We'll call it the Institute of Miscellaneous Research, IMR. Take on all sorts of odd jobs, the kind three smart college guys like us should be able to handle. I think we could start as male models specializing in rugged outdoor-type effects for a select group of advertisers. I can see it now—a fanfare of rugged music and on the TV screen there flashes a picture of a dirty, unshaven geologist in skivvy shorts cleaning down a section, or hauling a forty-pound grab sampler up from ten fathoms. With one last shovel full or, when the grab comes up streaming over the side of the boat, the dirty one hauls out a plug of Brown Mule and with a 16-inch Spanish bayonet cuts off a chaw, saying, 'Another short, snappy paper now, and science will be advanced by strong men using simple tools. Time now to relax with a chaw of Brown Mule, the old IMR standard for real men.' And the announcer comes on saying, 'Another typical day in the work of a rugged field geologist."

"Sounds good to me," I said. "Given how raunchy we get in the field we might want to do one for underarm deodorant, too."

"No," Henry responded. "I don't think so. I believe in soap and water for sweat, not those spray can things they advertise on TV. It's not natural not to sweat. Closing up the pores with alum has to be unhealthy. And, like someone said, how can you tell your friends from your enemies if they all smell like bouquets of lilacs. So I just sweat and take a bath at least once a day whether I need it or not."

We were spared the trauma of head-on confrontation with Mr. Dixon, the "meanest man in the county." When Henry reported our predicament to the Development Board, his superior, recognizing the potential political clout of Mr. Dixon, agreed to handle the matter personally. In a few days, a state highway crew with truckloads of dirt arrived at our yawning crater.

With the hole filled our future seemed secure, at least until the next disaster. The little schoolhouse and the country store had been spared and they lived on happily for many more years. Lake Evergreen never became a reality, but it and IMR have survived in our fantasies until the present day.

On the drive back to camp I was very aware that we had flirted with death that day. Had I believed in any sort of omnipotent being who looks after us all, I probably would have concluded that we had been spared for some greater purpose. As it was, I figured we were lucky as hell and I was overwhelmed with a strong sense of invincibility. It is true that ignorance can be bliss.

Our drilling often attracted the curious, who wished to learn what we were up to. It was important that we not tell them the complete truth, because any explanation which might carry overtones of the Darwinian theory of evolution or that suggested we harbored a notion that the rocks of the area might be older than "Noah's flood" had the potential of triggering violent responses from the red-necked fundamentalists who inhabit Carolina low country. Solliday's facial hair proved to some of these people that we were a pack of hippies and we were well aware of the generally held opinion that the only good hippies were dead ones.

Our favorite explanation went as follows: "We're just collecting soil samples for those smart college guys back at the lab in Columbia. We don't know much about that sort of stuff; it's just a job. They tell us it's got something to do with improving the tobacco yields. All we do is drill the holes and deliver the samples to the lab."

It didn't pay to suggest that we might be educated; everyone in the low country knows that college types are mostly pinko commie atheists.

I once made the mistake of telling a half-witted farmer that we were working for the federal government, whereupon he accused us of being "some of those fellas from Washington that won't let us pray in school no more." He then began to stride about the clearing where we sat eating our lunch and rapidly worked himself to a fever pitch over the godless types like us who ran the country. We tried, at first, to ignore him, hoping he would cool down and go away, but suddenly he reached down and grabbed my machete which had been lying on the ground near the rig. As he strode to and fro he waved the damned blade over his head, lashing out at imaginary Washington bureaucrats who, he was convinced, should be killed. He seemed completely out of control, a raving madman. The three of us, tense, and with eyes fixed on his every move, waited for the anticipated attack. He was a big, strong, 250-pound brute, and we knew he would not be brought down easily. It seemed likely he would decapitate at least one of us before we could subdue him.

Then, with no warning, he abruptly tossed the machete to the ground and walked off into the woods. We sat silent, motionless, looking after him and fearing he might return. Finally I arose, picked up the machete and everything else which might serve as a weapon and secured it all in the trunk of the Dodge. We completed the hole in a state of nervous anticipation, each of us casting furtive glances into the woods about us. Moving at last to the next drill site, we carried with us a common resolve to never again mention the federal government in the Carolina low country.

Later (1964-67) while I was with Esso in Houston, Henry and his crew sometimes drilled holes in the coastal plain to gather samples for my research. On one such occasion while drilling in Horry County, they were approached by a drunk. The man told them of a big rock nearby which had been drilled up out of the ground a few years earlier by three fellows, one of them sporting a flaming red beard.

He insisted on taking Henry and his crew to the site, which turned out to be the place where Henry, Solliday (who then had a full red beard) and I had drilled a hole in 1961. Sure enough, there beside the old drill hole was a big red rock. Apparently the slurry we had piled there beside the hole had oxidized through the years and had hardened into an ironstone mass four feet wide and a foot high.

Henry acknowledged that he and his men were the guilty ones. But the drunk would have none of that. He protested that there had been a man with a red beard. Giving Henry and his men a long, appraising look, he said, "Hell, ain't none y'all got a red beard."

Henry was rarely seen in the field without his Airedale. He and Rowdy found each other in the high country of Colorado in 1956. In those days Henry was a uranium explorationist for the USGS. One day while in the field he chanced upon a farm near Frieda. As he approached the house, two large Airedales bounded out to the road to greet him. When he was a little closer to the house, five dark, furry Airedales puppies darted from beneath the porch and began a wild series of romps around his feet. Later, tired of nipping his ankles, they discovered his shoestrings. Finally four of them ran off to better things. One chubby little rascal persisted; he couldn't get enough of Henry and followed him onto the porch.

Before Henry left the house he had purchased the puppy from the farmer for fifty dollars. It was the beginning of Henry's love affair with Rowdy and Airedales in general. Unfortunately and inevitably, Rowdy, who had shared so many of Henry's adventures, did not survive to share Henry's retirement years in Tennessee.

Rowdy's parents were bred to hunt grizzly bears and mountain lions, so it was not surprising that he possessed the instincts of a big game hunter. However, the Carolina low country is decidedly deficient in big game and much to Henry's chagrin and, at times, embarrassment, Rowdy, denied bears and lions, turned to the farmers' suckling pigs.

During the summer of 1968 Susan and I were working out of a rental house in Crescent Beach, South Carolina. Henry arrived rather unexpectedly early one evening. I was in the kitchen having a drink, feeling festive after a hot day in the field. As Henry walked toward me, I noticed he appeared a little pale and tight-lipped. Without a word he handed me something. For a moment I stared down at this strange thing in my hand; finally I realized Henry had given me a dog's leather collar. It was Rowdy's; he was dead.

We stood there, mute, for several seconds, tears welling in our eyes, my stomach gathering itself into a tight, painful lump. "How?" I asked.

"Our neighbor backed his car over him this morning. He was asleep in the neighbor's drive, too deaf to hear the car. I wrapped him in a blanket and drove him to the vet, but it was too late."

It was the only time I ever saw Henry cry.

Of my many memories of Rowdy, one emerges most vividly. We had been drilling somewhere in the interior and were taking a lunch break. Henry and I sat on the ground eating Vienna sausages, our backs propped against the trunks of two large live oaks. Rowdy sat on his haunches, gazing wistfully into the nearby swamp, his pink shaft pointed beseechingly skyward. At that moment man and dog shared common desires, common frustrations, and a common prayer, "Oh Lord, let there be a bitch in heat out there somewhere."

I was saddened when Henry left the Division of Geology in 1972. Our years together in the Coastal Plain, so rich in wonderful memories, were over. I'm told all good things must end one day. However, I could only agree that he had made a wise choice to go into consulting. Travel down a dead-end road carries few rewards. Even so, I couldn't resist a little gentle chiding when I sent him "Advice to the Wind":

> *So go inland, so leave the Coastal Plain and the sea. Go climb your mountain and pan your gold. Leave the stench of the salt air and the irritating roar of the surf. And chase from your memory the picture of foul, murky swamp water, dirty, narrow roads winding through dusty fields of tobacco, the scorching low country sun in August, and nasty little bugs and varmints that bite and sting and swarm over your hot, sweaty face. Drive from your mind that rasping, annoying sound of the drill bit vainly attempting to cut its way through PeeDee caprock and the foolish crunching as it works its way through an oyster bed at 38 feet.*
>
> *And if you have a mind to, put on a conservative, tailored gray flannel suit, white shirt and tie. Get yourself a big office and a big desk, and become an executive paper pusher.*
>
> *Perhaps as you pour over the latest stock market reports, and count your day's gains and losses, you'll be able to forget those grungy, disheveled, smelly oddballs and associated grizzly Airedales that, along with yourself, once proudly called themselves 'Kings of the Coastal Plain'.*

Soon after Henry left DOG to become a rich and famous consultant, our long-time faithful friend, the DOG Mobile Power Auger, passed on to drilling rig heaven. She had served us well. I was particularly grateful for the more than 1000 holes she had drilled for us between 1960 and 1972.

It was generally acknowledged among coastal plain geologists who had known her that she had died valiantly in the line of duty. However, it has always seemed to me that, having been abandoned by her loving and benevolent master who understood all her little quirks, she had died of a broken heart.

At the time of her death, Norman K. (Ole) Olson, Henry's successor as State Geologist, distributed the following memo:

To All Friends of the South Carolina Coastal Plain:

On July 18, 1972 there will be a wake held in honor of DOG power auger Mobile B-27. She drilled many holes, looking down into the hidden secrets of the Coastal Plain. She probed for the truth, despite the blue clay or the viscous Dovesville that would wrench her shear pins asunder, or the ever-present water table slurrying and mixing the real lithology.

Appropriately, she will be placed on Lot 1, leading the pack even in death. She'll be towed there after having thrown a rod through the engine block. Her friends will miss her.

Cordially,
Norman K. Olson
State Geologist
DIVISION OF GEOLOGY

The following excerpt from a letter written to me in 1966 serves as an example of Henry's repeated dream for his old age:

Have been thinking about the kind of outfit to have when the kids are on their own and a certain amount of freedom may be in sight. I want to get a big panel truck and put a cot or two in the back, and a table and a typewriter, and a rack and a boat on the top, and then set out to wander around the country a little.

Would also like to have a houseboat stashed away in a river or bay somewhere to serve as a base of operations and to provide a water capability when the road gets old or runs out.

Can you visualize coming topside in the early morning and taking a lung full of marsh air mixed with the aroma of eggs and sausage sizzling on the grill below?

And just over every skyline is adventure untold. And so what if we get too old and tottering, we can't get around. We will pick up a couple of Dadee's illegitimate sons (if we can't supply our own) to be crew and muscle, and to prop us up and fish us out if we fall overboard. However it went it would be better than Medicare. And before the end we have an obligation to put some of the things we have learned, and some of the adventures on paper for others to read in other days, so that old men can say, 'Yes, that's how it was.' And so sheltered hot-house plants of men can learn that there is more to life than 9 to 5 office hours and the commuter train.

Now (1998) alone in his golden years, Henry raises Airedales in western Tennessee and writes a regular column about Airedales for the magazine *Full Cry*. He has attempted to insulate himself from his past. In a recent letter he mentioned he had received an invitation to his 50th high school class reunion. The reunion committee asked on an enclosed questionnaire what life had taught him. He replied, "It taught me that life was out there in front of me, not behind me, and that you should forget your personal past, and live only by the hour, day and week. Past glories get you nowhere."

It seems ironic that, having renounced his former life, I now paint Henry into the dark nooks and crannies and shadowy corners of his past. One cannot entirely escape one's past. As someone once said, "My past intrudes my life, uninvited, willy-nilly."

> I've been a good fellow boys,
> I've earned all I spent,
> Paid all I borrowed,
> Lost all I lent,
> I once loved a woman,
> That came to an end,
> Get you a dog boys,
> He'll be your friend.

Written by Henry's father, circa World War I.

Face-Off at Dawn

One hot, muggy night in August 1961, we had been sitting around in the Deckers' kitchen drinking and telling tall tales for five hours or more. Molly had gone to California to her mother's funeral, and the kids had trundled off to bed hours earlier. It was 3:00 in the morning and long past the time we should have left for the Hideaway and needed shut eye.

But Jim and Deck had settled into a spirited discussion of one of their favorite topics—golf. Both were, when sober at least, excellent and highly competitive players. Each was positive he could beat the other any time or place with one hand tied behind his back. There was no hope of leaving now—this could go on for at least another hour.

Neither George Wilson (name has been changed) nor I knew a damned thing about golf. Neither of us had ever played and we shared a mutual disinterest in the game. George was draped in his chair in drunken oblivion as limp as wet toilet paper. But that was not a particularly unusual state for George. Whenever and wherever I had seen George during the past two years he was either already comatose, emerging from a stupor or on the verge of passing out.

The son of a prominent Conway banker, George was viewed by his family and friends as a hapless failure, a social misfit and an all-around pain in the ass. His father had expected George to attend college and to follow his daddy into the world of high finance. George had done neither. He had dropped out of high school, taken a job with a Georgetown paper company and married Lyla. Lyla was rarely sober.

Because George was unable to support both of their habits, Lyla was reduced to free-lancing. While George was busy cutting pine trees in Georgetown County, she regularly sold her services to any man in possession of a half pint. George confessed to me at one time that Lyla's four children had been fathered by four different men, none of them him.

As the debate droned on I turned my attention to memories of that first summer when we met George and Deck. On my release from the Wilmington hospital on July 14, 1959, Jim and I had driven to Conway, South Carolina, to begin work on the fossiliferous deposits exposed along the banks of the Waccamaw River in Horry County. A search conducted the next day for a suitable field camp led us to the Pure Oil Gas Station next to the Conway Post Office. From local inquiry we had learned that the station proprietor, Raymond Smith, made a practice of renting his cabin on the river to fishermen and weekend party people.

Smith seemed a little amused by my explanation for being in the area, but was not at all hesitant to rent his place to us for two weeks. Smith's description of the cabin, its location near Conway, its facilities, and most of all, the ten dollars a week rent convinced me to take the place sight unseen. We didn't have time for comparative shopping, and as it turned out the cabin was ideal for our purposes.

Smith, of medium height, but broad of shoulder and mean-eyed, struck me as a man with whom one does not trifle. As soon as we had consummated the deal Ray took us into his tiny office and with obvious pride pointed to a framed newspaper clipping hung on the wall behind his desk. The story told how his wife, upset over his most recent amorous affair, had showed up at the station with a loaded revolver and with clear-cut resolve to do him bodily harm. She fired six shots at close range but luckily for Smith she proved an incredibly poor marksman. Smith received only minor superficial wounds and was fully recovered and back to his old tricks in a few weeks.

In succeeding months we learned from a variety of sources that Ray Smith was a greatly feared small time hood who, with his redneck cronies, enjoyed bashing skulls and breaking up small town beer joints throughout the Carolina low country.

We managed to stay in Smith's good graces and came to warily regard him as a friend. Each time we were in town we stopped by the station with a bottle. On those occasions the three of us retired to the men's room and poured drinks into paper cups from the wall dispenser. While downing a few of these Ray would bring us up to date on his latest brawls, scrapes with the law and his female conquests.

We were still in Smith's office that July day in 1959 when a young man walked into the station. It was George Wilson, we learned, medium height, thin, wavy black hair, dark eyes and friendly like an abandoned puppy in a dog pound. When he learned why we were in town he invited us to his home for dinner. "You can follow in your car," he explained. "But I have to stop at the Piggly Wiggly to pick up a chicken."

Eventually we pulled up in front of a little white bungalow in a modest but attractive development. Pleasant enough on the outside, but a different story inside. Most of the furniture was concentrated in two small bedrooms. The bare pine floors of the living and dining rooms were strewn with a great clutter of old newspapers, comic books, dead beer cans, empty pop bottles, cigarette butts, dirty laundry and abandoned toys. Four small, unkempt, dirty kids eight and under bounded from one of the bedrooms and surrounded their tardy father, where they whirled and swirled and shrieked and shouted in frenzied competition for George's attention.

Lyla emerged from the kitchen with a beer can held in one hand, a lighted cigarette dangling loosely from her lower lip. She tried to calm the children, but her remonstrances, mostly shrill cries and screeched pleas, only served to energize the pack of dirty little beggars.

While unsuccessfully attempting to extricate himself from the band of baby primates now affixed to his back and legs, George managed a breathless and stuttering introduction and an entirely incomprehensible explanation of our presence in their home.

Stamping out her ciggie on the wood floor, Lyla took the chicken from her husband's outstretched hand and returned to the kitchen. We all, including George and the entangled mass of small bodies clinging to various parts of their father, followed.

In the kitchen I was surprised and relieved to find a small table and four chairs. As soon as the three of us succeeded in scraping the juvenile epibionts from George's torso, we gathered around the table as Lyla drunkenly proceeded to unwrap the scrawny Piggly Wiggly bird at the kitchen sink.

Enjoying a moment or two of silence I watched as George's eyes swept the impressive array of empty beer cans, half pint bottles and baby food jars on the counter near the refrigerator. Obviously embarrassed he said, "I'd offer you gents a drink but we seem to be fresh fuckin' out."

Accepting his reference to booze as my cue, I sent Jim to the car to fetch the bottle of Canadian Club we had brought with us from Wilmington.

While George and Jim drank and discussed the quality of life in Conway, I observed Lyla as she swayingly prepared our dinner. Pretty and vivacious once, I assumed, with bright, flashing blue eyes filled with hope and visions of love. But that had been before the union with George, before the disillusionment, before the babies, before the half pints and canned brews, before her self-esteem had slipped beyond her reach, before the juices of life had turned to dust and had been wafted off on the tepid winds of loneliness and despair.

Three or four drinks later dinner was served—chicken a la carte. Apparently the Wilsons also had been fresh out of food. When we saw the four kids hungrily waiting for their rations, Jim and I settled for another drink and the two scrawny wings. Unable to watch the little waifs pick at their plates of bones and lick their dirty little greasy fingers, I walked into the living room and stood at the front window and stared into the darkness of the small front yard.

After a while, Jim came into the room wearing a worried expression. "Is there a problem?" I asked.

"Hope to shit in your flat hat there is a problem. George is ransacking the house for his shotgun. Says he's going to kill us."

"What the hell are you talking about? What the fuck did you do to him?"

"Do to him?" he replied indignantly. "I didn't do anything or say anything. The fucker just went off his rocker—thinks I'm after his goddamned silly wife. Let's get the fuck out of here before he finds the damned gun!"

No further discussion seemed appropriate, so we hurried outside to the car and drove away.

A mile down the road I said, "I don't suppose you remembered to bring the bottle?"

With a clear expression of chagrin in his voice Jim responded, "Bring the bottle? Hell, you'll have to forgive me Big Daddy, but under the circumstances I figured possession was at least nine points of the law. Anyway, it seemed to me that George and Lyla needed it more than us."

Ray Smith's cabin was pleasantly isolated in a sandy, remote area at the edge of the Waccamaw River, but we soon learned that it was not the quiet retreat for which we had hoped. Our nearest neighbor, Thelma Throckmorton, owned the little place 200 yards upstream from our cabin. It was just a little shack where she sold bait (crickets) and served refreshments. Each evening after about 7:00 and until the wee hours Thelma's shack was the rallying point for most of the young, rowdy, male rednecks of the surrounding bottomlands. They lolled about on the ground in the yellow glow of the light that sifted through the screened windows of the bait shop, and drank beer and moonshine. They boasted, laughed, whooped and hollered, argued and sometimes fought. All this crude male bonding was accompanied by the ear-shattering sound of Thelma's "piccolo" (low country for jukebox).

Musical selections, limited to three or four favorites, were played over and over, hour after hour, day after day. The jarring notes vibrated the walls of Smith's cabin and pierced the most buffered recesses of our brains. By far the favorite of Thelma's patrons was *The Battle of New Orleans*, a piece for which I developed an intense aversion. In later years in the rosy glow of nostalgia, it came to be a favorite of both Jim and me.

Under the most optimum conditions I would have been little interested in spending time at Thelma's shack. As it turned out I couldn't have, had I wished. Soon after our arrival in Conway, I developed an extremely painful muscle spasm in the lower back. As a consequence our twelve-hour workdays on the river became, in short order, tests of sheer willpower for me. In the evening when we pulled the boat up in front of the cabin I typically had little desire to do more than eat, hit the sack, and read a book.

Solliday, on the other hand, was quite smitten by Thelma, whose husband was a soldier stationed in Germany. Jim was there each evening at least until midnight. George Wilson was also a regular at the shack and surprisingly he and Jim soon became friends.

Solliday burst into the cabin about 9:00 o' clock one evening. Surprised I tossed my book to the floor beside the bed and asked, "What brings you home at such an early hour? I didn't expect to see you until midnight."

"Never mind that Big Daddy," he said with a grin. "Just get your carcass out of that sack, we're going to Myrtle Beach."

"Oh hell," I moaned. "I can't do that. Riding in the car kills my back. Why do you want to go over there anyway?"

"George has been telling me about his friends, the Deckers. They live over there. They sound like the kind of people we need to meet. Besides, they've two good-looking daughters. Have a good stiff drink—it'll relax your damned muscles and getting out will do wonders for your back."

"Well, all right," I agreed. "Maybe you are right, at least I'll be free of that god-awful piccolo music for a short while. Just promise me that George won't try to kill us before we get back."

Suddenly I was startled by a brisk series of taps on the shoulder. It was Jim, standing over me. "Wake up, Big Daddy, We're getting ready to leave."

Lost in my reveries of 1959, it took a moment for my mind to jump forward two years. When it made it, I realized that I had completely closed out all the sounds of the great golf debate between Jim and Deck. Now I noticed that George was still inert in his chair but that there was no sign of Deck.

A little bewildered, I asked, "Where are we going, where's Deck?"

"Deck's coming. We're going to play a little golf. We're going to find out who the real pro is here."

At that moment Deck appeared carrying two clubs in one hand and a bulging brown bag in the other. Holding out the bag, he gleefully announced, "Sack of balls. A man can't play golf, or, for that matter, do much of anything worthwhile without balls."

In disbelief I asked, "What the hell do you guys think you're doing?"

"Why, Dr. Jules, my buddy," Deck said while attempting to feign a serious expression, "we're going to the course at Conway, where Jimbo and I mean to play three holes for the Horry County championship."

"I hate to be a killjoy," I said, "but how do you expect to play golf in the dark? Besides, both of you are too drunk to walk."

"Shit," Deck responded. "Drunk or sober, night or day, I can beat Old Jimbo. Anyway, it'll be getting light by the time we get there. Can't wait, gotta finish three holes before the groundskeeper arrives at 7:00 and calls security. Of course, we're going to need you and George to caddie for us."

"Caddie! Why the hell do you need caddies? All you got are two clubs and a sack of balls."

"Well, I know we're pretty fuckin good, Dr. Jules, but even we can't play one-handed. We need you and George to carry the drinks and the goddamned balls."

By then Jim had succeeded in propping George more-or-less upright against the wall, but he was having difficulty trying to prevent him from slithering to the floor. George leered at Deck and me and then limply flopped an arm in an apparent effort to signal us to move it along. Then slurringly, he called out, "Les get the fuckin' show on the road, men! I fuckin' never before in my whole life caddied a fuckin' championship tennis match."

As I watched Deck and Solliday dragging George to the car I decided it was best that I do the driving. "Hey," I called out. "Just dump George in the back. Deck can sit up in the front and be my navigator."

Deck unerringly directed me to the course and then, with Solliday at his heels, led the charge to the fairway where the classic contest would soon begin. George and I stumbled along behind somewhat encumbered by the full glasses of bourbon with which we had been entrusted. At the head of the fairway the four of us were silhouetted against a faint red glow that spread along the eastern margin. The sun was rising as Deck had predicted.

Losing no time Deck placed two tees in the grass about six feet apart. Then he and Jim each took a ball from the little brown bag I had carried from the car.

"This is it," Deck announced. "Jimbo goes first."

Placing the ball on the tee, Jim took one graceful practice swing. Then with a mighty crunch he sent the ball into the darkened sky where it soon disappeared from our view. Deck followed suit and his ball, too, disappeared down the fairway. I was impressed and could only wonder what they might be capable of sober and in the light of day. There was a downside, though. We had to walk down the fairway (not exactly a snap for a group of drunks in the dark), then we had to find the goddamned balls. After thirty or forty minutes of stumbling about the brush bordering the fairway we gave it up as a lost cause.

By then the sun was above the horizon and in the bright light of early morning we were conspicuously visible to anyone in the clubhouse who happened to look in our direction. Even worse, our heroes had exhausted the supply of bourbon and both Deck and Jim were now in worse shape than George had been when we left Myrtle Beach.

With no hope remaining that the match could be successfully completed, I suggested that the contest be postponed to another day and place before the paddy wagon arrived. George and Jim agreed but Deck had a different plan. He had come to play golf, and play, by God, he would! At the time we were twenty yards downslope from a rather large pond, with a putting green just beyond. Deck decided he would demonstrate his skills by driving a ball across the pond and onto the green. Ignoring our pleas to forget it, he teed up and a little shakily hit a Texas leaguer into the middle of the pond. Glancing over his shoulder he said, a little sheepishly, "Damned wet grass; lost my footing." In a moment another ball, with a resounding splash, followed its mate into the depths of the pond.

Failure only reinforced his determination. Reaching into the little brown bag he extracted another ball. This time, with the consummate skill possessed of all great golfers, he dribbled the ball through the grass, up the gentle slope, over the edge of the pond and into the cool, dark water.

In rapid succession four more balls were sent to watery graves. By that time I had become fascinated by Deck's performance. Sensing that I was witness to history in the making, something that might find its way into the Guinness Book of Records, I, too, ignored the now frantic pleas of George and Jim to get our asses out of there. *Some day*, I thought, *I will want to write of this night, so it is important that I remain until its conclusion.*

When two more balls had been propelled into the water, the little brown sack had been emptied. Gloomily Deck tossed it to the ground, retrieved his tee, and staggered down to me. His spirit, although a little bent, remained unbroken. "Wettest damn grass I ever played on. That son-of-a-bitch groundskeeper should take better care of this course!"

We left then. Two weeks later the Deckers had moved into their new home in Pacific Grove. The postponed match to determine the champion golfer of Horry County was never rescheduled.

I've never given much credence to the popular notion of a hereafter. Even so, there have been times when in my mind's eye I can see Jim and Deck standing in some distant place at the head of a fairway, clubs at ready, teed up for the long-awaited match. They wait there, their eyes sweeping the horizon in search of their two caddies who have fallen far behind. They wait for the water glasses of bourbon and the little brown sack of balls.

"A man," as Deck had aptly stated, "can't play golf or for that matter much of anything worthwhile without balls."

California, There They Go

Early in August 1961, when Molly returned from her mother's funeral in California, she announced to the family and to Jim and me that they would move to her mother's house in Pacific Grove. Molly and Deck had long considered themselves displaced Californians, whose stay in South Carolina was little more than an aberration to be remedied at the first possible opportunity. Even so the news of their impending departure from Myrtle Beach had a demoralizing effect on Jim and me.

For me it was the second phase of a double whammy. First it had been the loss of Karin and then, within ten days, the imminent separation from my adopted family. As a fighter I had learned the defensive moves necessary to blunt the onslaught of an opponent who had driven me dazed and rubbery-legged onto the ropes. I was considerably less prepared to cope with the effects of an emotional one-two punch.

We had taken some solace in the unwarranted assumption that the move would not occur before we broke camp and headed for Houston at the end of August. We had failed to accurately assess Molly's determination to remove herself and her family from South Carolina at the earliest possible moment, and her amazing faculty for the organization and facilitation of such a major undertaking. Within twenty-four hours all the furniture, home furnishings, appliances, and a large part of their personal items were advertised for sale. At the same time the five kids were assembled into a deadly serious and highly effective roving band of door-to-door salespersons.

During the next few days as Jim, Deck and I watched, pieces of furniture began to vanish from the house with distressing regularity. Within a week, when we were reduced to sitting on the floor and eating from paper plates, it had become evident that a going away party was in order.

With that purpose in mind I went to the Elks Club where, with the help of my waiter friend Johnny, I arranged a dinner for thirteen—the Deckers, Jim, me, Hobart Furbunch, and his most recent lady friend, Ma Earp.

They had met about three weeks earlier at the Elks Club (as my friend he had been given honorary membership in the Club). Hobart had been sitting alone at the bar. A lady whom he had barely noticed was playing the half-dollar slot. When the greedy little machine had devoured all her fifty-cent pieces without producing even a small reward, she sauntered over to where Hobart sat and introduced herself: "I'm Mrs. Earp," she said very sweetly. "All my friends back home called me 'Ma'—would you like to go to bed with me?"

Sizing her up and down for a few seconds, Hobart decided it was the best offer he had had all evening. He took her to his leased house on Cassandra, where she had remained as his "houseguest" for the past several weeks.

For Hobart, at least, there had proved to be only one small hitch to the arrangement—a small, feathered hitch, to be precise. It was Ma's traveling companion, Simpson, a particularly foul-mouthed parrot that had previously belonged to her late husband. Hobart had quickly developed an aversion to the bird who, he claimed, repeatedly told dirty stories that were funny only to Simpson and Ma Earp. Hobart had gradually become very jealous of Simpson and had come to believe the bird was actually Mrs. Earp's husband reincarnated in feathered form. For that reason Hobart had eventually banned Simpson from their bedroom.

To Hobart's great relief, I did not invite Simpson to Decker's farewell dinner.

At about six thirty on the evening of the big event, Jim and I arrived at the Deckers' nearly empty house. Hobart and Ma Earp showed up fifteen minutes later. The dinner was scheduled for eight o' clock, which allowed us plenty of time to sprawl about on the living room floor drinking great volumes of the white wine Deck had selected for the occasion.

At the Elks we were met by a young doorman who did not know me. When I identified myself and the purpose of the group which accompanied me, he gave me an embarrassed smile and waved us into the foyer. That is, all of us except Solliday, who at that time was sporting a flaming red beard. The young fellow explained very politely that beards were banned from the dining area. While I went in search of the manager, Jim, the only card-carrying, bona fide member of the club, was left sputtering outside on the door stoop.

When I explained our predicament to the manager, he went to the door and surveyed the then dejected and almost forlorn Solliday. "Well," said the manager. "I guess under the circumstances we can make an exception. Anyway," he added with a twinkle, "the book doesn't specifically forbid red facial hair."

As our festive group filed into the dining room Jesse Shaw and his five-piece combo arose to salute us with the customary *Georgia On My Mind*. The table seemed elegant, adorned with vases of bright cut flowers, a silver candelabra with three tall tapered white candles in the center, and, at the head of the table, a white card with large black printed letters which read: Dr. DuBar and Guests.

I motioned Deck to the seat of honor at the head of the table. Molly and her three daughters lined the table to Deck's left, and Keith, Lewis, Ma, Hobart, Jim and I sat to his right.

As Johnny took the orders for the first round of drinks I turned to Jim and handed him a fist full of coins. "I'm a little concerned about the cost of all this, Jim, so go back to the bar and hit a jackpot."

Before there was occasion to order a second round of drinks, Jim emerged from the back room. Grinning, hands cupped before his chest, pockets of his seersucker jacket and gray flannel trousers transformed to grotesque bulges, he struggled across the floor toward us. As he drew closer we could see that his cupped hands were heaped with silvery coins, some of which skittered to the floor as he walked.

Jim was still grinning when he edged up to me like a frisky, fuzzy feline feeding on fresh feces. With a dramatic flourish, he uncupped his hands and a great mass of dimes cascaded to the table beside my plate. A few of the most unruly coins scampered playfully across the table where they were gleefully pursued by the Decker girls. Then, as Jim began to add the contents of one of his jacket pockets, he gave me a smug look and said, "You told me to hit a jackpot and goddamn it I hit the biggest mother in town."

Feigning a cynical a look, I responded, "It's about time, Jim. What the hell took you so long?"

As Jim struggled to unload the remainder of his pockets, Johnny appeared with a large cloth bag into which he and Jim scooped the treasure trove. No one counted Jim's winnings; we were all too busy enjoying ourselves to take on such a tedious job. Later, when Jim had paid the dinner tab and bar bill and had covered the tips for the waiters, members of the band and the bartender, sufficient funds remained to permit him, for the final hours of the evening, to convincingly play his favorite role—the last of the big time spenders from the west.

At some point during the dinner Deck or Molly mentioned that their son Keith was then fifteen-and-a-half-years-old. This astounding piece of information called for a toast honoring Keith's advanced years and several lusty off-key renditions of *Happy Birthday Dear Keith*.

Later Jim and I decided that to send the Deckers off in regal style we would have Jesse Shaw's band play *California, Here I Come*. Perplexed by the request, Jesse turned to his musicians for help. None of them had ever heard of the piece. Deck and I tried to encourage them to follow our lead, but after a few half-hearted attempts they admitted defeat. The remainder of us, more determined to succeed, tried it *a cappella*, but finally had to give up when we discovered that none of us knew more than, "California, here I come, right back where I started from."

With dinner completed, Ma Earp and Hobart invited us all to Hurl Rocks Beach to go skinny-dipping. We unanimously declined so they wished the Deckers bon voyage and headed for the beach alone. It was then that I invited Bugsy, the Deckers' eleven-year-old daughter, to come with me to the back room to play the slots for a while. Excited with the notion of doing something so grown up she joined me without a moment's hesitation.

Within ten minutes a manager appeared at my side and politely suggested that, generally speaking, an eleven-year-old girl and one-armed bandits were by any measure a bad mix. He also commented that it was bound to be looked upon by the law as illegal. Following his advice, Bugsy and I returned to the dining room and found that her family had moved to smaller tables where they watched Jim dance with Molly and Linda, Gayle and any other female he could entice to join him on the floor.

We finally called it an evening about midnight. On our way to the cars I asked Jim how well his ill-gotten gains had held out. "Just fine," he said. "I came out even. I'm as broke as when we arrived. But wasn't it one hell of a night? The biggest jackpot of my life, and all those women! Hope to shit in your flat hat, it was a great evening."

I had to agree that it had been a success. Even though Jesse Shaw's band couldn't play our special request, it seemed the affair had skirted perfection. Of course the warm glow felt at that moment was in no way diminished by the knowledge that the Elks Club had, through their generous jackpot, sprung for it all.

On a warm mid-August afternoon a few days following the dinner at the Elks, the Deckers left for California. Hobart, Jim, and I watched from the front yard of their house as they drove up 38th N for the last time. The seven of them were somehow crammed into their little car, all their possessions towed behind in the smallest of the U-Haul trailers. As they turned onto U.S. 17 and disappeared from our view the vacuum created by their departure had already begun to envelop us.

In 1959 the Deckers had taken Jim and me (the two wandering troubadours, according to Molly) into their home, into their lives and into their hearts. They had provided us with companionship, solace and love.

Deck died in August 1979, almost exactly eighteen years following the Decker exodus from South Carolina. Deck was a remarkable man, a joy to know, a joy to be with. Tall and lean, an avid and excellent golfer, a first baseman good enough to have been given a tryout by the St. Louis Cardinals, he involved himself in life and with living. I am proud and I am fortunate to have been considered his friend. He was an incorrigible optimist, accepting everyone at face value, never critical, never judgmental, just there when needed. I cannot feel sad when I remember him. To think of Deck is to smile.

He gave his love to his family and they returned it in kind. A measure of that love is expressed in the eulogy written by his five children and read at his funeral at the Little Chapel By the Sea in Pacific Grove.

As most of you knew our Dad, you would know that he marched to a different drummer. He hated pretentiousness but adored his gold Cadillac, would have nothing to do with tradition, but put a ribbon around the Christmas tree to be cut at a special ceremony; was fiercely independent, but yet remained married for 42 years. His classic statement every anniversary was that he was still checking Mom out, but every now and then saying, "Ain't she a gem?" He had little patience with children, but had five and was expansively proud of every one of us, breaking up the audience at Keith's play when he called out, 'That's my boy and those are my shorts!' George Air Force Base was so impressed with him that they named him 'Father of the Year' in 1955.

He left us a legacy of such a strong moral code and sense of duty, when he would only deny that those things were important. He projected an image of 'who cares' but yet was in the service for twenty-two years and received many commendations for his excellent work. He was a very private man to whom every stranger was a friend, greeting everyone at the door with 'Have a seat and a seegar.' He hated sentimentality, but cried when we buried our kitten. He couldn't say 'I love you' but had special names for those he loved, like Cuz, Bugsy, Lindy Lou, Old Goat and Good Buddy. We knew what he meant. The grandchildren want to know who's going to call them 'Honyocks' any more or yell 'Out-out-out you lunkheads' when we got in his way in the kitchen.

He was a voracious reader, but delighted in telling the same stories time after time, interspersing his comments with his favorite phrases— 'case in point,' 'frankly,' 'I azume,' and 'you can't guarantee.'

Daddy never liked to plan ahead but whoever had a pasta dinner with him could never forget the hours of chopping onions and shredding cheese with every sliver perfect. He presented a gruff exterior but would entertain us with singing A Little Banty Rooster or joking about Hobart W.C. Furbunch.

We're here to say goodbye to our Daddy. We need him to know how much we really cared even though he didn't really like things like this. We're saying goodbye and we're saying we love you. We'll miss you so much, but we know you're playing golf at the 19th hole. We made sure you have a golf ball in your pocket and our love in your heart. As his grandson said, 'He didn't die alone. He died with himself'.

A letter written by Deck's oldest daughter tells of the funeral:

Dear Jules and Susan:
Jules you know us so well. We sent our Dad out in style. The five kids stayed perpetually boozy (not drunk) and we were able to cry and scream and take care of all the feelings that were tearing us up inside. Four days together, holding and loving each other and Mom. It was so crazy. We all knew this would happen, but none of us knew it would be so hard to say goodbye to Dad.

The minister of the Methodist church read the eulogy and it actually had people laughing. We wanted the funeral service to be something Daddy might have liked. So the background music was all Mario Lanza's Student Prince. It was so fabulous. The five of us sat with Mom in the front row of the chapel. We wanted to be there with all the people rather than in the special place reserved for the family. There we were singing softly through our tears and holding hands. Can you imagine Drink, Drink, Drink at a funeral service? We three girls came in red dresses—Daddy's favorite color. We all looked gorgeous—he was so proud of us. Just before the service we listened to I'll walk with God and at the end we heard Mario singing Ave Maria, Daddy's very favorite.

You and Jim (Solliday) were here with us in our hearts Jules.
You can imagine the memories that have been with us in all this.
Thank you for all you have meant to us.
  Love,
  Linda

9/3/79

Sometime following the funeral Deck's ashes were spread by plane into the sea off Pt. Lobos. Each year since 1979 the family, which now includes a substantial number of grandchildren who never knew their grandfather, gather at Pt. Lobos for a gourmet picnic. The fare includes Deck's favorite wine, cream sherry. After the meal the family, carrying glasses of the sherry, walk to the edge of the sea cliff and, while drinking a toast to Deck's memory, pour a glass of wine over the cliff into the ocean.

Elephant Hunt

Friday evening, November 18, 1961, I was sitting on the sofa in our den grading a huge stack of paleo exams when the telephone blasted me to reality. My first impulse was to ignore the thing—I didn't have time to talk to anyone and anyway, the ring had seemed to have a subtly sinister quality about it.

But I did answer it, only to confirm that I should not have. It was Tom Pulley's wife (Tom was then Curator of the Houston Museum of Natural History). A lady, Mrs. Beasley, had called Tom to report the discovery by her thirteen-year-old daughter and the family dog, of big fossil bones, probably an elephant, that had been washed from the bank of a drainage ditch near their house at the intersection of Ruthglen Drive and Chimney Rock in southwest Houston. She hoped Tom would come take a look at the site. "Tom's out of town until next Monday," Mrs. Pulley reported. "So I thought you might go out there in his place. I don't suppose it amounts to anything, but we really need to be a bit accommodating to the public, especially these days. Then, of course, if it is anything," she added, "it could be useful publicity."

I understood what she was saying. Trying to impart a note of enthusiasm in my voice I replied, "Okay, Mrs. Pulley, I'll take care of it in the morning and let you know how it goes; just give me the lady's name, address and phone number."

Before she hung up she tried again to reassure me that it probably wouldn't amount to much, but I wasn't so optimistic. I owed Tom a few, so I had to go through with it, but dealing with the public can be a pain in the ass, and if the news people get involved one's life can fray around the edges in a hurry.

Looking back on that evening I am reminded of stories of women in India who will patiently follow a domestic elephant until it deposits a huge, juicy load on the road. They then eagerly scoop the steaming excrement into a sack or basket to be used later as cooking fuel.

I probably wasn't going to end up sacking either fresh or fossilized elephant shit, but I did think there was a fair chance I would soon be crawling around in a mucky drainage ditch trying to retrieve the remains of a goddamned elephant that had been dead for God knows how long. Anyway I viewed the prospects it seemed that Fate had at last succeeded in shoving the broom handle up my ass.

I quickly dialed Solliday's number and explained the situation. "I can't go out there in the morning, Jim," I explained. "I've got that damned marathon six-hour Cenozoic Stratigraphy class until 2:00 p.m. I'll need you to fill in for me. Just get Mrs. Beasley, her daughter, or the goddamned dog to take you to the site and size it up. Let me know what you think when you get back. If necessary I can go out there Sunday or Monday with you and take a look. Anyway, I've got to tell Pulley' s wife something."

With a little luck, I thought, *this would be the end of it.* But all the luck I had that weekend was bad.

I didn't visit the site until Monday afternoon, so I insert here Jim Solliday's account of the events of Saturday and Monday mornings:

"The site was on the west bank of a drainage ditch tributary to Braes Bayou. Examination disclosed that this was a good find, consisting of the backbones, ribs and pelvic girdle of a large mammoth. Instructions were left with several young people to proceed very carefully with excavation of the overburden. A group from the university would return Monday morning to take over the operation. The children were very successful with their paleontological endeavor, and by morning all traces of the animal had been removed.

"All was not lost, however; in the mob of at least 300 people (a conservative estimate) that had dug into the banks of the canal one had planted a pick into the base of an elephant skull and when first observed by the team of 'trained vertebrate paleontologists,' three feet of double tusks had been uncovered. The new find was about 225 feet upstream from the original discovery and on the opposite (east) bank, essentially at water level and 22 feet below the street level."

The *Houston Post* had covered the story of the find in the Sunday morning edition, and the *Press* and *Chronicle* followed with stories in their Monday editions. I think the first TV coverage came on Monday evening. Thereafter all three newspapers and TV stations carried daily stories on our operation. This media coverage accounted for the large crowds that came daily to gawk at the site. Weekday afternoons and evenings and weekends were the worst. At those times up to four hundred people crowded both the east and west banks of the canal.

Solliday and several other of my graduate students had roped off and secured the site on Monday morning. When I arrived in the afternoon I was greeted with what seemed to be the site of a major catastrophe. My first thought was that a passing motorist had driven off the street and into the ditch. There were several hundred people milling about on both sides of the canal and I could make out three tripod-mounted TV cameras on the opposite bank. After I found a parking place two or three blocks from the site I walked to the crowd and worked my way past milling bodies of women, men and fidgety kids and down the bank to the restraining ropes. My students, assisted by seven or eight "volunteers" had removed much of the overburden and now I could see some volunteers pulling bones from the soft sediments while others behind them trampled some of the fragile bones. There was no doubt my worst nightmare had become a reality.

My first act was to order everyone to stop work and move slowly and carefully from the site. Then, when I had their attention I proceeded to deliver a brief, succinct lecture on how and how not to extricate a fossil elephant.

I explained that I appreciated and needed the help of volunteers, but that the work must be done carefully, scientifically, and under my supervision. Then I told them that to completely uncover the entire carcass would take a long time and a lot of work. I asked Solliday to take the names, addresses, phone numbers and days and hours of availability of those who wished to work at the site.

There were five or six reporters there with notepads and pencils in their hands anxious to ask questions. I explained to them that until I had studied the site there was little I could tell them. Then to make certain they would be kept informed of our progress I assigned Solliday to the *Houston Chronicle* and the NBC TV station, Ronnie Harlan to the *Press* and CBS, and I reserved the *Post* and ABC for myself.

I also needed to recruit more help from among our graduate and undergraduate students who had taken some of my paleontology courses. With my teaching and research load I knew I wasn't going to be at the site more than a few hours a day. To remove the bones as quickly as possible I needed a crew I could trust to do the work properly and who would stay with the job until its completion.

It would be necessary to work twelve hour days seven days a week and we would need to post guards at night after the work crews had left. In a day or two I had assembled a team of about ten geology students and ten volunteers who seemed to meet my prerequisite.

In a few days we had learned the crowds of spectators tapered off after nine o' clock in the evening and that some remained as late as midnight. By six in the morning new spectators would begin to trickle in and by noon we would have several hundred sets of eyeballs glued to us.

Reporters assigned to Harlen, Solliday and me called us at home each morning at six o'clock for the latest scoops and our TV stations discussed our progress and showed footages of our work every night on the 6:00 p.m. news for more than three weeks. On several evenings Shell Development Company sent out a mobile unit and showed their very entertaining film *The Fossil Story* to the gathered throng. Later I regretted that none of us had the presence of mind to set up a soft drink and popcorn concession at the site. We probably would have cleared a year's worth of beer money.

Working under the eye of the public and TV cameras was a new experience for all of us. We were accustomed to conducting our studies in boondocks where pissing on the outcrop was a time-honored tradition. Now we had to drive in a car several blocks to the nearest service station when the urge demanded. Even there we had become celebrities and usually were required to answer endless questions of the employees and customers as we stood cross-legged in front of the men's room. Also, our language, generally sprinkled with colorful expressions on the outcrop, had to be severely censored. During the time I spent at the site I think I heard more gosh darns, gee whizzes, and doggones than I had heard in the previous ten years. Unlike most big league baseball players, we did, with some considerable effort, succeed for the most part in suppressing men's basic instinct to scratch his crotch. But when the TV crews were on location some of my co-workers spent more time smiling at the cameras than digging out fossil bones.

One advantage of being media stars was that we always were provided with any supplies or equipment we needed. All I had to do was mention a need to the nearest reporter and a local business would come to our aid within twenty-four hours. During the time we were on the dig we were provided, free of charge, with a pump, a power saw, shellac, brushes, burlap bags, plaster of Paris, a flatbed truck and driver, and a crane and operator.

Work at the site progressed rapidly. Within a few days the excavation was twelve feet wide and ten feet deep. As we slowly uncovered part of the skeleton we found, to our surprise, that the head of the animal, now tentatively identified as an Imperial Elephant (*Elephas imperator*) was inverted—thrown back by an obviously powerful force so that the gigantic curved tusks pointed rearwards and penetrated the animal's rib cage. When we finally uncovered the intact tusks they were found to measure nearly thirteen feet in length, equaling perhaps the longest for this species yet recorded. Considering the current price of ivory from poached African elephant, we had uncovered a small fortune.

The soft sands in which the elephant was buried were generally thought to have been deposited on a deltaic floodplain during the most recent Ice Age of the Pleistocene Epoch. The sediments had never been radiometrically dated, but on geologic evidence alone they were considered to have been deposited at least 50,000 years ago. With hope of resolving the age question I had sent a fragment of one of the elephant's teeth to Shell Development Company in Bellaire for radiocarbon dating.

The analysis was run by Ernest Martin and W.O. Lease. They told me not to expect too much of them because my sample was undoubtedly much older than 30,000 years, the upper limit of accurate dating by the radiocarbon technique.

A week later I was surprised when Martin called to tell me that they had dated the tooth fragment at 18,700± 50 years. When I pressed him, he assured me that he had the utmost confidence in the accuracy of the date. "About as solid as they come," he said.

Of course the results of the test made all the local newspapers and TV newscasts. It also stirred up a bit of a controversy over its credibility. I had to agree that it was somewhat younger than I would have expected from my previous studies in the area but, in face of the evidence, I was forced to conclude that I may well have been wrong. A few weeks later, however, Shell announced that the tooth fragment Martin had analyzed had, on further inspection, been determined to be contaminated and therefore the earlier announced date was incorrect. The elephant, they concluded, must in fact be much older than 30,000 years. The question of the true age of our elephant was never satisfactorily resolved. My own opinion remains that Martin's date of 18,700 years could be basically correct.

Work at the site was time demanding, and with our other obligations my assistants Harlan, Solliday, Keller Davis, Jim Fowler, and Gordon Clopine and I were soon operating at the edge of reality. Under those stressful conditions a little comic relief was always welcome. One such event was recalled by Solliday. A lady who visited the dig peered down the slope and asked if the animal were there. Told by Jim that it was, she responded, "And you mean it's still alive down there?"

During the second week of our work I received a telephone call from Charles Allmon, Assistant Illustrator for *National Geographic*. He said he had heard of our discovery. He said *National Geographic* had been working on an article concerning fossil elephant finds in North America, so he was curious about our beast. I told him what I knew at the time and promised to keep him posted as we proceeded with the dig. From then on for several weeks he remained in frequent contact with me. At some stage he alerted Dr. Leroy Gazin, vertebrate paleontologist with the National Museum of Natural History. Gazin was interested in the possibility of sending a team to Houston to take over the work site, but eventually he had to leave the country on another assignment so that option died on the planning board.

It became obvious that *National Geographic* had a direct line to Houston and to our operation. One day when I arrived on the site a reporter grabbed my arm and asked, "Would you say this is the largest fossil elephant ever found anywhere in North America?" I replied, "Well, I haven't seen all the elephants discovered in North America, but I'd say it is the largest one yet found in Texas."

The pipeline between our excavation and Washington may have been impressive but it was not infallible. The next day Charles Allmon called and asked me if it were true that ours was the largest fossil elephant ever found in North America.

Sometime during the second week I was invited to do an interview for Alec Dryer's news program on the local ABC TV affiliate. A young lady taped my segment in their studio. She asked me questions about the site, the elephant, its significance, age, etc. and I responded as best I could. It all seemed very routine. Then she reached over, snapped off the recorder, and said, "Well, that's it then. Good job." Before I could respond she leaped up and ran from the studio and down a hallway screaming very loudly, "A star is born, a star is born!"

I was still sitting alone and puzzled at the interview table, trying to understand what the hell was going on when she re-appeared with two male employees who stared at me as if I had just emerged from the abyssal depths of the Gulf with slimy green algae dripping from my ears.

"How would you like to have your own show?" the young lady asked, and without waiting for my reaction, she continued, "We want you to do a regular science show for the station—once each week. How does that sound?"

I really didn't know what to think or say, uncertain that she was even serious. "Well, I, ah, I, er, that is I don't think I know. I'm pretty busy these days. It does sound interesting; perhaps it could be managed."

"Great!" she exclaimed with a broad smile. The two staring males smiled benevolently. "That's it, then. I'll call you in a few days with the details. We'll need, of course, to run this by Alec, you know."

I never learned exactly what happened. Apparently old Alec had nixed the proposition. I was told simply that the TV station had decided not to go forward with the idea. As things turned out it proved to be as close as I would come to paving the way for Carl Sagan.

Our elephant, we soon discovered, straddled the local water table. As a result the skeletal bones which lay above the water table were well preserved but those below it had been softened to varying degrees by the corrosive effects of the groundwater. Except for foot-long segments at their tips the great, curving, 13-foot ivory tusks lay above the water table and were, therefore, in excellent condition. The tips, long in contact with the acid waters, were rotted and extremely fragile. It was clear that successful retrieval of these delicate tip segments would require great care and considerable patience as well as a liberal sprinkling of good fortune.

With the hope of enhancing our chances for complete, intact retrieval of these two magnificent tusks, I gave the job of reinforcing the decayed tips to Jim Fowler, one of my graduate assistants. To accomplish our goal it was necessary for Jim to remove, very carefully, and bit by bit, the encasing sediment from around the decayed ivory. When a small surface area had been exposed it was thoroughly dried, glued and shellacked. It was a tedious, slow-going job which required Jim to squat for many hours in a small, cramped muddy hole. But to his credit he persevered and, in the end, because of his efforts we were able to retrieve the two beautifully complete tusks.

After two and a half weeks we had just about reached the point of both physical and mental exhaustion. Someone had been working at the site or standing all night watches continuously since day one. We each had other responsibilities so I knew we could no longer maintain the killing pace. With that in mind and having achieved most of our primary goals, I decided to close down the operation sometime within the next two or three days.

We constructed a large, heavy-duty wooden platform and slid it with great difficulty under the colossal head of the great pachyderm. Once in position and secured to the platform the head was ready to be hoisted from the excavation.

To raise the tusks presented a special set of problems. First, the tusks were shellacked and then reinforced with splints made of slender boards wrapped in several layers of burlap soaked in plaster of Paris. Completion of this task had required about 104 feet of boards, 50 burlap bags, and 900 pounds of plaster of Paris. Even so, we discovered that any attempt to move them resulted in unacceptable levels of damage. Reluctantly I decided the only way we could get them up to the truck without losing them altogether was to cut each tusk off about five feet from the jaw and then raise the freed segments independently. I could only hope that we might devise a satisfactory method of re-attaching the severed ends when they were safely in our lab.

When all was ready we arranged to remove the elephant from the excavation and to transport it to the campus on Saturday, December 9. A local construction firm volunteered a crane and operator to do the hoisting, and another company provided a flatbed truck and driver for transportation.

On Friday night Solliday and I drew guard duty at the site. We had decided to stay on in the morning to supervise the removal of our great beast. It was winter then, and even in Houston it gets cold. So we gathered firewood from along the banks of the canal and started a campfire to keep warm. We had no sleeping bags or blankets, so just lay on the ground at the base of the bank, huddled as close to the fire as we dared. About 10:30 Ed Pyeatt, a geology major, showed up at the site. He hailed us from the top of the bank waving a large bottle of Chianti. "This is the stuff to keep you warm," he cried.

We called him down and the three of us hugged the fire and passed the bottle as we chatted. Ed was the son of Lloyd Pyeatt, a micropaleontologist with Sohio. His parents insisted he follow in daddy's footsteps and enroll at the University of Houston where he was instructed to major in geology. I knew Lloyd pretty well, so I had ample opportunity to hear of his hopes for his son. The problem the Pyeatts had was that Ed wanted no part of a career in geology. What he really wanted was to be a rock star. He played gigs with a local band and carried his guitar in a case just about everywhere he went—even to class.

Lloyd and Mrs. Pyeatt couldn't understand how Ed had turned out so badly, how he could disappoint them in this manner. They demanded that he give up all such foolish notions and get down to serious business and prepare himself to do something respectable, something in which they could take pride.

Ed tried to please them, but his heart was not in the effort. He cut classes, slept through lectures, got drunk with his buddies and finally, to the horror of his parents, flunked out of college.

Mr. and Mrs. Pyeatt came to me then and pleaded that I intervene, that I try to turn him around and see that he receive another chance. So I talked with Ed about the dreary situation and made a pitch for giving geology one more shot, but I had no more influence on him than his parents, probably because deep inside I thought they were making a mistake. It was obvious that Ed was in open rebellion against parental domination and I could understand that.

We sat around the glowing embers drinking and talking of his gigs and his plans to go to California to make it big. About midnight when the bottle mysteriously had gone dry Ed left and Solliday and I stretched out on the ground, hoping the inner, wine-induced warmth would allow a little sleep. It did but the effects quickly wore off. When we awoke it was a little past 1:30 a.m. Lying there, complaining about how miserable we were, we suddenly became aware of a person on the bank above. A lady stood there barely visible in the dull glow of the corner streetlight. She stared down at us and we with our lolling, purple-stained tongues returned her stare. Finally she placed her hands on her hips and declared, with obvious distaste, "Life's other side." Then she turned and vanished, just an ill-tempered apparition in the night.

At about three o'clock we were awakened by voices approaching up the street. Several males were headed toward the site. Alerted now we rose to defend our treasure when three young high schoolers with picks and shovels in hand appeared over the crest of the bank. When these would-be grave robbers saw us they halted in their tracks and without a word turned and fled. Once again we had saved the pachyderm, but I paid the price for our heroics. By 6:00 a.m. feeling like six pounds of dung in a five-pound sack, I told Jim that I would have to leave him as soon as relief arrived. Someone was supposed to show up in an hour to help get things prepared for the big move.

"Hell," Jim said magnanimously. "Go ahead, you look half dead. I'll stay. It's only an hour or so."

Too sick to argue, I left and drove the 30 or 40 miles to my house in southeast Houston.

When the phone jangled at about 10:30 I was near death and had no desire to talk with anyone. Reluctantly I lifted the receiver from the phone beside the bed. It was Jim reporting that they had successfully removed the elephant and trucked it to the department foyer where it now resided in all its plaster of Paris glory.

"Fine," I said, not really giving a damn. "I'm dying, so if it proves to be a new species maybe you can name it in my honor or at least my memory."

Having waited patiently for me to finish with the sarcasm, he burst forth with a blend of incredulity and excitement, "Guess what we found beneath the elephant?"

"How the hell do I know?"

"No, I'm serious, guess!"

"Well, all right, if you insist. You found a female elephant beneath and the two of them had fucked themselves to death."

"No, no," Jim said a bit irritably. "It was a goddamned entire horse skeleton beneath the elephant."

"God, our old boy must have been queer for horses. Have you told anyone?"

"Only you."

"Well," I said, slowly, clearly and with deep conviction. "Don't. Especially don't mention it to any of those goddamned reporters. Now then," I continued, "listen carefully. Can you see the head of the horse?"

"Well, yes, most of it."

"Good. Can you see if there are teeth in its mouth or nearby?"

"Sure," Jim replied. "I saw at least three teeth in the jaws."

"All right then, remove the teeth, pack them carefully and bring them to my office Monday morning. When you've done that, fill the fucking hole and get out of there."

I slept then, and dreamed of a land where no one had ever seen or heard of an elephant or a horse. I slept until Sunday.

On Monday morning, still ill but compelled by a sense of duty, I drove to the campus. As I came abreast the plaster-clad behemoth residing now in our departmental foyer I stopped to stare at it for a few seconds, but hurriedly moved on when beset by a powerful surge of nausea. At my office I spotted Jim holding a small white sample bag.

"The teeth?" I asked.

"Yes," he replied. "Two of them."

"Good," I said. "Just lay them on my desk. I'll send them to Jim Quinn at the University of Arkansas for identification. He knows more about fossil Texas horses than anyone else." Then I abruptly asked, "Did you get the excavation filled?"

"Sure did. We buried the Chianti bottle with the horse and the remainder of the elephant."

Later, sitting at my desk I had to smile as I considered the possibility that one day in the dim future another paleontologist might accidentally re-excavate our site. What would he think when he found that Chianti bottle with the fossils? That the beasts had died during some sort of Ice Age drunken orgy?

A few weeks later Jim Quinn informed me that the teeth I had sent belonged to the horse, *Equus caballus*. He also said that contrary to what anyone else might think, the horse was no more than 25,000 years old.

At that moment I might have imagined that, following nearly a month of living with an extinct elephant, I could once again settle into my normally hectic routine. Not true.

The attention given our elephant hunt by the press had, it seemed, sent half the population of Houston into a frenzied search of the area bayou banks for traces of fossilized bones. Each week I received calls from local citizens who thought they had made an important fossil discovery. Usually Gordon Clopine, Solliday, or I were forced to visit with these people and examine their finds. Most commonly they had nothing of scientific value; however, a few had found something of special interest. For example, one family in north Houston had several parts of the skeleton of a giant turtle four times as large as the modern Galapagos species. However, they had decided their find was worth a great amount of money and expected us to make a substantial offer on the spot. Although we attempted to convince such persons that the fossils had only scientific value, we rarely succeeded. There were also individuals who were only interested in publicity. I took a call one afternoon from a local gravel pit operator who claimed his workmen had uncovered a "truly interesting fossil bone." He wondered, innocently, if I could come to the pit at 4:00 p.m. for a close-up look. I couldn't, so I sent Gordon Clopine. Gordon later reported that when he arrived at the location a TV crew was already in place. The quarry owner stood with the bone proudly displayed in one hand, next to a large billboard advertising the company's name, its services and the telephone number. Gordon was certain that a passing dog had buried the bone in the pit.

Not everyone expected us to come examine their discovery. Some people brought them directly to us. One Saturday morning I was working in my office when a middle-aged man and his teenaged son appeared at my door. Having introduced themselves they told me of their fantastic fossil discovery—a horse they had dug from a Houston bayou. "The bones are right outside in the pickup," the father said, "and my boy and I will bring them up here right now if you' d be willing to examine them." I had little interest in horse bones that morning, but in the interest of public goodwill, I foolishly agreed to take a look.

In a few minutes they were back with two large rolled tarps. In a flash they unrolled the tarps on my office floor. It was a horse skeleton all right—the whole damned mud-caked thing. But it sure as hell wasn't a fossil. Most of the bones were still articulated, held together by semi-rotted, stinking cartilage. It was clear that the animal had died during a flood not more than six months earlier.

It was necessary to be diplomatic in breaking bad news to neophyte fossil hunters such as they, who tended to be very proud of their discoveries. They had gone to considerable length to recover them and often only wanted to be duly praised and patted on their heads. I explained as best I could why the horse was not a fossil, pointing out the cartilage and even a few tufts of hair that clung tenaciously to a leg bone. They countered that the horses had been found "pretty well buried" 10 feet below the bank top so they were certain it had to be very old. Then I explained that all sorts of animate and inanimate objects were carried down the bayous during flash flooding and were left partially buried in silt and sand along the bayou banks when the water level dropped. They really didn't want to believe me, and perhaps never did, but while gathering up the smelly carcass they politely thanked me for my time and then left in apparent good spirits. I could only hope that instead of taking it home with them they would transport the skeleton to a remote corner of Harris County and give the poor beast a decent Christian burial.

There were times when, in similar circumstances, my efforts at diplomacy failed spectacularly. Late in February I received another phone call. The man's voice at the other end identified itself as Lewis A. Manson, president of a Houston-based manufacturing company. He said he had a collection of fossils he wished to donate to the department and asked if it would be all right if he brought them around the next day at about 4:00 p.m. When I agreed to see him he added, "I have a very special fossil I'd like you to look at." I said that would be fine, just bring it along and I'd take a look.

True to his word, Manson arrived the next afternoon with a small box of invertebrate fossils he had collected from Cretaceous outcrops in central Texas. But he was not alone. He had brought with him a *Houston Post* photographer he introduced to me as Ed Valdez. Ed came equipped with a large, heavy camera bag that hung by a leather strap from his left shoulder. When I saw that, I became moderately wary. Then Manson opened a small box held in his left hand and very carefully removed an object wrapped in tissue paper. Denuded of its wrapping, it appeared to be a white spherical object the approximate size of a baseball. Smiling proudly Manson handed the thing to me. "Here it is," he announced, his face aglow. "Have you ever seen anything like it?"

"Well," I shrugged. "Well, well, it truly is interesting. Er, ah, it certainly is a fine one but I' m not exactly sure just what it may be." Then, as I held the sphere in my hand, I was blinded by a flash of light from Ed Valdez' camera. The historic moment had been captured for posterity.

Blinking, I asked, "What do you think it is, Mr. Manson?"

Manson looked a little surprised at my admission of ignorance. "Why," he said almost indignantly, "it's obviously a Pterodactyl egg!"

"A Pterodactyl egg!" I exclaimed, unable to hide my amazement. "If it were true it certainly would be a most remarkable find."

"Oh, it's true all right. Dug it out of the side of the Braes Bayou—buried 10 feet below the surface."

"That's a bit odd," I said. "The sediments in Braes Bayou are Pleistocene in age—only tens of thousands of years old. Pterodactyls became extinct at the end of the Cretaceous Period, roughly 65 million years ago. Anyway," I added, "this doesn't really look like a fossil at all—something man-made, I think."

Defensive now, Manson drew himself up to his full 5' 4" and, with great firmness, re-stated his amazing claim. "Oh, I don't know about that age stuff, I just know that without doubt it is a Pterodactyl egg and that it could well be the first ever discovered."

Valdez, who had remained standing behind Manson, edged forward for a closer look at Manson's egg. Directing my attention to Manson, I said, "You probably are right, as far as I know no one has ever found a Pterodactyl egg. I think as important as this might be we should seek a second opinion." Manson seemed to approve of my suggestion. As I spoke he picked up the egg and carefully returned it to the little box. "Right below us," I said, "on the first floor, we have in residence a very famous biologist, Dr. Joseph Bequaert from Harvard University. He certainly will be able to tell us whether or not your specimen is a Pterodactyl egg."

Joe Bequaert was working on the pulmonate snails of Texas and I had helped him make some of his collections. He had been born in Belgium about 70 years earlier and was strictly of the old European school. Stiff, formal and usually quite gruff, he loathed any interruptions of his work. As the three of us headed for his office, I thought, *This should prove interesting.*

As always Dr. Bequaert was at his worktable poring over scores of tiny gastropod shells. "Pardon the interruption, Dr. Bequaert," I began. "I have a gentleman here who has collected an object from Braes Bayou that he thinks is a Pterodactyl egg. I don't agree with him so we thought you might be willing to offer an opinion."

Joe looked up at us as if we were a traveling pack of escaped lunatics. "A Pterodactyl egg," he repeated in disbelief. "Let me see that thing."

Manson carefully handed him the sphere. Bequaert whipped a hands lens out of his pocket and examined the surface of the object for less than ten seconds before he slammed it to the table, proclaiming loudly in a tone of bitter disgust, "It's a damned styrofoam ball!"

In that moment my careful efforts at diplomacy disintegrated to dust. Manson, with reddening cheeks, grabbed the ball from the table, dropped it unwrapped into its little box and then, wheeling abruptly, charged into the hall. Stunned, Valdez and I followed him to my office where, without a word, he picked up the box of fossils he had donated to the department and with Valdez at his heels rushed down the hall toward the stairs.

My meeting with Manson hadn't worked out well at all, but I took some solace in the certainty that this was one peculiar episode in my recent life that would not make the newspaper. Dead wrong one more time. The next morning when I picked up the *Post* I was astonished to find on the front page a headline which read: "A non-petrified, non-egg—no glory for Harris County."

On an inside page there was the Valdez picture of me, frozen in time, staring quizzically at Manson's stupid styrofoam egg. Actually I had been desperately attempting to figure out how to handle this obviously deranged individual who had invaded the sanctity of my office.

It was a tongue-in-cheek story—clever, humorous, well written by the veteran newsman Hubert McWhinney. I sighed when I finished it—a sigh of relief. Surely, I though, this will be the end of it, the end of the exasperating series of events that had beset me for the past three months. Of course it didn't end entirely, but the worst had passed. In March I would escape to San Francisco for a week at the annual AAPG convention. Then in June I would be off to the Carolinas to begin a new NSF research project and, best of all, in September I would leave Houston to take up a new position as Associate Professor of Geology at Duke University.

Fu Manchu Strikes Again

In November 1961, we were deep into the fall semester and I was trying to keep a hundred balls simultaneously suspended above my head. When I had time to think about it there seemed a fair chance that all the balls would plummet to my office floor at any moment. At such times in my life, the words of the old Chinese philosopher usually pop into mind: "If I shoved a broom up my ass I could also sweep the floor."

In addition to teaching courses in invertebrate paleontology, Cenozoic Stratigraphy and Physical Geology, I was supervising seven or eight master's theses, working every available moment on my NSF research project, trying to set up a departmental doctoral curriculum, finishing off two Florida manuscripts, holding down a seat on the faculty senate, completing a study of Duplin fossils with Solliday, and working on the Pleistocene stratigraphy of the Houston area. I was also preparing a paper with Solliday and Chaplin on the Neogene stratigraphy of Horry County, South Carolina to be presented at the AAPG Annual Meeting in San Francisco in March. In addition, I was trying to arrange a trip, delayed by an airline strike, to southwest Florida in January to study a newly discovered fossil site reported to me by Eric Van Tolenen of Harvard University.

Solliday and I had formed a fossil supply company in the fall we called "Barsol." The purpose was to provide fossil specimens to universities, museums and private collectors for classroom study, research and display. Our biggest jobs had been to take inventory of the existing stock and to organize the fossil suites for sale. We had mailed fliers to more than a hundred institutions announcing our services and merchandise, and now that the orders had begun to trickle in we spent one night each week packaging and shipping them. This was a strictly clandestine operation. Our return address was a P.O. box and only our wives knew that Jim and I were "Barsol". By spring business had boomed, producing a substantial supplemental income, but with my departure from Houston in August 1962, we terminated the operation.

The evenings when we packed fossils for shipping were special for me because on those occasions I called Martha Anzueto in Silver Spring, Maryland. She was a Guatemalan who worked at the Pan American Union in D.C. and shared an apartment with her brother, a student at the University of Maryland. We met one evening in 1960 at a Hawaiian nightclub near the capitol building. At 5' 5" and 97 pounds she struck me as a Latin Audrey Hepburn. Her fragile appearance, however, belied a fiery revolutionary spirit and fierce devotion to the cause of Fidel Castro.

She was a female comfortable with her own sex and not fearful of mine. She possessed a firm and realistic sense of self and of universal justice and fair play, and she had a commendable deep-seated pride in her origins—in her family and countrymen. She was also conscious of her olive skin, skin she found to be despised by bigots in the United States. "Americans," she observed defiantly. "They call themselves Americans. We are all Americans: North, Central, South, white, black, brown—all Americans!"

In the beginning our encounter had been romantic, enhanced for me by my observation that she never mentioned the word "germs" when we kissed. In a short time, though, romance turned to a comfortably warm friendship, rooted in mutual respect and shared views. When I called her on those evenings from Houston, we always professed our mutual love, each fully aware it was the love of brother and sister.

In July, 1962, while in D.C. to do some work at the Museum, I drove to Silver Spring only to find that Martha and her brother had moved, leaving no forwarding address. With the faint hope that she might still work at the Pan American Union I went there at 5:00 p.m. and waited outside where I scanned the faces of the employees as they headed home. She was not among them.

I knew then that she had returned to Guatemala, returned there, I knew, to fight for the rights and human dignity of her countrymen.

In the short time that she had known me she had detected something beneath my pale skin, something she had considered of value. It was something my wife had overlooked or ignored. It was something probably only intuitively sensed by Martha—a nebulous blur like a shadowy figure reflected in a mirror at dusk. But whatever it had been she had felt it and she had made me feel it. She had given me a sense of self-worth and the hope that tomorrow merited more than casual anticipation.

There had been no slowdown in the inexorable deterioration of my marriage and for some time I had known that it could not be salvaged. In September Phyllis, Betty and Charlie Quinn and I had spent two disastrous days in

Matamoros, Mexico. When we returned to Houston I asked Phyllis for a divorce, but she had been stubbornly unreceptive to the idea. At that time I decided to drop the subject until I could determine the status of my relationship with Karin Zeisig, if indeed one existed. But there was little I could do about that until spring break in March when I would have the opportunity to talk with her face to face in Myrtle Beach.

By November 1961, the suicidal war that had been waged for two years between two factions of the Geology Department was essentially resolved. My side (the good guys) had lost. It had been a replay of the Stenzel Affair of 1956-57, with similar results. Each of us who had faced off against the Wang regime had been marked by him for extermination.

The first casualty had been our structural geologist, Jim Taggard. Jim, a student of Marland Billings at Harvard, had failed to complete his doctoral dissertation in the two-year period granted to him when he had been hired. Bill Berry was next. Bill, a brilliant student of the renowned Yale paleontologist Carl Dunbar, had been subjected to a calculated campaign of lies and harassment by Wang. He left Houston of his own accord to take a position in the Department of Paleontology at the University of California at Berkeley.

George Sommers, our aging geophysicist who had failed for years to keep abreast of new concepts and methods in his specialty, was an easy target for Wang. Not long after the day Wang had strangely announced to me that Sommers was "…Obviously senile and professionally incompetent," George, confused and bewildered, walked into my office and told me that he had just learned that he was being forced by the administration to retire.

At that point only three of us were left to lock horns with the wily Chinaman: Carl Rexroad, Bob Greenwood, and myself. Firmly aligned with Wang were Mary Pope(name has been changed) and Karl Keital. Frank Barber was a bit of a wild card. All of us had frequently heard him proclaim his undying devotion to the very highest of academic standards, but it was difficult for some of us to forget that he had supported the purge of Stenzel, who had insisted that all staff members actively engage in research and publish at least one paper a year.

Our situation had become even more critical in late 1959 when we learned that Wang had informed Carl Rexroad that his contract would not be renewed for the 1960-61 academic year. Wang had hired Rexroad in the summer of 1958 while I was in the field. On my return to the campus Wang visited my office one day and apologized for hiring Carl without consulting me. But then he explained with an enigmatic smile "Carl's specialty, conodonts, is exactly what this department needs, and besides, he has such a completely irresistible personality."

The official explanation given for the dismissal of Carl was that his specialty, conodonts, did not at all fit into the plans of the department and that he had a very abrasive personality.

Fortunately for Carl the Vice President for Faculty extended Carl's contract until the spring of 1962 so that he would have ample time to seek new employment.

In 1959, several influential geologists from major oil companies in Houston and a segment of the Alumni Association urged me to try to unseat John Wang as department chairman. Although I agreed to try I had no idea how to comply with their wish. Shortly thereafter Wang had himself presented me with a possible answer.

On a fateful fall morning in 1961 John Wang stunned at least a few of us when he proposed that the department drop the thesis as a prerequisite for a master's degree in geology. Predictably Mary Pope and Karl Keital quickly proclaimed their enthusiastic support for the startling proposal.

Then, as now, a thesis was required of master's candidates by all certified geology departments in the country. The purpose was, of course, to test the ability of a student to initiate and conduct original research. To omit this requirement would have been interpreted throughout the profession as an overt attempt to subvert acceptable academic standards. There was little doubt that the adoption of John's proposal would prove devastating to the reputation of the geology department, its faculty and students, as well as an embarrassment for the university.

It seemed that at last Wang had made the mistake for which I long had waited. Even Frank Barber, I thought, would be forced to stand against Wang on this one. And if Frank joined forces with us we would have the votes to defeat Wang's proposal. If Wang were thwarted on this critical issue it should demonstrate rather dramatically that he had lost the confidence of his staff. Under those circumstances he would almost certainly be obliged to step down as chair.

Wang never really revealed the reasoning behind his proposal to drop the thesis requirement. However, it was fairly easy to deduce the reasons he would consider most compelling. At that time there was a large number of entry-level young men who worked as technicians for local petroleum and service companies. Most of them, with only a B.S. degree, were locked into low-paying positions with little hope of promotion or significant salary increases. Some of these people had realized they could greatly enhance their professional position if they had a master's degree in geology. It was these individuals Wang wanted to pull into our graduate program. We taught a full suite of required graduate courses at night and on weekends for such people. The problem was that most of them didn't want to take the time to complete a thesis research project.

When I arrived at the university there were 60 or 70 of these men from industry enrolled in the graduate program. It was my observation during the first year there that the majority of those who took my courses were not qualified academically or intellectually to handle graduate-level work. Furthermore, most were motivated solely by the hope of eventual financial gain. They also tended to lack any sort of work ethic, intellectual curiosity, or significant sense of excellence. Typically, having worked in the petroleum industry they considered themselves experts on the type of training they required. They were quick to point out that none of us knew our asses from a hole in the ground about the industry. It is a gross understatement to say I had no desire to try to teach such people. We also discovered there were a number of these people, according to existing departmental records, who were currently working on theses but who seemed not to have indicated the subject of their research, had no major professor of record, and had not been seen or heard from in more than five years. During the first year Greenwood and I weeded out many of these so-called students and began to replace them with qualified young people recruited from universities throughout the nation.

Then suddenly with Wang's announcement, our work seemed to have been conducted in vain. Part of Wang's motivation may have stemmed from his apparent aversion to anything that smacked of work for himself. The direction of a student thesis project requires considerable time and effort on the part of the major professor, effort not always properly recognized by university administration. Also, by standard convention, the major professor is expected to be an expert in the field of research chosen by his student.

The word "expert" is generally reserved for those who have, in the judgment of their peers, published a significant body of meaningful papers in his field. Wang, Pope, and Keital had accumulated virtually no tangible record of any kind of research, meaningful or otherwise. More to the point, it seemed quite clear that they never would.

Rexroad, Greenwood and I privately discussed the significance of Wang's proposal at some length over a period of several days. To block Wang's scheme we needed the support of Frank Barber. With him on our side we held a four to three edge in the upcoming voting. Because Bob had known Barber much longer than Carl and I, he was elected to sound out Frank. We all feared that even if Frank agreed with us he would lack the backbone to stand up to Wang. In a day or so Bob reported to us that he had spoken with Frank about the situation and had explained why it was necessary to preserve the thesis requirement. To our surprise and great relief, Frank had declared that he was solidly in agreement with us. With this development we had acquired the means to thwart Wang.

Had we won? Well, we were as filled with confidence as one dared to be under those circumstances. Through the years Lord John and Lady Mary had repelled all assaults directed at their citadel of academic mediocrity. The attackers invariably had been strewn bloodied, battered and humiliated across the Elysian Fields of higher education. Considering the number and caliber of the vanquished heroes, our task, at best daunting, was made doubly difficult by the fact that Wang would know we were coming. There would be no element of surprise. Fu Manchu with the Dragon Lady at his side would be waiting for us with a full bag of cunning and lethal tricks.

At our staff meeting a few days later Wang moved immediately to put the primary issue to a vote. Calmly and with surprising confidence he began to poll the staff starting with Lady Mary, seated to his right. Her "Yes" came as no surprise to any of us. Moving counterclockwise around the table, Keital, who was next, responded with the obligatory "Yea." With the nay votes of Carl, Bob and me, and Wang's "Yea" the vote was deadlocked.

All eyes turned to Frank Barber, seated at the far end of the table. For all of us I suspect it was a dramatic moment, staged no doubt by Wang himself. With Frank's expected (by us) "Nay" vote we would carry the day. Then to my horror, instead of voting Frank began slowly and hesitantly to speak. "I've given this, ah, matter, a great deal of thought during the past few days. Our decision will, ah, long affect the quality of our program and, ah, the professional lives of our students. We must carefully weigh the pros and cons of such a serious decision." Suddenly I was possessed by the sinking feeling of defeat. *He's giving a fucking speech,* I said to myself. *The son of a bitch has sold us down the river and now he's fucking rationalizing his fucking betrayal.* Even before he sheepishly uttered the dreaded "Yea" I knew we were dead—that I was doomed. My name, along with those of Rexroad and Greenwood, would soon be added to the now long and perhaps illustrious list of those who had preceded us to a low-rent geological Valhalla. Wang had done it again. He was good, I thought—one had almost to admire the son of a bitch.

We didn't have to wait long to learn how Wang had done it. A few weeks following that meeting, our Dean announced that Frank Barber had been selected as the new Assistant Dean of the School of Liberal Arts and Sciences.

There was a bizarre epilogue to my tale. One day early in the 1962 spring semester, John Wang appeared at my office door obviously quite distraught. "Can you imagine, Jules," he began, "I just had a long talk with the Vice President and he told me that the university would not permit us to drop the thesis requirement?" John Wang had amazed and baffled me many times, but never more than at that moment. To this day I've not figured out why he had chosen to break this news, shattering for himself, to his chief antagonist rather than Pope or Keital. I had, of course, been delighted that the thesis requirement had received a last minute reprieve. At the same time, however, I knew that for me this would change nothing; my days at the university remained numbered.

A few months later Rexroad had joined the Indiana Geological Survey and Greenwood, on leave of absence, was preparing for a trip to India. Wang, it seemed, had been forced by the administration to step down as departmental chairman. But even so, "Wily One" had grasped victory from the jaws of ignoble defeat by somehow engineering the formation of a puppet regime chaired by his stooge Karl Keital. Now from the dark recesses of his inner sanctum, secure in the snug, warm, cocoon of his own making, Fu Manchu was free to conjure dark schemes, weave intricate intrigues and cast unearthly spells.

When Fu required room service he had only to pull a few strings and his puppet attached at the other end would begin to squirm and to sway. Then the creature with its piggish little reddened eyes and with yellow drool oozing from the corners of its evil mouth would creep into his master's den and obsequiously await its orders. "Yes, master, yes, master." Orders received and acknowledged, the thing would clasp its bony fingers over its sunken chest and bowing repeatedly slowly back from Fu's chamber hissing as it departed, "Kill, kill, kill."

I was alone then, properly hosed down and cut off at the knees, a highly vulnerable target. I had only to await the coup de grace.

Dejected in my office, I could almost make out the face of my grade school principal, "Old Lady Swopey" frowning from the ceiling and saying in the well-calculated tone she had always reserved just for me, "I told you years ago that little boys who stand on one foot never amount to anything."

But I need not have been despondent. At that moment the forces of my liberation, spear-headed by R.C. Moore and Carl Rexroad, were mobilizing and my succor was imminent. I was beginning to hear a faint voice in the back of my head; it told me, "Keep the faith, baby." So I did.

Free at Last

Monday morning, March 26, 1962, I was on a Delta flight to San Francisco. Jim Solliday was in the seat beside me. Jim Chaplin, then a geology professor at Morehead State University in eastern Kentucky, would meet us at the airport when we landed. The three of us had co-authored a paper on the Pleistocene geology of Horry County, South Carolina. We were scheduled to present a summary of our work at the annual convention of the American Association of Petroleum Geologists on Wednesday afternoon.

The pilot informed us we were 35,000 feet above the Grand Canyon and clipping along at 600 mph. I looked down at that marvelous slit in the earth's surface. As a boy I had dreamed of one day running the treacherous Colorado River in a small boat. At the time only half of the one hundred daredevils who had tried to conquer the canyon had survived to tell of their adventure; my old professor R.C. Moore, had been one of them.

I had anticipated Martin Luther King's "Free at Last" speech. I was definitely feeling free—free of my wife, free of the fucking geology department, free of John Wang and Karl Keital, free of Houston, where mid-summer heat and humidity enveloped and threatened to suffocate the city in mid-March—free at last, but only for a week.

We had it all planned. Monday afternoon we would make an appearance at the convention center, register, and then meet with Henryk Stenzel to discuss the mess at the University of Houston. Monday evening Deck and Molly would drive up from Pacific Grove and meet us at the St. Francis for drinks, laughs, and talk of the good old days we had shared in Myrtle Beach.

For Tuesday evening, Bob Greenwood had arranged a date for me with a former girlfriend, a nurse from Denmark. Wednesday was reserved for the technical sessions and our presentation. Thursday we would pick up Linda Decker at the University of San Francisco, where she was a student, and drive south for a two-day visit with the Deckers at their Pacific Grove home.

Six glorious days! With a little luck the Russians would nuke Houston in our absence.

As a counterbalance to my high spirits there was the reminder that, as anticipated, I had not been granted tenure by the University of Houston. Unless I succeeded in securing a position by August, I would be faced with a big bunch of freedom, more than I could handle.

Sometime in February Karl Keital had requested my presence in his office. When I arrived he looked up from his desk and motioned me to a seat. I noticed that his small, beady eyes seemed dilated. He looked, I thought, like a man who had just defecated in his best Sunday-go-to-meeting trousers. His vacuous eyes peered at me for several seconds as he seemed to search for a beginning point. He chose the direct approach.

"The university has decided not to grant you tenure. There seems to be a, ah, general consensus that you are an eccentric, and that you will only grow worse with time."

I had been called a lot of things during my life, but eccentric had not been one of them. Even worse, my particular affliction seemed to be terminal. But I could guess why he would think me eccentric. In the fall he had gone into my office one day while I was at lunch and had removed my favorite swivel chair from the back room and replaced it with some kind of ratty-looking, broken down mess that I was afraid to sit in. Pissed by his high-handedness, I carried the old, moth-eaten thing into the hall and smashed it to bits against the wall beside his office. After that he insisted that I had a propensity to make mountains of molehills. To emphasize the point he gave me a very small folding wooden stool at the departmental Christmas exchange party. Actually it is a cute little thing for which, through the years, I have found many uses. At the moment it sits on the deck outside my office painted a nice, bright, canary yellow.

He moved on then to my deficiencies as a teacher. "Too demanding of your students," he declared. "You really pile on the work." To illustrate the assertion he turned to the handout on report writing which I gave to each of my students in advanced courses. "It's longer than the reports you make them write. We got a lot of complaints from students about that."

The handout was actually a hybrid of instructions for scientific report writing given to me as a student by R.C. Moore and Carl Savage. They were excellent and essential instructions which most of my students fully appreciated. In fact, I had to keep extras on hand, because the most frequent first communication from graduates was a frantic request for a copy.

276

However, I had long known that Keital loved to expound on teaching methods. He firmly believed that the art of effective teaching had been his exclusive creation.

"One thing does puzzle me," he said. "Despite everything, more than half of our graduate students have chosen to do their theses under your direction. They seem to be devoted to you for some reason."

As he droned on I imagined that creepy spiders were crawling in my shorts, and I constantly fought a strong urge to cut a raunchy fart to clear them away and Keital with them.

Later in my office I tried to put some things in perspective. It was true that Keital had savored his role as my Lord High Executioner, but there could be little doubt that the scenario had been written, directed, and produced by John Wang. No matter who or what had brought me down, the fact was that for the first (and only time) I had been fired from a job, and I found that deeply disturbing.

I was especially disturbed to have been characterized as an eccentric. I had always associated the word with weird behavior. I certainly did not consider myself weird. Hell, I was unconventional all right, offbeat, candid (perhaps to excess), commonly impulsive and, on occasion, even volatile, but definitely not weird. Weird people howl at the moon and I had almost never done that. He surely hadn't based his assessment of me solely on that stupid chair episode. There had to be other things I had said or done that he also considered eccentric. Perhaps everything I did seemed eccentric to him.

As we winged our way westward I began to recall a few things I had done that Keital could very well have considered a bit peculiar.

On February 20, 1962, John Glenn was scheduled by NASA to attempt the first orbit of the earth by an American. Lift-off was to take place in the morning during my Historical Geology lecture. I didn't want to miss this historic event and I didn't think my students should either, so during the lecture I had a graduate student in the back of the room monitoring a radio. As the countdown began, he gave me a pre-arranged signal and turned up the volume. We all listened to the successful lift-off. It had been a monumental moment in the history of space exploration, and in the study of the earth. Keital probably thought that I had wasted valuable lecture time.

There was a wet lab close to my office where I did some of my research. The space was shared with two or three other faculty members and their graduate students, with the result that several different research projects were usually in progress at the same time. Under such crowded conditions it was essential to allocate a specific work area for each research project to avoid messing up each other's work.

I made a special effort to work only in my assigned area and to keep it as clean and neat as possible. Some of the other guys weren't always so considerate. Sometimes they encroached on my space or, more commonly, left their own space in chaotic disorder.

About once a month, when the mess in the lab had exceeded my level of tolerance, I'd go in there and clean and organize the entire place. As soon as someone heard my banging around and cursing, the word would be passed that DuBar was cleaning the lab. In minutes the hall would clear, office doors would slam shut, and everyone would hide until I was finished. There seems little doubt that Keital regarded these episodes as examples of eccentric behavior.

One evening I was in my outer office with Jim Fowler and several other graduate students. We were attempting, unsuccessfully, to explain some small aspect of a geological hypothesis to Doug Lewis, one of our master's candidates. Following ten or fifteen frustrating minutes, Doug finally got the point.

Relieved, Fowler said, "I think he's got it."

That brought the obvious response from me, "By George, I think he's got it!" whereupon we all filed out of the office and snaked down the hall singing loudly, "The Rain in Spain …" The door to Keital's office suddenly slammed shut.

Some idiots in the administration decided that maybe the university should require all professors to use the Bell Curve system of grading students. Employing this system, we would have to hand out ten percent A's, 20 percent B's, 40 percent C's, 20 percent D's, and 10 percent F's in each class we taught. It's a neat system of grading which eliminates the element of common sense. A professor would be required to use this illogical scheme even though, in his judgment, all the students in his class earned an A or if he thought they deserved an F.

I'm certain Keital would have enjoyed seeing me forced to adopt the Bell Curve because he had long contended I failed too many students.

The Psychology Department was commissioned to make a feasibility study of the proposed plan. A couple of psychologists prepared a questionnaire and sent it to each of the faculty members to poll their reactions to the use of the Bell Curve. After filling all the appropriate blanks with my caustic observations, I returned the form and promptly forgot it.

A week or so later a coed appeared at my office door. She told me she was a graduate student in Psychology and that the head of the Psychology Department, after reading my responses to the questionnaire, had asked her to see me. She said that if I didn't mind, she'd like to do a study of me.

"Well, I suppose that would be okay. What do you have in mind?" was my reply.

"Oh, I'll ask some questions, but mostly you can tell me about your philosophy of teaching, or anything else you wish."

After that the young lady came to my office one hour each week. As she had suggested, I talked and she asked an occasional question and took a lot of notes. I never did have a clear idea of the purpose of these meetings, but I did think that one day a couple of guys in white would come to my office and haul me away. It all ended undramatically and I heard no more of it and never saw the coed again. However, if any of the girl's notes reached Keital, it is reasonable to assume that what I had said might have been regarded by him as further evidence of my eccentricity.

Eventually, the university decided to experiment with TV credit courses. The first course done by the School of Education was a test case to see how it would work and how it would be received by the public. Faculty members were asked to watch some of the lectures and pass on their reactions and comments to whoever was in charge of the project.

The lectures were presented live at 6:00 p.m. I watched one of them one evening while having dinner at home. The next day I sent my opinion of the lecture to the project director: "It spoiled my dinner and made me want to barf. Unless it is a course for the mentally retarded, it is an embarrassment to the university and to the city of Houston."

This time no psychologist appeared at my door. However, as far as I know, no more university credit courses were aired on TV while I remained on the faculty. Even Keital might have agreed with me on that one.

Robbie Moore, a research geologist with Texaco, taught a night course in marine geology at the university. I met him in the hall one evening and he told me that our faculty members needed to loosen up a little with their students. "All these professors here are too stiff, remote and formal. That's bad for student esprit de corps," he confided. He was right, but I wasn't sure what could be done; besides, I couldn't do it all alone. Robbie suggested getting the students out of the classroom environment and into a less formal setting—a bar, perhaps.

The thought was both intriguing and appealing. I decided to give it a try with my paleoecology class, a group of five graduate students that should just about fit into one of the booths at the Algerian Club, a student hangout across the street from the campus.

Thereafter I met the class at the Algerian Club one evening a week from 6:00 p.m. to 7:00 p.m. We sat squeezed in a booth at the rear of the room, ate Polish sausages, drank draft beer, and discussed papers on paleoecology reviewed by the students. I soon found that a one-hour session under those circumstances was just about right—any longer and we all had difficulty making much sense of the subject.

One evening Keital was to give a talk to the faculty and graduate students at 7:00 p.m. The six of us, full of sausage and beer, arrived about ten minutes late. Keital interrupted his talk, and, scowling, watched our laughing and chattering group take our places in the back of the room. Doubtless he long retained a vivid memory of that incident.

It must have been the winter of 1962 when a snowstorm blew into town while I was lecturing my paleontology class. The flakes were big and wet, and they came in such abundance that within 15 minutes they covered the campus with a soft, glistening white blanket.

It almost never snowed like that in Houston, so I stopped lecturing and we all walked to the windows to watch. Behind me a male voice said, "Looks like good stuff for a snowman." I agreed and asked how many of the students had ever made a snowman. To my surprise none had.

"Your education is sadly lacking," I declared. "Everyone should make at least one snowman during his life. I think you should all grab your jackets and follow me outside, I'll show you how it's done."

Quickly 30 students and a lone professor were rollicking, frolicking in the white stuff in front of Roy Cullen Building. Slipping, sliding, skidding, tumbling in tangled masses, tossing snowballs, with flushed faces glowing bright pink and gloveless hands sporting pale blue fingers, they rolled up mighty globs of grassy, wet snow and stacked them one on another until a great frozen creature rose from the ground seven feet toward the gray, chill sky. No wondrous work of art this thing, only a crude pagan born of joy and exuberance, the child of red-blooded young animals exuding the joy of collective youth in a celebration of life. That hour of unbridled passion would be long remembered after dull lectures, draped in the cobwebs of time, had become only distant echoes of an old man's ramblings.

Had Keital watched from his office window he would have seen only a milling entanglement of irresponsible young heathens and one professor gone mad.

At the airport the Jims and I grabbed a cab to the St. Francis. As soon as we had dumped our gear in the room on the eleventh floor we walked the twelve blocks to the convention hall. There was a steady flow of arrivals at the center, so we had to wait in line to register and receive our information packets. Before we could pin our nametags to our lapels, we were accosted by a group of four or five geologists, all strangers to me. One large, ruddy-faced guy about my age grabbed me by an elbow and drew me to him. His face shoved close to mine, he asked, "Do you know what those bastards at the University of Houston have done to DuBar?"

I thought it was a joke, but quickly realized he had no idea who I was. Blinking with astonishment, I stammered, "Well, no, what did they do to, ah, him?"

"Sacked him," he responded indignantly. "That's what the bastards did, just like they screwed old Henryk Stenzel!"

"Sacked him?!" I repeated, trying to inject a note of surprise in my voice. I shook my head in dismay. "Damn, that's terrible. Something needs to be done about people like that."

With an ominous smile, he hissed, "Something sure as hell will; you bet your goodies on that."

Moving toward the convention floor, I could hear Ruddy Face somewhere behind me. He was grabbing everyone he met and asking, "You know what those bastards at the University of Houston did to DuBar?" I was a hot topic in San Francisco.

For nearly two months Carl Rexroad, R.C. Moore and I had joined in a nationwide campaign to alert the profession to what the bastards at the University of Houston had done to DuBar. It seemed our efforts had met with success.

I was scheduled to meet with Henryk Stenzel a little later in the afternoon. Our department had offered an Assistant Professorship to Harvey Blatt, a recent Ph.D. from UCLA. Henryk and I planned to corner Harvey and to try to dissuade him from taking the job.

I met Stenzel near the registration tables. Although he barely knew me, he wrapped a stubby arm around my shoulder and guided me onto the convention floor where he introduced me to many of his friends. In our meanderings we eventually bumped into Harvey Blatt. Pinning him between us we spent 30 minutes trying to convince him that the Houston geology department was an academic cesspool which he should avoid at any cost. I think he believed most of what we told him but, as it turned out, it was his only job offer and he had to take it. He left the university a few years later, but I am unaware of the circumstances which shaped that decision.

At about 5:00 p.m. the Jims and I headed back to our hotel. On the way I made my first purchase with my newly acquired American Express card, a fifth of Canadian Club.

Jesus Loves to Cha, Cha, Cha

As we walked we concluded that it would be sensible to establish a working relationship with a hotel employee who, for a reasonable gratuity, would be willing to look after our interests during our sojourn in San Francisco.

The bellhop who had handled our luggage when we arrived, a bright young fellow, probably with an eye for a little extra cash, seemed the likely choice. In the lobby we cornered him near the elevator, where, for twenty dollars, we quickly closed a deal.

When we went to the desk for the room key, a striking black couple was checking in. The woman was probably in her mid-twenties, the man a decade older. Their clothes, obviously expensive, were flashy enough to attract a lot of attention, even in sophisticated San Francisco. I recall little of the man, but the woman (I assumed she was an actress or model) was one of the most sensually beautiful and beguiling women I had ever seen. A mere glance was sufficient to fill my mind with a clutter of carnal thoughts and an array of embarrassingly erotic images.

Solliday, rising to the occasion, had quickly engaged the couple in friendly, chatty conversation. When I heard the woman accept his invitation to join us later in our room for a drink I assumed she was politely humoring him. I was puzzled, though, to note that her male escort remained strangely silent and seemingly disinterested.

In our room we poured drinks and called the Deckers in Pacific Grove. They would be at our door, Deck promised, with two bottles, two glasses and two Carolina thirsts, no later than 8:00. With the assurance that there would indeed be a hot time in the old town that night, we proceeded with the business of self-embalming.

In what seemed only a fleeting moment the contents of our fifth of Canadian Club had become dangerously low. Drinking on an empty stomach had led to rather advanced states of inebriation and starvation. While Solliday busily and suspiciously checked the bottle for a leak, Chaplin, with a more firm grip on reality, suggested we go out for hamburgers.

In minutes we were somehow on the street, confused but determined to find food and booze. I have no idea which we found first. The next recollection was of the three of us standing in the hotel elevator, Chaplin possessively hugging a large box of burgers and fries against his massive chest and Solliday beside him, a brown bag hiding two fifths of Canadian Club snugged under his left armpit.

We pressed into the tiny space with eight other passengers who stood silently staring directly and impassively at the elevator door. They looked like a bunch of department store mannequins.

As the elevator started up my eyes wandered to a space just above the control panel. There a small metal plate modestly declared, "Maximum load capacity 1100 pounds." Turning my head toward Solliday I saw instantly that he, too, had just read the message. When we made eye contact I instinctively knew his train of thought was identical to mine. If one added our combined weight of 340 pounds to Chaplin's 350 pounds, it quickly became evident that the three of us accounted for roughly 63 percent of the elevator's maximum safe load. It followed that unless the remaining eight passengers averaged no more than 51 pounds each, we were in serious violation of someone's ordinance. It struck me that if the cable should snap our heirs would have a firm basis for a class-action suit.

Under the circumstances I found the prospect of a free-fall to the hotel basement outrageously humorous. It was then that the first giggle escaped my lips. It was followed quickly by a rapid-fire succession of mixed giggles, coughs, and sputters as I desperately attempted to suppress the demon which had possessed me. The effort failed altogether when Solliday, who at first had been startled by my outburst, joined in the fun. Chaplin, who had no idea what had set us off, was soon caught up in the contagion of the moment. Now there was a trio of gigglers.

It seems certain that at that moment our fellow travelers concluded they were trapped in a mobile cage with three raving lunatics, who could turn violent at any moment. To their everlasting credit they resolutely kept their eyes riveted to the elevator door, and, except for an initial fleeting moment, the implacable expressions on the faces remained uncompromised.

At that point all restraints were shed and we advanced rapidly to a complete meltdown. Such a loss of propriety in a rigidly dignified and solemn setting usually occurs with little warning and is typically uncontrollable. Such an affliction seems to possess a life of its own, drawing sustenance from every desperate attempt at suppression and from expressions of disapproval registered by offended onlookers. There is really little to do except allow the thing to run its natural course.

The remainder of the ascent was an unmitigated disaster. By the fifth floor we were out of control, shrieking convulsively, slapping our knees and thighs, our eyes leaking streams of salty tears. The harder we tried to regain control, the worse it all became. At the eighth floor we could only clutch one another to avoid falling down.

The last of the passengers disembarked on the ninth floor. In the absence of a disapproving audience, the need to maintain any semblance of self-control ended. Thus freed we lapsed into a savage volley of frenzied, gasping laughter necessary to exorcise our demons.

Once we were in the hall outside the elevator the paroxysms gradually subsided in intensity and ferocity. Still giddy, giggling and completely spent, we stumbled into our room. Even before we attacked the burgers and fries we each swore never again to ride the St. Francis elevator.

When we finished eating we had sobered sufficiently to justify a return to the Canadian Club. At about 7:45 our now devoted bellboy arrived at the door with the beautiful black female in tow. By that time Chaplin and Solliday had convinced me that, rather than the actress or model I had imagined, the woman was a high-class hooker and her male escort a pimp.

Normally I had made it a practice to avoid prostitutes, but this female was different. Her name, she said, was Chico, and she wore something dark, tight, short and low-cut. Whore or not, I was prepared to pay her price.

Chaplin poured her the promised drink and the four of us sat on the edge of one of the double beds and talked. In ten minutes we had finished the drinks and Chico and I had reached a mutually agreeable arrangement. As the two of us rose to go upstairs to Chico's room, the Deckers arrived. It was 8 o'clock.

Without introducing Chico I embraced Molly and Deck and excused myself assuring everyone I would return when my business had been satisfactorily concluded. The Deckers had known us long enough and well enough that little any of us might do was likely to surprise them. Even so, as Chico and I walked out the door I was conscious that Molly's eyes trailed Chico with an expression of wonderment and critical appraisal.

In the room on the twelfth floor Chico motioned me to the bed and went directly into the bathroom. When she returned she was naked; I was still wearing my boxer shorts. "Shy?" she asked, as she slipped them down over my knees.

Afterward she put on a sheer, pale green dressing gown and sat at a small table by the wall. I lay on the bed watching as she took stationery from the drawer and began to write a letter. Curious, I rose up on an elbow and asked, "You're writing a letter?"

Smiling, she said, "Yes, to my mother; she lives in Texas." She named the small town in south Texas where she had been reared.

"I know the town," I said.

"You do? Hardly anyone does, it's just a tiny place in the boonies."

I explained that I lived in Houston and drove through there sometimes on my way to the coast. "Do you have brothers and sisters?" I asked.

"Six: three sisters, three brothers. My youngest sister still lives with Mother, but she graduates from high school in June and I suppose Mother will be alone then."

I'm an only child," I said. "But I've often wondered what it would be like to have brothers and sisters."

"Oh, it's fine, at least most of the time, but it can be hard, too."

"Do you write often to your mother?"

"When I can," she replied a bit wistfully. "Like now. I have half an hour before I must go out and work the street." She returned to her letter then, and I began to dress. Almost immediately she paused, turned, and surveyed me. "I like you," she said.

"Oh, and why is that?" I asked.

"You're not like the others. You have personality."

On the eleventh floor sounds of gaiety, peals of laughter, fragments of amusing conversations seeped from behind the door of our room. The reunion was progressing better than I had anticipated. If the noise level continued to amplify it was certain to attract angry complaints from neighboring guests.

When I rejoined my friends I was the only one relatively sober. During the next hour I did my best to catch up with them, but I was interrupted by the first faint twinges of one of the damned cluster headaches which had plagued me intermittently since 1946. The headaches are bona fide bastards. At their peak the intense pain is controlled only with a shot of morphine. During a full-blown attack Dr. Jekyll becomes Mr. Hyde. Social discourse at any level is impossible, and suicide seems a rational option.

That evening I decided to fight the thing without resorting to the pain pills my doctor had provided for the trip, so I climbed into one of the beds and propped my head up on two pillows. In that position I could watch my friends and give the illusion of only resting. To my surprise and great relief the alcohol

I had consumed and continued to imbibe held the pain to a marginally acceptable level. In less than an hour I had rejoined my companions and no one was aware that there had been a problem.

Soon, with the clamor already dangerously high, we spontaneously broke into one of the rituals reserved for such occasions. Forming up into a single file, each participant except the leader grasped the left shoulder of the person in front. Then while weaving drunkenly about the room and rhythmically stomping on the floor we sang at the top of our voices, *Jesus Loves to Cha, Cha, Cha; Arthur Murray Taught Him How.*

Following numerous erratic circumnavigations of the quarters during which chairs and small tables were sent careening across the floor, we became aware of a gentle but firm and persistent knocking at the door. It was our bellhop. He was there to warn us that an elderly couple in an adjoining room had registered a complaint about the noise. "Nothing to worry about," he assured us. "I'm on my way now to talk to them. I'll let you know how I make out."

Hot, sweaty, and a little subdued, we gathered up the toppled furniture and sat down to our drinks and relatively sedate conversation while we waited for his return. In a short time he was back, this time wearing a smile of self-satisfaction.

"Everything's taken care of," he announced jauntily. "They were pretty pissed and threatened to call the police. Odd couple, wouldn't listen to reason at all."

"So what happened?" I asked impatiently.

"Well, there wasn't much we could do except ask them to leave the hotel. Can't have troublemakers like that upsetting the guests. They're down in the lobby now, checking out."

I could only admire his style—definitely my kind of man. We hadn't been in the hotel twelve hours and he had already earned the twenty dollars I had given him.

About one o' clock the Deckers decided to drive back to Pacific Grove. Solliday left with them. In the afternoon he would drive Deck's car back to the hotel and on Thursday we would pick up Linda at San Francisco University and the four of us would drive to Pacific Grove.

From Solliday's later report I learned that Deck had flawlessly negotiated the fogged in, cliff-bound coastal route to Pacific Grove at an unrelenting 80 mph. It didn't surprise me at all. Several nights, carrying high blood-alcohol levels, Deck had driven us at racing speed across foggy back roads of the

Carolina lowlands. On those trips Deck leisurely sipped a beer from a can held in one hand while, with consummate skill and self-confidence, he steered with the other. We had never been close to having an accident. It called to mind occasions during his Air Force days when he and his crew had been abruptly summoned away from heavy duty drinking bouts to fly extended and always successful missions.

One night in February, 1979, while driving to Pacific Grove from northern California where he had spent the day visiting and drinking with his eldest son, he decided the straight-through drive he had planned was too much so he checked into a small, roadside motel for a few hours rest. The maid found his body in the morning. He had died, not as some may have predicted, in a flaming crash on the highway, but peacefully in bed of complications related to a long and losing battle with emphysema.

Drunk or sober, but especially drunk, E.P. Decker was the best damned driver I have ever known.

Science Confronts Chaos

Chaplin and I spent most of Tuesday morning nursing thumping heads and quavering stomachs. We still had not fully recovered when Solliday breezed in from Pacific Grove at about 10:00 p.m. I had, despite the pain, managed to call Kristine at about seven o'clock, but her roommate told me she would not be home from work for another half an hour. I left my name and number and promptly at 7:30 Kristine returned my call. During a brief conversation we agreed that she would meet me at the main entrance of the St. Francis at 6:00 p.m. on Wednesday.

Wednesday morning the Jims and I remained in the room and worked on our presentation until lunchtime.

We arrived at the convention hall at about two o' clock. Our paper was scheduled for 4:15, which we thought provided plenty of time to relax and take in several papers scheduled prior to ours. We had not inspected the room where the stratigraphic sessions were being held, but earlier in the year the AAPG had provided me with the room dimensions and had clearly stated that two large screens would be located at either side of the speaker's lectern.

In February, when our slides had been inspected by the slide committee in San Francisco, I had been assured that the two large screens required for our talk would indeed be in place as advertised.

In retrospect I've wondered how I could have accepted these assurances at face value. I'd been around long enough to know that pre-convention plans and promises commonly are not met. Nevertheless we approached the session room with the innocence of three small boys who had been promised cookies if they would get into the car with the nice man.

As promised there actually was a fine looking screen to the right of the lectern, but only a large void to the left, which afforded an unobstructed view of the wall behind the stage. I cried out to my companions, "Goddamn, there is only one fucking screen."

"My God," echoed Chaplin. "This fucks up our entire preparation. Everything is geared to two screens. Shit, we have to reorganize all the slides and the entire goddamned talk in an hour and a half."

In sulking silence we turned and found our way to a quiet alcove off the hall where we sat on the floor and went to work. My job was to prepare a new set of crib cards which, with luck, might coordinate to some reasonable degree with the revised slide arrangement now underway by Solliday and Chaplin. In about 45 minutes we were satisfied that detectable constructive progress had been achieved. By then, however, I had begun to hyperventilate. Fortunately I had learned never to attend a convention without a pocketful of Compose tablets. It occurred to me that the time had arrived to delve into my supply.

At four o'clock time had run out and we could only hope our frantic efforts to salvage our talk had been successful. I sent Solliday to the projection room with the tray of slides and instructions to stand over the shoulder of the projectionist and make certain he did his job properly. Projectionists, I had learned, can foul up a slide presentation with stunning virtuosity in ways baffling to the ordinary man.

Chaplin's assignment was to sit in the front row with a narrow-beam flashlight and move things along by acting as my pointer. Convinced that the Compose tablet had been a dud, I washed down another at the fountain in the hall, after which we returned to the session room and took places in the front row.

A few moments later I heard the voice of the section chairman who had risen to introduce us to the audience. "I think," he began, "it is noteworthy to point out to everyone that the first two initials of each of our co-authors of the next paper are *J.R.*"

My God, I thought, *that's true. Why hadn't I noticed that?* I racked my mind to find something profound, or even ominous in the coincidence of our initials, but found nothing. Puzzled, but making a mental note to look into the matter later, I walked to the stage. At the lectern I noticed that the Compose tablets had locked into place. I was surely the most relaxed person in the room. Actually, relaxation was no longer a problem—staying awake was. As I gazed out into the expectant faces of the audience I fought an almost overpowering need to lower my head to the lectern and take a short nap.

The room darkened and the first slide burst forth in splotches of brilliant color on the screen over my right shoulder. Ready or not, here we go! Adrenaline poured into the blood stream, and the mouth, if not the brain, swung into action.

To this day I have little recollection of just what it was the mouth said, or if any of it was intelligible. As it babbled on, the projected bolts of color splashed on and off the screen, and Chaplin, from the front row, probed elusive targets with his zap gun. Synchrony between words and projected images was in the hands of the gods.

Finally, I flipped aside my last scribbled cue card, the room was again awash in light and the session chair was at my side. His request for questions from the floor was met by 500 upturned and silent faces. A thousand dark eyes which seemed riveted on me probably had been left glazed and sightless by my rambling ravings.

Eventually a solitary figure rose from somewhere deep in the crowd and a loud, sonorous voice identified itself as a geologist employed by the USGS. In softer, reassuring tones similar to those employed by psychologists attempting to placate a dangerous maniac, he praised the quality of the presentation and the character of our research. Without asking a question he managed to alert my defense mechanisms. It is a time-honored technique of clever interrogators to soften the victim, build his confidence, disarm and blindside him.

When the question eventually came it took me completely off guard. It had nothing to do with the talk or our research. It appeared he hadn t listened to or understood a word I had said.

"How much," he asked, "have you learned about the origin of Carolina bays during the course of your work?"

For a moment the mouth, so active a few minutes earlier, became stony mute. Then, making a serious effort to avoid any suggestion of sarcasm, I replied, "Well, I know how intriguing those things are and, of course, we have an interest in their origin. The fact is, however, we haven't seen any way to fit them into the present project. Perhaps at some time in the future we'll find time and funds to examine them in the detail they deserve." (I've since learned that the focus of the research is unimportant—if a geologist gives a talk on some aspect of the Carolina coastal plain, there's *always* a question about the Carolina bays.)

Disappointed, I suspect, the fellow slumped down into his seat. Following another twenty seconds of silence the chairman requested and received the perfunctory round of applause. At least everyone was wide-awake for the next speaker.

The Yellow Rose

The meeting adjourned at 5:30, leaving just about time to walk to the hotel where I was to meet Greenwood's Danish friend, Kristine. Solliday, clutching the tray of slides, met us in the lobby. But before we could work our way through the crowd to the exit I noticed a small, dark-eyed, scowling young man shoving his way directly toward me. No need to be clairvoyant to figure that he was pissed, but before I could take evasive action he was on me. He offered no introduction; the scowl was frozen in place.

"Have you read van Straaten's latest paper on intertidal processes in the North Sea?" he demanded.

"Oh well," I said. "I'm familiar with van Straaten's work, of course. He's certainly done some outstanding stuff, but I've not seen the paper to which you refer." In an attempt to appease the little man, I assured him I would make every effort to locate and study the paper on my return to Houston. But that wasn't good enough for this guy. In his mind I had already committed a cardinal sin, and for me there would be no redemption.

"Well, you should have read it before you left Houston," he scolded. "If you had you would have had a better understanding of your own research project."

Now *I* was pissed. I didn't have time for such nonsense, so I glowered down at the fellow and said, "If I took time to read every damned paper on nearshore geology I'd probably be just like you and never complete a research project, present a paper, or publish a report." Then, forming a wedge with Chaplin at the apex, we moved around the little prick and charged outside onto the street.

We were nearing the hotel, but we were late. I wondered how long Kristine would wait on a street corner to meet a stranger from Texas. Then Chaplin called out, "There she is, Jules."

When she spotted us Kristine glided from her position near the hotel entrance and gracefully, but with firm steps, moved toward us. Even at twenty feet I could see the features of her face, the sun-kissed, shoulder-length hair flowing in the soft March breeze, the broad, friendly smile, and perhaps most of all, the white skin. A few more strides and I was affixed by two smiling, pale blue, Scandinavian eyes.

We picked up her car in the basement garage of the St. Francis and drove to Oakland. "I want to take you to a restaurant in Oakland," she said. "I think you will enjoy it. It's quite unusual; water ballet on a stage with beautiful colored lights, a rosé fountain where you can fill your glass as you please, and the food is delicious."

The restaurant had been as promised—completely delightful. But with this charming Danish lady as my companion, I might well have said the same had we gone to a fast food joint.

On the Bay Bridge during the return to San Francisco I carried with me visions of multi-colored plumes of dancing lights, a warm rosé glow, and a sense of contentment I had rarely experienced. Had the evening ended at that moment I would have long judged it memorable. But it had only begun.

We rode a clanking cable car to Fishermen's Wharf, then searched the darkened streets for an espresso shop fondly recalled by Kristine. Along the way she asked directions of a passerby, embarrassed for having usurped my God-given male role, she begged my forgiveness.

At the espresso shop we sat on stools at the counter sipping a vile, black liquid from tiny cups. It was my first and last espresso. And as we drank, a strange, monkey-like man in coveralls seated at a piano in the middle of the room, with impressive skill, played Beethoven's *Moonlight Sonata.*

A hippie couple seated beside us introduced themselves. When they learned I was a paleontologist they asked if I had read *The Phenomenon of Man* written by the rogue French priest Pere Teilhard de Chardin. They were shocked that I had not, and admonished me to do so at my earliest convenience. It was my second reading assignment in six hours. I felt humbled.

The evening had been so fabulous I had no wish to see it end, so I decided to ride with Kristine to Oakland and catch the midnight bus back to San Francisco. A half hour early at the station, we sat in the car and talked.

She told me she had been born in a small town in Denmark, but had spent much of her adult life in Copenhagen, where she had worked as a nurse. In 1960 she accepted an offer to come to Houston to work in a children's hospital. For more than a year she lived near the Rice Institute campus at the home of her American sponsor. She said it was a shame she had not met me there. I could only agree. Though she never mentioned Bob Greenwood, she did speak of several people she had met in America. They had all disappointed her in one way or another. Then she turned to me and said very earnestly, "I think you are my only friend in America."

It was nearly 12:00, the bus was due any minute. "Before you go," she said, "I have a gift for you. I want to sing a song for you, *The Yellow Rose of Texas,* in Danish."

Looking directly into my eyes she sang the words sweetly and softly, as I held her gloved hand in mine. Then as she finished a great roaring hulk, huffing and puffing toxic fumes, squealed to a halt in front of the station.

My mind and the bus soared over San Francisco Bay. The evening had been an unexpected delight. Warm, caring, giving Kristine. She was a joy, a balm to soothe my weary, ragged soul. Could I just walk away? Return to the shambles of my personal life, bleak and empty? Return as if nothing had happened? A nice evening with a nice lady. Nothing more? I tried to concentrate on other things. Failed. The smile, the warm soft voice, the Yellow Rose rode with me.

But what about Karin? She had declared our relationship to be over, at an end. And even though I feared only an echo of our love remained, I had, nevertheless, held a glimmer of hope. An unrealistic glimmer, faint and flickering. A friend once told me, "It's real hard to let go, even if it's the right thing to do." Right? Wrong? Only stupid words without significance? Or are they?

Confusion draped itself over my slumping shoulders. Karin would be waiting tomorrow night for my call. Perhaps then it would all come clear.

Like to cut it close, do you?

At noon Thursday Solliday, Linda Decker and I were enjoying abalone steaks at a Monterey waterfront restaurant. Chaplin had elected not to join us in Pacific Grove when he learned that Linda's sister Gayle, with whom he was greatly smitten, had become engaged to a young Californian. Jim had made the reasonable assumption that his presence at the Deckers would be awkward for everyone and painful for him. But we didn't feel too sorry for him when later we discovered that in our absence he had met Scott Brady, a well-known movie star, who had taken him along to a party given by Alfred Hitchcock at his San Francisco apartment.

It was Linda's twenty-first birthday, so I proposed a drink to the occasion. Embarrassed, Linda declined, explaining that her father had long looked forward to serving her first legal drink. That ceremony was scheduled by Deck for later in the afternoon at the Pacific Grove Elks Club where he worked as a bartender. However, when Jim and I swore never to tell Deck of her transgression, Linda accepted my proposal.

Later in the afternoon the three of us joined Deck at the Elks Club. Wasting no time he introduced Linda to the gathering throng and explained the ceremony to be performed. The news itself was sufficient cause for drinks all around. At about that moment I happened to glance at my watch, and was abruptly reminded of my promise to call Karin at her sister's apartment in Myrtle Beach. By the time I found an empty phone booth, and had dialed the number I was five minutes late.

I was relieved to hear Karin's voice, "Irma and I have been sitting here on the sofa knitting while we waited for you to call. You're late, you know, we thought you had forgotten."

"Well, yes," I said tentatively. "I had a little trouble finding a pay booth."

"But," she said reproachfully, "you are an hour late."

"No, no," I protested, "only five minutes. What time is it there?"

Her response stunned me. "It's ten minutes past 8:00, Jules. You said you would call at 7:00."

Horrified, I realized I had miscalculated the time difference between the two coasts. I tried to explain this, but it was obvious she wasn't buying. I knew as I spoke that the thread which connected us had been stretched to its limit.

The crowd noise was loud enough to reach Myrtle Beach without the benefit of a telephone. There was little doubt Karin would assume I was at a wild party. If she really had any doubt it was removed a second later when Linda, laughing and giggling, leaned over my shoulder and handed me a drink. In an attempt to be heard over the background noise, she shouted into my ear and the receiver, "Deck's afraid you will miss all the fun."

I could almost hear the thread snap. Karin's next words remain indelibly imprinted on my memory. "Is this the way you are, to have a girl in every port?" No satisfactory explanation existed. I knew then that our relationship was forever ended. She had, in her own way, pronounced me dead. All that remained was for a Good Samaritan to close my eyelids, fold my hands over my torso, and draw a sheet over me.

More than a year later, when we were camping out in the old Brockhurst Place in south Myrtle Beach, I tried to recall when Karin and I had been together.

"And when I walk the streets at night I can still hear the voices, the laughter, the hushed, intimate whispers of lovers. In the shadows I see a slim girl and I can smell the lingering, faint scene of her hair. As I move toward her I can almost make out the contours of her soft lips, and I can imagine her eyes beckoning to me. But when I reach out for her hand she fades into the darkness and I hear the tinkle of laughter trail off into the night. Was she ever there at all?"

Jim and Linda and I left then for the Decker house on Funston. Molly and the kids were preparing a cookout to celebrate our arrival. Deck, still on duty at the Elks, would join us later.

After dinner Molly assigned cleanup chores to her offspring. She was taking us to a neighbor's house where a group of Bohemian types had collected for a party. Neither Jim nor I had been to such a gathering, but tales we'd heard suggested they were never dull.

That there would be no chance that we might be left dry, Jim stuffed the pockets of his seersucker jacket with cans of cold beer. Thus prepared, Molly led us into the night. Several blocks down the street we reached our destination, a dimly lighted, strangely quiet and sedate little bungalow tucked, half hidden, in a thick stand of shrubs and small trees. An unlikely place, it seemed, for unbridled debauchery.

A middle-aged, conventionally dressed lady, the hostess, I assumed, greeted us at the door with a whispered "Hello." Inside she pressed a finger to her thin lips to solicit our silence as she led us to a room utterly devoid of furniture. Fifteen or twenty long-haired, bizarrely dressed young people squatted on the bare wood floor. Offering no acknowledgment of our presence, they stared straight ahead, as if entranced, at an oil painting mounted on an otherwise empty wall. With an air of confidentiality our hostess whispered that they were contemplating the artist's subtle, but profound message.

Uncertain of the rules of etiquette which might apply in such an unusual setting, we remained standing just inside the door. With nothing better to do, we attempted our own independent assessment of the painting on the wall. At least our upright positions permitted a slightly different perspective than that of those on the floor.

Following a few minutes of scrutiny it struck me that if the artist had a subtle and profound message to convey it seemed likely to go with him to the grave.

More determined than I, Jim leaned forward at the waist for a closer view. In a minute he straightened up, pulled a can of beer from a jacket pocket, opened it with a church key, put the can to his lips, and took several long, loud, obviously satisfying gulps. Then with an enormous belch, reminiscent of the foghorn on the New London Ledge Lighthouse, he turned to Molly and me. In a voice which reverberated off the bare walls he announced, "I think I've got it. In fact I'm positive I have. It's clearly a Samurai warrior afflicted with dysentery, taking a shit in a snake-infested swamp. However, if there's a hidden message there it beats the fuck out of me."

His candid appraisal was met by a sea of reproving glowers from the indignant squatters. At the same time our hostess quietly, but firmly, suggested it would be wise if we were to leave at once.

On our return we were surprised to find Deck gloomily slouched on the living room sofa. He had arranged for a buddy to take over the balance of his shift, only to arrive home and find his wife and two best friends had run off to some sort of weird party without him. But Deck was constitutionally incapable of sustaining for long either a grudge or a serious sulk. Ten minutes and one bourbon later he was once again his usual carefree, congenial, gregarious self.

Gradually our small group: Molly, Deck, the five kids, Gayle's boyfriend Jerry, and Jim and I migrated to the kitchen. There, emulating the hippies, we squatted on the floor along the baseboards of the walls. For most of an hour we laughed and joked about our days together in Myrtle Beach. Eventually the conversation drifted to the unique character of the Decker family. We worked together to compile a list of the personality traits required of anyone wishing to become a part of the family.

To Jerry's discomfort we unanimously concluded that he did not measure up. We all laughed then, considering it a great joke on Jerry. Later Gayle and Jerry were married, and as we had jokingly predicted that evening, Jerry never did quite measure up to Decker standards and in the end the marriage failed.

I was bright eyed and alert the next morning. It was 6:00 a.m. and except for a chorus of snores and wheezes emanating from various recesses of the houses, all was quiet. Following my pre-dawn decision to call Kristine before she left for work at the hospital, I had packed in three delicious hours of sound and restful sleep.

I dialed her number on the kitchen phone and when I heard her sleepy voice I rapidly explained that I would like to see her again that evening. I would be leaving for Houston at 11:30 a.m. Saturday, and this would be my last opportunity.

She was delighted that I had called, but explained there was a slight complication. The annual Scandinavian variety show and general bash was scheduled for that evening at the Swedish-American Hall, and Kristine was committed to serve as a hostess. "But don't worry," she reassured me. "I'll leave a ticket for you at the table in the lobby. You can enjoy the show until I come off duty at about eleven o'clock. I know a very nice Japanese restaurant where we can have a late dinner."

My movements about the house had been detected by Molly. By the time I finished my call she had bacon and eggs cooking on the stove. I excitedly explained that I would return to San Francisco later in the day if I could find a way to get there by 6:00 or 7:00 in the evening.

Molly was ahead of me. "You can catch a bus from Monterey to Salinas, and pick up a train there to Frisco. I'll check the schedules while you have breakfast." She had the information before I finished the bacon and eggs. "The bus leaves Monterey at 1:30 and is scheduled in Salinas at 3:00. That will give you plenty of time to catch the train at 3:30. You'll be in Frisco by 5:30. Since you won't be leaving here immediately you might enjoy a tour of Cannery Row."

"Cannery Row? I'd love it. Wanted to see it for years. You know I'm a big fan of Steinbeck and old Ricketts seems to have been a fascinating guy."

When we were ready to leave the house an hour later, bodies had begun to stir but none of them belonged to Jim or Deck. On the way to the car Molly briefed me on the morning schedule.

It occurred to me that if someone walked up to me at Cannery Row and asked if I'd read Steinbeck's stuff I could say, "Hell yes, just about everything he's written, and I think the movie version of *Grapes of Wrath* is a true classic. And by the way, did you know Joel Hedgepeth is doing a revision of Rickett's *Between Pacific Tides?* What do you think of that?" Maybe if I did that I wouldn't be given another embarrassing reading assignment.

With an enjoyable tour of Cannery Row behind us, a little time remained before the bus was due to arrive. At Molly's suggestion we walked out on the point, admired the flowers blooming among the craggy rocks, and at the edge of the headland with the crisp sea breeze in our faces, we watched divers splash about offshore like playful otters in search of abalone.

The bus was waiting when we returned. As I grabbed my bag from the back seat Molly patted me gently on the shoulder and reminded me that she, Deck, Linda and Jim would meet me at the airport at 10:30 Saturday morning.

"If I'm not there by 11:30," I grinned, "tell Jim I've defected to Denmark."

In the bus the three or four passengers slouched low in their seats watched indifferently as I chose a spot by the window four rows behind the driver. I waved to Molly who remained standing by the car. Then I leaned back and allowed a pair of leaded eyelids to slip down over a pair of bloodshot eyeballs. My body began to relax, to grow heavy and limp, but only for a half-minute. I was abruptly brought back to the world of the living by piercing shrieks of steel desperately grinding against steel. When the driver had engaged the gears the guts had been torn from the great metal monster. Not satisfied, the driver, with stolid determination, gave it another try. This time the mortally wounded behemoth bolted forward a few yards, and jerked to a sudden stop, emitting a bone-chilling wail which seemed to originate from a very large animal just castrated by a jagged chunk of metal.

The ensuing brief interval of silence was broken when the understandably embarrassed driver announced that there was a problem with the engine. It would be necessary to call in for a replacement unit. "Just relax, folks, we'll have another bus here in fifteen minutes." With a growing sense of impending doom I rejoined Molly in the front seat of her car. "Damn!" I hissed. "This could cut things close in Salinas. I can't miss that train."

"Well," Molly said. "You'll still have a 15-minute cushion."

True to the driver's word, the replacement bus hove into view in 15 minutes, but another ten minutes passed while the passengers, mail and luggage made the transfer and we were finally on the road to Salinas. My cushion had been reduced to five minutes, a prospect which kept me awake, one eye on my watch, the other on the road until we arrived at the train station.

By the time the bespectacled guy behind the ticket window had taken my hastily proffered money and given me a ticket, my cushion had shrunk to something close to ten seconds. As I bounded out onto the loading platform the train was moving slowly out of the station. Luckily a door of the rear car remained open. Tucking my bag under an arm football style, I made a wild dash down the tracks. At the open door a conductor reached down, grabbed my outstretched hand and hoisted me aboard. Then appraising me head to foot, he drawled, "Like to cut it close, do you?"

April Fool

In my room at the St. Francis I idly flipped on the TV, striped and took a shower and, a little precariously, shaved standing in the bedroom while watching a boxing match. It was a few minutes past 7:00 when I walked out onto the street.

Too nervous to eat, I picked up a pack of menthols at a corner drugstore and hailed a cab. To my relief the cabbie had not only heard of the Swedish-American Hall, he knew how to find it.

I recall a long drive through dark streets to what appeared to be a residential area, unknown to me. The driver stopped the cab in front of a dimly lighted, unattractive, two-story, concrete block building. "This is it, buddy," he said. "The Swedish-American Hall."

"Are you sure?" I asked, a trifle incredulously. "Looks like an abandoned warehouse."

"This is it, all right," he declared with a tone of conviction. "I've been here before with Scandinavian fares. Not likely to forget that."

A low-wattage bulb dangling loosely from a rusty metal fixture lighted a heavy wooden door bearing neither number nor identification. Tentatively I turned a big brass knob and gave the massive structure a firm yank. It swung open revealing a long, carpeted, poorly lighted corridor leading to a small table behind which a nondescript female sat stiffly on an uncomfortable-looking wooden chair. Clearly a no-frills establishment. At one end of the table I saw a tray of assorted currency, a well-worn ledger beside it, and at the opposite end an old shoebox held a few multicolored cards I assumed to be tickets.

Reassured that I was at the right place I told the woman my name and explained that Kristine Villumsen had promised to leave a ticket in my name.

"Oh, yes, indeed," she said smiling broadly as she handed me a small envelope bearing my name. "I'll go see if I can find her, I know she wants to see you for a moment."

A minute later the door behind the table opened and Kristine, wearing a starched white apron and a gossamer scarf about her head walked toward me.

"I'm so happy you could make it, Jules. I'm working now, so I can't stay to talk. The show begins in 30 minutes, and there is a bar where you may have a drink while you wait. I'll be finished about 10:30, then we can have a nice dinner at the Japanese restaurant I mentioned this morning." Before I could do more than smile and nod my head, she was gone.

I needed food, not alcohol. Starvation had conquered mind and body, so I went back outside to search for a restaurant. But it really was a residential area, and there were no restaurants, cafés, diners, grocery stores, or even a gas station with a vending machine. For several blocks around the hall I found only dark, deserted streets, inhabited, it seemed, only by bodiless, wispy, transparent beings, ethereal spirits without apparent need for food.

Defeated, I gathered together my pangs of hunger and retraced my steps to the hall. Perhaps the entertainment would direct my attention from my empty stomach.

The show was in progress, and, except for the stage lights, the room was a black cave. I stood just inside the entrance and waited for my eyes to make the necessary adjustment. Gradually lumps of coal, arranged in orderly rows, began to emerge—human heads silhouetted in the yellow glow of the stage lights.

In the middle of one of the back rows, I spotted a headless gap and groped my way toward it. As I worked down the row, past the seated guests, two men on stage were doing a comedy routine. I understood only the laughter of the crowd, the universal language.

Easing toward the headless gap, I inadvertently stepped on someone's toes. A Swedish groan oozed up from the darkness. I tried to apologize but gave up when I realized the victim wouldn't understand my English. Then moving ahead I tripped over another extended foot, pitched forward, groped a matronly lady (or a fat man). There were no complaints. At last I reached the seat and plummeted down. It was not, as I had feared, occupied by a Norwegian dwarf.

To avoid becoming a conspicuous target I slouched deeply into the cushions and attempted to blend into the shadows. The comics pranced off the stage accompanied by the roar of the Nordic crowd. Then, to the apparent delight of everyone, they were replaced by a troupe of young men and women in traditional native attire who sang and stomped their way to and fro about the stage. The audience, caught up in the festive spirit of things, joined in the singing and clapped their hands and stomped their feet in delight and ethnic fervor.

The troupe was followed by a pretty young lady in a regal evening gown befitting a princess. She sang several lyrical melodies sweetly and with touching tenderness. The crowd cried. In the middle of one of her songs I decided to light up a menthol. While placing it between my lips with one hand I groped in my pockets in search of a book of matches. Successful at last I proceeded to strike a match, but in the darkness somehow forgot to close the book. In a blinding flash, not unlike a fireball from outer space, the entire book of twenty matches burst into scorching flames. Instinctively I closed my hand over the book, smothering the fire. Summoning up reserves of willpower heretofore unknown to me, I managed not to succumb to an extremely urgent need to emit a succession of blood-curdling screams which surely would have cleared the house.

After that I tried to settle into my seat hoping those near me would attempt to ignore the strong stench of brimstone and burned flesh. It seemed sensible that I not move again until the show ended.

When it was all over, the house lights came up and I saw that the stage and seating area were confined to only one end of a gymnasium-like, rectangular room. At the far side, free of seats, a crowd had begun to gather in a large circle. Five attractive young ladies and a man with a microphone in one hand stood in the center of the ring.

My guess was that we would soon witness a beauty contest, but I resolved to view whatever it might be from the comparative safety of my seat in the deserted theater section.

At length one of the girls, a petite, dishwater blonde in a long, loose-fitting dress, was introduced by the man with the microphone. For a few seconds the girl stood alone and motionless while the crowd watched and waited in tense anticipation. Then, without warning, a small combo I hadn't detected burst forth in a frenzied and ear-splitting rock song. At the same moment the girl's body quivered and then began to undulate to the beat of the music.

Picking up the pace, the girl soon displayed an amazing array of bumps, grinds, gyrations, pelvic thrusts, and innuendo rarely seen outside the confines of an old Tangiers bordello. To my astonishment, when the music came to an abrupt halt, the young lady collapsed to the floor, breasts heaving, perspiring, spent, in a convulsive orgasmic heap.

Crowd response was exactly what I might have expected from a gang of horny cowhands just off the trail relieving pent-up tension in a bawdy dance hall in the golden days of the Old West.

My long-held perception of the cold, aloof and reserved Scandinavians was shattered. I could only suppose it was in this manner that the Norsemen of old passed the long, cold winter nights before the advent of central heating.

Each participant who followed seemed to wholly commit their physical and imaginative resources to the purpose of outdoing the achievements of her predecessors. The last girl was a remarkably endowed blonde in a low-cut, flaming red, knee-length shimmering dress. Judging from the crowd clamor evoked by her presence in the center of the human ring, I assumed she was the popular favorite, perhaps a past champion. If this was indeed a contest I was sure the lady in red had already been declared the winner.

At that point, convinced that an additional dose of erotica would be detrimental to my mental health, I headed for the bar.

The bar, I discovered, was a makeshift affair, uncarpeted, with bare walls, a rectangular room. It reminded me of the workout room in the Ohio YMCA where as a lad of sixteen I learned the rudiments of boxing and the discipline of hard work and intense pain. Several long tables with folding legs covered for the occasion with a nondescript white cloth were aligned in a row near one of the long walls where they served as the bar. Table tops held a clutter of napkins, ashtrays, plastic stirring rods, pitchers of orange juice, and quart or liter bottles of vodka.

There were perhaps thirty young men in the room. Conservative tailored suits, white shirts, silk ties, expensive shoes polished to pass a military inspection proclaimed their affluence. They were, I guessed, men saturated and bored with squiggling asses and jiggling boobs, who had retreated to the bar for good booze, cigars, and the ritual of man talk and genial male bonding.

They were grouped in small, fluid clusters, hands holding tumblers of vodka and expensive, aromatic cigars. Conversations were animated, punctuated by ripples and bursts of male laughter, slaps on the back, playful probes at nearby rib cages. In the flood of male voices which enveloped the room not a word of English, only a blend of Swedish, Norwegian and Danish.

To obtain a drink one had only to pick up an empty glass from the table and direct it at arms length to the nearest bartender. With commendable efficiency the tumbler would be filled nearly to the brim with crystal clear, and almost odorless vodka topped with a tiny splash of orange juice.

While standing at the bar a slightly sodden guy brushed against my arm splashing some of my drink onto the table. I acknowledged his Scandinavian apology with an American smile.

Out on the floor I joined one of the clusters of men. They nodded congenially and returned to their conversation. Soon bored by not understanding a word said, I returned to the bar for a refill.

Turning to leave with my fresh drink I was approached by an earnest, thin-faced young fellow who seemed to have something of an urgent nature to report to me. Unable to identify the topic I found I could hold my share of the discussion with a carefully selected and timed assortment of head nods, smiles and noncommittal grunts. It was easy, just like a conversation with my mother.

His final comment, as he turned to leave, I assumed to be a Scandinavian goodbye. I responded with my very best combination of smiling nods and a friendly wave of a hand. It worked perfectly. So far no one had discovered that I was a foreigner and it was my intention to keep it that way. It proved to be a wise decision.

In a few minutes two guys began to descend the stairway from the second floor. At a casual glance they appeared as the other men in the room. The fellow in the lead, however, differed in two ways. First he carried a drink in each hand, but more importantly, he was speaking a Scandinavian version of English. When he paused dramatically on the lower step, conversational chatter in the room trailed off rapidly and all eyes were directed to him.

By then I had heard enough to deduce he was somehow connected with the fur business.

"Americans," he said, spitting out the word contemptuously. "They are so very stupid. Americans, they know nothing of quality. It is so easy to take their money. They are so stupid."

Each use of the word "Americans" triggered a chorus of sniggers and guffaws from his audience.

With a sneer he went on. "Just this morning a stupid American lady came to me. She wanted to purchase a fine fox fur, the very best we had to offer. Americans always want the best, the finest, the most expensive. If it is expensive they know it is the finest. The value of everything is measured by its price tag in America. They have no taste, no sense of quality. Very stupid indeed." He paused for dramatic effect; the audience hung on his words.

"'Good,' I said to the stupid lady. 'I sell only the best.' I say this to all Americans who cannot distinguish mink from cat dung." He paused again to savor the roar of approval from the men on the floor.

"So then," he sneered, "I showed her a coat. I told her it was the finest fox in all of Sweden. She took it into her fat arms, rubbed her ugly cheeks against the collar, and wet her panties in ecstasy." Another burst of boisterous laughter erupted from the floor.

"I told that fat pig, 'Just write a check now and you will be the envy of all

San Francisco. Beauty such as yours deserves no less than the finest.' American women cannot resist flattery, you know. She groped in her purse then and finally found her checkbook and pen. Paid me in full, there and then."

He paused again, to heighten the suspense, holding his subjects transfixed. "It was all so very amusing. I could barely suppress my need to laugh aloud. The stupid bitch had just purchased the very best rabbit I had in stock."

When he stepped onto the floor he was greeted by his comrades with shouts of approval, laughter, and finally a rousing round of applause. A Nordic hero for the evening.

It occurred to me then that it was time to become as inconspicuous as possible. Fifteen minutes later Kristine popped into the room dressed in street clothes and ready to leave. Noting that her presence beside me had directed considerable attention to both of us I took her arm and began to hustle her to the door. She was completely uncooperative. "This is my American friend," she called out. "He's a professor from Texas."

A battery of critical eyeballs rotated in my direction, scanned me from head to foot, and, I feared, prepared to launch a succession of death rays at my stupid American crotch. Under the circumstances I was compelled to face the firing squad.

"Gentlemen," I said theatrically, "it has been a lovely party. We must do this again sometime." Then, addressing the fur salesman, I added, "If I ever require a bunny coat I'll look you up." I bowed then, an utterly stupid American gesture, and led Kristine outside to the car.

As we drove into town an impatient driver cut closely across our bow. "Naughty, naughty," Kristine scolded. A charming response, I thought, to someone who had nearly taken the front end off her car. Had I been the driver it is certain I would have given the guy a stiff middle finger, followed by several unflattering comments about his mother.

Bellies pacified by Japanese cuisine and warm saki, we drove to Seal Rock where we sat in the car looking out at the black Pacific, talking softly, intimately, for two hours. Mostly I listened to her. Her voice was soothing and filled the car with the essence of the things I needed most: warmth, tenderness, and caring understanding companionship. It had been too long since I'd had any of those things.

Somewhere around three, Kristine, with a note of resignation, reminded me that she had to be at the hospital at eight. We drove in near silence, neither wishing the evening to end. We parked at the curb opposite the hotel, and Kristine began to say goodnight. I interrupted her, "Would you come with me to my room?"

"You mean you want to be with me?"

"Yes, I do. Very much so."

In the morning when I opened my eyes the room was dark and I couldn't make out discrete objects. For a moment I thought it was night, but there was a dull orange glow around the window frame, and a single dust-laden ribbon of light penetrated a slit in the lower left corner of the drawn window blind. The sun was up. It was 7:00 a.m. Saturday, April 1, in San Francisco.

Gradually I became aware of rustling sounds in the far corner by the TV set. Kristine was dressing. I laid my hand on her side of the bed, felt the lingering warm dampness where she had lain in my arms moments earlier. In the car at the ocean side she had said wistfully, "All I want is to lie in your arms, but it won't be that way, will it?"

When we had made love later she held me tightly and in an almost inaudible whisper said, "I sank you." It had seemed so strange to be thanked for something so wonderful, so satisfying for me. We slept then virtually as one, with bodies fitted together and did not move again.

Now the sounds of the outside world were creeping into our sanctuary, raucous horns, screaming tires, clanking bells, roaring engines, a clock striking seven. We were passing through the transition from the deep bliss of love to the demands, stresses, and anxieties of our separate lives.

While I was still in the process of awakening, Kristine walked to the bedside. "Good morning, Jules." I tried to grab her hand and to hold her, but she eluded my clumsy efforts. "I'm late for work," she said. I knew she was slipping from me, that I was losing her to the world outside, the world I dreaded. A surge of depression and doubts raced through my body, my mind. How many times had this happened before? I didn't want to believe it could happen again.

She stood before me now, fully dressed, prim and proper, her hair drawn back into a knot at the back of her neck, a cold contrast to the long auburn tresses which had framed her beautiful face a few hours earlier. She was a creature apart from me now, no longer mine, a growing stranger with obligations elsewhere.

She kissed me gently on the cheek. "I'll call you later from the hospital. I'm afraid you'll go back to sleep and miss your plane."

I found it difficult to speak. Finally, I managed a muffled goodbye. She was gone then. I never saw her again.

Inside the room the faint female scent of her lingered, but it was dissipating rapidly as the outside ugliness and urgencies continued to seep through the walls. Soon all that had been would become only a memory.

In a few hours I would step off that damned jet in Houston to be greeted by an angry, scowling, frigid wife with demands for accountability. In that week I had been exposed to a world of serenity filled with laughter, joy and the sublime feeling of being wanted and loved. It was ending now like a macabre joke on April Fools' Day.

I packed my bags methodically and before leaving stood in the open doorway for a few seconds to record a mental image of the room and its contents. It was a picture that remained with me for a long time. I saw it each time I heard Tony Bennett sing *I Left My Heart in San Francisco.* Each time I would try to find a little Danish girl in the room, but she was never there. There is, I suppose, no way to hold onto such a moment. No way to preserve it. It is an intangible thing which passes briefly between two people and then evaporates, or, perhaps, it merely changes form and becomes a small but enriching part of each person touched by it.

Return of the Specter

I reached the air terminal at eleven. Deck, Molly, Linda and Jim were working on their third round of drinks. I joined them with a whiskey sour. Soon we were encased in a cocoon of our own making, a portable environment brought with us for all such occasions.

Two hours later, I became aware of a muffled voice, soft, but persistent, somewhere in the distance, in another world. In time, the receptors of my subconscious registered an alarm. The voice had been announcing the last call for our flight to Houston. Adrenaline flowing, I leaped to my feet, bade the Deckers a hurried farewell, and raced off. Solliday took a more loving and leisurely leave of Linda.

The plane, poised to taxi to the runaway, was at least 50 yards from the terminal exit. A stewardess stood at the open hatch above the still lowered boarding ladder. I waved and shouted to hold it. The stewardess returned my wave. Then as I ran, I gasped, "Another one is on the way."

Mounting the steps I caught sight of Jim emerging from the terminal.

The plane was packed with high-spirited geologists returning from the convention. When we were safely in the air we all joined in a three-hour, standing-in-the-aisle cocktail party.

When the plane began its approach to International Airport the tension, left behind six days earlier, stealthily crept back into its dark, moist lair in the pit of my stomach. Mounting pressure behind my right eye signaled an oncoming cluster headache.

A tall, gaunt creature, wearing a flowing, floor length black coat and a black, floppy-brimmed hat slipped into the seat beside me. Slowly it turned its face toward me and I caught the phosphorescent glow of its eyes. It was my specter. For years it had come to my bedroom at night when I was asleep. Shrouded in black, it stood silent at the foot of the bed, the eyes watching me. I always awoke screaming, thrashing, sweating, terrified, desperately attempting to escape those glowing, penetrating eyes. The specter never spoke.

The wheels of the plane touched the runway, with a short screech; the plane bounced back into the air once or twice. Then the grinding sound of brakes that would gradually slow the racing monster and bring it to submission far down the landing strip.

I was home, inexorably drawn back, as always, to the reality of my life. San Francisco had already begun to blur. The seat beside me was empty, my specter was gone. I shuddered, knowing that when I stepped off the plane it would be there. It would have taken the form of my wife. Waiting.

A day or two after my return to the office someone asked, "How was the Frisco trip?"

"Oh!" I replied, "Just another convention. You know, a few beers and a lot of boring talks."

He grinned. "Yes, I know what you mean."

Kristine and I corresponded after that, letters between friends and confidants. In May she told me she would soon return to Denmark with a short layover in Greenland. I asked her if she might delay her departure and meet me in New York City in June. She responded that she would love to do so, but that her brother in Copenhagen had purchased her ticket as a gift and she thought it would be unfair not to do as he wished.

Sometime later I received a small package from Greenland. It contained an assortment of igneous and metamorphic rock fragments Kristine had collected along a Greenland beach. I was as touched by that gift as I had been with her Danish *Yellow Rose.* She had walked on a beach and stopped and picked up a handful of glacial pebbles and put heart and meaning into them and had sent them across a thousand miles of sea to me.

Her last letter reached me in Durham. She was distressed that she had so little of herself to give to the world. She asked if I might arrange to come to Copenhagen to be with her long enough to give her a child. In that way, she thought, she would have something that would survive her, something for which to live. She feared she would die and leave nothing of herself for posterity.

I was surprised to learn that this most giving person should think she had nothing to give. I was flattered that she would choose me to father her child. One more gift, one my wife had denied me. But it was too late for that. My life by then had turned in a new direction. At long last I had found the path to my future, a future without a place for a "little lost Danish girl" in Copenhagen.

Even so, if things had been different, I could not have fathered a child who I would never know, and who would never know me.

When I wrote to Kristine I tried to explain my feelings. Did so very badly, I suspect. In the end all I could do was to wish her the best, to thank her for all she had given me and to say goodbye.

Anchors Aweigh

Unlike our modest presence in South Carolina where we maintained a relatively low profile while drilling with the small DOG mobile power rig, our operation in southeastern North Carolina in July of 1962 took on the proportions of a traveling circus.

I had hired the Hartsfield Water Company to drill my holes with their big rotary rig. In addition to the heavy-duty drill truck, we were accompanied by a large water tank truck, a pickup, a truck-towed, trailer-mounted generator, two passengers cars, and a four-man drill crew. My field assistant that summer was a strapping fellow from Iowa, Jim Fowler.

The youngest member of the drill crew, a lad of eighteen, had graduated from high school in June. As a reward for this achievement, his parents gave him the choice of a college education or a new, bright red convertible. Each day he drove up to the drill site in his shining machine, donned his coveralls, hard hat, and boots, grabbed a pick and shovel and dug the drainage ditches for us.

When the Hartsfield drill was operating, water from the tank truck was circulated down the hole bringing to the surface the tiny rock and fossil fragments cut loose by the rotating drill bit. As the water flowed from the hole onto the ground it was directed through a shallow ditch to a wider, circular depression previously prepared by the boy with the red convertible. It was there in that shallow gathering basin that Jim and I scooped out and bagged the mud which settled from the water. Later, this sediment, dried and scientifically processed, would be studied in our Houston laboratory. Overflow from the little pond found its way into another ditch dug to drain the dirty water away from the highway and into a nearby field or swamp.

The individual drill rods were ten feet long and four inches in diameter, making them heavy enough to seriously challenge the combined lifting capability of Jim and me, who at this time were a pair of husky 200 pounders. To our embarrassment our roughneck, a muscular 130-pound ex-Navy man, lifted and stacked the damned rods all day, hardly working up a sweat in the process.

His pace was slowed slightly for several days following a weekend mishap. While sitting in his car in a drunken stupor, Barney had attempted to light a cigarette, but dropped the flaming lighter into his crotch, setting fire to his pants. By the time he managed to beat out the flames, his genitals had been nearly charcoaled. After that, for a week, he walked a little strangely. But despite considerable pain, he never complained and continued to hoist the heavy rods nearly as adroitly as ever.

Barney became awed of me when he learned I had written a book. He had never known anyone who had managed such a feat. Most of his family and friends, as well as himself, were hard pressed to write their own name or to read the daily comic strips.

When the drilling project was finished I invited the crew to our motel room in Whiteville for a modest party. During the evening Barney and I swapped sea stories and joined in rousing, off-key renditions of seafarer's songs. At midnight, the bottle empty, Barney stood on unsteady legs near the door and told me it had been a night he would always remember. "Never before have I sung *Anchors Aweigh* with a man who wrote a book," he declared. It was something he hoped one day to tell his children, providing the circumstances of his recent misfortune permitted him to have offspring.

Long before we had commenced drilling I had requested and received permission from the North Carolina Highway Department to drill on state right of way land. My contract with the Hartsfield Company stipulated that I would select all drill sites subject to the approval of the drill foreman. To drill a hole without his approval would have meant that I would have been liable for time lost due to equipment breakdown. With drilling costs of $250 per day, I was strongly motivated to follow the foreman's advice. During the entire drilling period the only equipment failure occurred at a site approved by the foreman.

As anticipated, our activities and the odd assortment of vehicles with which we traversed the countryside attracted considerable attention wherever we went.

Each day, fifty to one hundred people from nearby farms and hamlets gathered to watch the hottest show in the area. At some point the local population became convinced we were prospecting for oil. I never confirmed or denied this misconception despite the fact that many of the onlookers obviously expected to see a gusher of oil explode from the ground at any moment.

There was, however, one little man among the onlookers who had no interest in oil. Each morning for several days he appeared carrying a wooden apple crate. He always placed the crate on the ground somewhere near the center of the crowd. Then he would climb up on it, and from his lofty vantage point he would deliver a two-or three-hour spirited lecture on naval engagements of World War II. As the little man rambled on, no one in the crowd paid the least attention or ever indicated in any way that they considered his behavior a bit odd. We could only assume that these were his friends, relatives and neighbors who were well acquainted with him and who had heard all of his material in the past. For Jim and me and the crew, the little guy provided a welcome distraction. It was our unanimous opinion that his lectures were both informative and amusing, and that he was as mad as a hatter.

One day a man pulled his car up near the rig, poked his bald head out the window, and motioned to me to come over. When I walked to the car he said, "I'm John Soandso. I sell Goody's Headache Powders." He pointed to the back seat. It was packed with boxes of the stuff. "I just wondered what you gents were up to."

I was busy so I gave him an abbreviated version of my usual routine. He laughed, and as he began to drive away, he stuck his head out of the window and called out, "To each his own. Ha, ha, ha!"

The first leg of our drilling traverse extended sixty miles seaward from the town of Orrum in Robeson County, to Shallotte, in Brunswick County. I had originally expected to go all the way to the ocean at Holden Beach, but was forced to stop short of that goal because of the danger that the rig might become bogged down in the loose sands of the coastal dunes.

Following the trail to the sea I was sometimes reminded of Sherman's march through Georgia. But it was only an analogy and perhaps not a very good one. We burned no cities and with but one exception, left no carnage in our wake.

At a site about ten miles inland from Shallotte we had attracted an unusually large crowd. At about ten that morning the assemblage of gawkers suddenly parted like the Red Sea, and a big black sedan drove through the gap and parked near the rig. The head of a well-dressed, middle-age man popped from the open window. With a big vote-for-me-I'm-a-jolly-good-fellow smile, the guy identified himself as the Brunswick County Commissioner.

"What you fellers up to?" he asked. I stepped forward, told him who I was, and gave him the standard one-minute bullshit explanation of our intentions. Then I produced my drilling permit. He wasn't interested in looking at it so I read it to him. While I folded the paper and returned it to my wallet, a particularly seductive political grin crossed the commissioner's rose-cheeked face.

"Well now, that sounds right interestin'." He had tried to inject a note of conviction in the words, but it seemed clear he really didn't give a damn what we were doing. He was there only because he hadn't been able to suppress his politician's instincts to make an appearance before such a gathering of his constituency. With a cheery, "Ya'll have a good day," and a friendly wave to the crowd, he once again crossed the Red Sea and disappeared down the road in a cloud of dust.

At the time, neither the commissioner nor I could have known that as we had been chatting, our drill bit had cut through one of the main telephone cables in that part of Brunswick County.

The next morning we were set up on U.S. 17 a few miles north of Shallotte. For the first time we were alone, no crowd. It was too dangerous there on the busy highway for idle onlookers. In an hour or less, a pick-up pulled off the road just behind us. A man in work clothes walked toward us until he was close enough to ask who was in charge. He seemed friendly, so I identified myself and prepared to give him my little speech. Instead of asking what we were doing, he said, "Looks like you fellows cut one of our telephone cables over by Ash yesterday morning. None of the people have had any service since yesterday morning. We'd like you to come over there and make sure it's the place where you fellows were drilling."

I followed his pick-up in the Dodge, leaving Fowler in charge of the drilling. I had no doubt that our drill had severed the cable. As I drove, a series of distressing words bounced around in my mind: liability, disaster, big bucks, screwed, fucking mess.

At the old drill site I found a crowd somewhat larger than the one which had unknowingly watched us take out their telephones. We were still the biggest show in town. Excitement such as this, I was sure, had rarely descended on the town of Ash.

I walked to the spot where we had drilled It was occupied by a rectangular trench, the approximate dimensions of the standard grave. Mine no doubt. A workman crunched down in the hole returned my inquisitive gaze. In one hand he clutched an impressively large bundle of tangled and frayed copper wire. Against my better judgment I told him who I was.

"Oh yeah," he said, as he sized me up. "You're the one."

"Good Lord," I said. "That looks pretty bad. How much will it cost to repair?"

With an ominous deadpan, he replied, "A lot. They want to see you over at the Shallotte office."

Resolved to face the music I drove into town to the office. The receptionist, who apparently was expecting me, smiled sweetly and directed me to Mr. Thompkins' office. I found Tompkins, red hair, red walrus mustache, in a room at the rear of the one-story building where he was busily pouring over a large stack of blueprints spread over his desk.

"Come on in, Mr. DuBar," he said.

Geez, I thought, *I'm famous around here, everyone knows my name.* I started to grope for words to explain our presence in the area and some way to demonstrate that we were merely innocent victims in this ugly affair. But before I could utter a word in my defense, I realized that Tompkins was talking and, to my amazement, he sounded apologetic.

"I told those people to do a map of the underground cables in that area a dozen times. Hell, I assumed it had been completed some time ago. Now, I find they never managed to get around to it!"

He walked around to the front of the desk, then, and stood facing me. "I'm sorry as hell about this, sorry about the inconvenience we've caused you. I'm really embarrassed, I know how busy you must be."

"Well," I replied, soothingly. "It's no real problem for us. My assistant is running the operation in my absence. He's a good man. We won't lose a minute." Then I added, "But you are right about the map. If we'd had one that showed the locations of the cables, this all could have been avoided." Clasping his hands to his chest as a gesture of anguish, Tompkins said, "True, true, it certainly could have been. If we'd had that map we wouldn't have this problem. But we'll get that map now, and maybe nothing like this will happen again."

There was little more we could say on the subject, so we shook hands and I left Tompkins to his fretting duties.

I didn't fully understand what had gone on in there, but it was clear my ass was off the hook. After all, it was we who had cut the cable, but it was the telephone company doing the apologizing. When I reached the car it occurred to me that, considering how guilty old Tompkins had acted, we might be in a position to sue for negligence. Immediately overwhelmed with a surge of good will and uncommon benevolence, I said to myself, "Hell, no, that won't do. I think I've introduced sufficient grief into poor Tompkins' life for one day." Anyway, for all I knew we could have been cutting another cable out there on U.S. 17 at that very moment. After all, we still didn't have that map.

The following week we were at a site on the shoulder of U.S. 70 north of Whiteville. Our boy with the red convertible had dug the drainage ditches and the drill bit was down hole five or six feet when a car pulled off on the shoulder in front of the rig. A man, very obviously upset, strode purposely toward us.

Addressing no one in particular, he demanded in a booming voice sufficient for all to hear, "What the hell do you people think you are doing here?"

Calmly and softly, I told him what we thought we were doing, but he wasn't listening.

"I want you people out of here, and I want you out right now!" Face scarlet, the guy looked as if he might explode at any moment.

"Well," I said. "That's not possible. You see we're drilling this hole, and until it bottoms out we're not leaving. Anyway, I have a permit from the State Highway Department to drill any of the right of way I wish." While I spoke I lifted the well-worn permit from my wallet and attempted to show it to the guy, but he just brushed it aside. Choking on his words, he yelled, "The state does not own this land. When their people came here trying to buy it I refused to sell. They can't grant you permission to trespass on my property."

"Okay then," I responded. "I guess the best thing for you to do is to call the highway department and hash it out with them. In the meantime we'll drill this hole."

He turned abruptly and walked off in a rage. Watching the car disappear down the road I was confident the telephone of Mr. Babcock, the highway commissioner, would soon jangle.

In two hours the guy was back. Friendly this time, and he had brought another middle-aged guy with him who tried to act friendly too, but his sour face could not handle friendly. With the apparent change in mood I figured Mr. Babcock had set him straight. Hell, maybe he had come back to apologize.

The two men stood stoically at the edge of the collection basin and watched as Fowler and I bagged and labeled samples. Then our friend asked a question. It was one I had heard before.

"How do you suppose all these shells we find around here got this far inland?" It was strictly a rhetorical question; he already had the answer. I waited breathlessly to hear it.

"Noah's flood, of course, just as the Lord's word tells us." He cast a pontifical glance at the two of us, sinners slopping in our private little pool of blue mud. I should have responded with something like, "The wonders of the Lord never cease to amaze." Nine years in the Bible Belt had taught me to say as little as possible under such circumstances. Unfortunately, experience and

317

common sense forsook me. I stood up, and while vainly trying to wipe the ooze from my hands and arms, said, "You know that before we finish we will have drilled to rocks that were deposited along the inner edge of an ocean that was here about 70 million years ago. There have been many floods since then and Noah's is one of the most insignificant."

At that moment the man lost all semblance of self control. Face flushed red, bloated and distorted, he spewed out his rage. "Atheists! Blasphemers! Scum of the earth! Commies. No right to live in this Christian land!" And there was some sort of suggestion that we go live with the godless devils in Moscow. The tirade continued for two or three minutes. I said nothing. Couldn't have gotten a word in edgewise, had I wished. I just measured the man with my eyes. I wondered how nearly his body would fit into our drainage ditch. I knew I had screwed up. Maybe the Devil had made me do it.

As suddenly as it had begun the man's outburst ended. Drained of his venom he glared at me with cold, steely hate in his eyes.

"I want you off my land. I want this mess cleaned up. And I want you to plant grass seed wherever you disturbed the surface."

He grabbed the arm of his silent partner and the two of them returned to the car and drove away.

During the entire bizarre episode neither Jim nor any of the drill crew had moved or made a sound. They looked like frozen wax figures in a driller's museum.

"All right," I called out. "Let's get the job done before he comes back." No one asked if I intended to drive into town for grass seed.

A Wise Decision

On my return from San Francisco I found, due in large part to the efforts of R.C. Moore, I had solid shots at four positions in southeastern USA. There were associate professorships at Duke, Florida State, and the University of Georgia and a dual appointment as Assistant State Geologist with the Alabama State Geological Survey and Professor of Geology at the University of Alabama.

My hands down preference was Duke. I had done graduate work in ecology at Duke's Beaufort marine lab in 1951 and had liked what I had seen there. The campus in Durham, North Carolina, was near to my research area, the geology department was small but seemed to have considerable potential, and the university, with Ivy League academic standards, attracted only quality students.

In mid-April I arranged a May 2-4 interview in Durham with the department chairman, E.W. Berry. On my arrival I was met at the front door of their home by Willard and his wife, Dorothy, who asked if I wished something to eat. When I explained that I had been served dinner during the flight from Houston, they invited me into the parlor for drinks.

We drank and talked for hours, Willard presiding from his Archie Bunker chair at the front of the room, Dorothy directly opposite near the stairwell, and I at my assigned station in the shadows near the fireplace. The only light source was a depression-era floor lamp at Willard's side.

Somewhere around one o' clock Dorothy informed us that it was well past her bedtime and with that staggered up the stairs to her bedroom. Willard and I were left alone, drinks in hand, faced off in the living room. I had been aware for some time that the Berrys were subjecting me to a test—a test calculated to determine my ability to handle hard liquor. In a sense, this was the Berrys' weird version of a job applicant's interview.

However, I wasn't much concerned. The drinks, a mix of one shot of

Cream of Kentucky bourbon to a large tumbler of warm water, were foul-tasting and weak. It was very unlikely I could become sufficiently inebriated to go into a Mr. Hyde routine in the wee hours. At the same time I had no wish to drink my prospective boss under his own table.

So about three o' clock I purposely placed my empty glass on the coffee table and with a gesture of resignation announced my decision to call it a night, reminding Willard of our appointment with the dean at 9:00. I left him then with the reassurance that I was a socially acceptable drinker and with the ego-stroking illusion that he had just out-distanced a much younger man.

Before nodding off that evening I spent several minutes savoring the warm comforting conviction that the Duke job was mine.

During the two days in Durham I learned a lot about the Berrys—especially Willard. He smoked a pipe but had no objection to my cigars. He peered with poppy-eyes from beneath heavy-rimmed glasses, had a full head of dark hair and chin whiskers to match. And he was a chunky, out-of-condition 62-year-old diabetic under strict orders from his doctor never to touch alcoholic beverages. I also learned that he collected old hubcaps and rusty, bent nails and that he preferred to use empty institution-size fruit and vegetable tins gathered from the university cafeteria trash bins as beakers in the geology lab.

I also discovered that Willard was not only the departmental chairman but also its chief maintenance and repairman. He personally took care of broken windows, damaged venetian blinds, faulty electrical outlets and cantankerous office furniture.

Willard was the son of E. Wilber Berry, a famous paleontologist who had served as Professor of Geology, Dean of the School of Liberal Arts and Sciences, and Provost of Johns Hopkins University in Baltimore.

Along the way to earning his undergraduate and graduate degrees at Johns Hopkins, Willard sat for endless hours, year after year, in courses taught by his domineering father. When he finally left the family home and the university with his doctorate in geology, Willard was doomed to live his life in the shadow of old E. Wilber.

As a young man Willard felt compelled to emulate his father's achievements in research. But his slim record of published papers bore testimony to the fact that he had failed. And despite his frequent protestations that he was actively engaged in study of Gondawanaland coals, while at Duke I saw no evidence of this in either his office or his dusty, unused research lab.

During Willard's boyhood many of the famous geologists of the time visited in the Berrys' Baltimore home. For me, he became a fascinating link to the men who had pioneered geological study of eastern United States. His many stories of these people, boring old man's ramblings to many of his colleagues, never failed during the two years of our friendship to absolutely mesmerize me.

Dorothy, his frumpy wife of thirty-seven years and mother of their three children, was born in Virginia, a fact which seemed to have left her with a life-long inordinate interest in smoked Virginia hams. Bleached blonde, hard features, tight lips painted red, rouge-caked cheeks, chain smoker, and hard drinker, she could curse like a longshoremen and loved to tell shockingly filthy stories at social functions. Had she been an actor she would have been typecast as a madame of brothels in sagas of the old west.

The Berrys were financially independent, ultra-conservative Republicans, who were deeply offended by the presence in the White House of the young, liberal-assed Jack Kennedy. Each day, as devout Quakers, they prayed for Kennedy's demise, but were greatly shocked and guilt-ridden when he was assassinated.

They had devised a rather curious method by which they paid bills. Stock dividend checks, which arrived in their mail with considerable regularity, were casually placed in a drawer of the dining room table. When a bill came due they merely sorted through the accumulated checks for one which adequately covered the debt and deposited it in their checking account.

By just about any measure, Dorothy and Willard would have been considered alcoholics. They had wine with breakfast, lunch and dinner. For coffee breaks, Willard kept a bottle of whiskey in an office filing cabinet under B for booze. Following dinner they retired to the parlor where each evening they polished off a two dollar fifth of Cream of Kentucky before bedtime at eleven.

I don't recall ever having discussed pornography with the Berrys, although it was clearly a topic of considerable interest to them. Just about any place one looked in their house—coffee tables, end tables, night stands, magazine racks, bookshelves, the john—there were copies of girlie magazines, elegant "art" volumes featuring nudes, and books of dirty jokes and stories. And Willard was rarely without a copy of the Frederick's of Hollywood catalogue of sexy feminine undergarments in his briefcase.

On May 10, I was offered a position of Associate Professor of Geology at Duke University. I accepted by return mail. In retrospect I can say it was the wisest decision of my life.

Early in July I drove to the Duke campus from my field camp in Myrtle Beach to inspect my new office and adjoining laboratory. While there I had the opportunity to visit with the geology staff and to meet some of the undergraduate majors.

A day or two later on my return to Myrtle Beach I did not travel alone. I was accompanied by the disturbing image of two dark and very beautiful eyes—they were the eyes of a young coed, a geology major, I had met at Duke. I could not then, of course, have known that they were also the eyes of the young lady who in two years would become my life-long partner and the mother of our two beautiful children.

But, as I think someone else has said, that is another story.

The Godfather

The Myrtle Beach Elks Club was a popular gathering place for the major crime figures of the Grand Strand, the men and women who controlled prostitution, gambling and the flow of illegal booze. The only prominent member of the underworld who I never saw there was the mob's godfather, Cuter Jennings, the owner of the Oasis Club on U.S. 501.

Cuter didn't look much like the stereotypical criminal. To the casual observer he probably seemed a fifty-ish, pudgy, kindly, grandfatherly type. But anyone who had looked into the gray, hard-core depths of his eyes would know better. No one who knew Cuter well regarded him as a kindly grandfather. There were even those who would have been pleased to see him dead. It was for the latter reason that he was never without his burly bodyguards and it was why he preferred to remain in the relative safety of his club, his downtown motel suite, or the back room of one of his Grand Strand restaurants.

Though I had talked with Jennings on numerous occasions I knew nothing of his background. When once I asked him why he had a framed photograph of Reverend Billy Graham on the wall opposite the Oasis bar, I learned that he and Billy were friends, had grown up together as boys, and attended public school together in Charlotte, North Carolina.

Two of the most interesting underworld characters I met at the Elks were the Prince and the Princess, a husband and wife team who handled interstate prostitution for Cuter. The Prince made no claim to royal blood, but he assured me that his wife was, indeed, a member of the Russian royal family.

Royalty or not, they were a handsome pair in their late forties, expensively and tastefully attired, and well educated. They brought an air of class and an aura of elegance to the Elks. Even their girls exuded class. They were brought in from Virginia early each Saturday during the tourist season. All were in their early twenties, exceptional beauties, elegant, bright, refined, excellent conversationalists, impeccable decorum. They could easily have been products of an expensive finishing school. Possibly they were. The girls served the needs and desires of well-to-do, respectable gentlemen, lawyers, judges, businessmen, doctors, in town for business and "a little golf at the Dunes." On Sunday afternoon they returned home to their wives and families with carefully preserved score cards recording their prowess on the golf course.

In time Jim and I established a friendly, platonic relationship with the girls, whose company we found more rewarding than that of the typically boorish, provincial, narrow-minded tourists in town from the hinterlands for a big hoot and holler.

In 1960 we were working out of a cabin on the Waccamaw River. There was a wonderful deep and cool hole in the river at the edge of the backyard where Jim and I spent a relaxing half hour each evening when we returned from the field hot, sweaty, dirty and tired. When the girls learned of our swimming hole they all wanted to come to our place for a dip. It sounded like a good idea so we invited them to drop by in the morning. At ten a carload of the girls arrived at the cabin ready for a swim. For the next two hours Jim and I hosted the happiest little whorehouse in Horry County.

Sometime in late 1961 or early 1962 the Prince and Princess and their bevy of beauties disappeared from the Grand Strand. No explanation was forthcoming, and we discreetly asked no questions.

For a time Cuter, using inferior local talent, managed the hookers himself. I don't think the operation went very smoothly during that period. His merchandise was clearly second rate, and I suppose he hadn't the time or perhaps the touch for the business.

While having a drink at the Oasis Club one afternoon Cuter invited me to join him for dinner at his downtown motel suite. I had never seen the place, and, except for his close, most trusted associates, I think few people had been invited there. I tried to guess why I had been so honored, but I knew it was impossible to anticipate Cuter's mind.

I watched while Cuter cooked dinner for us in his compact little kitchenette. After dinner he finally worked around to the reason behind the invitation. He told me he wanted me to take charge of his hooker business. I only barely concealed my astonishment at this unexpected and seemingly bizarre proposal. The pay, I knew, would far exceed the salary of a lowly professor, but I had never aspired to become a pimp at any price, and this sudden opportunity to do so did nothing to alter my mind. For one thing, I was completely satisfied with my life as a geologist, and for another, I had no wish to end up in prison, or worse, encased in a concrete slab.

To my considerable relief Cuter accepted my refusal with grace and even a trace of a friendly smile. We shook hands then and I complimented him on a delicious meal. The bodyguard, who had hovered in the background all evening, showed me to the door. Outside I walked to my car still a law-abiding citizen, but with a vague sense of guilt for having been just a little flattered by Jennings' offer.

A short time later my friend Zeb Berry was made manager of the Elks and the mob's chief pimp. It was a bad deal for both Zeb and Cuter. Zeb proved to have a severe problem with his hands. When they weren't in the till they were on one or more of the girls.

Early the next spring I discovered that the Elks had a new manager. No one would or could tell me what had happened to Zeb. A search of Myrtle Beach and the entire Grand Strand uncovered no trace of him or any member of his family.

My efforts thwarted, I made the risky decision to ask Cuter if he could tell me where Zeb had gone. If foul play were involved, the odds were that Cuter was behind it, and my nosing around would make him edgy.

The next evening I found Cuter and Hack, his devoted muscle, at the Oasis bar and asked my question. For several seconds I received only looks of disapproval. Then a tight-lipped Cuter said, softly but firmly, "He's gone to Florence, South Carolina." Another few seconds of cold stare and he added, "Don't ever ask another question about Zeb Berry, and never mention his name to me again."

A few years later when Susan and I were in Florence we looked for Zeb, but found no trace of him. But then, I hadn't expected we would. The answer to the question of Zeb's fate had not been in the words of Cuter, but rather in his cold, deadly eyes.

One of the first indications I had that the local police were on Jennings' payroll came one evening in 1959 at the Elks. Jim and I were at a table having a few drinks and listening to Jesse Shaw's combo when the manager walked into the dining room and announced that the police would raid the club in about ten minutes. We were to remain calm and continue to enjoy ourselves, there would be no problems. It was obvious that most of the patrons were undisturbed, so, following their lead, we settled back in our chairs and relaxed.

As promised, three uniformed officers came through the main entrance ten minutes later. They strode purposefully through our area and into the bar in the back room where about 25 one-armed bandits were arranged on counters halfway around the room. Apparently they left later by a back door; we saw no more of them that evening. Later I went into the bar and looked around. Nothing seemed changed so I asked the bartender what had happened. He told me that one of the dime slots had been confiscated. In time I learned that these raids by the city police were prompted by pressure exerted by the state police and the FBI, who were attempting to shut down all gambling operations in Horry County. During each raid one machine was taken in an effort to demonstrate that the city was doing its best to bring crime in Myrtle Beach under control.

None of the slots were ever replaced at the Elks, so by early 1962 the last one had been removed. By late summer of 1963 all of Cuter's gambling operations, including those at the Dunes and Ocean Forest had been terminated, and, in addition, he was no longer permitted to serve hard liquor at any of his establishments.

My drinking habits were little altered by the ban. While tourists at the Elks sipped iced tea or guzzled cold beer, I enjoyed my usual glasses of bourbon and water served to me by my friend Johnny, who explained with a mysterious smile that the drinks were prepared in "the room upstairs." It was the only reference ever made to me of the room upstairs. I could only suppose it was another of Cuter's secret places, but putting my curiosity aside, I drank my bourbon and asked no questions.

During those dreary days in Cuter's life the Oasis was an empty shell, dark, and silent. A wonderful watering hole turned to dust. The midnight to dawn floor shows a blurred memory, the dazzling array of bottles once displayed on the shelves behind the bar confiscated and impounded, the fun-seeking crowds of weekend sinners doomed to wander endlessly in futile search of illicit pleasure in the sterile confines of their personal Bible-thumping hinterland purgatory.

From time to time I dropped by the dormant Oasis to visit with Cuter and Hack. On those occasions the three of us, enveloped in the dull, hazy orange glow of the bar light, talked, smoked and sipped drinks mixed by Hack in the back seat of his car parked in the shadows behind the club.

Cuter usually spoke of better days to come when the FBI, weary of its crusade against him, would pack their attaché cases and quietly slip out of town. "Then," he would declare, "I'll be able to reassemble the business and bring back free enterprise to the Grand Strand."

Finally one day, following Cuter's scenario, the FBI, satisfied they had snuffed out big time gambling in Myrtle Beach, packed up their operation and left the area. In their wake the Oasis soon reopened, and Cuter's far-flung enterprises, featuring booze, girls, good food, and good times, were once again in full swing.

I have no knowledge that Cuter ever again attempted to bring gambling back to the Grand Strand. Even so, he remained for another decade the Godfather of the Myrtle Beach underworld.

An Arabian Night

By 1962 I was well known at the Oasis Club and seemingly in the good graces of its owner, Cuter Jennings. As he was a master of understatement with a face frozen into a perpetual deadpan, it was difficult to accurately gauge Cuter's true feelings about anything.

In 1961 Jennings had, in his usual cryptic manner, passed the word to me through one of his close associates that having observed me for some time he had reached the conclusion that I was "Okay." However, this judgment was put to a stringent test by the events of a 48-hour period in June, 1962.

The strange episode, as many things I experienced in those days, began at the Elks Club. It had been a quiet Friday evening so the club closed an hour early at midnight. When the last of the boozy patrons had straggled into the warm, humid night, Jim Fowler and I wandered to the bar in the back room for a drink and a little conversation before hitting the road to McCumber.

There were two men behind the bar: Mike, a young man recently hired by the Elks as a bartender, and an older man of forty or so, well dressed, tailored, steel gray suit, white shirt, dark blue silk tie, diamond-studded stick pin, pale blue eyes, hair dark brown, neatly coiffured, freshly manicured nails, one hundred eighty pounds, 5'10", an ex-athlete or fitness freak.

The third person, a woman, also forty-ish, slim, attractive in a dark way, dark eyes, dark skin, black hair, shoulder length. She sat on a stool at the bar engaged in earnest conversation with the man in the gray suit. They were both strangers to me. It seemed odd they would have after-hours access to the club.

Fowler and I moved to the bar close to the dark lady and introduced ourselves. She smiled, reached out her hand and said, "Anna Culver; actually everyone calls me Annie."

The name was a surprise; I'd expected something Arabic or Turkish. Reading the surprise in my eyes, she laughed, "It's my ex-husband's name, Colonel Edward L. Culver, U.S. Air Force. We met in Florida, had two children and two years ago were assigned to the Myrtle Beach Air Force Base. We'd been married twelve years, but he found greener pasture along the Grand Strand."

"I'm afraid," I responded, "that divorce has become a way of life these days. I don't think most marriages survive ten or fifteen years."

"That's true," she agreed. "But it's not completely bad. Edward at least provides child support."

While we were speaking, the man behind the bar in the gray suit laid a deck of cards on the counter and fanned them out like a Vegas dealer. As he did, Mrs. Culver waved her hand limply in the direction of the deck. "Harry and I are going to have a little game. Care to join us?"

We both declined.

"Small stakes," she said, invitingly.

"Another time?" I suggested. "Jim and I are planning to hoist one and pack it in." It had been an invitation that Jim Solliday would not have refused, but neither Fowler nor I were gambling types and, in fact, I never even played cards socially. I suppose it was a holdover from my fundamentalist training as a boy. My mother and her wacko friends at the First Brethren Church regarded all card playing as sinful. Perhaps I had simply inherited my father's view that card games were interminably boring.

As the little game commenced beside us at the bar, Jim and I turned to our drinks and to a discussion of some of the finer points of Jim's thesis project. He had started on a paleoecological analysis of waterway Pleistocene deposits as a companion study to the work completed by Jim Chaplin in June.

So far we had made only modest progress with Fowler's field studies. This was because schedule constraints had obliged us to give priority during the first two weeks of the field season to the work of another of my graduate students, Jim Howard. Howard planned to study the microfossils of the James City, Waccamaw, and Duplin formations, but it was impossible for him to commence this work until he had properly collected samples from the three formations under my close supervision.

Since we had packed up Howard and his samples and sent him off to Houston a week earlier, there had been barely time for Fowler to develop a real feel for the character of his study. We needed to move right along because in three weeks we were locked into a major month-long drilling project in southeastern North Carolina.

It is probably a noteworthy oddity that the first four students to complete masters theses on the geology of the Carolina Coastal Plain Province under my direction were named James (Solliday, Chaplin, Fowler, and Howard).

There was a time at the University of Houston when it was generally believed that for a student to qualify to do a thesis under my direction it was necessary to change his name to James. This, however, was a flawed hypothesis which failed to take into account that at the same time as the Jims toiled in the Carolinas, the two graduate students working on Florida-based theses for me were Donald Taylor and Donald Beardsley.

I must admit that there were times when dealing with four Jims simultaneously proved perplexing. This was particularly true of their correspondence to me. Each wrote on lined yellow legal paper and signed letters simply "Jim." On numerous occasions I would spend several minutes pondering the identity of the author of the letter I had just read.

In about 30 minutes we pushed our stools aside, stood up and announced our intention to call it a night. Annie looked up at us, surprised, "Already you're leaving?" Abruptly she laid her cards down on the counter, picked up her purse and stood up beside us. With an apologetic expression, she said, "I hope I can hitch a ride with you gentlemen. My escort had to leave early and I've been stranded all evening. It won't be far out of your way—just south of 501 and a few blocks west of U.S. 17."

Although her request came as a surprise to us we assured her it would be no problem to drop her off. But I couldn't help wondering why she had waited until we were leaving before she had asked for a ride. I wondered, too, how she would have gotten home had we refused. And then there was her friend, Harry, the stranger in the gray suit. Why hadn't he offered to take her home? I had no answers so I stopped wondering. I shouldn't have, but then how could I have suspected that I was the mark in a complicated scam?

During the drive to Annie's house she asked if we would like to join her for lunch later in the day at her uncle's restaurant in North Myrtle Beach. "He's a fine cook," she said proudly, "and of course you will be our guests." Tired of our own cooking, I hastened to accept her offer and agreed to pick her up at ten in the morning. When we dropped her off in front of her house she turned to Jim and, smiling, said, "And don't you worry, Jim, there will be a pretty young lady waiting there at the restaurant just for you."

As I had promised we gathered up Mrs. Culver at her house and drove to her uncle's place near Crescent Beach. There, to my surprise, we found not one but two attractive, blonde, blue-eyed young ladies waiting at the counter for Fowler.

I had little opportunity to dwell on the possible ramifications of Fowler's bountiful good fortune. With introductions in progress a door at the rear of the dining room was suddenly flung open and a tiny, dark, wizened, gray-haired man of about sixty-five flitted across the room toward us. It was Annie's Arab Uncle Ali who had just returned from Little River with the catch of the day. He was very excited that the catch had included an angel fish. When I was forced to admit I knew nothing about angel fish the little man took my arm and led me to the rear of the dining room. "You must taste an angel fish to understand," he declared. "No man should die until he has eaten at least one angel fish. So that your life will not have been in vain I will prepare the fish especially for you. Just sit down at the table. I'll bring you a beer, the cooking will not take long, but it will be perfect."

While the others sat at a table near the front window eating whatever the hell the catch of the day happened to be, I sat alone at the back of the room drinking beer and devouring one of the best fish fillets I had ever tasted. Old Uncle Ali was right about his heavenly fish.

Shortly after joining my group at the front of the room Annie asked Jim and me if we were familiar with the new private club off south U.S. 17 in Myrtle Beach. When we responded that we were not, she said, "Well, it's very nice and it occurred to me that perhaps we could all go there this evening for dinner and drinks."

"Well," I said. "That sounds appealing, but if it's a private club how do we get in?"

"Oh, that's all right," she replied. "My cousin Joey is one of the owners. I'll just call him later and arrange everything."

We agreed to take the women to Annie's house and to return for them at seven-thirty. Though some of the events of that morning had seemed a bit odd, neither of us had noted anything we could consider sinister. Nevertheless, as was later apparent, while Jim and I worked that afternoon at McCumber, Mrs. Culver and her friends were busy refining their scheme to separate me from my money.

Jim and I assumed that we would all ride together in my Dodge, but at Annie's house she told us that she and the girls would ride in her car and that we were to follow in ours. It struck me as a strange arrangement but I agreed. I think Annie's explanation was that two cars were best in case some of us might want to leave early.

The club, about 100 yards deep into a stand of tall pines, was not only private but effectively isolated. And it was hardly what we had expected—a sort of forlorn, neglected little one-story frame building just barely short of qualifying as a shack. There were no windows that we could detect and only one door. The club crouched almost apologetically in the shadow of a quite large, gray, two-story house with an outside staircase that suggested it could have been a duplex.

As we crossed the shelly sand parking area I recall thinking it odd that although two or three cars were parked in front of the big house, ours were the only ones at the club. A dismal showing it seemed for the nice place Annie had described earlier in the day.

The club door came fitted with a prohibition peephole from which a dark and searching eye monitored our approach. When we were within a step or two of the door it swung open almost as if we had broken the beam of an electric eye.

The only eyes, however, were those of our doorman, and we had already met one of those a moment earlier. The man, dark, pocked skin, a red, three-inch scar along the left cheekbone, a flattened nose with a large orange mole near the right nostril, hair steel gray, frizzled to add two inches to his 5' 5" frame. Arms askew at his sides to accommodate a massive chest, he wore a brown and tan checked sport coat that seemed at least one size too small, a dark brown shirt, cream tie, brown slacks, brown and white sport shoes. If there wasn't a holstered revolver snugged against his left armpit, all the George Raft characters I had seen in the movies were only figments of the screenwriter's fantasies. A sneer that creased his hard mouth was intended, I assumed, as a warm smile of welcome, but it brought the hair on the nape of my neck to a bristled alert.

Then from behind me Annie said, "Jules, this is George. George is the bartender." George's large hairy hand clasped mine. George was a knuckle buster. George was good at it. I tried, with only modest success, not to wince.

Inside we found two poorly lighted rectangular rooms separated by a thin wooden partition. Along the outer wall of the room in which we stood was a row of four or five booths, all empty, and at the far end at the room a large, silent jukebox. The open area of the bare wood floor served, I speculated, as a dance floor or boxing ring as dictated by the mood of the guests.

A short, narrow passageway at the front of the building led past the end of a bar into the adjoining room. The bar stretched along the partition for eight or ten feet. At the back of this room were two small tables around which six or seven rough looking men shrouded in a blue haze of cigarette and cigar smoke joked, cursed, and played cards.

When George had mixed and served the drinks we had ordered, Jim and the girls returned to a booth in the outer room. Annie, leaving me at the bar, strolled to the gaming tables and struck up an animated conversation with several of the men whom she obviously knew.

Left with George and his Peter Lorre smile, I said, "George, I came here with the impression that you folks served meals and I find there is nothing except stale potato chips at the bar."

"Well," he said, not quite able to meet my eyes. "There has been some talk of putting a restaurant in, but that would go next door in the big house. So far, though, that's just talk. Most fellows come here to drink, gamble and fight." Then dropping his voice as if he feared someone might overhear him, he leaned toward me and said, "Just between us, you know, we get some tough customers in here—get a little drunken up and they start feeling their oats." He reached beneath the bar then and pulled up a holstered 38 cal. revolver. "Keep this thing handy for guys like that." Then he pointed the holster toward the floor behind me. "See that hole down there? Bullet hole from this gun. Had a wild bunch in here from Conway a couple of weeks ago that wanted to break up the place. Those guys rather fight than fuck. A couple slugs around their feet cooled ' em off. Can't have that sort of stuff in here—this is a respectable place."

Annie came back then and we joined Jim and the girls at their table in the outer room. While I was trying to think of a diplomatic way of suggesting we get out of the place, Annie turned to me and said, "I think Jim should take the girls out somewhere for dinner and then get them back to Crescent Beach. I've got some business with a fellow next door, Jules. As soon as I take care of that I'll take you to dinner if you wish. Sorry about there being no food—I was sure they served meals here."

I should have refused and left with Jim and the girls but though I had realized the situation was weird I still didn't see it as threatening. I'd been away from the street too long—the instincts had dulled.

We had been alone only a minute when the door swung open and a tall, lean and mean-looking Arab-type walked into the room and headed for our table. He was wearing a mustard colored suit, the standard dark brown shirt, a revolting flowered tie and a sinister smile. The bulge under his suit coat near his left armpit had a familiar look. Somehow I didn't need to wait for Annie to tell me that this was Cousin Joey.

At the table he stood over us and, ignoring me, directed a knowing look at Annie. "He's up there now, if you want to see him you better go now."

Annie stood up and thrust her purse toward me. "Hold this for me until I get back. I won't be long. Perhaps in my absence you and Joey could go up to the bar and play a little Black Jack."

As she disappeared through the door Joey turned to me and with his natural sneer said, "Well, fellow, you do know how, don't you, or don't they gamble where you come from?"

Fighting back an urge to drive my fist into his family jewels, I smiled instead. There could be no harm, I thought, in humoring the prick and I sure as hell had no wish to piss him off. So reluctantly I agreed to try my hand at a little Black Jack. A minute later I was at the front end of the bar in the passageway and Joey was behind the bar with a deck of cards in one hand. George, all but hidden behind Joey, was doing his best to peer around him so he could watch me get cleaned out.

Just then the door opened again and three ugly characters stepped inside, walked through the passage and took up positions behind me. Hired muscle, I thought, stupid, but deadly. Walking away from Joey's game might not be easy. For the first time I sensed that I had been set up.

As expected I won the first three or four games. I wondered how long this would go on before they went for the kill, but I had no intention of finding out. I knew if there was any chance of quitting it had to be right then, before things became serious. I had won only a few dollars so there were no grounds for them to complain that I was quitting without giving them a chance to get even. I was hardly close to breaking the bank.

When Joey began once again to deal the cards, I brushed them aside. "That's it, Joey, that's all for me. I think I'll blow my winnings on a couple of drinks."

"Hell," he said. "You been doing okay, why would you quit now? That's no way to play this game. You should never quit when you're hot."

"Well, I've heard that refrain before. It's a song sung by every loser I've ever known."

Frowning, Joey shrugged his shoulders. "Maybe you'll change your mind later. Either way, I'll be around."

I considered his last words a threat. Shoving my way past the goons behind me, I walked around to the front of the bar and ordered a bourbon and water from George. While working on my second drink I checked my watch for the twelfth time. It had been nearly 45 minutes since Annie had left and I was becoming pissed around the edges.

A few minutes later a man came into the club, walked to the bar and spoke softly into one of George's hairy ears. When the man left George came over to where I stood. "You might as well relax, fellow. Annie's got herself into a game upstairs in the big house and I doubt she'll be back soon."

Now I was pissed all over. What the hell did the damned broad think I was supposed to do in this shit hole? Then a feeling of wariness crept over me. What the hell really is going on here? It was then I knew that I'd like to leave before I found the answer to my question.

It was a realization that immediately raised the question of transportation. My car had gone with Fowler, but Annie's should be just outside the door of the club and the keys would be in her purse she had left to my safekeeping.

Not wishing to alert any of the men at the game table or George behind the bar, I strolled into the outer room and slid into a booth where I could not be observed as I made the necessary search of her bag. At first I placed the bag on the seat next to the wall and groped through it with my right hand. When this technique failed to reveal the keys, I dumped the contents of the bag onto the seat, only to confirm what I had feared—there were no keys.

Before the brain had fully formulated the question, "Why the hell did she take the keys with her?" it spit out the answer. I had been set up. There were no keys in the purse because I wasn't expected to go anywhere. And the brain had an observation on the girls as well. Involuntarily or otherwise they were a part of it—decoys used to separate me from Fowler and my car.

My mind was racing now, trying to play catch-up. The other guys were far ahead, and I didn't know who all the players were, or for that matter, I didn' t even know the name of the game. But it didn't require a Ph.D. to figure out that it was I who carried the game stakes in my left hip pocket—at least two thousand NSF dollars.

As I attempted to think rationally, I realized I did know two of the players— Annie and Cousin Joey—and it seemed safe to add a third party, the man in the gray suit, Harry. Harry had barely said a word as he stood behind the bar at the Elks—a picture of detachment. When Annie announced she was stranded he was the logical one to have offered her a ride, but he didn't. Why? The answer seemed clear to me at that moment, he hadn't made the offer because it was his con. He was the coach and he hadn't written the game plan that way. But if it was really Harry's con, where was he now? The answer to that one came with surprising ease. Hell, he was where he had been all evening, in the big gray house next door. He pulled the strings, his puppets did his bidding. Annie and Joey were over there with him because they had a little problem. According to the plan I was to have permitted Cousin Joey to clean me out at Black Jack, but no one had provided me with a copy of the script.

Worse yet, I had made it clear that I was no gambler and it must have been obvious that it was unlikely that anyone would succeed in involving me in one of their cute games. With unwitting docility I had taken their bait piece by programmed piece, and had just as unwittingly screwed up the role in which I had been cast.

I sat there and stared blankly at the silent jukebox as I fought off repeated surges of embarrassment, anger and fear. Since the aborted Black Jack game no one had attempted to engage me in a game of cards. But then, why should they? I was alone, and unarmed (usually I carried an Armi Galesi 6.335 cal. pistol, but that evening I had left it for safekeeping in the nightstand beside my bed at McCumber), and outnumbered maybe ten to one. There seemed no need to waste time on tedious games of chance; they could take my money at their leisure.

I was trapped, the only way out was the way I had come in and for all I knew the door was locked. But I had little choice—I had to take a shot at that door. Once outside I could move quickly to the cover of the pines and work my way north to McCumber. I was a good runner and I was in excellent shape, so I felt confident I would be able to out-sprint or out-endure anyone who might pursue. Even so, I couldn't out-speed a bullet. It was important that I get through the door unobserved. Once outside, the greater my lead time, the better my chance of escape.

With the door to the club squarely centered in the middle of the front wall of the outer room, it was essential that the room remain unoccupied. There had been no customers all evening and no one, except me, had been in the room since Annie and Cousin Joey had gone next door nearly an hour earlier.

Actually it seemed the only reason anyone might venture into the room would be to play the jukebox and so far none of the men at the game table had indicated any interest in music. To be on the safe side, though, I decided to feed the machine quarters until I managed to engineer my escape.

The door was not visible from the game tables, but George, who also served as doorman, had it under loose surveillance most of the time.

Nevertheless, I was counting on George and the helping hand of Mother Nature to provide me with a passport to freedom. A devoted beer drinker, George had been hitting the men's room at the end of the bar with frequent regularity and it had been at least fifteen minutes since his last response to necessity.

As the victim of a con for the past 24 hours, I felt it was definitely time to turn the tables. Although I was a novice in the execution of this subtle art form, it seemed apparent that the potential success of a con is directly dependent on the creation of a compelling illusion.

My plan, if nothing else, had the beauty of simplicity. I had only to convince Annie's friends that I was completely unaware of any threat of foul play and was prepared to await Annie's return until Hell iced over. Relieved of their fear that I might attempt an escape, my movements about the club would, I hoped, soon be perceived by George and the men at the game table with nothing more than a collective, complacent, ho-hum.

To create the desired illusion I tucked Annie's purse under my right armpit and began to slowly and repetitiously pace the floor in an arc that took me from the bar, where I was in full view of everyone in the club, through the passageway to the outer room and back to the bar. My movements were calculated to be, if not hypnotizing, at least non-threatening and boringly uninteresting.

To condition the men to my repeated absences from their view I lingered a little longer in the back room with each traverse of my arc. Thirty minutes later my plan suddenly began to produce benefits. Arriving at the bar for probably the twelfth time, I found it untended—George finally had succumbed to the call of nature. A quick glance directed to the back of the room told me that, as hoped, the men at the tables had become oblivious to my seemingly mindless meanderings.

With sweaty armpits and thumping temples I fought off a powerful impulse to break ground and run like hell; instead, I forced myself to walk slowly and deliberately through the passage. At the door I paused and without contemplating the consequences if it were locked, I grasped the knob firmly with my left hand and gave it a sharp twist. The door opened and I stepped outside.

Sucking warm, wet air into my lungs, I quietly closed the door and tossed Annie' s purse to the ground. With the glow of the lights along U.S. 17 over my right shoulder and the fading strains of Ray Charles singing *I Can' t Stop Loving You* at my back, I sprinted into the comparative safety of the pine woods.

Winded after several hundred yards I dropped down into a brisk walk, avoiding U.S. 17 in case some of the gang decided to pursue me by auto. Eventually I broke out of the woods and into a grassy field. In a few minutes the shadowy silhouette of the Woodland Esso Station loomed ahead. I knew then that I was opposite McCumber Place.

Approaching the highway with deliberate caution, I didn't cross it until I was as certain as possible that no suspicious cars or men on foot were nearby. A few minutes later I was at McCumber.

Looking fresh and relaxed, clad only in his boxer shorts, Fowler sat at the dining room worktable writing a letter. Utterly unaware of any of the drama and danger of the past twenty-four hours he looked up at me as I walked into the living room and asked how things had gone. At the moment it seemed sinful to contemplate encroaching on such equanimity with anything approaching the truth, so I shrugged and said, "A real drag, Jim, so boring, in fact, I decided to walk home alone."

When I crashed into my sack that night it was with the gratifying conviction that the sequence of bizarre events had at last run its course. However, the last chapter (so far as I was concerned) was written the following night.

I had stopped by the Oasis Club for a drink. In a very short time I was joined by Hack, Cuter's chief bodyguard and for five minutes or so he and I and Jack, the bartender, engaged in the usual desultory banter. Then, with no warning, Hack asked about my visit to the club in the pines. The question took me totally off guard. While I struggled to imagine how he could possibly know of my little escapade of the previous evening, Cuter, who had been across the room a moment earlier, suddenly slipped onto a stool beside Hack. Waving Jack to the opposite site of the bar, Cuter and Hack in tandem launched a non-smiling, full-scale interrogation. The questions were fired in rapid succession, almost before I had answered one, another was posed. How did I meet Annie? How long had I known Joey? Who else was in the club? Who was in the big gray house? Did I go there to gamble? How did I get home?

All the time I had an eerie feeling they already knew the answers and were only gauging my willingness to level with them, and were trying to judge if I were friend or foe. I could only assume that one of the men in the club was on Cuter's payroll. One of the men at the game table? Or could it be George, the bartender? Very clever; very spooky.

Then, as abruptly as it had begun, Cuter's quiz show ended. At the same time the mood at our side of the bar changed from one of tense confrontation to congenial comradeship. My answers, none of which I now recall, had apparently satisfied him. In an almost fatherly manner, Cuter began to explain the reasons for his concern about my recent activities.

"You should know," he began, "the people you were with last night are a dangerous, untrustworthy lot of thieves and cutthroats. These are people who'll stop at nothing to get what they want." With a thin smile he added, somewhat parenthetically, "You were lucky, you know, to get out of there last night with your wallet."

He crooked his left arm over the bar then and leaned toward me while Hack wagged his head in agreement. Cuter continued, "These gentlemen moved up here from Miami in the winter. Moved into the big gray house you saw last night and they built the little clip joint next door. All that was just a starter— a toehold until they have time to get better positioned. They mean to take over all the gambling operations along the Grand Strand. That in itself means trouble for us, but the worst part is that they came up there with a reputation and now they have the FBI nosing around with some idea of closing us all down." Fixing me with his steely eyes he said, "You understand that we must be very cautious. Things are heating up and it's certain someone is going to be burned."

It was quite a speech for a man who normally was as loquacious as a cold stone. Even more interesting, he had for the first time in my presence identified himself as a major player in the Grand Strand gambling scene.

When he had finished there were questions I wanted to ask but I knew better. In Cuter Jennings' world, Cuter asked all the questions and those around him, if they wished to remain around him, provided the answers.

On the return drive to McCumber I felt particularly thankful that we would soon wrap up our 1962 field studies in South Carolina. I had no wish to become further involved in a gang war or to become the subject of an FBI investigation. In a few days we would move our base of operations to Whiteville, North Carolina and later to New Bern where we expected to spend two weeks re-examining exposures along the Neuse Estuary. Then we would close out the season in Washington, D.C. with a study of Neogene mollusk collections at the National Museum of Natural History. In late August I would return to Houston, sell my house on Bessemer Street and head for Durham, North Carolina to begin my duties as Associate Professor of Geology at Duke University.

Mustang Sally

In August, 1964, I joined Humble Oil and Refining Research Lab in Houston as a Senior Geologist. My research assignments were interesting but only moderately challenging and a 40-hour week left a lot of the tiger tail in my tank. One result of all this was that I was soon suffering from terminal boredom. To help remedy the problem I set up an office and a small laboratory at home and re-activated my Carolina research projects working evenings, weekends and holidays. At the same time Henry Johnson, still the State Geologist of South Carolina, agreed to continue drilling holes for me in South Carolina and to supply me with a steady stream of sediments for analysis. I also continued to work on unfinished manuscripts and in the fall of 1964 I completed a paper written with Hobart Furbunch on the Waccamaw fossils of the intercoastal waterway in Horry County, South Carolina.

In the summer of 1965 I arranged with Henry to meet me in Myrtle Beach to do some drilling during my September vacation. Hobart, whom I contacted at the same time, agreed to join us and help out on the rig.

Henry responded to the impending reunion with Hobart and me with comments expressing his keenness to get back into the field:

> *Am making plans and getting gear together in hope of plunging back into the Coastal Plain with you fellows and can feel the small, never-dying seed of excitement and enthusiasm and life stirring inside me at the prospect of what may come in the steaming hot summer days and the insect-ridden nights. I think it is man's basic instinct to seek after something, he knows not what. To see what lies beyond the next mountain range, and over the horizon on the sea. Not knowing what is there is what moves and stimulates him. The mixed emotions of fear, greed and desire are involved in this reaching for the unknown. In many cases it is like a moth drawn*

to the flame that consumes him. But it gives a spice to life that is not found in known things and known ways and known places. Treading old familiar trails and dealing only with old familiar situations from day to day and week to week is a deadly thing and chokes and suffocates a man, and his life stagnates and he is not really alive. Our mores and system create this stagnant environment, and most of us go down—as Thoreau says, breathing our own breath over and over again.

On the afternoon of September 20 Susan and I, with our six-month-old daughter, Nicole, checked into the Pines Motel in North Myrtle Beach. Hobart and Henry showed up with the mobile drill rig about eleven in the evening. Working from topo maps, Henry and I decided that our first hole in the morning would go down at Little River Neck schoolhouse in the northeast corner of Horry County.

On the following morning Hobart, Henry and I received our first surprise when we pulled the rig into the schoolyard at 7:00 a.m. The flimsy clapboard, one-story building that had at one time served the black boys and girls of Little River Neck as a schoolhouse had been converted to a nightclub.

In bold, free-style, multicolored letters a sign painted on one wall declared the establishment to be the "Bellamy Rooster." Smaller letters below, which identified the proprietor as "Mustang Sally" were accompanied by a gaudy portrayal of a scantily clad, well-endowed, black female astride a bucking, nostril-flaring, wild-eyed mustang.

On a Saturday night it was a place black men freed the evils in their guts, where cheap wine flowed like a river, where voices were raised in joy and anger, where knives flashed and the floor and walls were splattered with human blood. On that warm, peaceful weekday morning, it was as quiet as death.

With the place apparently deserted we were uncertain how to proceed. Drilling on private property without the owner's permission can, at times, prove hazardous. Casting our fate to the winds, however, we agreed to set up and drill the damned hole as planned.

When the bit was about fifteen feet down the hole a young female with the body of a Tina Turner materialized in the doorway of the Rooster.

For a long moment she stared at us with the dark, smoldering eyes of a cat sizing up its intended prey. Slowly then, and gracefully she glided over the dew-laden grass toward us, exuding an aura of animal sexuality that drifted up into

341

the low hanging, gnarled branches of the live oaks and spread before her, soon enveloping the drill rig and the three of us who stood transfixed in hypnotic wonderment. When she reached the cab of the truck she stood watching us, silent and motionless.

A trifle belatedly, Henry recalled that the bit was still noisily rotating in the hole. Shutting down the engine, he climbed down from his perch at the back of the truck, walked around to the young lady and introduced himself as the State Geologist and Hobart and I as his two trusty hired hands. Then he asked, "Is this your property?"

With an expression of mild puzzlement she replied, "Yes sir, the Rooster is mine." Then, hunching her right shoulder in the direction of the sign on the side of the building she said, somewhat proudly it seemed, "That's me—I'm Sally."

At that precise moment Henry's facade of nonchalance and composure began a meltdown. With his eyes riveted on Sally's cleavage, he launched into a faltering fumbling, and entirely incomprehensible discourse on our work in Horry County which ended finally with a declaration of why drilling a hole in her backyard would indubitably advance the cause of scientific research by several decades.

Through all this Sally listened politely, wondering, no doubt, whether she was dealing with a potentially dangerous madman or another redneck honky who wanted to lay her, but was too dumb to know how to properly propose a fairly simple business transaction.

When she had satisfied herself that he was quite finished with his unintelligible monologue, she smiled invitingly and asked, "Would you care to take a tour of the Rooster?"

Henry immediately accepted the invitation and the two of them headed for the Rooster. As we followed well behind, Hobart leaned toward me and, in a hissing whisper, said, "Perhaps the old girl dispenses free samples to visiting dignitaries."

"What's with the free stuff?" I hissed back. "A man with your financial resources could buy the whole damned setup—Sally and the Bellamy Rooster."

He actually seemed to consider my suggestion for a moment and then with a reflective expression on his crusty face said, "That's a thought, old man— that's a thought."

There really wasn't much to see inside the Rooster. The door opened into a modestly large room where at one time young people of all eight grades assembled to receive an education and to slowly, I suspected, push the teacher over the edge of sanity. Now a six-foot long bar flanked the middle of the inner wall. Rough plank shelves behind it were essentially empty. If Sally kept booze on the premises, it must have been stored under the bar. But then, this was the kind of place where the customers probably tended to import their own brand of poison. Picnic tables and crude benches lined the other three walls. The center of the room remained open, as Sally explained, to be used for dancing. At the far end of the bar there was a jukebox and beside it a door that led, we learned, to a small kitchenette equipped with a four-burner propane gas stove, a small, dilapidated old fridge, and about four square feet of counter space. Adjoining was another small room which served as Sally's living quarters. A cot, small table, a little lamp, a well-worn dresser, and an old trunk made up the furnishings. Two more very tiny rooms adjacent to Sally's bedroom were equipped only with cots. She offered no explanation for these rooms and none seemed necessary.

When the tour had ended we each thanked her and Henry, probably to Sally's amazement, explained that if she had no objection we would return to our drilling. She registered no objection but she came outside and watched as we eventually bottomed on the PeeDee surface, pulled the rods, sacked our samples, cleaned up and prepared to leave. When we were all in the cab of the truck Sally walked to the driver's side, poked her head inside the window and invited us to visit again whenever we were in the area.

As we drove down the sand road toward the next drill site near Little River, Hobart, who sat to my right, sighed deeply and almost to himself, said, "You know, that was quite a lady back there."

Henry, without lifting his eyes from the road but with a trace of a smile he thought we wouldn't detect, responded, "Not bad, not bad for a black madame."

Smiling inwardly I was warmly reassured to note that in my thirteen-month absence from Horry County, nothing much had changed.

Printed in the United States
17584LVS00003B/182